PENGUIN BOOKS

THE ACTOR'S BOOK OF GAY AND LESBIAN PLAYS

The Actor's Book of Gay and Lesbian Plays marks the third collaboration by Eric Lane and Nina Shengold for Penguin Books. Previously they coedited *Moving Parts: Monologues from Contemporary Plays* and *The Actor's Book of Scenes from New Plays*. In addition, Mr. Lane edited *Telling Tales: New One-Act Plays* and Ms. Shengold edited *The Actor's Book of Contemporary Stage Monologues*.

ERIC LANE's plays have been performed at LaMama, One Dream, the Circle Rep Lab, and other theaters in New York and around the country. Plays include *Lights Along the Highway, It Must Be Him*, and *The Heart of a Child. Dancing on Checkers' Grave* was named Best Play in Love Creek's Annual Gay and Lesbian Festival. His screen adaptation of *Cater-Waiter*, starring David Drake, is currently in production. For his television work on *Ryan's Hope*, Mr. Lane received a Writer's Guild Award. He is artistic director of Orange Thoughts, a not-for-profit theater and film company in New York City. Mr. Lane is a graduate of Brown University. Honors include the first LaMama Playwright Development Award, finalist in the Actors Theatre of Louisville National Ten-Minute Play Contest, and two-time winner of the Lamia Ink! International One-Page Play Competition. He has received Artist-in-Residency Fellowships at Yaddo, where he worked on two new plays, *Times of War* and *The Gary & Rob Show*.

NINA SHENGOLD won the ABC Playwright Award and *L.A. Weekly* Award for her play *Homesteaders*, and just received a Berrilla Kerr Foundation grant for her work-in-progress *Grown Women*. Her short plays have been commissioned by the Actors Theatre of Louisville and performed all over the country. Ms. Shengold has written TV scripts for all three networks, including the Hallmark Hall of Fame presentation *Blind Spot*, starring Emmy nominee Joanne Woodward. She adapted Jane Smiley's *Good Will* for American Playhouse, for whom she is currently writing *Running on Faith*. Other screenplays include *The Lady from Montana*, for Disney, and *Labor of Love*, an independent feature about a nontraditional family which was recently given a reading at Lincoln Center. Ms. Shengold is a founding member of the theatre company Actors & Writers. She lives in upstate New York with her daughter Maya and two fat cats.

The Actor's Book Of

GAY AND LESBIAN PLAYS

Edited by

Eric Lane and Nina Shengold

PENGUIN BOOKS

PENGUIN BOOKS
Published by the Penguin Group
Penguin Books USA Inc., 375 Hudson Street,
New York, New York 10014, U.S.A.
Penguin Books Ltd, 27 Wrights Lane,
London W8 5TZ, England
Penguin Books Australia Ltd, Ringwood,
Victoria, Australia
Penguin Books Canada Ltd, 10 Alcorn Avenue,
Toronto, Ontario, Canada M4V 3B2
Penguin Books (N.Z.) Ltd, 182–190 Wairau Road,
Auckland 10, New Zealand

Penguin Books Ltd, Registered Offices:
Harmondsworth, Middlesex, England

First published in Penguin Books 1995

1 3 5 7 9 10 8 6 4 2

LIBRARY OF CONGRESS CATALOGING IN PUBLICATION DATA
The actor's book of gay and lesbian plays/edited by Eric Lane and
Nina Shengold.
p. cm.
ISBN 0 14 02.4552 9 (pbk.)
1. American drama—20th century. 2. Gays' writings, American.
3. Gay men—Drama. 4. Lesbians—Drama. I. Lane, Eric.
II. Shengold, Nina.
PS627.H67A28 1995
812'.54080352064—dc20 95–339

Printed in the United States of America
Set in Garamond No. 3
Designed by Claudyne Bianco

EDITORS' PREFACE

The past few years have seen an explosion of queer theatre. Gay and lesbian plays are finding homes everywhere from Broadway to Off- and Off-Off-Broadway, at regional theatres, with gay companies and in downtown performance spaces. Are producers becoming more enlightened? Or have they simply discovered that these plays make money, often appealing to both gay and straight audiences? Whatever the reason, queer theatre is booming as never before.

Tony Kushner's seven-hour epic *Angels in America: A Gay Fantasia on National Themes* was the most eagerly anticipated play to arrive on Broadway in recent years, with sold-out performances across the United States and abroad. The published version of the play continues to sell at a phenomenal pace, no doubt aided by the work's Pulitzer Prize and Tony Awards. Terrence McNally's *Love! Valour! Compassion!* broke box office records at Manhattan Theatre Club before quickly transferring to Broadway and winning the Tony Award for Best Play.

Recently actor/director Joe Mantello and playwright Jon Robin Baitz were hailed by *The New York Times* as theatre's "couple of the '90s." Hollywood producers, encouraged by the success of high-profile gay-themed films like *The Crying Game* and *Philadelphia* (not to mention art house favorites like *Paris Is Burning*, *Go Fish*, and *The Wedding Banquet*), are snapping up Off-Broadway hits like Paul Rudnick's Obie-winning *Jeffrey* and David Stevens's *The Sum of Us*. Major regional theatres are including gay and lesbian plays in their seasons. The 1994 Actors Theatre of Louisville Humana Festival featured several exciting new works: Tony Kushner's *Slavs!*, Tina Landau's *1969*, Susan Miller's *My Left Breast*, and Wendy Hammond's *Julie Johnson*. Paula Vogel's *The Baltimore Waltz* has received major productions at Circle Rep and theatres around the country. And playwrights Claire Chafee (*Why We Have a Body*), Cherríe Moraga (*Giving Up the Ghost*), Phyllis Nagy (*Weldon Rising*), and Kate Moira Ryan (*The Autobiography of Aiken Fiction*) are beginning to receive critical and public recognition.

Queer theatre is thriving outside the mainstream as well. Performance collectives like the Five Lesbian Brothers and Pomo Afro Homos have enthusiastic cult followings, as do drag artists like Charles Busch, Lypsinka, and Everett Quinton, heiress apparent to the late Charles Ludlam's immortal Ridiculous Theatre. We're also seeing a profusion of queer downtown performance artists. David Drake's *The Night Larry Kramer Kissed Me* ran off-Broadway for over a year, with productions in San Francisco, L.A., London, and Australia. Holly Hughes, John Kelly, Lisa Kron, Marga Gomez, and countless others are developing challenging work at theatres and alternative spaces around the country.

Gay and lesbian playwrights have always been a part of the commercial theatre as well as the fringe. But for centuries they struggled under a veil of silence, funneling their wits and passion through the mouths of straight characters. When gay characters belatedly started to emerge onstage, they were invariably punished for "the love that dare not speak its name" by death, dismemberment, alcoholism, or—for the lucky—a lifetime of repression and loneliness as a "maiden aunt" or "fussy bachelor." Sometimes gay characters were killed off before the play even started, like Blanche DuBois's suicidal husband in *A Streetcar Named Desire.* Sometimes they were rescued from their aberrent urges, like the "sensitive" youth in *Tea and Sympathy*, or the spinster schoolteacher in Lillian Hellman's *The Children's Hour*, who hangs herself after merely *admitting* that she may have felt "that way" about her friend. Audience members could identify with these characters, but they were dealt a stern warning as well: stay in the closet, or pay with your life.

For many gays and lesbians growing up, the stereotypes of earlier works were the only images to cling to. They may have been distorted mirrors, but they were mirrors nonetheless. Many of the melodramatic excesses of these older plays are so familiar they now seem funny. The Five Lesbian Brothers brilliantly parody such "lesbian tragedies" as *Mädchen in Uniform*, *The Group*, and *The Children's Hour* in *Brave Smiles*. What a surprise when the actress rehearsing the Hellman play reads the lines inserted in her script by the director, "Rub me. Rub on me, baby. Let me be a prostrate worshipper in your grotto of love. . . . Did Lillian write this?"

If the first generation of gay playwrights labored in the closet, the next—the Stonewall generation—often wrote *about* the closet. Groundbreaking works like Mart Crowley's *The Boys in the Band*, Jane Chambers's *Last Summer at Bluefish Cove*, and Harvey Fierstein's *Torch Song Trilogy* featured defiantly gay characters in a gay environment. They were targeted toward gay and lesbian audiences, though, significantly, they sometimes reached a straight one as well. Most were domestic dramas, in which the struggle to proclaim or defend a gay identity was central to the plot. And they created new clichés. Scenes of suicidal anguish were replaced with countless renditions of "Mom, Dad, I have something to tell you."

Then the AIDS plays hit, and with them a tidal wave of grief and rage. Plays like Larry Kramer's *The Normal Heart* and William Hoffman's *As Is* lambasted the media and medical establishment and tried to find a way to live with dying. Writing became an act of witness, a matter of life and death. The plays in this anthology represent a new generation of gay and lesbian playwriting. In contrast to the past, the very fact of being gay or lesbian is no longer the dilemma of these works. In essence, today's playwrights are saying, the characters are gay, let's go from there—as the street chant has it, "We're here, we're queer, get used to it." These post-closet plays cover numerous issues from living with AIDS to outing to sexual/cultural identity to the boundaries of friendship and love to finding a date. We have moved from plays that equated homosexuality with death to plays that proclaim that Silence = Death.

When we began seeking submissions for this anthology, the first question we had to answer was, "What do you mean by gay and lesbian plays?" Would we consider all plays by gay and lesbian playwrights, regardless of subject matter? What about plays with gay themes and characters that were written by straight or bisexual writers? After much discussion, we evolved a broad definition that included plays dealing with gay and lesbian themes and issues, plays with gay and lesbian leading characters, and any play we felt would speak to gay and lesbian actors or audiences—admittedly a very subjective barometer—regardless of the playwright's own orientation. We looked for both full-lengths and one-acts, with strong roles for actors, requiring simple sets and costumes. The plays were to be performed as well as read. Well-written. Interesting. In a range of styles and cast sizes. We received a wealth of terrific material from which to choose.

The seventeen plays we selected run from comic to dramatic, with most navigating the waters somewhere in between. The authors include celebrated playwrights Constance Congdon, Craig Lucas, Susan Miller, and Paula Vogel, as well as the award-winning screenwriter of *Philadelphia*, Ron Nyswaner. Many contributors, including Victor Bumbalo, Keith Curran, Steven Dietz, and Joe Pintauro, have been widely produced across the country. Others, like Linda Eisenstadt, Edwin Sánchez, and Will Sheffer, are being published here for the first time.

You'll find a variety of cast sizes, from one in Linda Eisenstadt's *At the Root*, a haunting monologue about a lesbian mother's sacrifice for her son, to ten actors performing forty-five roles in Keith Curran's *The Stand-In*, a hilarious take on homophobia in Hollywood. Voices range from the lyrical precision of Claire Chafee's *Why We Have a Body* to Cherríe Moraga's Chicana-inflected blank verse in *Giving Up the Ghost* to the gritty street rhythms of Times Square hustlers and runaways in Edwin Sánchez's *Trafficking in Broken Hearts*.

AIDS plays a central role in many of these plays. Sometimes it is depicted directly, as in Victor Bumbalo's shattering *What Are Tuesdays Like?*, set in the outpatient waiting room of a hospital. Other times it is represented metaphorically, as in Paula Vogel's exquisitely dizzy *The Baltimore Waltz* and Steven Dietz's Ionesco-inspired *Lonely Planet*, in which a map store with no customers slowly fills with the chairs of the dead. Often it is simply a part of the world the characters inhabit. Nearly all of the plays dealing with AIDS incorporate humor in the work. Maybe it is the horribleness of the disease that makes humor a necessary element of these plays. Ultimately the humor heightens the devastation. Moments of great beauty and ugliness, humor and tragedy exist side by side. For many of us who have experienced AIDS, whether firsthand or through the struggles of our friends, family and lovers, this juxtaposition presents an accurate reflection of our lives.

We also chose several small-cast, ten-minute plays that can easily be performed in acting class or on a bill of one-acts. These include Eric Lane's *Cater-Waiter*, a story of two gay cater-waiters at a Republican fund-raiser in Connecticut, Craig Lucas's *Bad Dream*, a powerful depiction of fear, sex, and intimacy in the age of AIDS, Ron Nyswaner's *Reservoir*, in which a fervently religious teenager copes with the aftermath of his first sexual encounter, Joe Pintauro's searing *Rosen's Son*, the story of a gay man trying to move on after his lover's death and the father-in-law who refuses to let him, Will Scheffer's *Falling Man*, a poetic monologue about destiny, passion, and the Cha Cha champion of the world, and Shay Youngblood's *There Are Many Houses in My Tribe*, an exuberant African-American celebration of sensuality and community.

In addition, Susan Miller's beautifully written *It's Our Town, Too* reinterprets the Thorton Wilder classic from a gay and lesbian perspective. And Constance Congdon examines the emotionally intimate friendship between a gay man and a straight woman in her poignant, uproarious *Dog Opera*, which recently premiered at New York's Public Theatre.

The nineties' explosion of queer theatre corresponds to an increased visibility of gays and lesbians throughout our society. Bill Clinton's first major issue upon taking office was his disastrously equivocal "gays in the military" policy. Lesbians made the front cover of *Newsweek* and other national magazines. Gay couples turned up on sitcoms; RuPaul worked MTV. At the same time, attacks on gays and lesbians escalated as the Far Right continued its campaign of fear and hatred. With the end of the Cold War, the Right shifted its focus from the Evil Empire to the perceived erosion of "family values." Communism is no longer a threat. Now it is anyone from

Murphy Brown to Robert Mapplethorpe to the NEA Four. Even *Sesame Street*'s Bert and Ernie have been attacked for promoting a "homosexual lifestyle." Maybe the vehemence of these attacks is an implicit acknowledgment that gay men and lesbians are becoming an increasingly powerful political force. In a world of rising censorship, telling our stories becomes an essential, affirmative act.

This is an exciting and scary time we live in. The theatre community has lost countless artists to AIDS. Republicans and conservatives are making gains in their attempt to abolish the National Endowment for the Arts. The financial rewards of a life in today's theatre are painfully few. Yet theatres continue to flourish, and the playwrights in this collection and their peers continue to create works that are vibrant and alive. Their plays are full of joy and sadness, rage and hope, desperation and delight. We hope you enjoy bringing their words to life.

—Eric Lane and Nina Shengold

July 1995

ACKNOWLEDGMENTS

We'd like to thank the many people who contributed to this anthology, especially Actors & Writers, Martha Banta and Greg Gunter of New York Theatre Workshop, Beth Blickers, James Conrad of OUT Magazine, Steven Corsano, Donal Egan, Peter Franklin of William Morris, Anne Harris of the Lesbian Exchange for New Drama—LEND, International, Jessica Hagedorn, Morgan Jenness of the New York Shakespeare Festival, Joyce Ketay, the Lane family, Cherri Magid, John McCormack, Carl Mulert, Orange Thoughts Theater Company, Mark Owen of 3$-Bill, Michael Warren Powell of Circle Rep, Dave Robinson, Susan Schulman, the Shengold family, Sonya Sobieski of Playwrights Horizons, Eleanore Speert of Dramatists Play Service, Phyllis Wender, and Peregrine Whittlesey.

Thanks again to our editor at Penguin, Michael Millman, and his assistant, Kristine Puopolo. Also to all the agents and their assistants for their submissions and help in securing permission to include the plays in this collection. Much appreciation to the theaters that continue to develop and present exciting gay and lesbian plays. Most of all, we deeply appreciate the playwrights who have generously shared their work.

CONTENTS

WHAT ARE TUESDAYS LIKE?

Victor Bumbalo

WHAT ARE TUESDAYS LIKE? had its world premiere at the Contemporary American Theater Festival in Shepherdstown, West Virginia, on July 6, 1994. The cast and creative contributors were as follows:

HOWARD	Jeremy Lawrence
JEFF	Jerry McGonigle
SCOTT	John Hollywood
GENE	Greg Stuhr
DENISE	Althea Lewis
RANDY	James Cassidy

DIRECTOR	Ed Herendeen
SCENIC DESIGN	Michael J. Dempsey
COSTUME DESIGN	Garry D. Lennon
LIGHTING DESIGN	Tina Gallegos
SOUND DESIGN	Kevin Lloyd
PRODUCTION STAGE MANAGER	Valerie Gramling
MANAGING DIRECTOR	Gabrielle Buck Seivold

WHAT ARE TUESDAYS LIKE? is dedicated to Robert Chesley.

~

SCENE I

The Out-Patient Waiting Room of a Hospital. Tuesday Afternoon.

At this time every week only people with AIDS are scheduled for services. Four men are in the room. Two of the men, SCOTT and GENE, are seated close to each other. The other two, HOWARD and JEFF, sit apart from the couple and from each other.

HOWARD is gregarious and commands authority. His chatty nature stems from a genuine interest in people. There is an inner calm to this man that people find attractive.

JEFF is obviously frail. Although he tries to hide it, the fear JEFF lives with is evident.

SCOTT is attractive and intense. He holds on to his individuality by hiding his true nature from most people.

GENE likes to be in control.

At the moment no one is speaking. GENE has his arm around SCOTT. HOWARD is watching JEFF who is staring at a page of a magazine.

HOWARD: Excuse me, may I ask, what is it you're reading?
JEFF: What?
HOWARD: I know it's none of my business, but you've been staring at the same page for over thirty-five minutes. I was just curious what was so fascinating.
JEFF (*Showing him the magazine*): It's a picture of the Grand Canyon. I was meditating on it. Trying to put myself into the picture. (*Pointing to a specific spot in the picture*) I was standing there.
HOWARD: You weren't planning to jump in?
JEFF: Why? Do I look suicidal?
HOWARD: No. I was kidding.
SCOTT (*From the other side of the room*): Just what we need in this room—a comic.
HOWARD: Excuse me?
SCOTT (*From the other side of the room*): Nothing.
JEFF: I don't understand. I was scheduled fifteen minutes ago for my chemotherapy, and there's no one here to give it to me. I can't be waiting around here all day.
HOWARD: It's usually not like this on Tuesdays.
SCOTT (*From the other side of the room*): I don't want to do this.
GENE: It won't be as bad as you think.

SCOTT: How do you know?

HOWARD (*To JEFF*): Does it work?

JEFF: What?

HOWARD: Your meditation.

JEFF: No. Maybe. I don't know. It passes the time. I can't be waiting all day for them. If they don't take me in a few minutes, I'm going to have to go.

HOWARD: You shouldn't do that.

JEFF: I'm going to have to.

HOWARD: Why don't you go back to your picture.

JEFF: I can't concentrate anymore. (*Offering HOWARD the magazine*) Would you like to try?

HOWARD: No, thank you.

SCOTT (*To JEFF*): Excuse me, what's it like, the chemotherapy?

JEFF: It probably isn't as bad as you imagine.

GENE (*To SCOTT*): See.

SCOTT: But you've lost some hair.

JEFF: Not everyone does.

GENE: (*To SCOTT*): See.

JEFF (*To HOWARD*): What are you here for?

HOWARD: To see Louise. She's a therapist.

JEFF: Is she nice?

HOWARD: Very nondirective. But she can use some help dressing.

JEFF: I used to see Don, the other therapist.

HOWARD: Was he nice?

JEFF: Wonderful. Very humane. Had these sparkling eyes. But he flipped out.

HOWARD: I can understand.

JEFF: One day I arrived here for my appointment and he wasn't here. He disappeared. Never even gave the hospital notice. My lover, Mack, tried to track him down, but he wasn't very successful. The last thing any of his friends heard was that he was getting in his car and just going. I hope he's all right.

HOWARD: He's probably at your Grand Canyon leading those donkey tours.

JEFF: That would be great, wouldn't it?

SCOTT (*From the other side of the room*): Or maybe he jumped in.

GENE: Scott!

JEFF: I'm going to check to see how much longer I have to wait. This is not right. I told them I had to be taken on time. I called them twice and told them.

HOWARD: Try to relax. Let's find you another picture.

JEFF: I'm going to find out what's going on.

(*JEFF exits.*)

HOWARD: He's a nervous little thing, isn't he? (*No one responds.*) I'm sorry, I'm disturbing you. I had nothing else to do this afternoon. So I got here early. That's why I'm waiting. That kid made me edgy. Sorry. I'm disturbing you.

GENE: It's all right.

SCOTT (*To HOWARD*): Do you get chemo?

HOWARD: No, I'm sorry.

SCOTT (*Sarcastically*): What do you have to be sorry about?

HOWARD: I'm sorry I can't tell you anything about it. You seem worried. I'm sure the nurse will answer all your questions. (*He picks up JEFF's magazine.*)

SCOTT: I bet she will. (*To GENE*) You're going to be late getting back to the office.

GENE: It's okay. I told them what I was doing.

SCOTT: You told them what I was coming here for?

GENE: Of course. What's the secret?

SCOTT: Goddamn it, Gene. I don't want people to know about my treatment.

GENE: Why not?

SCOTT: Because it's my treatment.

GENE: People want to know what's going on with you.

SCOTT: Why? They're not my close friends.

GENE: They're mine. And I need their support.

SCOTT: Your office friends are arrogant bastards.

GENE: You don't like anybody these days.

HOWARD (*Putting down the magazine*): I wish I had my book with me. I forgot it at home. I'm reading *Middlemarch*. It's fat and glorious. I only read thick books now. I figure nothing bad can happen to you when you're in the middle of a long, long story. It's been working so far.

(JEFF enters.)

JEFF: They're going to start taking people in a minute. (*Referring to SCOTT*) They said you're ahead of me.

SCOTT: You can go first if you want.

JEFF (*Suddenly*): I have to go. I've waited too long. You know, the pay phone is broken. I have to call home or get home. I better go.

HOWARD: Do you think you should?

JEFF: I have to. I told them they had to take me on time today. I told them.

HOWARD: What's the matter?

JEFF: I have to go. Maybe I'll see you next week.

(JEFF exits.)

GENE: That guy is setting himself up for a coronary.

HOWARD: I wonder how he's going to get home? Should somebody have gone with him?

GENE: Is he a friend?

HOWARD: No. I just met him today.

(They are interrupted by a VOICE coming from the public address system.)

VOICE: Mr. Donnelly. Mr. Donnelly, please report to room 4. Room 4.

SCOTT (*Frightened*): I don't want to go!

GENE: Come on, you have to.

HOWARD: I should have helped him home.

VOICE: Mr. Donnelly . . . room 4. Room 4.
SCOTT: I don't want to go!

Blackout

SCENE 2

Another Tuesday.

JEFF is alone in the room. He is staring intently at the postcard he is holding. After a few seconds, HOWARD enters. He has been shopping. He is clutching several packages and his copy of Middlemarch.

HOWARD: Well, hello. What's the picture this week?
JEFF: It's a painting. By Monet. (*Showing HOWARD the postcard*) Of his gardens at Giverny. Wouldn't you love to live in this painting?
HOWARD: Never. The pollen would kill me.
JEFF: That's too bad.
HOWARD: Did you get home all right last week?
JEFF: Yes, thank you. They promised they would take me exactly on time this week.
HOWARD: That's good.
JEFF: On Tuesdays I'm on a tight schedule. I have banking to do. I have to go to social services, get shopping done, come here. I can't afford to waste any time.
HOWARD: You sound busy.
JEFF: I don't like being away from my apartment too long. My lover's there. He's sick. Quite sick. I don't like being away from him. These are precious moments, right?
HOWARD: Right.
JEFF: At this point, he only likes me to take care of him. When he's up to it, sometimes we sit together, hold hands, and listen to music. Or maybe watch a movie on the VCR. Our friends chipped in and bought us one. That was good of them, wasn't it?

HOWARD: Yes.

JEFF: We know lovely people. On days when we both have a resurgence of energy, I play for him. He loves that. I used to be a concert pianist.

HOWARD: What a comfort your music must be.

JEFF: I love the very idea of it. Selecting sounds from the universe. Giving them an order. They apologized for last week. Did I tell you they said they might even take me early?

HOWARD: Great.

JEFF: You've been shopping.

HOWARD: I've been depressed. This morning I was paying bills. I used to make a good income, but now even the telephone bill terrifies me.

JEFF: May I ask what you do?

HOWARD: Right now, I'm bartending a few days a week. Off the books. But I used to be a therapist. Both occupations are frighteningly similar. All you have to do is listen, and people will throw money at you.

JEFF: Did you have fun shopping?

HOWARD: I should have done this a few weeks ago. I'm sure those T-cells of mine are dropping through economic fear. I've been pinching pennies for too many months now. So this morning I gave myself a good talking to and then went out on a spree. I just handed the cashiers my credit card and never peeked at the bills. I figured I'll take a look while I'm in session with Louise. Let her deal with it.

JEFF: Let anybody else deal with it.

HOWARD: Wouldn't it be fabulous if you could wrap AIDS and all that comes with it in a box and hand it over to a friend? Just for a day. How about a week? A month?

JEFF: That would be mean.

HOWARD: I mean temporarily. It would give us a break. They would learn something. Know what it's really like. It would be fabulous. Maybe for a year.

(They are interrupted by a VOICE coming from the public address system.)

VOICE: Mr. Ferris. Mr. Ferris, please report to room 4. Room 4.

JEFF: See, they kept their word. They're taking me early.

HOWARD: So it's Ferris.

JEFF: Yes. Jeff Ferris.

HOWARD: Howard Salvo.

JEFF: Good meeting you. I've got to run. I don't want to keep them waiting.

(JEFF begins to leave.)

HOWARD *(Calling after him)*: When you gave concerts, did you specialize in anything?

JEFF: Yes. The French. I was known for my French repertoire.

Blackout

SCENE 3

Another Tuesday.

When the lights come up, SCOTT and GENE are the only men in the room. They are in the middle of an argument.

GENE: It was four-thirty. Four-thirty in the morning. An ACT-UP meeting my ass.

SCOTT: After the meeting, some of the guys took me out for a beer.

GENE: A beer? You smelled like a brewery. What kind of jerks do you hang out with? Don't they know you're sick?

SCOTT: They know.

GENE: Then they're fools.

SCOTT: Why don't you leave and go to work.

GENE: You shouldn't be drinking.

SCOTT: Gene, two beers.

GENE: You should be in bed early.

SCOTT: I had fun last night.

GENE: Doing what?

SCOTT: Go! Just leave!

GENE: You don't know how to take care of yourself. That's always been your problem.

SCOTT: What do you mean by that?

GENE: Just that I want you taking better care of yourself.

(HOWARD enters carrying a package and his copy of Middlemarch.*)*

HOWARD: Well, how are my sweet ones?

SCOTT: We're not your sweet ones.

HOWARD: Missy is sour today.

SCOTT: God, what a tired queen.

HOWARD: I hope your chemo makes you bald.

SCOTT: Take that back!

HOWARD: Twirl on your own finger!

SCOTT: Take it back!

HOWARD: Bald!

(SCOTT leaps at HOWARD and grabs HOWARD by his shirt.)

GENE (*Trying to separate the men*): Stop it!

SCOTT (*Not letting go*): I'll clean this room with you if you don't take it back.

HOWARD: Little tough boys bore me. Move those hands.

SCOTT: Take it back. (*Beginning to break down*) Please. Please, take it back.

(SCOTT releases HOWARD.)

SCOTT (*Breaking down*): Please.

HOWARD (*Trying to calm SCOTT down*): I'm sorry. Really. I am.

SCOTT: Please.

HOWARD: I take it back.

(SCOTT is sobbing. HOWARD takes him into his arms.)

HOWARD: I take it back.

Blackout

SCENE 4

Another Tuesday.

HOWARD is reading his book. DENISE is pacing back and forth. She is an attractive black woman who is trying to conceal her nerves.

DENISE: You can't smoke here, can you?
HOWARD: No.
DENISE: That's too bad.
HOWARD: I don't think so.
DENISE (*Suddenly*): You have AIDS don't you?
HOWARD: Why?
DENISE: I want to make sure I'm in the right place.
HOWARD: You're in the right place.
DENISE: Good. What kind of treatment do you get here?
HOWARD: I talk to a therapist.
DENISE: I like therapy. I'm in a group. It's a lot of fun.
HOWARD: Fun?
DENISE: All you do is talk and listen. It's fun. People are usually polite. They make you feel good. But I don't take it too seriously. I mean we all have to leave and go home. And these days, that definitely is not fun.
HOWARD: Where do you live?
DENISE: Out on Long Island. I had to take that goddamn train to get here. I've been selected to be in some study. Some experimental drug. My family is all excited. But to tell you the truth, if I had to win something, I would have preferred the lotto or a scholarship to Yale. Experiments make me nervous. My doctor said I should be delighted. But I can't help wondering, Why me? Is it because I'm black? When I said that to my doctor, she said I was getting paranoid. Perhaps. Then

she told me that a lot of gay men were going on this drug. I asked her to show me one straight white man who would be participating. Then maybe I would show more enthusiasm.

HOWARD: You're too much.

DENISE: Denise.

HOWARD: Howard.

DENISE: I wish we were meeting somewhere else.

(SCOTT and GENE enter.)

SCOTT: Not one hair. Not one hair has fallen out.

HOWARD: Terrific.

(HOWARD and SCOTT embrace.)

SCOTT: I appreciated your call. It helped.

HOWARD: Don't isolate yourself.

GENE: He's not isolated.

HOWARD (*Purposely leaving GENE out of the introductions*): Denise. Scott.

DENISE: Hi.

GENE: Gene.

DENISE: Hi. (*To SCOTT*) You're on the chemotherapy? You look terrific. You don't even look sick? (*To GENE*) What are you here for?

GENE: I'm not sick.

DENISE: Really?

GENE: What do you mean? Do I look sick?

DENISE: I was just wondering what you were doing here?

GENE (*Indicating SCOTT*): I come with him.

DENISE: Aren't you kind.

GENE: But I'm not sick. As a matter of fact, I'm not even HIV positive. I test negative. Every time.

(SCOTT starts applauding.)

GENE: Stop that!

SCOTT: I'm proud of you. You refrained from mentioning that here for over a month. (*To* DENISE *and* HOWARD) Usually it's within an hour of meeting someone new that he makes his announcement.

GENE: That's unfair.

SCOTT: You practically carry a banner.

GENE: I'm leaving.

SCOTT: Fine.

GENE: To treat me like this in front of your friends.

DENISE: I just met him.

GENE (*Referring to* HOWARD): I meant him.

SCOTT: Gene, go to work.

GENE: Aren't you relieved I'm negative?

SCOTT: Of course. But you advertise it the same way you advertise your condos. You're relentless.

HOWARD: You own condos?

SCOTT: He sells them.

DENISE: So does my sister-in-law. She loves it. Says it's a real cushy job.

GENE: I work hard.

DENISE: I'm sure you do. But she used to teach in a city school.

GENE: May I say something?

HOWARD: No.

GENE: Why not?

HOWARD: Because whenever someone starts a statement like that, they are about to tell you something you don't want to hear.

GENE: I'm going to say it anyway.

HOWARD: I knew you would.

GENE: You people can be pompous and self-righteous. There. I said it.

DENISE: What people does he mean?

HOWARD: Sick people.

GENE: I'm sorry, but I had to say it.

HOWARD: Bravo.

(GENE walks over to SCOTT and awkwardly gives him a kiss.)

GENE: I'll see you at home. (*He waits for SCOTT to respond.*) I said . . .

SCOTT: I heard you.

(GENE leaves.)

SCOTT: He didn't used to be like that.

HOWARD: It's the pressure.

DENISE: It's men. God, I'm glad I'm taking a break from them. (*To HOWARD*) You live with somebody?

HOWARD: I used to.

DENISE (*To SCOTT*): What you need, honey, is a vacation from him.

SCOTT: Impossible. At the moment he's supporting me.

DENISE: That's a bitch.

HOWARD (*To SCOTT*): Aren't you still working?

SCOTT: My employers forced an early retirement on me. I worked at Fairyland.

DENISE: Is that a dance club?

SCOTT: No, it's a preschool. They told me they didn't want me deteriorating in front of the children's eyes. Forcing concepts on them that they weren't ready for. They said at my kids' ages only bunny rabbits should get sick and die. So I let them buy me off. They told the kids I was going on a trip. They gave me a bon voyage party and kept me on the payroll for six months. Maybe I should have fought them. I miss the kids.

DENISE: Anytime you want, you can take my two.

(They are interrupted by a VOICE from the public address system.)

VOICE: Mrs. McMillan, report to room 3. Mrs. McMillan to room 3.

DENISE: They better answer all my questions.

HOWARD: They'll try to rush you, but see to it that they don't.

DENISE: See you later.
HOWARD: Good luck.

(DENISE exits.)

SCOTT (*After a moment*): How do you keep it together?
HOWARD: Linguini and clam sauce. Any time I want it.

Blackout

SCENE 5

Another Tuesday.

GENE is standing away from SCOTT thumbing through a magazine. SCOTT is seated staring at the door that leads to the treatment center.

GENE: Maybe we should think about Europe next year.

(SCOTT starts to cry.)

GENE: Oh babe, please don't.
SCOTT (*Trying to control himself*): I'm okay. I'll be okay.

(GENE goes over to SCOTT.)

Blackout

SCENE 6

Another Tuesday.

HOWARD, SCOTT, and GENE are seated.

HOWARD: I'm worried about that guy. The pianist.
SCOTT: Jeff?

HOWARD: I haven't seen him in weeks. I tried calling him, but he's not listed. And they won't give me any information here.
GENE: Confidentiality. You should be glad.
HOWARD: His lover is sick.
SCOTT: I don't think I want to know.
HOWARD: I hope he's all right.
GENE: He said he doesn't want to know.
HOWARD: Maybe they're listening to music.
GENE: Did you hear him?
SCOTT: Gene, chill out.
HOWARD: Sorry. (*To SCOTT*) How are you doing?
SCOTT (*Cheerfully*): Pretty good.
HOWARD: Great.
SCOTT: How about you?
HOWARD: Getting along.

(Pause.)

SCOTT: It's a fine day out there, isn't it? So clear.

(Pause.)

HOWARD: Do you think he's got somebody to take care of him?

Blackout

SCENE 7

Another Tuesday.

HOWARD, DENISE, GENE, and SCOTT are sitting almost totally still listening to JEFF. JEFF is in a state of near hysteria.

JEFF: . . . I kept repeating, over five thousand times a day, "This isn't happening to me. This isn't happening." In one month my entire life . . . gone. It disappeared. Everything. And where to? Mack's death wasn't what I expected. And what happened afterwards I just wasn't prepared for. "This isn't happening to me." He was home. He slipped . . . that's the expression people used . . . slipped into a coma as if by means of a slate of ice. He slipped. I was afraid to be alone. Afraid I was going to do something wrong. Hurt him in some way. Friends stayed with me around the clock. Took shifts. I could tell they were praying for him to die. Some of them had done this before. They knew what to do. They were sad. I know that. It just wasn't that special to them. Not anymore. "It's time," they said. I knew they had said that in some other room. In someone else's home. "This isn't happening to me." Still, I was holding on to him. Didn't want him to die. I couldn't imagine living in a world where Mack wasn't breathing. "This isn't happening to me." I was exhausted when he died. Had been up for three days. Harry was with me. He made a mistake. Instantly he called 911. The police came. Since the apartment wasn't in my name, they told me they would have to seal it up until the official cause of death was documented and Mack's next of kin arrived. Mack's brother—Mack never liked him—would be handing me back our things, my things. "This isn't happening to me." As they were taking Mack away—they put him in a bag—Harry was putting some things together for me in my overnight bag. Everyone was rushing around as if we were running to catch a plane. "Mack, we're not taking a plane anywhere. We're not going on a vacation. This isn't happening to me." Our friends were in a fury at my being locked out of my home. That's what they kept talking about all evening. Not the obvious. Mack was dead. I would never see him again. "This isn't happening to me." A quick cremation. I scattered his ashes near the boat pond in Central Park. A little place where we picnicked. His brother and mother were furious. They wanted a body. Lots of ceremonies. But I did what Mack wanted. They were as much a part of his death and illness as they were a part of his life. They were no part. They wanted things. In the apartment, once I was allowed back in, they kept asking me, "Is this yours?" How does "ours" get split into "yours or his or mine?" What right did they have to ask me? "This isn't happening to me." I didn't want to fight them. I let them have so many of our things. The truth was—what was I going to do with a complete household and no home. The landlady thought she was being so loving by letting me stay one more month. Nine years in that apartment. I made it a home. Our home. My home. "This isn't happening to me." My lover's dead. I'm sick. I don't have much money. I have to find a place to live. I'm living out of a suitcase in a friend's living room. Did I tell you, I had to sell my piano?

Blackout

SCENE 8

Another Tuesday.

HOWARD *and* GENE *are seated on opposite sides of the room.*

GENE (*After a moment*): I've joined a support group for guys who have lovers with HIV.

HOWARD (*Barely paying attention*): Good.

GENE: We've started a bowling league.

HOWARD (*Sarcastically*): You guys really know how to get down and dirty.

GENE: You can't stand me.

HOWARD (*Friendly*): You're right. And it's so upsetting to me. You can be rude, but God, I live in New York. I should be used to it. I spent my entire last session with my therapist only talking about you.

GENE: I wish you hadn't.

HOWARD: Oh, I had to. I have to get to the bottom of this. I must say I was disappointed in Louise's first analysis. She jumped to the obvious. That I was attracted to you. Who does she think she's talking to? Of course, I had already thought of that. In fact the other night I even tried getting up a fantasy about you. I tried to picture you undressed. . . . My sitting next to you . . . But I swear, nothing, nothing happened. But don't worry, I'll figure it out.

GENE: I don't care. This is not my problem.

HOWARD: You're absolutely right. I was talking to my friend Willy about you . . .

GENE: Next you'll be on Oprah. . . .

HOWARD: Relax. Willy is such a hoot. You'd love him. But maybe you wouldn't. He said it was our past lives. That you must have been a real prick to me in one of them. And that it's sort of spilled over into this lifetime. Who were you Gene? Attila the Hun, the Marquis de Sade, Medea. . . .

GENE: She wasn't real.

HOWARD: You're right. Very good. Oh, don't look so worried. Maybe I was the prick.

(SCOTT enters from the treatment center.)

GENE: That was quick.

HOWARD: They think they're working on an assembly line in there.

SCOTT: I didn't take my treatment today.

GENE: Why?

SCOTT: I want to go for a bike ride.

GENE: I know what this is about. A few hairs. You lost just a few hairs.

SCOTT: They were mine.

(SCOTT exits.)

GENE (*After a moment*): He'll be back.

Blackout

SCENE 9

Another Tuesday.

HOWARD *is seated.* DENISE *is pacing.*

DENISE: I want it just like the old days. I want a good old-fashioned public hanging. You know the kind where people would bring their sewing. I don't sew, but maybe I'd file my nails. I'd get there early. Sit right in the front row. He would scream and cry. I know it. I'd be humming while I was filing my fucking nails. I'd even give the bastard a smile when he climbed the platform.

HOWARD: And I'd be sitting right next to you.

DENISE: What would you be doing?

HOWARD: Reading my book. I'd glance up a couple of times. I'd pretend I was bored. That his execution didn't matter that much.

DENISE: We'd act just like he did. Social services, my ass. Social abuse, that's what they should call his department. He was filling out his appointment book while he was talking to me. (*Imitating a man's voice*) "I'm going to have to bring up something that you're avoiding. Have you thought of your children, Mrs. McMillan? Where will they go when you're not here? It's best not to wait until the last minute for these kinds of things. We better start making plans." We? That scumbag doesn't think I have a brain in my head. What does he think I think about day after day after day? My mother is old. She may go first. What's he think I am? Some dog? Some bitch that has a litter that has to be disposed of? (*In a fury*) He wasn't even looking at me. He was writing things down in his appointment book.

HOWARD: He'd hear us. Talking about a new restaurant we'd be going to as soon as the show was over.

DENISE (*Breaking down*): He glanced up at me, maybe twice. Like over his glasses. Checking me out. Seeing if the animal had a reaction.

HOWARD: I'd tell you a joke.

DENISE (*After a moment*): And I'd laugh as I looked at him.

Blackout

SCENE 10

Another Tuesday.

HOWARD is staring at SCOTT who is beaming.

HOWARD: Give me some.

SCOTT: What?

HOWARD: Whatever it is you are on. You look euphoric.

SCOTT: Not quite. Almost. Where's our little friend?

HOWARD: Jeff? He's moved away. Down to Florida. His mother has taken him in. He said he would write. I hope he does.

SCOTT: I hope she's good to him.

HOWARD: I'm sure she will be. She's a piano teacher.

SCOTT: Good. They'll have something to talk about. What time is your appointment?

HOWARD: In a few minutes.

SCOTT: Do you want me to wait around for you? And then maybe we could do dinner—cheap of course.

HOWARD: Of course.

SCOTT: . . . and maybe a movie or something.

HOWARD: That would be lovely.

SCOTT: Great.

HOWARD: I don't believe it. This is fabulous. I have a date.

SCOTT (*Suddenly worried*): It's not a date. We're just going to be like buddies—hanging out.

HOWARD (*Nervously*): I know, I know.

SCOTT: No date.

HOWARD: Right. We're just friends. Spending some time together.

SCOTT: I just didn't want you to expect something that's not going to happen.

HOWARD: You *are* feeling good.

SCOTT: What do you mean?

HOWARD: You instantly jumped to the conclusion I was after your ass.

SCOTT: But you said date. . . .

HOWARD: Don't worry. You'll be safe with me.

SCOTT: Let's just forget it.

HOWARD: No, please. I'd love to go out with you. But not on a date. Be assured, I'm not going to think of it as a date.

SCOTT: Am I acting like a slimeball?

HOWARD (*After a moment*): No.

SCOTT: It's just that I never imagined I'd be feeling like this again. Alive. Almost—do I dare say it—hot.

HOWARD: Somebody must have had an awfully good time last night.

SCOTT: No. It's just that I'm going to be free from all this. Free, Howard. Forever more free.

HOWARD: Then what are you doing here? I thought you had come back.

SCOTT: I'm getting my records.

HOWARD: Please, please don't do this.

SCOTT: My Tuesdays are going to be spent in a more pleasant place. Screw their charts. Screw the number they've turned me into. Screw their claim over this body. It's mine again.

HOWARD (*Worried*): Scott, this is the only help there is for us.

SCOTT: I don't believe their medicines are going to make me any better. I don't believe their drugs will retard my virus.

HOWARD: But they do.

SCOTT: In my soul I don't believe it.

HOWARD: What the hell are you going to do? Get a crystal and start chanting?

SCOTT: Maybe that too. I'm going on a totally holistic trip. Under a doctor's supervision. I'm blowing this joint.

HOWARD: You're playing with your life.

SCOTT: And you're not? You've been brainwashed. I'm going a different way that's all.

HOWARD: Oh, Jesus, I'm scared for you.
SCOTT: For the first time in ages I'm not.

Blackout

SCENE II

Another Tuesday.

HOWARD and DENISE are seated. Both are eating a piece of cake and seem to be enjoying it.

DENISE: God, it's good. Are you sure you didn't buy this?
HOWARD: Made it from scratch. I'm totally talented.
DENISE: Will you marry me?
HOWARD: Are you neat?
DENISE: Forget it. Listen darling, can I ask you a question?
HOWARD: Shoot.
DENISE: Have you had any intimacy lately?
HOWARD: A friend came over to dinner the other night, and I couldn't believe how close we got. We talked and talked. . . .
DENISE: And then?
HOWARD: That's all. We just talked.
DENISE: I'm talking about the old push-push.
HOWARD: Oh.
DENISE: Yes, oh. Well?
HOWARD: No.
DENISE: Don't you want to?
HOWARD: Sometimes. I guess so.
DENISE: Then why aren't you getting anything?
HOWARD: You sound like my therapist.
DENISE: I'm making you nervous. I'm sorry. I just thought you were all liberated. . . .
HOWARD: I am.
DENISE: . . . and being a shrink yourself you were able to talk easily about all sorts of things.

HOWARD: I can.

DENISE: You are lying. You are as uptight as any of us.

HOWARD: I am not. It's just that I'm ambivalent right now.

DENISE: Same as being uptight. Do you feel unclean?

HOWARD: Sometimes . . . yes.

DENISE: That's how I usually feel. That was until the other night. Two of my girlfriends took me out. They're in the drug program with me. I usually say no to them, but this time I felt—why not? They act superior sometimes. They don't have AIDS. But generally they're nice. What a party crowd we make. We don't do drugs or drink. But we chain-smoked our cigarettes and tried to act "with it." The music was loud. I was about to get a headache when this guy asked me to dance. It was the first time in over two years that a man had his arms around me. That dance depressed the hell out of me.

HOWARD: Why? Didn't you like the song?

DENISE: I felt like an old lady. There could be no follow-up to the dance. Not even a dream of one.

HOWARD: Of course there could be.

DENISE: Get real, girl. What was I supposed to say? "Let's get to know each other? Should we go to a movie next week? How about dinner. . . ."

HOWARD (*Interrupting her*): Yes.

DENISE: ". . . But don't get too interested in me, because I have . . . Should I give you three guesses? Let's just say it begins with an A, and it's not asthma."

HOWARD: What happened?

DENISE: Nothing. I pretended I was from out of town. I feel like I'm from the moon.

HOWARD: We know how to be safe. We can't stop living.

DENISE: It's fucked.

HOWARD (*After a moment*): We have to do something.

DENISE: Well Einstein, think on it. When you get a vision, give me a call. You wouldn't consider going straight, would you?

HOWARD: That's your second proposition tonight.

DENISE: I'm getting desperate.

HOWARD: Thanks a lot. Maybe you should take out an ad.

DENISE: Where? In some porno rag?

HOWARD: No. In a classier publication. Something like *The New York Review of Books*.

DENISE: You need a CAT scan. The virus has hit your brain.

HOWARD: You have a pen?

DENISE: Yes.

HOWARD: Okay. As fast as you can, write an ad for yourself. I'll write one for you. We'll see what we come up with.

DENISE: I wonder how long you have after the virus enters your brain.

HOWARD: Come on.

(HOWARD starts writing on the back cover of his book. DENISE picks up a magazine to write on.)

HOWARD: And make sure you give it a bit of spark.

DENISE: Of course. "Poor Black Diseased Woman with two children. . . ." Won't that send them beating down my door.

HOWARD: That's not all you are. You're also attractive, witty. . . .

DENISE: Okay. "Poor Witty Diseased Black. . . ."

HOWARD: You are not diseased . . . so to speak.

DENISE: So to speak.

(GENE enters.)

GENE: Hi guys.

HOWARD: Is Scott coming back?

GENE: Howard, you have to talk to him.

(Although HOWARD and DENISE seem to be giving GENE their attention, they still continue, at various moments, working on their ads.)

HOWARD: How is he?

GENE: Fine. For the time being.

DENISE: Good.

GENE: No, not good. With all this seaweed nonsense, he's endangering his life. He won't listen to me. But he respects you Howard. Why don't you give it a try?

HOWARD: This is not my business.

GENE: But you've become his friend.

HOWARD: And I'd like to stay that way.

GENE: Your friend is standing on a train track and a train is speeding towards him. You're not going to suggest that he might get the hell out of its way?

HOWARD: This is different.

GENE: Do you believe in what he's doing?

HOWARD: No. But he does.

GENE: Don't give me this New Age nonsense.

HOWARD (*To DENISE*): Do you like books?

DENISE: Who's got time to read?

HOWARD: Do you like them?

DENISE: I guess so.

GENE: What are you people doing?

DENISE: We're writing an advertisement for me so I can get a boyfriend. You got any ideas?

GENE: You people are no longer playing with a full deck.

DENISE: This is a hell of a lot more fun than thinking about the new drug they're going to shoot me up with today. I think I'm going to say I'm sophisticated. It sounds more high-toned.

GENE: My lover is killing himself. . . .

HOWARD: That's not necessarily true.

GENE: And you guys are in lulu land.

HOWARD: Let go Gene.

GENE: These goddamned cliché phrases. "Let go." I'm not talking about an idea here. I'm talking about a man. My lover. Because of all this wheat-grass shit, he no longer trusts me. Doesn't think I have his best interest at heart. Lumps me in with the government, the medical profession. We can't even sit in front of the television without there being some kind of tension. My home is no longer a pleasant place to be.

HOWARD (*Not paying attention*): I'm sorry.

GENE: My kitchen now looks like a laboratory. He can't take on a part-time job because of his health. But he spends five hours a day cooking up this slop. Did you know, he has to bleach his vegetables with Clorox?

HOWARD (*Not paying attention*): I'm sorry.

GENE: We can't even go to a restaurant together anymore. We used to love going to restaurants.

HOWARD (*Not paying attention*): I'm sorry.

GENE (*Furiously*): Listen to me goddamn it!

(GENE grabs the book out of HOWARD's hand and rips the page HOWARD has been writing on.)

GENE (*Trying not to break down*): My whole life I dreamed of a having a lover. A partner. A sane, whole one. I wanted a lover with a future. I wanted us to have a future.

HOWARD (*Meaning it*): I'm sorry. I am.

GENE: Like hell you are.

(GENE exits. HOWARD and DENISE watch him leave.)

DENISE (*After a moment, looking at the crumbled page from HOWARD's book*): What did your ad say?

Blackout

SCENE 12

Another Tuesday.

JEFF appears excited. On the other side of the room a young MAN sits filling out forms. After a moment, HOWARD enters. When he does, JEFF jumps up, pulls out a toy horn, blows it, and shouts.

JEFF: Surprise!

(The MAN appears shocked by this behavior.)

HOWARD: I don't believe my eyes.

JEFF: I'm back.

HOWARD: For how long?

JEFF: Forever. Two more weeks in Florida and I would have been up for matricide.

HOWARD: Your mother and you got along that well?

JEFF: Don't get me wrong, I love my mother. She's a decent human being. Brimming with humanity. But my AIDS made her hyperactive. It was like she was on speed. She talked constantly. I fell asleep and woke up to the sound of her voice. She became obsessed with becoming the greatest mother who ever lived. She was out to prove that Jesus got gypped with that lightweight mother of his. By the time I arrived she was an expert on AIDS. NYU Medical Center could use her. She cooked all the time. Special foods for the immune system. My mother can't cook. Never could. Have you ever tried to digest charcoal-broiled, burnt, bean curd? Did I ever tell you when we were children, my sister and I had ulcers. Little baby ulcers. They're back. Only this time they're great big ones. She developed a routine. She became kind of a positive thinking Miami Beach Cassandra. Always talking about how fabulously I was doing. Peppering all talk with a kind of Walt Disney spirituality. Introducing me to everyone—"This is my brave, wonderful son. He has AIDS, you know." By the end of two weeks we were more famous than Regis and Kathie Lee. I was beginning to forget my own name. I was just the son with AIDS. I knew I had had it the night I dreamt my mother was puréed to death in a juicer. The next morning she was doing her act in Kmart. (*Imitating his mother*) "What's your name honey? Fay Ann. Fay Ann, this is my son. Do you see the light in his eyes? That's because he's special. He's been given a special burden, and he's conquering it. He has AIDS." I lost it. I turned to her and said, "Mother you have to stop telling that story up and down the beach. You have to accept that you're the one with AIDS." The poor woman just started screaming. It was the first real feeling she had since I arrived. She screamed all the way home. Even up the elevator. I told the ladies who were riding with us that she had just heard Lucille Ball was dead. She so wanted me out of Miami that she believed the most stupid lie. I told her that the Academy of Music—whatever that may be—was giving me a rent-free apartment in New York. She said she would visit. In a few months.

HOWARD: Where are you staying?

JEFF: With a friend. I told him it's only for a week. He thinks I'm just visiting from Miami. I don't want to freak him out.

HOWARD: Jeff, you have no money. What are you going to do?

JEFF: I don't know. I'm just happy to be out of Miami. I never thought I would do anything like that. Just pack up and leave. I'm getting daring.

MAN (*Under his breath*): Fool.

JEFF: What?

MAN: Go home.

JEFF: This is my home.

HOWARD: Honey, now this might not happen, but suppose you get sick.

JEFF: There's no reason for anyone to worry, because I have health insurance. I have no money. But I do have health insurance.

MAN (*Nervously*): I'm trying to fill out these forms. Will you please keep it down?

JEFF: Sorry.

HOWARD (*To the MAN*): This is a public space. People can talk.

MAN: Well, I just don't feel like listening to other people's problems at the moment. Okay?

HOWARD: Then go somewhere else. Try another planet.

MAN: But I may need their help.

HOWARD: Then you're just going to have to concentrate harder.

JEFF: Maybe we should continue this conversation over coffee.

HOWARD: No, we'll have it now.
JEFF: Later. After you're finished with Louise.
HOWARD: I'm not seeing her today.
JEFF: Then why are you here? Who are you seeing?
HOWARD: Doctor Willis.
JEFF: But he's the cancer doctor.
HOWARD: A couple of spots. That's all.
JEFF: Not KS too.
HOWARD: Please don't get upset.
JEFF (*Obviously shaken*): Can I hold you?
HOWARD: I'm all right.
MAN: They expect me to fill out their damn forms with the two of you in the room. Well, the hell with them. I shouldn't be here. I'm not like you guys. I'm not going to make a career out of this disease.
HOWARD (*To the MAN*): Good for you.
JEFF (*To HOWARD*): How long have you had KS?
MAN: I'm getting out of here.
HOWARD (*To the MAN*): Do you need help with the forms?
MAN: Why do they need to know some of these things?
JEFF: Howard, I just asked you a question.
HOWARD (*To the MAN*): What things?
MAN (*Ripping up the forms and giving them to HOWARD*): If they come looking for me, tell them here are their forms.
HOWARD (*To the MAN*): Oh, sit down.
MAN: And tell them they can shove every one of their questions.

(The MAN exits.)

HOWARD: Denial.
JEFF: What about yours?
HOWARD: And yours?
JEFF: That you can't lay on me.

HOWARD: You have no place to live.

JEFF: How long have you had KS?

HOWARD: Over a month. (*Strongly*) I don't want to talk about that right now.

JEFF: Fine. (*After a moment*) And we're not going to talk about my living situation.

HOWARD: Fine.

JEFF: So what are we going to talk about?

HOWARD (*After a moment*): What are you doing tonight?

JEFF: Nothing.

HOWARD: How about a movie?

JEFF: I'm watching money.

HOWARD: My treat.

JEFF: Are you sure?

HOWARD (*Jokingly*): But no popcorn.

JEFF: Cheap.

HOWARD: What should we see?

JEFF: Oh . . . something new. . . .

HOWARD: And terrible. . . .

JEFF: And funny . . .

HOWARD: With young people.

JEFF: Something where the people look forward to the future.

HOWARD: Something that has nothing to do with life.

Blackout

SCENE 13

Another Tuesday.

JEFF is seated. He has a suitcase near him. HOWARD seems agitated.

HOWARD: You can't keep living like this Jeff. Permanent plans have to be made.

JEFF: That seems to be impossible.

HOWARD: You're much too passive.

JEFF: No, I'm not. I left Miami.

HOWARD: For what? To be out on the streets?

JEFF: Things have a way of turning up.

HOWARD: Oh, for Chrissake.

JEFF: Look, Scott said he had a place for me. For a whole month.

HOWARD: Where is this place?

JEFF: I don't know.

HOWARD: Are you going to be living with somebody?

JEFF: I don't know.

HOWARD: I don't believe you.

JEFF (*On the verge of tears*): What am I supposed to do? Please stop this.

HOWARD: I want you to wake up.

JEFF: I'm awake Howard. I'm handling all that I can. I got through the last hour. I'm getting through this one.

HOWARD: There's something wrong with you.

JEFF: They tell me I have AIDS. (*He laughs.*)

HOWARD: How many social service agencies do you have working on your case?

JEFF (*Yelling*): Shut up!

HOWARD: I'm glad to see you yelling.

JEFF: But I'm not.

HOWARD: However, I shouldn't be the object of your rage.

JEFF (*Imitating Bette Davis*): "But you are Howard. You are." Let's change the subject.

HOWARD: To what?

JEFF (*After a moment*): Who do you think Cher's next husband or steady will be?

HOWARD: You're impossible.

JEFF: Or do you think she'll play the field and keep people guessing?

HOWARD: We're talking about your life.

JEFF: And I'm trying to get through the next hour.

HOWARD: And I'm trying to be a friend.

(*SCOTT enters.*)

JEFF: Then leave me alone.
SCOTT: What's going on guys? (*Jokingly*) Did Howard make a pass?
HOWARD: We were having a dispute.
JEFF: About Cher's next beau.
SCOTT: Really?
JEFF: Really.
SCOTT: Whatever gets you off. Jeffrey, wait till you see the place I've got for you.
JEFF: Yes.
SCOTT: With a room of your own. Rent free. For six, count them, six weeks.
JEFF: Amazing.
SCOTT: It's a small two bedroom, but real cozy.
JEFF: Is anybody else going to be living there?
SCOTT: Yes.
JEFF: Who?
SCOTT: Me.
HOWARD: Oh, for Chrissake.
JEFF: What happened?
SCOTT: He won't let me live the way I want to live. He criticizes everything I'm doing. (*Imitating GENE*) "Do you want to die? Is that why you're not going to your doctor? Do you want to die?" I can't take it anymore.
HOWARD: You've got to talk to him. Reach some sort of compromise.
SCOTT: It's impossible. It has nothing to do with the holistic stuff I'm doing. When that man looks at me, all he sees is a corpse. I'm not that.
HOWARD: So what are you going to do?
SCOTT: This friend of mine is going to be out of town for six weeks, and he's giving me his place.
HOWARD: After that?
SCOTT: I don't know.

HOWARD: You two can't afford "I don't knows" anymore.

SCOTT: Listen Howard, I'm alive, and while I am I want as much freedom as I can handle. I can't kiss ass and turn over my treatment to somebody for a roof over my head.

HOWARD: That roof is worth a lot.

SCOTT: Not my life.

JEFF: Where's the apartment?

SCOTT: In Chelsea. It faces a courtyard. Gets tons of sun.

JEFF: Does my room have a window?

SCOTT: Yes. A large one.

JEFF: That's good.

HOWARD: It's terrific. In six weeks you can open it and jump out.

(JEFF laughs.)

SCOTT: Lighten up Howard.

Blackout

SCENE 14

JEFF is thumbing through a magazine. HOWARD, appearing nervous, is writing a letter.

HOWARD: Damn! It's just not coming out right.

JEFF: What?

HOWARD: My letter.

JEFF: Not another one to the President.

HOWARD: No, to my sister.

JEFF: You have a sister?

HOWARD: Is there anything wrong with that?

JEFF: You never mentioned her.

HOWARD: Didn't I?

JEFF: Therapists are so secretive. They just love dragging stories out of everybody, but they act like it's a major intrusion if you ask them what they had for lunch.

HOWARD: A stuffed pepper.

JEFF: Are you and your sister close?

HOWARD: Used to be. It's our family reunion next weekend. There's going to be party.

JEFF: Will it be fun?

HOWARD: I can't go.

JEFF: Why not?

HOWARD: Because I don't want to. And this letter's all wrong. Would you listen?

JEFF: Of course.

HOWARD: "Dear Janet, So sorry this note has taken so long . . ." I wrote that "so sorry" part because that's how our Mom starts all her correspondence. Even her Visa bills. Anyway . . . "So sorry this note has taken so long. I will not be coming to the family reunion. You see, I'm redecorating my bathroom this weekend, and I'm in a conflict as to what color the shower curtain should be."

JEFF: Howard, what the hell is going on?

HOWARD: "I know you understand why I can't make it to this place you call home. Because wasn't that your same predicament the week that my Greg died? Oh Howie," you wrote. . . . "So sorry . . . you actually used Mom's expression. . . . But they just started the construction on our kitchen. . . . Now, after the funeral, come home and I'll take care of you." (*To JEFF*) I haven't been able to talk to her for a year. And now, all I can do is quote her own letter. (*Tearing up the letter*) I can't send this. It's humiliating. Too fucking needy. (*Breaking down*) But not one cousin showed up.

JEFF (*Going to HOWARD*): It's all right Howard.

HOWARD (*Furiously*): What the hell is all right?

Blackout

SCENE 15

Another Tuesday.

DENISE is pacing. JEFF is reading a magazine.

JEFF (*After a moment*): Is anything wrong?
DENISE: I don't want to be here today.
JEFF: I don't either.
DENISE: Is it interesting?
JEFF: What?
DENISE: What you're reading.
JEFF: It's about the renovation of castles. It's the latest thing the European yuppies are buying.
DENISE: So . . . how's it going?
JEFF: I don't think I'd buy one. Too damp.
DENISE: I mean with you.
JEFF: Great. I just wish it would stop raining.

HOWARD, who is walking slowly, enters.

HOWARD: So that's what's bothering you these days.
JEFF: Say "hello" before you start on me.
HOWARD: Hello. (*To DENISE*) And hello stranger. Where'd you disappear to?
DENISE: Scranton.
HOWARD: The one in Pennsylvania?
DENISE: I pray to God there isn't another one.
HOWARD: Were you there on vacation?
DENISE: I'm not tasteless.
HOWARD: You look great.
DENISE: I'm okay. Yes. I think I'm doing okay. I took my kids there.
HOWARD: Why?
DENISE (*After a moment*): They've moved in with my sister and her husband.

HOWARD: Oh God, no.

DENISE: Yes. But I'm okay. I should be grateful. Now, I know where my kids are going to be. My sister—Colleen—is very loving. So is her husband. They have a baby of their own. Now, they'll be a family of five.

(HOWARD starts to cry.)

DENISE: Howard, don't cry, please. I'm okay. We decided it was best for my children to do this now, while I'm doing well. This way, I can go down there—once a month if I want—to see how they're adjusting. I can still be a part of their lives. Howard, don't cry. It doesn't help. Look I've brought you a coffee mug. It says, "Scranton, PA." Classy, isn't it? I took a bus back. That's how you get back from Scranton. You take a bus. The man next to me wanted to chat. Wanted to get to know me. "You're not very friendly are you?" That's what he said. He said it twice. I just stared out the window. Listening to him furiously turning the pages of his magazine. Thousands of people have taken bus rides like mine. Coming from their doctors after they find out. Coming from their families after they've told them. Staring out of windows wanting it to be yesterday. My little one—my boy—when I kissed him good-bye, he immediately left my arms and went and sat in front of the TV. What do you think that poor boy was thinking? My daughter—she acts all grown-up—gave me a big hug and said, "Everything is going to be fine." Sure darling. Sure. They've seen too much already in their baby lives. I hope some day they're happy. Don't cry Howard. It doesn't help.

HOWARD: Again and again. It happens again and again.

JEFF (*Jumping up*): Howard!

HOWARD (*Yelling*): When will this stop?!?

JEFF (*Opening the door to the treatment center*): Get somebody!

DENISE (*In her own world*): Will they ever be happy?

HOWARD (*Yelling*): How much more can we take?!? How much more?!?

(*HOWARD lets out a scream. DENISE remains seated. JEFF remains frozen.*)

Blackout

SCENE 16

Another Tuesday.

(*HOWARD is asleep on the floor. JEFF is watching him.*)

JEFF (*After a moment*): Howard . . . they called you.
HOWARD (*Waking up. After a moment*): I was dreaming.

(*HOWARD struggles to get up.*)

Blackout

SCENE 17

Another Tuesday.

(*HOWARD appears to be engrossed in his book. JEFF is watching him.*)

JEFF: Is it good?
HOWARD: *War and Peace.*
JEFF: That should keep you going for a year.
HOWARD: These days I can lick a book like this in a week.
JEFF: You've been that social?
HOWARD: How's Scott?
JEFF: Good. He's fun to live with. He sings. Like around the house. It puts you in a good mood.
HOWARD: When you have to move, do you know where you're going yet?

JEFF: I'm working on it.
HOWARD: What about Scott?
JEFF: He's working on it.
HOWARD: I guess that's good.
JEFF: I wish you'd drop by and visit us.
HOWARD: I don't think so.
JEFF: Why not?

(GENE enters.)

GENE (*Tentatively*): Hi guys.
JEFF: Hello. What brings you here?
GENE: Howard left a message. Said he had to see me. That it was urgent.
HOWARD: I'd like to talk.
GENE: Yes.
HOWARD: Over dinner soon.
GENE (*Awkwardly*): Oh. Well, I'm taking off for a while. A vacation.
HOWARD: Okay. When you get back.
GENE: I'm not sure when that will be. I'll give you a call. I guess I'll be seeing you guys.
HOWARD: Wait! Gene—do—do you miss Scott?
GENE (*Embarrassed*): That's not your business.
HOWARD: I'm worried about him.
GENE: I try not to.
HOWARD: You care for him, don't you?
GENE: You're embarrassing me.
HOWARD: I know you do. So you've got to take him back.
JEFF: Howard!
GENE: It's over.
HOWARD: Then be a friend. Love him as a friend.
JEFF (*To HOWARD*): Stop it! Have some pride.
HOWARD: Screw it!
GENE: I've got to get back to the office.

HOWARD (*Grabbing GENE's arm*): The office? What the fuck you talking about?

JEFF: Howard, don't do this.

GENE (*To HOWARD*): Let go.

HOWARD (*Holding tight*): Someone you once loved is sick. Has no money. And in a few weeks will have no place to live.

GENE (*Shoving HOWARD away from him*): I can't think about it anymore.

HOWARD: You have to.

GENE: No! No, I don't. Right now, I can't. I've had enough.

HOWARD (*Begging*): What about Scott?

GENE: I'm not Scott, and I'm not you. The last two years have been a nightmare. But there's a way out for me, and I'm taking it.

HOWARD (*Pleading*): What about us? People have to help, don't they? You have to help.

JEFF: Shut up Howard!

GENE: All I have is one life. I want some pleasure.

HOWARD (*Desperately*): But what about us?

GENE: I pray for you.

(HOWARD hauls off and slaps GENE across the face. GENE just stands there.)

JEFF (*To GENE*): Get out of here.

GENE: I'll still pray.

JEFF: Go!

(GENE backs out of the room.)

HOWARD: Look at me. I'm going crazy. I am. We all are. Every single damn one of us.

Blackout

SCENE 18

Another Tuesday.

DENISE is alone. She looks around and seems uncomfortable. A VOICE comes over the public address system.

VOICE: Dennis McMillian report to room 3. Dennis McMillian to room 3.
DENISE (*After a moment. Softly, almost crying*): It's Denise. Denise.

(She slowly gets up and heads for the treatment center.)

SCENE 19

Two weeks later.

JEFF is seated next to HOWARD. HOWARD appears dazed. He has a book in his lap.

JEFF: You were home. I know you were there.
HOWARD: I probably went out for milk.
JEFF: You were in there. You don't even answer your phone.
HOWARD: I'm just going through a hermit phase. That's all.
JEFF: Why don't you want to be with your friends?
HOWARD: Jeff, lay off, please. Let me get back to my book.
JEFF: Look at me Howard.
HOWARD: No, I can't. I love you Jeff. I love Denise. But I don't want to be with you now. I don't want to think about Denise and her children. I'm like Gene. I don't want to think about you. Your lover. All my dead friends. I just want to read my book.
JEFF: What about you? What kind of thought are you giving yourself? Aren't you sad at what's happening to you? I am. Don't you want to tell me?
HOWARD: Tell you what?
JEFF: That you're getting weaker. That you're losing weight. That

you're sleeping all the time. That you're having trouble walking.

HOWARD: Please let me read my book.

JEFF: Talk to me.

HOWARD: Why don't we just forget it.

JEFF: Because we can't. Come on . . . please . . . talk to me.

HOWARD (*After a moment*): Last night . . .

JEFF: Yes . . .

HOWARD: . . . when I came out of the bathroom, I didn't know where I was. I stood there in my apartment, among my things, and I didn't know where I was.

JEFF (*Lovingly*): Now, say it. Please.

HOWARD: What?

JEFF: You know.

HOWARD: I'm . . .

JEFF: Yes.

HOWARD: Afraid. I'm so afraid.

(HOWARD begins to cry.)

JEFF: Don't do this alone.

HOWARD: I don't know how long I stood there. Shaking and wondering where I was.

JEFF: You don't need to do this alone. I'm a terrific nurse.

HOWARD: I can't ask you. You've done it already. I can't ask you to do it again.

JEFF: I'd do it again and again and again if it would help.

HOWARD: You'd come live with me?

JEFF: I'm practically homeless.

HOWARD: Are you neat?

JEFF: I have no idea what a dust ball looks like.

HOWARD: You've got yourself a roommate.

(JEFF takes HOWARD in his arms.)

Blackout

SCENE 20

Two weeks later.

SCOTT and JEFF are listening to DENISE.

DENISE: The kids are doing okay. Teddy has made a good friend so he's busy and happy. Jeff—you'll appreciate this—Michelle is taking piano lessons and loving it. It was a crazy weekend. My sister and I cooked and drank gallons of coffee. The only problem is Bill, my brother-in-law. He's a beautiful human being—don't get me wrong. This is awful, but I've got to say it. He's the most boring person I've ever met. After dinner one night he was talking a blue streak. I sat there trying to listen, but I fell right to sleep. Had a good doze. The poor guy was embarrassed. I said—this is the worst—that people with AIDS fall asleep constantly. He believed me, thank God. Colleen is so vibrant. What could she see in him?

SCOTT: Maybe he's great sex.

DENISE: I doubt it. If I have insomnia now, I picture him talking to me and within minutes I'm in Never Never Land. I hope his personality doesn't rub off on my children.

JEFF: He can't be that bad.

DENISE: He's a beautiful person. I'm grateful to him. I should keep my mouth shut. He's in hardware. Maybe he's the Michelangelo of light fixtures.

SCOTT: Maybe at night, in his basement, he's working on the great American poem.

JEFF: Or the cure for AIDS.

DENISE: You've got it. You guys are so perceptive. Bill doesn't want to see me get too excited. His boring nature is all a disguise. He's going to come up with a cure for AIDS.

(HOWARD, who is now using a cane, walks in slowly and looks in pain.)

HOWARD: Somebody better. And soon.

JEFF: You finished?

HOWARD: Yes. Thank you for coming here Scott. You look good.
SCOTT: Still walking around.
HOWARD: How have you been living?
SCOTT: Sponging off a lot of people.
HOWARD: Is that okay?
SCOTT: Not all the time.

(HOWARD strokes SCOTT's face.)

HOWARD: I'm glad you're here. I need you people today.
SCOTT: Are they going to put you in the hospital buddy?
HOWARD: Not yet.
JEFF: Great. Then let's get out of here.
HOWARD: I have to sit for a minute. What a day. I got stuck with blind Belinda.
JEFF: I'm sorry. How many times did she stick you before she found a vein?
HOWARD: My arm can now be used as a colander.
JEFF: What did Dr. Willis say?
HOWARD: The news is not good. I may refuse to believe him. I'm wasting away. Disintegrating. I'd rather think of it as a process of evaporation. Do you think I'll be in the air like H_2O?

(DENISE embraces HOWARD. JEFF and SCOTT lovingly watch them.)

HOWARD: You smell good.
DENISE: Thank you.
HOWARD: Don't let go yet. I have blossomed into a sentimental sponge.
JEFF: He's even taken to watching the reruns of *The Waltons.*
HOWARD (*Leaving DENISE's embrace*): And you promised you'd never tell.
JEFF: I lied.
HOWARD: Denise, do you believe in God?
DENISE: No.
HOWARD: Shit.

DENISE: Did I give the wrong answer?

HOWARD: I was hoping you did. It would have thrown a nice monkey wrench into my atheism.

SCOTT: I believe in God.

HOWARD: You do?

SCOTT: Why are you surprised?

DENISE: What God do you believe in?

SCOTT: There's only one God.

DENISE: He's a Catholic.

SCOTT: Not anymore. But I am a Christian.

JEFF: No!

SCOTT: Yes.

JEFF: I'll be damned.

SCOTT: I can't believe how shocked you people look.

JEFF: It doesn't seem to fit.

SCOTT: With what?

JEFF: With your politics.

SCOTT: That's narrow-minded.

JEFF: Sorry. Maybe if you told us you were into some New Age philosophy where they read auras and build pyramids we wouldn't be so surprised.

SCOTT: Well, get ready for this one. I go to church.

JEFF: No.

SCOTT: I take communion. I always have, and I always will.

HOWARD: Even before you got sick?

SCOTT: Yes, Howard.

DENISE: Well, I'll be damned.

JEFF: I lived with you. How come I never knew? Why would you keep it a secret?

SCOTT: What secret? On Sundays I told you I'd bring home bagels after church.

JEFF: I thought it was a poor joke.

DENISE (*To SCOTT*): You believe in heaven?

SCOTT: Yes.

DENISE: Well, I'll be damned.

SCOTT: If I told you people I was a serial killer, you would be less shocked. Come on Jeff, come out of the closet and admit you're religious too.

HOWARD: You?

JEFF: Not religious. Spiritual. There were rare moments, when I was on stage playing, I would enter another world. There has to be something beyond this. Many other worlds.

DENISE: Well, I'll be damned.

HOWARD: I envy you guys.

DENISE: I don't.

HOWARD (*To* DENISE): Not even a bit.

DENISE: No. I think some of the stories are nice, but if I believed that there was someone in charge and this is what that person had come up with—I'd walk around pissed all the time.

SCOTT: That's not how it works.

DENISE: I have no interest in any of it. It's better for me to focus on this life and get through it as best I can.

HOWARD: Jeff, I don't think I know how to do this?

JEFF: Do what?

HOWARD: Die.

JEFF (*After a moment, lovingly*): You're not dying yet. When the time comes, I'm sure it's real easy. Let's go home.

HOWARD: I don't want another night falling asleep in front of the TV.

JEFF: Then we won't turn it on.

HOWARD: I'm sounding like a pain in the ass.

DENISE: You sound drugged.

HOWARD (*Smiling*): Well, I am . . . a little. I'd love to be sitting on a porch—looking at something green.

JEFF: Now, you're sounding trite. But if you want, I'll read you an Andy Hardy story.

HOWARD (*Referring to* JEFF): Do you believe the mouth I live with?

SCOTT: I know a place.

HOWARD: What place?

SCOTT: A place where you can sit on a porch and look out on beautiful farmlands.

HOWARD: Scott, you're not going to take my hand, and we're not going to start a meditation.

SCOTT: But I know a place. Upstate. We can all go for a few days. It's owned by two guys I know. Doctors. They only use it on weekends. They're real generous. I know they'll give me the keys. Let's all go.

DENISE: All of us.

SCOTT: Why not?

DENISE: How do we get there?

HOWARD: We rent a car with my credit card. (*Handing his wallet to JEFF*) Here. Jeff, you arrange it.

SCOTT: I'll call my friends.

DENISE: Do I have time to go home and pack?

SCOTT (*Exiting*): No.

JEFF: Howard, are you sure you want to do this?

HOWARD: Why not? If I croak while you're getting the car, take me to the country anyway.

JEFF: We'll stuff you in the trunk. This way I'll be able to stretch out in the back seat.

(*JEFF kisses HOWARD and exits with SCOTT.*)

DENISE: Aren't we something.

(*The young MAN who appeared in Scene 11 walks in and sits down nervously.*)

MAN: Hi.

HOWARD: Hello.

MAN: Randy.

HOWARD: Howard.

DENISE: Denise.

RANDY (*To HOWARD*): Do you remember me?

HOWARD: Yes.

RANDY: I'm back.

HOWARD: I'm sorry.

DENISE: I'd better call my mother and tell her we're going on a trip.

(DENISE exits.)

RANDY: A vacation?
HOWARD: Sort of.
RANDY: I'm handling things better.
HOWARD: That's good.
RANDY: How have you been doing?
HOWARD: Not well today.
RANDY: I'm sorry.
HOWARD: You look good.
RANDY: I'm handling things better.
HOWARD: Attitude is important.
RANDY: That's what they say. *(Nervously)* What's it like coming here every week?
HOWARD: I've made some wonderful friends.
RANDY: But what's it like?
HOWARD: Different for everyone.
RANDY: That's evasive.
HOWARD: What do you want me to tell you?
RANDY: The truth.
HOWARD: No. You want me to lie and tell you that you'll never get like me.
RANDY: No. I want to know. What's it like? Please.
HOWARD: I can't answer that. Maybe you'll never get as weak as I am. Things are changing.
RANDY: Not fast enough. Tell me something. Anything.
HOWARD: Try to stay in charge.
RANDY: I feel lonely. So separate from everyone I know.
HOWARD: You've moved. You now live on the other side of the street. People on our side are forced to think about and look at things most people are blind to. I know you're thinking about death. Well, look at it. And then go about the business of living.

RANDY: You're a kind man.

VOICE: Mr. Tompkins, please report to room 4. Mr. Tompkins to room 4.

RANDY (*Not moving*): That's me. I'm so scared.

HOWARD: Of course you are. Why don't I stay here until you're finished with your treatment.

RANDY: Would you come in with me?

HOWARD: Of course.

VOICE: Mr. Tompkins, room 4. Room 4.

RANDY: I haven't told anybody yet.

HOWARD (*Getting up*): You'll feel better after you do.

RANDY (*Getting up*): You're probably right.

HOWARD: Are you going to be coming on Tuesdays?

RANDY: Yes. Is it a good day?

HOWARD: The best.

RANDY: Will you be here?

HOWARD: Maybe.

Blackout

WHY WE HAVE A BODY

Claire Chafee

This play is dedicated to the actors in the original cast . . .
for their passion.

WHY WE HAVE A BODY was first presented at The Magic Theatre, San Francisco. It was directed by Jayne Wenger, Mame Hunt as dramaturg, with the following cast:

LILI . . . . Amy Resnick
MARY . . . . Alice Barden
RENEE . . . . Jeri Lynn Cohen
ELEANOR . . . . Nellie Cravens

Author's Note

This play was written in three months from a wellspring of fragments and ruminations, conscious and part-conscious. I made an effort to reflect the "lesbian brain" in form as well as in content . . . therefore letting the plot be driven by memory, lust and hammering doubt. In doing so, however, I do not pretend to represent anyone else's lesbian brain but my own.

Characters

LILI a woman in her early thirties. A private investigator.
RENEE her lover, a married woman of forty. A paleontologist.
MARY Lili's sister. A criminal. Late twenties.
ELEANOR mother of Lili and Mary. Mid-fifties. Explorer.

~

ACT I

PROLOGUE

MARY, *in an orange mechanic's overall, stands center stage, pointing a semiautomatic handgun with both hands.*

MARY: OK, FREEZE! OK, OK, no comedy. Let's go, FREEZE! (*Pause.*) Yes this is a holdup. Now. Listen: I will only say this once. I am the way things go.

I've been called, The Lark, La Pucelle, deceiver of the people, sinner, murderess, saint, invoker of devils, an idolatrous, cruel, dissolute heretic, so I think this gives me some ground to talk. And I can tell you this: I am tired of putting my mood at the mercy of strangers. (*Cocks gun.*)

Take all the money out of the drawer . . . (*Points.*) that drawer . . . and put it in a to-go container. (*Watches him.*) Any size.

Is this your first time, you're very nervous. Are you kidding? This is my fifteenth 7-Eleven. So you can trust me here. Now I want you to put the cup on the counter and slowly turn to face the wall. I am not going to shoot you. You are a very negative person. Since I came in here, it's been worst-case scenario in your mind, boom-boom-boom, down the line. The world is going to get to you if you keep on going like this . . . and let me tell you—there is very little Prozac can do for you, when push comes to shove, as it did in my case. (MARY *motions for him to throw to-go container.*)

Now I'm gonna back out of here and I want you to close your eyes. Close . . . Your . . . Eyes. If you think that you can love me unconditionally, press 1, NOW. If you love me a lot but you just can't take my moods, press 2, NOW. If you're calling from a rotary phone, wake up. This is the 90s: go and get yourself a Touch-Tone—something to lean against. It's important that you pay attention. I will not repeat myself. You cannot return to the main menu at any time.

There will be no pitons on which to hook your rope, no themes, no easy contradictions. You are skidding sideways on the ice, and there's nothing you can do about it. It's not your fault that you don't listen to your own unconscious mind. That's why it's there. (*Blackout on* MARY. *Lights up on* LILI.)

SCENE I

Music: Scarlatti, Pastoral in C major. LILI *is in bed, asleep. An alarm goes off: digital.*

LILI (*Turns off clock.*) When I was in the womb, my mother listened to nothing but Scarlatti. Scarlatti. Over and over.

All day long she would rock by the window . . . in the dead heat of morning . . . in a lemon-colored dress. She would look out at the desert and picture different forms of transportation. (*She finds her silk bathrobe and puts it on.*) She'd tilt her head to one side and I was the thought that she was having. She thought me up. (*She finds her slippers.*)

She wanted something different. That is why she called me "Lili," thinking it was French. That is why, when she got mad, she'd say, *"mais, Qu'est-ce que c'est que ça?* (*Pronounced: may kesskuh seh kuh sah? hand-on-hip.*)

The voice of my grandmother was all around me; told me details I would not remember but nevertheless just know. "A pound of butter equals four sticks." Things like that. "Never use the inside fork." "You can make a tasty dip from sour cream and a stirred-in packet of onion soup mix." "Seat your guests boy, girl, boy, girl." "Always let a frozen cake completely thaw before you serve it." Things like that.

When my mother put her hand against her belly, I could feel her pat me on the head. She was working on a promise, the details of which she would not remember but nevertheless just know.

I can hear her heartbeat going "thud, thwat, thud, thwat." I can hear the crunch of Dorito chips that she is chewing aimlessly. I can see the pictures play against the inside of her rib cage . . . those home movies of the heart . . . I become the shape of things my mother never tried. Things my mother gave up on to have me. I can see that there's a highway, I can see that there's a suitcase. And I start to get a restless feeling like I want to get born but I don't know how. (*LILI closes eyes. Lights up on ELEANOR.*)

Before I attached myself to the womb, in that tiny fall, when I was both, when I was anything, and could be anything, before the loss of becoming specific . . . when I was single.

Before I became this shape of wanting you.

SCENE 2

ELEANOR: Compare the brain of a perfectly normal woman, with that of a lesbian. The Lesbian Brain is divided into three sections, as opposed to the subdivision into two sections of the normal brain. MEMORY . . . LUST . . . and HAMMERING DOUBT. (*Points to small circle below Lust.*)

Because the lesbian is born without a future, the Lesbian Brain is born with more past to remember and has developed a larger location in the prefrontal cortex, specifically for this function.

It is still not clear however whether this area develops in utero, therefore forming a certain predilection to be a lesbian, or whether this extended capacity for memory develops later, simply as a by-product of years of living without a future and more past than one can possibly manage. It is confusing. I sincerely try to pierce that question. At one time I did blame myself that Lili was a lesbian . . . but she just told me: "Why should you take all the credit" so I guess that finally just sunk in. Now I live by the great words of Ophelia: "Lord we know what we are, but know not what we may be."

And as you know with science, once you start to ask there are just more questions than there are answers. However, it is safe to say that, . . . since the dawn of time, we have been mostly sleeping. (*Lights out on* ELEANOR *and* LILI. *Music: Ella sings "Honeysuckle Rose."*)

SCENE 3

Lights up on MARY *in the desert, putting on makeup. She has propped up a little mirror on her travel makeup case. She has on handcuffs. A slide of the desert is behind her.*

MARY: I swear to God you are my only friend. (*Putting on lipstick very carefully.*) When I talk to you I want to be glamorous. Now . . . I can hear you tell me . . . "you don't have to be glamorous when you talk to me," but . . . if you sat by the highway and hallucinated for days at a time, you would want to at least be good-looking.

People ask me when did Joan of Arc surrender . . . the truth is (*Blots lips with a Kleenex.*) there were many surrenders.

What's the definition of insanity . . . say it . . . say it! Doing the same thing over and over and expecting different results.

I've got my session tape. Travel therapist, for the patient on the move. (*Presses* PLAY *on boom box . . . hears recorded lines.*)

"How do you feel? What's come up for you this week? How does this relate to your mother? And how does that make you feel? Have you expressed any of this to her? And what do you feel about me? Do you see a pattern here? Can you forgive that in yourself? Is there a way to integrate the two? Well I guess that's all the time we have this week." (*Presses* STOP.)

Usually I actually answer the questions on the tape. It helps you more than it looks like it would . . . (*Continues to make herself up.*) I just love that they call this "making yourself up."

SCENE 4

LILI: When I was growing up, they taught you very young to tell them right away if you were a boy or if you were a girl. And from then on you were sent to live in two different worlds. Even before you were born, they asked this question over and over, and from in there you can't imagine what the problem is. "In our family," Grandma said, "the men pass down the name, the women pass out hors d'oeuvres." Boys had shop. They got to bring home breakfast trays made out of plywood: things you had a use for. We sewed those pictures with the poked out holes. A picture of a rabbit done in yarn. We all did the same picture of a rabbit. The good part about living in the world of the girl is it prepares you for absurdity. Centuries from now, they are going to dig up those things and wonder: "What culture, what form of life, what pattern too intricate to discern created the need for these?" (*Lights on* MARY, *who looks in makeup case and takes out a bent hairpin, starts to pick the lock of one of her handcuffs.*)

SCENE 5

MARY: The thing about leading an army, any army, is they don't just follow out of duty . . . it's the back of your head they watch. And if you haven't made that adjustment . . . inside . . . they can tell. (*One handcuff opens easily. She leaves the other one on as a bracelet.*) I was out collecting firewood when I first heard my Voices. I was thirteen years old. A shepherd girl, with nothing but the sheep to watch, gets ideas in her head. "Don't get nervous" I told myself. "Miracles happen." I told myself. "You're out collecting firewood, you hear your Voices. There they are." Who was I to judge their motives?

SCENE 6

LILI: The first lesbian I ever met was Harriet the Spy. The second was Margaret Mead. I knew she didn't fit in. It was obvious. She had thick ankles and she took herself seriously. Around about that time I was also aware of girl actor Jodie Foster, girl actor Tatum O'Neal and that lady on *The Beverly Hillbillies* . . . Miss Hathaway . . . all of whom also took themselves seriously, and were sturdy in one way or another. All of them: investigators.

I think that is because they learned so well from an early age to do surveillance. I fell in love four times before the age of eight . . . each time it was with a girl . . . and no: I did not want to be like them. I did not want to write romantic letters from camp. I did not want to share their skates. What I wanted was to take them on the rug. Of their parents' bedroom. Exactly. So, I had no other choice than to be a spy. (*A telepathic fax appears. She watches it.*) That must be Mary.

I still can't figure out how she does that. Every time she hits another 7-Eleven, she faxes a confession. Telepathically. (*She nods.*) Mary. (*We see* MARY, *at a pay phone in the desert, as* LILI *reads.*)

"Pulled another job. Some complications: cashier a novice. Was chased and apprehended. But . . . leapt out back of van: angels slipped inside the car lock . . . Ran into a crowded mall . . . Lost authorities in a gourmet jellybean store . . .

I love you and you know that, Mary." (*The telephone rings.* LILI *looks at it.* MARY *stands still, hands down.*)

OPERATOR VOICE: Will you accept a collect call to anyone, from Mary?

LILI: (*Staring straight ahead.*) Yes.

MARY: Lili? Lili hi. Hi. Listen . . . would you get me out of here? I need you to get me outa here. (*Pause.*) My roommate's got a walkman that she plays that thing so loud I can hear it coming outa her eyes . . . she's got that knob on ten, you know, and you wanna know what she listens to Lili? (*No answer.*) Willie Nelson. Willie Nelson day and night and night and fucking day, and I told her, "If I had the authority and the money right now I would go to Willie Nelson . . . to his house or mansion whatever and ask him, "How much money will it take for you to stop singing altogether? I'm talking permanent retirement, no comebacks. What's it gonna take for you to never sing another note?" And I bet you he'd do it too. You live in a lousy city for an operator call. (*Long pause. She lights a cigarette.*)

If you love me anywhere at all in your being, you will pay someone to get me out of here. I don't care what it takes. Where's our mother? I'm just trying to reach my mother. Where's our mother?

LILI: She's in Palenque. In the Yucatán. Paddling a canoe.

MARY: (*As before.*) Where's our mother?

LILI: Getting a manicure in Sri Lanka.

MARY: Where's our mother?

LILI: Completing a co-pilot's training course for American Airlines, where are you? (*Pause.*)

MARY: I just feel like I have to get in touch with my family. I just feel like I have to make contact.

LILI: What's it mean, the part, "was chased and apprehended," Mary? (*Silence.*) Where are you? You sound like you're by the highway, in the desert and distinctly NOT in a group home.

MARY: You are so good at what you do. What was it, the background sound?

LILI: I don't hear upholstery, Mary. I don't hear wall-to-wall. What I get so far is pay phone, desert, with a hot dry wind.

MARY: Where am I?

LILI: I'm not sure, but I hear handcuffs.

MARY: You're an artist Lili, never let anyone fucking tell you otherwise.

I love you, Lili. I love you and Mom. You know that. You shouldn't have to ask yourself over and over if you are great. That can be dangerous. You are great. You are great. You have the emotional calcium for that somehow . . . you know what I mean.

LILI: I may not be able to get you out of trouble this time.

MARY: I'm going to order some clothes from this catalogue. Do you want me to order you anything?

LILI: What catalogue?

MARY: (*Pulls it out from back pocket.*) L. L. Bean.

LILI: That's OK.

MARY: Are you sure? I'm getting myself some lightweight hiking boots. Are you sure you don't need anything? A canvas tote bag? Some turtlenecks?

LILI: No. I don't need anything.

MARY: What do you WANT? I want to send you something! A present or something. You're my sister. I love you and you know that.

LILI: You could send me a letter.

MARY: I don't know you well enough. Look, I'm just taking a wild guess here, but . . . do you want me to pick you up a parrot or a fish tank or something? It would be simple. How about a surfboard? Do you surf?

LILI: No, I don't think so.

MARY: Well when you look out at the water, does it look like you would want to? (*MARY spreads out hand. LILI stares out.*) OK let's not drag this out, let's not deface the moment. Do you want to take my case?

LILI: Mary. You hold up 7-Elevens in broad daylight with a semiautomatic—there aren't a lot of blanks to fill in.

MARY: Do not be so sure . . . What's my motive?

LILI: Look, I'm in the middle of something here. Can I get back to you?

MARY: You have work to do.

LILI: Yes.

MARY: I'll call you later. I'll call you in an hour. (*Starts to hang up.*)

LILI: (*Loudly.*) Mary? Call me later on than that, OK? A while from now. OK?

MARY: I keep thinking over and over about that they burned her, Lili.

LILI: Ya? (*Pause.*) I know. It's hard to imagine.

MARY: They tied her to the stake. The flames crackled and rose.

LILI: You're still reading that book?

MARY: Ya.

LILI: Well. It was a horrible way to die.

MARY: It wasn't the flames. It wasn't the smoke. It was the shame of being naked in front of so many men.

LILI: That's probably right. (*They hold still, facing forward, then both put the phone down.*)

SCENE 7

RENEE: (*Points to slide.*) Brontosaur. Any of a genus of sauropods of the Cretaceous period, weighing about 30 tons. They lived . . . they died . . . they left their bones. Part of a lost and restless generation. Most species, in fact some 99 percent of all species that have ever lived, are now extinct. When a species disappears, it cannot easily be discerned whether it is through extinction or evolution. Without extinction, evolution would be impossible. Extinction, therefore, is not a failure. (*Clicks slide.*)

This is a picture of Gloria. Hence, the "Gloria Project" . . . Gloria being the name given an immature female whose incomplete neckbone fragments I had virtually tripped over in a parking lot in the Kalahari Desert . . . (*Takes off glasses.*) that just did not belong that far from Montana. (*Clicks to a slide of the galaxies.*) . . . But . . . during the Mesozoic period . . . what with meteors, slamming into the earth . . . at a variable speed of 4,000 miles per minute . . . (*Clicks to slide.*) And with Triceratops, the vicious vegetarian, always on your tail, if I had been a baby duck-billed dinosaur, well I would want to migrate too.

SCENE 8

LILI: (*Having entered and watched* RENEE.) It is just amazing that she found a job in science.

She is an ardent fan of free association. The wild guess will always be more accurate for her . . . and contradiction is her genius. Look at her hair: it is short in a long kind of way. She has kept the sense of flowing. She's held on to the memory (*Gestures.*) of when it was long (*Gestures.*).

RENEE: (*Mirroring these gestures.*) The whole notion of going to remote places to look for dinosaur bones captivated my childhood so completely, I never questioned that was how I'd spend my life . . . and it's on my knees, at work, with that hydraulic airbrush in my hands, easing a scapula out of its rocky cradle . . . that I just think: "We're ancient beings—we're pretty spectacular and could be anything."

LILI: We have a flashback relationship: everything takes place in memory. Making everything seem strangely familiar.

I have no way of knowing this is true, but somehow, I feel so sure that she will never have the courage to keep loving me, and that there is nothing I can do about it. And that the memory of how she did love me, at the start, is the only thing still keeping her here . . . in a sort of state of regret. We are taught we are an absence and mistake this for a longing to be found.

SCENE 9

ELEANOR: Any woman has within her a profound hatred for sex. Even if, by some fluke, she herself escaped some direct violation through any number of assaults on her dignity, her desire and her view of these two things . . . then surely she will have experienced an indirect assault on her dignity, her desire and her view of these two things, while playing jacks with her friends in the school courtyard.

INHERITED, at the very least in the tissues of her sex, a collective shame passed down through tiny chinks in her mother . . . happening in imperceptible increments every night as the mother wipes up crumbs from dinner with a damp sponge.

The daughter watches. The sound of the fork against the mixing bowl, the sinking feeling the shine on the kitchen floor can summon . . . these are things that pass through her mind while having sex. Or trying on a bathing suit. Every woman has a day when she hates the form that she has taken on so much that she makes plans to have it destroyed. The will to change is somehow hindered by her body. The doubt of God exists behind her ear. Her unmet strength collects around her hips and makes them sore for no apparent reason. She feeds herself too much . . . she feeds herself too little.

She steals, she flirts, conceals the truth.

She counts the beans on her plate. She adds up numbers with phenomenal speed, the approximate number of calories in the plate that's put before her. The speed of her equations impresses astronomers. She is calculating just how much she can expect from things . . . and at what speed. This is the New Math. Her own world asks her to undress. The father's glance, the brother's trap, the mother's disbelief. Every woman is an incest survivor, if you count the thoughts of the world . . . if those count.

SCENE 10

MARY: (*Fishing through a hole in the ice.*) I've changed a lot since I was waiting for everything to happen based on love . . . the "getting your needs met" department anyway.

I was a soldier for her. I love battle. But I don't have a saviour thing—I have a hero thing. Because: she is a regal person. Let's face it, Who can actually stand to be saved? It feels disgusting. Rescue is a different matter: heroes rescue . . . rescue's not your fault. It's an emergency. And it was my particular crusade, to rescue my mother. Because she is a regal person. May not be France, but she was just as difficult in her own small way.

But, of course, I was thwarted in my attempts. She just . . . wouldn't . . . budge.

I kept misplacing myself in her mood swings. Let's put it this way: there was a possibility of a metamorphosis, but it passed. Turns out few can stand to be rescued either.

I had to accept my own mediocrity . . . even as a mental patient. I just kept telling myself: I chose these parents.

I slipped between their grief. I parachuted into their neglect. I came back to work on this, I told myself. I know the world is round. I also have an advantage in having a background in puppetry. I can make things happen. And all my life I've had those two consuming fears, that (1) I would never make something of myself, and (2) that I would one day make something of myself. It is unlikely you can actually learn anything from success, anyway. Failure: It's like the desert, it's like Windex, it makes everything clear.

SCENE 11

Music: tablas duet. Lights up dimly on a plane at night. LILI *sits by a window, the seat next to her is empty. The reading light is on overhead, a blanket is across* LILI*'s lap, one hand is clutching the armrest. In her other hand is a mini tape recorder. She is looking out the window. Sound of a plane taking off.*

LILI: (*Softly, into recorder.*) Dear Renee. (*Looks out window.*) I miss you. (*Presses* PAUSE *button. Unpresses it.*) I can't stop thinking of you night and day and crave your body always. (*Presses* STOP. *Rewinds tape. Begins again.*) I'm airborne, above a vast landscape of . . . snow. Either that or the moon is making the ocean look white. There are no lights and still the ground looks surprisingly close. I've been practicing my takeoffs and my landings: breathing, like you showed me, but it hasn't made that much difference. (*Pause.*) It's almost impossible to hope for this but I picture that you leave your husband. I play that movie again and again. I've scored the soundtrack . . . (*Presses* STOP. *Rewinds that much and listens to it. Erases it all. Starts again, looking at the recorder like* RENEE*'s inside.*) Renee? Renee. I feel kinda like Dick Tracy here. I feel . . . very private. There is no one next to me. No one can overhear. I am kissing you. Can you feel me? Renee? I want to wear lingerie. (*Smiles.*) I want you down around me. And I want to fuck you . . . and I mean that in the nicest possible way. (*Clicks off tape. To audience.*) I had written letters like that to her for a long, long time before we met. I was thinking her up. (*RENEE enters, walks down aisle and finds her seat next to LILI. To audience.*) I met her on a plane. She was sitting next to me . . . and . . . I could tell immediately that she was a good conversationalist from the way she crossed her legs, took out her novel and sent out the message, "Please don't talk to me." (*RENEE does this. Pause. Weird airplane sound.*) But after takeoff, this sound kept happening, like they were . . . pressing a button over and over, like they were trying to retract the landing gear and couldn't . . . and it was the niggling fear of death that made us start to talk.

RENEE: (*Still looking out the window.*) What's your line of work?

LILI: I'm a private investigator. (*They both nod.*) You?

RENEE: Paleontologist. (*They both nod.*)

LILI: (*To audience.*) And that was that. We started talking. There was a lot of turbulence as we climbed up to our cruising altitude.

RENEE: (*Looking into LILI's eyes.*) So. It is your job to notice little, imperceptible things that most of us would overlook, that tell the story of a person's curse . . . or shadow . . . that which they cannot help but be attracted to—yet that which they cannot permit in themselves and therefore strive to conceal. And, in doing so, of course, reveal it all the more.

LILI: (*To audience.*) I mean I knew just what she meant but I would never think to say it all at once like that.

RENEE: Are you in crime or insurance?

LILI: Well, both. But I prefer the intricacies of adultery.

RENEE: Oh I see.

LILI: I work for women who want evidence. I track down husbands.

RENEE: That must be exhausting work.

LILI: I actually find it quite relaxing. I'm a lesbian. (*RENEE, piecing it together.*)

RENEE: So . . . you don't get . . . overinvolved . . .

LILI: I travel blind. Being an outcast helps. In my work, a preconceived notion is a flat tire.

RENEE: Do you carry a gun?

LILI: Yes I do.

RENEE: Well. For what it's worth, just seeing you at the gate, I would never take you for an outcast.

LILI: (*To audience.*) Was she flirting with me? (*To* RENEE.) Well, nobody looks much like an outcast anymore. These days, we take great pride in looking not at all the way you would expect us to. At least in the business world. (*Looks at* RENEE.) How long have you been separated from your husband?

RENEE: Four months. That's pretty good. That's pretty sharp.

LILI: (*Picking up her hand.*) You've got a faded tan line on your ring finger, your luggage tags say "MRS.," and you're reading *Sylvia Plath: The Complete Works*. Something's going on . . . (*Pause.*)

RENEE: When I'm with men they all complain I always lead. (LILI *looks at her.*) I always lead. Out . . . dancing.

LILI: Well, you can't just go all limp . . . and let a man drag you across a dance floor. (*Pause.*) You have to hold a bit back from a man. They have no sense of the subtle distance required between them and you. (*Pause. They both look at separate places in the plane.*)

RENEE: Does your mother know?

LILI: Ya.

RENEE: . . . and does she approve?

LILI: It threw her for a loop at first. For some reason she had a hard time imagining what we do in bed. (*Pause.*)

RENEE: I don't have trouble with that part.

LILI: (*To audience.*) She was flirting with me. She had to know that she was definitely flirting with me.

RENEE: I'd be scared I wouldn't want to get up the next morning. That it would bring out some strange, victim love-haze thing in me. (LILI *looks at her.*) . . . sleeping with a woman . . . Did you know you were gay? I mean early on.

LILI: Three years old . . . in play group. I was inexplicably drawn to the superman cape. I ran around at nap time rescuing all the girls . . . who didn't seem to mind, they were already kinda lying down . . . but it set the boys on edge. They would start to cry, and Miss Appleyard finally had to call up my mother to get me to share it.

RENEE: And did you?

LILI: I never wore it again. It took all the fun out of it: being exposed.

RENEE: While other girls were guessing what each other's favorite color was . . . I was constructing a geodesic dome out of my brother's Lego set.

LILI: Well, that's unusual . . . A geodesic dome out of Lego. That sounds impossible.

RENEE: It was. (*Lights bump down.*)

SCENE 11A

Lights up again. It's darker, there's a blanket across their laps.

RENEE: (*Looking out the window.*) I've always wanted to try parachuting. As a sport.

LILI: As a sport. Oh.

RENEE: Have you ever wanted to?

LILI: Try parachuting? No. Me? No. I'm a little phobic. No, I might try . . . maybe . . . ballooning. I would maybe try ballooning.

RENEE: Maybe ballooning. Maybe. Maybe ballooning. (*She leans over to check if* LILI*'s smiling. Blackout.*)

SCENE 12

Lights up on ELEANOR, *downstage, in a pith helmet, in the bow of a canoe, paddling up a remote river. Shadows fall across her face. She paddles. Music fades out. Sound of water.*

ELEANOR: I am convinced there is something in the female psyche that gets stuck. And it just circles in and circles in like a 747 over Chicago, trying to land and can't. We just don't think it's our turn. For five decades, I have struggled to say something more than, "Where could I have put my pocketbook?" which is the central thing I remember my mother saying. "Where could I have put my pocketbook?" She would say it like it meant . . . Like she meant to say, "Now where could I have put my . . . mind?"

We haven't thought big enough. Our thoughts are small. We retrace our steps constantly.

(*Resting paddle, taking off helmet.*) Once you wake up . . . once you come to . . . you have no place to start from. Nothing here will make any sense to you. Nothing here will make any sense.

Including becoming a student of history. Including becoming a student of the female brain. Including becoming a feminist archeologist/historian/bilingual student of the female brain. You will be stuck without a ride.

(*She starts to paddle again.*) At this point your only recourse is to choose between the following methods of transportation: falling into madness, falling in love, committing suicide or burning at the stake. Which is by far the trickiest one to engineer. You have to get somebody else to do it to you. But . . . that's also what makes it the elegant choice . . . Leaving you free to signal through the flames.

SCENE 13

A huge, blow-up slide of a photograph of the AIRPORT HILTON *sign. Music: Duke Ellington's "Stompy Jones."* RENEE, *in a black coat, stands opposite* LILI, *whose jacket is off.* RENEE *reaches out her hand and starts to dance to the music with* LILI. *She spins her out. They dance till the song ends. Pause.* RENEE *sits in a chair facing* LILI, *who sits on the still-made bed.* RENEE *has her head in her hands.*

RENEE: I can't believe I'm here with you. I cannot believe I'm here.

LILI: (*Pause. Looks at* RENEE.) Why don't you take off your coat?

RENEE: I think I'm not going to stay.

LILI: Oh. (*Pause.*) Do you wish I were a man?

RENEE: Don't be ridiculous. I'm married to a man.

LILI: Did the bellboy make you nervous?

RENEE: I think he thought that we were gay. I don't want to disappoint you. Did you think I was gay? . . . when you saw me on the plane?

LILI: I didn't think about it. (*Lie.*)

RENEE: But would you think that I was? If you saw me . . . just . . . on a bus?

LILI: Probably not. Maybe a little. Around the mouth.

RENEE: The mouth? That's really odd.

LILI: Maybe it's more the walk.

RENEE: The walk. You're saying you could tell . . . you would think I liked women if you saw me walking . . . toward a bus?

LILI: It's possible. I could tell there was a possibility.

RENEE: A possibility I like women. (*They smile.*) That's really odd. Maybe I'm a man. Is that a possibility? I feel like a man . . . (*She looks right at* LILI, *who is absolutely still.*) Men keep their change in their pockets. They have smooth, heavy desk accoutrements where they plunk down their pocket change and collar stays after a long day of getting somewhere. Feeling like a man means: wanting it direct, to the point and now.

LILI: Is that at all how you feel?

RENEE: Yes. A lot of the time.

LILI: Then maybe . . . you are . . . a man. And maybe I'm a man too . . . and that is why . . . you can't tell we are gay.

RENEE: If we're both men we'd still be gay.

LILI: True. Why don't you just let it out Renee. (RENEE *gets up, goes to her purse, takes out a changer, points it to the wall, a slide comes up.*)

RENEE: These are my parents, just after they married. (*Click.*) This is my mother with her best friend Zelda. (*Click.*) This is my mother as a girl. (*Click.*) This is my mother with me. (*Click.*) This is me. I am not a child, but a nuclear physicist trapped in the body of an infant. This is not my mother, but an orchestra . . . swelling to the night's crescendo . . . (*Slide fades.*) bows crossing strings, saxophones thick like a layer of cinnamon . . . high-hat like a match hitting water. This is not my mother but instructions transmitting through the big band sound.

Tables seated boy-girl boy-girl glimmer with the hope that it takes two to tango. My mother taught me: think the words "please ask me" till he hears you . . .

LILI: . . . and when he takes you in his arms you will be light . . . you'll be astonished . . . you'll make it look like you aren't leading as he spins you. You're a flower, not a person. Like a daisy. He becomes your future, he becomes the thought you're thinking when you put yourself to sleep . . . he's become the dreams that you are having . . . how can you not love your own dreams?

RENEE: That is what I started with. I just think that you should know.

LILI: I know. (*LILI leans in and kisses her. It takes a while. She kisses her again. Lights fade. Music: Aretha Franklin's "I Never Loved a Man."*)

SCENE 14

Lights up on MARY in an orange coat with a small hard suitcase on the floor next to her, sitting at a table in the Airport Bar. She lip-synchs to Aretha. Music fades. She looks for LILI. She arranges herself. She angles the empty chair away from the table to make it seem more welcoming. She waits. She switches chairs. She hails cocktail waitress.

MARY: "WATER WATER EVERYWHERE AND NOT A DROP TO DRINK." Yes. Let's see. (*Examines a huge drink menu.*) Why don't you bring me . . . I'll have two grasshoppers, please. I'm expecting somebody. (*She looks at her watch.* LILI *walks in.*) Lili.

LILI: Hi Mary. (*Blackout. Lights up again. They are both seated, drinks half empty. We hear constant ambient airport noise. The lights are cocktail lounge red. They are mid-conversation.*)

LILI: The thing is . . . sometimes life is very strange. Very strange. (*She takes a handful of peanuts.*)

MARY: I'm not exactly sure what it is I want to ask. The thing is hard to pinpoint. The idea. It's hard to pinpoint.

LILI: Take my collection of love affairs, for example. (MARY *nods.*) Each situation, completely unique . . . all totally different people, yet . . . uncannily alike. (*They both sip from tall drinks through straws.*) I mean, how do we spot each other from across a crowded room . . . (MARY *nods.*) and infallibly find the one who's going to make us crazy. (*She looks at* MARY.) Not literally . . . but . . . (MARY *nods gracefully.*)

And there were signs, little tip-off points about them that could have clued me in. Some of them had the same last name, or identical family structures, or a freckle in the same place. I mean I coulda spotted it. But, instead . . . those signs, instead of being like warnings, or signals . . . and this is what I'm getting at, those signs became sort of like little arrows pointing to something familiar . . . to something . . . erotic.

MARY: . . . looking for a place to happen.

LILI: The repetition compulsion is by far the most evolutionarily cruel phenomenon we've ever had, don't you think?

MARY: Yes, I do.

LILI: I mean the desire to do it over and over again, in the vain hope of getting it right is . . . well, it's pathetic. Especially considering we take such pains to accurately reproduce, in loving detail, the original situation which brought us to our knees in the first place. Seeking some sort of deliverance from the same fucked thing. (*Pause. Looks at* MARY.) Where did you fly in from?

MARY: Nowhere. Took the bus here from downtown.

LILI: So why'd you have me meet you at the airport?

MARY: It's my favorite bar. I love the atmosphere. (*Feels the texture of the air.*) The mix of terror and boredom. It's what drinking's all about . . .

LILI: Are you going to be coming home with me?

MARY: (*Reaching into her bag.*) I did order you something . . . small. (*Brings out a badly wrapped parcel.*) I know you told me not to. (*Puts it in front of* LILI.) Just a token. A little nothing that caught my eye. Just something that reminded me of you.

LILI: (*Not touching it.*) I guess there's nowhere else. Hm? At least until we contact Mom.

MARY: (*Joining in.*) And figure out what's next.

LILI: That's right. And as usual our agreement is: it cannot be a long-term thing here, Mary.

MARY: (*Taking out inhaler.*) Granny used to breathe like this: ">>>>>>>>>>>>>." (*Uses inhaler.*)

LILI: Are you OK? (MARY *nods.*) Are you agitated or anything? (*Pulls out a prescription bottle.*) I still have extras from before if you feel, and I quote, disoriented and/or violent toward yourself and/or others.

MARY: No, I actually feel quite well. (*Thinks.*) Ever listen to Don Cherry? Trumpet player? I used to try to listen to this album by Don Cherry in the 10th grade, out there, free form jazz-thing . . . and people felt great pressure to live that way . . . like they were bumping into things . . . like they were free . . .

LILI: Without a past . . .

MARY: . . . and a lot of people faked it . . . and now live in apartments, and are holding down jobs, and I, who hated this music, I, who was made nauseous by it, somehow, inadvertently . . . I don't know. Somehow this became the way my life went. (*Long pause.*)

LILI: Life does separate out, eventually, the ones who have real trouble from the ones who are looking for it.

MARY: Which is something else entirely. (*Pause. Pointing to present.*) I got Mom a harmonica and a luggage lock. And I got you this and some shampoo. I don't know what happened to the shampoo . . . but . . . (*Gestures.*) open it. (*LILI starts to unwrap the present. It is a toaster oven. Lights fade. Music: cocktail piano.*)

~

ACT II

PROLOGUE

In darkness.

VOICE: HOW TO MAKE LOVE TO A WOMAN: start with the throat. Start there. Look at this place. Is it open? Is it closed. Notice the Adam's apple. Place of the great fall . . . (*Their matches go out. They strike a new one.*) The face may be the road map, but the throat will show you all your shortcuts. (*Holding matches up to each other's mouth.*) Look at her lips. Now kiss them. Here, the rules of the road apply: If you go into a skid . . . steer right into it and for God's sake keep your foot off the brake. (*She kisses LILI.*) Take all the hard right-hand turns you want, but always always signal. Pass a hand across her belly, travel south. Slow down on the entrance ramp. Cross the isthmus of her down-below . . . as lost and as convinced as any Columbus.

SCENE I

Lights up on RENEE, in Mexico in her bathing suit and shirt.

RENEE: The other day I went into the supermarket . . . and all I could see were women. Now, I go into the supermarket all the time . . . but I never noticed women. There are women everywhere . . . picking out heads of lettuce, picking out cans . . . standing behind their metal carts they stare at the frozen foods in their own little world. And I wanted to go up to them . . . any one of them and say: "Excuse me, but I made love to a woman, and I could probably make love to you too, if you would like me to." I could barely control myself not to do that. I think I'm losing my fucking mind. I made eye contact with every woman in there. I would stand beside them, wait till I got their attention and look them straight in the eye. I think they thought I was psychotic. I especially made eye contact with the checkout girl who I swear imbued the question, "do you want paper or plastic" with the vague feel of sex. I would have never noticed this before . . . but now I do. There is a subterranean life that runs just beneath and below the normal life, and you only see it if you fall in there . . . and you either fall in there or you get pushed in, but you really don't go there for just a little excursion . . . because there really is no way back . . . to not noticing once you start. So I really don't know why they call it sexual preference. (*Lights of* LILI's *apartment come up behind her.* MARY, *in white gloves and orange crosser-guard straps, sits with a small* STOP *sign on her lap.* LILI *goes to desk and starts looking for a set of keys.*)

SCENE 2

MARY: At the time of her trial . . . Joan of Arc was expected to be a terrified, humble girl. Her first words revealed a different disposition: when asked to swear upon the Gospels that she would answer nothing but the truth, she said, "Perhaps you'll ask me things I will not tell you." (*Pause.*) There's a girl who trusts her voices.

LILI: . . . Hmmm-mm.

MARY: The only modern version of this I know of, is bulimia. (*Pause.*)

LILI: (*Throws her keys.*) Here's an extra set, top and bottom lock front door, top and bottom lock back door. The Medeco is the downstairs front door. The police lock's only used at night, from the inside. I do that. I expect you to come right back here after work, at 3:15. I expect you to report to me about your whereabouts at all times. And I assume it is clear without my even specifying this: convenience stores are out of bounds. When are you due at work?

MARY: Not for another hour. (*Looks at her equipment.*) I just wanted to be ready . . .

LILI: Remember when Mom'd drive us to the pool and you'd already have your bathing cap and goggles on in the car? You were always like that. That was very embarrassing.

MARY: . . . but that way, you're already on vacation. That way it starts before you get there.

LILI: You are just so literal. You are incapable of metaphor.

MARY: Remember when you begged Mom to send you back to that camp, because you were so moved by the candlelight closing ceremony at the end of the summer that it completely wiped out the memory of how much you hated that place?

LILI: What's your point?

MARY: . . . just that all your capable of is metaphor. This whole investigator stuff's just an overcompensation. Deep down everything always reminds you of something else . . . (*Looks at her.*) What's her name? (*Looks at* LILI.)

LILI: Renee. (*MARY looks at her.*) She's straight.

MARY: Of course she is. What's she do?

LILI: Paleontologist.

MARY: (*Shaking her head.*) That is a very sexy thing for a woman to do. You have my sympathy.

LILI: She's married.

MARY: Of course she is.

LILI: She's with her husband now in Mexico, trying to patch things up.

MARY: (*Smiles at* LILI.) I bet it's going badly. I bet she's hitting the rum. She misses you.

LILI: It's in this place . . . (*Draws a square in the air.*) over here. It's what it is.

MARY: Well, that's OK then.

LILI: Ya, but I'm just tired of compartmentalizing.

MARY: Be grateful you can compartmentalize. To me emotions are like a big wind. A tornado with people and garbage and furniture whirling around . . . (*LILI takes out wallet, pulls out a photo of RENEE and gives it to MARY, who studies it.*)

MARY: (*Looking at photo.*) Looks like she's got fruit in her hair. Is that fruit?

LILI: (*Looking on.*) No . . . I don't think so. That's just her hair.

MARY: It looks as if she's turning half away from you . . .

LILI: She's at a dinner party . . .

MARY: But, see how her . . . face is pointed at you but her shoulders are sort of tilted away to one side? Like she's about to get up and get herself a snack? (*Pointing to photo, does pose.*) See that? Looks like she's gonna bolt. (*Hands back photo.*)

LILI: Well, I don't know how you get that from a snapshot of a person eating paella.

MARY: You always pick somebody busy not-noticing you.

LILI: It's a conversation I am having with my past. (*Spot up on RENEE in a robe, the phone in her hand. The phone rings. LILI looks at it. She goes over and answers it. RENEE hangs up. Dial tone. RENEE's light goes out. LILI hangs up. Sits staring at phone.*)

MARY: (*Looking at LILI.*) Last night I had another in my series of Celebrity Nightmares. Like the one where I was supposed to drive Cindy Crawford and Richard Gere to the airport? Well, this time I'm with . . . Omar Sharif, only sometimes I am him too, just a different version of Omar Sharif . . . and I'm supposed to help him choose a wardrobe . . . only we can't decide if he should go Arab or Western.

LILI: And?

MARY: Well, that's about the end of it. Those dreams just have that snapshot feeling. It's nice though. It makes me wake up feeling like I touched something magic. That's what the famous do: they make you feel half-famous for a split of an instant. That's their job. It's hard work.

LILI: I think it's depressing. The whole thing.

MARY: Well, that's because you don't enjoy yourself. You gotta just enjoy the human dilemma, Lili. That's why it's there. (*Blackout. Music up immediately: Jane Siberry's "Are We Dancing Now?" Lights up on RENEE in a poolside chaise lounge, in a bathing suit, holding a sun reflector under her chin. Next to her is another chaise, with a man's robe and towel and a copy of* Esquire *on it. A pair of men's flip-flops face the foot of it. On a little table beside her is a man's watch and a wallet. She suns awhile, then shields her eyes and watches a figure swim laps, left to right, in the first row of the audience.*)

SCENE 3

RENEE: (*Music fades.*) What sweetheart? (*Speaking up.*) No. I don't want to come in right now. I'm reading my book. (*She leans back. She picks up* Esquire *and flips through it. Very loudly.*) Do you want me to order you another Tecate? (*She picks up his watch and looks at the time. She looks at him again. Shielding her eyes, nodding.*) I can see. You going for half a mile? Great. (*Shakes her head.*) No, I don't want to come in again . . . the sun's starting to go down. (*Puts on her flip-flops.*) I'm going to go order another drink. (*Puts on robe.*) Do you have any cash? (*He can't hear.*) Cash. (*He can't hear.*) Never mind, honey. You keep swimming. See you up in the room. (*She gives a tiny wave. Picks up his wallet. She picks up his watch and puts it on. She feels it's weight on her wrist . . . feels what it's like to wear a man's watch. She stares out.*)

SCENE 4

Cross-fade. MARY *in white gloves and crosser-guard straps, stopping traffic at an intersection. We still see* RENEE*'s fade out as scene begins. Sound of city traffic mixed with sound of planes taking off.*

MARY: (*Waving someone forward.*) Hold up, hold up, hold up. You. Hold up. Stop! (*Points to other group.*) You. Come on. Go. Go! Hurry up here, keep it moving. OK, OK, if you're going to make the turn, make it, but blend. Blend with this guy. Are you blending?

And you. Yield. He has the right of way. (*Back to other*

group.) OK., you guys . . . go. Move up into the intersection, you're blocking this whole lane. YOU—IN THE TOYOTA . . . MOVE!!!!!!! Go around him. Go. Make a choice! This is the 90s . . . choose a lane and fill it . . . pull out and be hopeful. Ya, all right . . . that's it. We got a flow going now. Very good.

Don't worry about the traffic lights—I'm superceding the traffic lights. I'm the way things go. (*Motions for new lane to pull forward.*) Lady, why are you stopping . . . You see me standing here. Would they put a traffic engineer out here if they wanted you to pay attention to the lights?

(*To a honker.*) What's your problem? You see me talking to her. (*Shakes her head.*) Hold up. It's not your turn. Oh, jeez . . . what, I don't exist now? Is that it? (*Pulls out gun.*) Which part of "hold up" did you not understand? (*Puts it back.*) It's amazing how they listen to that. (*Lights up on* ELEANOR.)

SCENE 5

ELEANOR: I suppose my girls are mad at me. I imagine I did a number of horrible things to them growing up. Whole entire lapses of concern . . . In fact I spent the whole time that they would describe as their childhood in a sort of fog. I was in a light trance at the time. And now I honestly do not remember when I said, for instance: "—" (*Makes a silent gesture.*) which apparently turned Mary into a criminal . . . or the time I asked the salesgirl for help in Bloomingdale's and completely mortified Lili, to the point where she still hates being naked. I take their word for it but I don't remember.

If it's true that we replace each cell entirely every seven years, and if the soul does progress across the sky, like the planets . . . then it's fair to say I was a different person. Someone I no longer am. The person you have come for is no longer here. And the little girls they were, are no longer here. So . . . it is just a memory talking to a memory.

There maybe should be a statute of limitations on this

kind of thing, but there isn't. (*Cross-fade to* LILI *and* MARY. *Back in her apartment,* LILI *is working on her computer, compiling evidence.* MARY *enters, taking off her uniform.*)

SCENE 6

LILI: (*Not looking up.*) How was work?

MARY: Fine.

LILI: I'm working on a menu for the next three days. Do you still not eat meat?

MARY: No meat. No fish. Nothing with a face. Have you seen my *Sylvia Plath: The Complete Works* anywhere?

LILI: You're reading that book?

MARY: Ya. Why not?

LILI: Well, it's just I wouldn't recommend her for people with a tendency toward depression.

MARY: I find her hysterically funny myself. (*Looks for book.*)

LILI: Sylvia Plath?

MARY: She is one of the great comic writers of the twentieth century.

LILI: Prove it.

MARY: (*Finding book.*) It was in my bag. (*She walks to the center of room, and "delivers" the twelve-line middle section of Sylvia Plath's poem "Lesbos." She delivers it, loudly and as one sentence. Then pauses, sits down, closes book.*)

LILI: That's not funny.

MARY: To each his own. (*Pulls out another book.*) When I'm done with her I'm starting on, *The Encyclopedia of Amazons.* (*Reading cover.*) "Women Warriors from Antiquity to the Modern Era." "Absorbing . . . a fresh, sometimes surprising look at the role of women in the world's long history of combat."

Did you know that Joan of Arc's father had this premonition dream that she went off dressed as a soldier, and the next day he told his sons that if that were ever to happen in reality they were to take her and drown her in the river? Some people really get upset at cross-dressing.

LILI: No wonder she took on the English. There was no going back . . .

MARY: After they burned her, they also tried to burn her heart and every entrail . . . because it was rumored that her spirit could still escape and live—if she really were a witch . . . but they couldn't set them on fire no matter how much lighter fluid or whatever they used . . . and they ended up having to just throw them in the river . . . and that is how the executioner went mad . . . because that meant he burned a saint. That is a fact. If you watch the Ingrid Bergman movie, you can see him get upset and beat his fist against his head, but they don't explain why or anything. I guess they didn't think it was integral to the story . . .

LILI: They shoulda gotten you to play her.

MARY: (*Looks at* LILI.) Ya well. I know I'm not really her.

LILI: I know you do.

MARY: There were just so few examples of a woman I would want to be when I grew up.

There was Harriet the Spy. There was Margaret Mead. Those were yours. Besides . . . I mean they were nice, but you couldn't qualify them as warriors. Tintin and Go Speed Racer were the only two I liked and they were boys.

LILI: And both cartoons.

MARY: And both cartoons. (*The phone rings. Spot up on* RENEE, *in robe, with a phone in her hand.* LILI *looks at the phone. She goes over and answers it.* RENEE *hangs up. Dial tone.* RENEE*'s light goes out.* LILI *hangs up. Long pause.*)

MARY: (*Looks at* LILI.) The thing you want to say is: "I am not a thought you're having. I am not a thought of yours." Am I right? What ever happened to that U.P.S. delivery woman?

LILI: She moved out. We're not talking. I sent her her stuff in a cardboard box. There wasn't much evidence: a toothbrush, her perfume, an extra T-shirt, photographs of her naked, photographs of me naked, a pair of dangly earrings and a map.

MARY: Did you send it U.P.S.?

LILI: (*Breaking into a smile.*) I certainly did.

MARY: Why do you live like this?

LILI: Why do you commit crimes?

MARY: I think we need to bring Mom back here. Where's our mother?

LILI: Shearing sheep in Turkey . . .

MARY: Where's our brother?

LILI: Carrying on a dialogue with the Dali Lama.

MARY: Where's our mother?

LILI: Intercepting ham radio broadcasts in Outer Mongolia.

MARY: (*Kneeling by the TV and sending a fax by pressing her forehead to the screen and concentrating.*) "Come home. We need you for verification. Huge chunks missing . . . make haste, your daughter Mary, and your daughter Lili." Have you got a satellite dish?

LILI: Where are you going to send it?

MARY: Telepathic fax: just punch it in, and it goes to where she is. Angels . . . (*Looks at* LILI.) . . . slip inside the lock.

LILI: (*In unison.*) Slip inside the lock. (*ELEANOR in her own spot, is staring into a pool of water, which casts a blue light on her face.*)

SCENE 7

ELEANOR: I wish I was in a pool right now, one where the lights come up off the bottom, where the steam comes up off the surface at night, as you do your breaststroke. Aquamarine.

That used to be my favorite color. Many, many things used to come in that color: sofas, refrigerators, cardigans . . . evening gowns. I love those ads for the Caribbean where that color bumps against the uninterrupted sand. I wish I was in a pool right now, under a palm tree and beginning a whole new life, as of tonight.

There was a lot of ice in my background. Ice fishing, iceberg lettuce . . . the sound of ice in a highball glass. When I think of my childhood I am skating an awful lot of the time. It's all I remember really. Every day I do the exact same thing: I lace my skates up on the bench. I try to be safe. I try to push off. I take little trips, little half-circles on the ice. Like the marks left on cocktail napkins by our mother's martinis: half-circles on the ice over frozen lakes with Indian names.

Little trips. Try to make it look like you're practicing. Never ever let it look like you are actually doing this.

I can feel them. I can feel them pulling . . . but I won't go back.

SCENE 8

RENEE holds LILI in bed. LILI is sleeping

RENEE: (*Staring at LILI's face.*) I am watching her for signs. Something crucial. Something slow.

The body holds grudges, the body is old. (*To audience.*) In dreams the fathers still are stalking us in the woods, daggers at their sides like tiny flames.

The past. The space between her teeth. The unremembered memories of fierce assaults and slow betrayals . . . place-of-all-places, soft tongue pressing on it . . . pressing till it hurts something crucial, something slow begins. (*Blackout. Lights up immediately. RENEE is running her hand down LILI's thigh.*) When I was in Mexico, all I could think of was your hipbone against my cheek. (*Pause.*)

LILI: When you were in Mexico . . . all I could think of was: what aftershave does that guy use? Mennen? Old Spice?

RENEE: I'm leaving him.

LILI: Eternity for Men? Aramis?

RENEE: I've left him.

LILI: Brute? Fabergé?

RENEE: I left him a while ago. I may have never been with him.

LILI: I have to tell you something right now. I may be a first for you . . . but you are my one-too-many times. I may be your wake-up call, but you are just the bell that sounds the hour. Hour after hour. It's the same ache. What's missing is the same.

You want to play missing persons? You pretend you're missing and I search for your whereabouts? I trail you, do surveillance . . . dust for prints . . . run a credit check . . . figure out if you're gay? So that you are my subject . . . and I deliver you back explained. I have stared in people's eyes until they bloom their secrets . . . took their private puzzles on and solved them. I have cracked the hard ones, Renee. I became a private investigator . . . but what I wanted, with something approaching despair, was for somebody to figure me out. That I could just for once be the subject . . . of an investigation. That it would be my turn to be the mystery. It is my turn to be the fucking mystery. (*Long pause.*)

RENEE: Then stop figuring everything out. (*Pause.*)

LILI: It better not turn out that you're fickle.

RENEE: I cannot think of a moment . . . of the many I have had on earth, when I have felt anything approaching fickle. But if I had had that moment . . . this would be it's polar opposite.

LILI: Are you making love to me?

RENEE: It is your turn to be the mystery. That's why you're so pissed off. (*They kiss.* RENEE *breaks away for a moment.*) I always wondered why I wanted to be a paleontologist so badly.

But I think now, having kissed you I might have made that my career. (RENEE *and* LILI *start to make love. Blackout.*)

SCENE 9

Lights up on MARY, *in her own spot, awake late at night, in the living room. She has a sleeping bag, her boom box and a camping lantern. She drinks hot chocolate.*

MARY: I can't believe I'm here again. I cannot believe I'm here. I have proof . . . that I seem to be permanently stuck in a misconception.

I am trying to remember childhood. I remember the brown sand road and me alone on it. I remember the cove, and the swimming pool but nobody touched me. I would dive beneath the waves all day, touch the bottom, push off, climb back up, feel the blue rush past me, like a slow embrace. Repeat. All afternoon. Every afternoon. Diving under in a one-piece: lunatic daughter called in for lunch . . . sitting on a lawn chair in a bathrobe eating tuna-fish sandwiches but nobody talked to me, nobody touched. (*LILI enters, on her way to get some water.*)

LILI: How long have you been up?

MARY: A while. I just keep drinking hot chocolate. (*Shrugs like there's no explaining it.*) I don't think she's coming. I don't think she's coming back.

LILI: Ya. This time I think you're right. I think she's gone.

MARY: Are we talking about our mother?

LILI: Ya.

MARY: So. I guess this is pretty much it then. I guess we are the next generation.

LILI: Ya.

MARY: . . . Well all I can say is: this is a small world.

LILI: You know what's stuck in my head? *Mission Impossible.* (*She hums.*)

MARY: I just want to be part of this family. This family is the shrapnel flying out in a million directions. This is Life After The Blast. There's too much energy in my hands. There's no where for it to go. I feel like they're gonna clench up on me . . .

LILI: What helps?

MARY: It feels like they're gonna fly off the ends of my arms. Like they're separate.

LILI: What helps?

MARY: I guess if you could hold them down . . . hold on to them . . . (*LILI holds MARY's hands.*) Tighter. (*LILI does that.*) Tighter.

LILI: Like that? (*MARY nods.*)

MARY: I've been trying to remember my childhood. I think I need a better past.

LILI: You just have to know what it is, apart from everything else.

MARY: We split. We divided, like one cell; you and me. We each took on only one attribute for simplicity.

It's limiting enough to be a human being, it's fucked enough without having to split the traits with someone else. Why couldn't I be fierce for example? Is it your opinion that I was never capable of being fierce? Wasn't it in my column? Life is hard enough without having to lop off an entire column of human attributes in order to survive.

LILI: I think you are as fierce. I think of you as fierce all the time.

MARY: (*Furious.*) What I'm lacking is an achievement. Of any kind.

LILI: You are not. (*Pause.*) You have sailed through practically an armada of therapists . . . virtually unchanged. That has got to count for something.

MARY: (*Stopping in her tracks.*) . . . didn't touch me did they?

LILI: They shoulda paid you.

MARY: . . . for the privilege.

LILI: . . . of your company.

MARY: Is there someone in your bedroom? I think I heard some Spanish music . . .

LILI: (*Getting up.*) She came back early.

MARY: Well if she tries an escape . . . you know what the King of Spain once said, on how to put down a coup d'état . . .

LILI: No. What did the King of Spain say?

MARY: (*LILI starts to leave.*) (1) Stay in the palace. (2) Hold your ground, whatever the cost. (3) Do not leave under any circumstances, whatever they promise, whatever they threaten. (*LILI starts to go . . . comes back.*)

LILI: Well. It's different. (*Exits.*)

MARY: It's going to have to be.

SCENE 10

Starting to collect her stuff to leave.

MARY: My two favorite subjects growing up were slavery and the Holocaust. I wanted to find out about a thing I had something in common with. Every day I practiced leaving in some form or another. Sometimes I would practice getting out of the car, and slamming the door. Sometimes I'd practice stepping out of the school bus onto the curb, I'd picture I was somewhere else . . . somewhere in Europe. Or I'd get in an elevator, and watch the door close behind me and focus on the sound it made "ssshhhh-hhtt . . ." and then I'd press any floor other than the one I was going to . . . little things like that. Little trips.

I thought I couldn't be the first to go, 'cause someone beat me to it. But I knew one day it would be my turn. It is my turn.

I'm gonna turn myself in. I'm gonna serve my time. (*MARY clicks on her own handcuffs. Speaks to LILI in absentia.*)

No offense, Lili, but living with you makes me lonely. Very lonely. By the time I get out, I don't know . . . I'll be a shining example to late bloomers everywhere.

You have your own disaster. God gives us each our own disaster. Believe me, you'll be fine. (*MARY goes. Lights out.*)

~

EPILOGUE

Lights up on LILI. Morning. Weeks later. LILI is sleeping, the alarm goes off, she turns it off and sits up. She takes a stethoscope out from under the covers, and listens to her heart.

LILI: There's something's happening to my heart. There's something irregular going on. It's missing a beat. The extra beat born into me. The one that held me back and made it race . . . The one that made it hurt to run too fast. The extra beat . . . the extra hopeless one that made me think: "Am I having a heart attack?" So I always took precautions. I have managed not to use too much of it at any one time. (*Gets up, puts on robe.*) But now . . . it's so loud . . . I think that you could hear it from across the room. And it's different. (*Lights up on MARY, in prison orange, by a pay phone. Sound of coins dropping.*) I have somehow got a different heartbeat—and there's nothing I can do about it. (*Phone rings.*)

VOICE OF OPERATOR: "Will you accept a collect call to anyone, from Mary?

LILI: (*Into speaker phone.*) Yes, I will.

MARY: Hey, Lili. Hi. Hi, it's me. How's it going?

LILI: Holding down the fort.

MARY: Good work. Remember what the King of Spain said . . .

LILI: (*Interrupting.*) I remember.

MARY: Listen, I just wanted to tell you . . . I think my roommate . . . whatever you call 'em in here . . . I think she's a multiple. (*Pause.*) Personality.

LILI: What's she in for?

MARY: Credit card fraud. She's really touchy that you use the plural. You don't say, "She's nice," you say, "They're nice." Or, "Do they want to sit down." Like that. So I wanted you to know. In case you come to visit. I just wanted to warn you.

LILI: I'm coming Tuesday. I told you. (*Pause.*) You sound good.

MARY: You sound: (*Thinks awhile*) spectacular. (*Long pause.*) At first I was really afraid to be locked up. I thought: I'm too individually directed for this. "I can't take the organization." I told myself. But I found out it is a big relief.

LILI: Listen. I'm going to order myself something from this catalogue. Do you want me to order you something?

MARY: What catalogue?

LILI: Smith and Hawkins.

MARY: Gardens! I love garden equipment. Listen—you know me better than I do myself. You pick it out.

LILI: They have some trowels here from Sweden that are very nice.

MARY: What about those plastic clogs? Do they have any of those yellow plastic clogs?

LILI: They have them but they come in wine, periwinkle blue or ochre.

MARY: . . . No . . .

LILI: How about an outdoor grill specifically for salmon that's shaped like a salmon?

MARY: That reminds me why I called you. That reminds me why I called you up. Last night I had another in my series of Feminist Nightmares.

LILI: Like the one where you're in a big circle and you have to come to a unanimous decision?

MARY: Right right . . . only in this dream we were fishing, Lili. The two of us. We were back in Minnesota. We had cut a hole in the ice and made a fire right there to stay warm. On the ice. And we were fishing.

All of a sudden you caught something big. It felt really big. You reeled it in. It was Virginia Woolf. And she was angry, Lili. She was furious. She told you to throw her back in and you said are you sure? And she said, "Yes" so you did. And we just sat there and looked up at the stars . . . the monogamous stars . . . until I felt a tug, a tiny tug . . . it felt like I had caught something big, and so I reeled it in. And it was . . . it was Ophelia. In the dream I caught Ophelia.

And she was nicer about it but still, she said to throw her back. And I said, "are you sure?" and she just said: "goodnight . . . goodnight goodnight goodnight" and started singing. And so I threw her back. We could hear her singing as she sank back under. And we both thought, this is some motherfucking river here we picked. (*Listens to LILI's silence.*) It really creeped us out. So we turned to the fire to stay warm, but pretty soon we heard something pulling my pole across the ice, so I picked it up and reeled it in and out of the ice came this bright red blob. It was a heart, Lili. Joan of Arc's . . . and it was frozen solid.

I held it in my hand until it got warm and started beating again. It got all red and then it spoke. It spoke to me, and what it said was really simple. It told us "fish somewhere else." (*Silence.*) Is that amazing? Huh? Is that a message?

LILI: That is a bonfire. That is a sentence in the sky.

MARY: (*In a tiny voice.*) "Surrender Dorothy." Listen . . . do they have any outdoor lights in that catalogue? Any like . . . torches . . . like the Tonga Room?

LILI: Well . . . let's see. They have some patio bonfire holders. They have a Lu-Au kit, "complete supplies and instructions for a traditional Lu-Au."

MARY: What I'm thinking of are lights. A string of lights.

LILI: I can get those anywhere. Those are easy.

MARY: Why don't you send me those. I'll have to ask my roommate if it's all right with her . . . (*Hits her forehead.*) if it's all right with "them" . . . if I hang them in our cell. On the ceiling. That way I'll have some stars. That's what I need in here, some stars. You won't forget to send them, will you?

LILI: No, I won't.

MARY: I like a bonfire. I like a good bonfire . . . you know that . . .

LILI: I know you do.

MARY: But I think I'd like those little lights. You know? 'Cause small fires everywhere are harder to put out. (*Lights hold for a minute on* LILI *and* MARY, *then out.*)

DOG OPERA

Constance Congdon

DOG OPERA received its premiere at the New York Shakespeare Festival (George C. Wolfe, Producer). It opened at the Joseph Papp Public Theater/Martinson Hall on May 10, 1995. It was directed by Gerald Gutierrez; the set design was by John Lee Beatty; the costume design was by Toni-Leslie James; the lighting design was by Brian MacDevitt; the sound design was by Ottis Munderloh and the production stage manager was Marjorie Horne. The cast was as follows:

PETER SZCZEPANEK . . . . Albert Macklin
MADELINE NEWELL . . . . Kristine Nielsen
JACKIE . . . . Kevin Dewey
BERNICE/RUBY/DALE/DORIS/MAUREEN . . . . . Sloane Shelton
CHARLIE SZCZEPANEK/BRAD/SANNY . .Richard Russell Ramos
STEVEN/CHRIS/DAVID/TIM/HANK . . . . Rick Holmes
JOE'S LOVER/MAN ON STREET/STAVROS/
ARAPAHO . . . . Eduardo Andino

Cast List

MADELINE NEWELL, age thirty-five or so
PETER SZCZEPANEK, age thirty-five or so
JACKIE, age sixteen
All the other parts are doubled and tripled, etc.:
MOTHER ACTOR, character woman, fifty-five and up
CHARLIE ACTOR, character man, fifty-five and up
BOYFRIEND ACTOR, age thirty-five or so
CHARLIE ACTOR also plays: Joe's Lover, Brad, Man (in the Village), Male Voice on Porno Film, Egret narrative

BOYFRIEND ACTOR plays: Steven, Chris, David, Tim, Hank, Stavros, Mac, TV Voice, Male Voice on Porno Film, Lawrence Welk, Man in elevator, Arapaho

MOTHER ACTOR plays: Bernice (Mother), Ruby (male transvestite), Doris, Dale Williamson, Sanny (male), Woman in elevator.

Setting

The action takes place in the present, in areas around Manhattan, and, briefly, in Greece.

This play is dedicated to Greg Leaming

Acknowledgments

The Gathering at Bigfork, Jahnna Beecham, Malcolm Hillgartner, Cliff Fannin Baker, Joe Kell, Marie Mathay, Ken Marshall, Brad Williams, Kim Simmons, Elizabeth Huddle, David Mong, Dann Florek, Zouanne Leroy, Victor Pappas and the Intiman Theatre, Phyllis Somerville, Chloe Webb, Mitchell Feinstein, Kevin Dewey, Michael Lombard, Jack Stehlin, Morgan Jenness, Steve Alter, Joanne Akalaitis, Peter Franklin, Gerry Gutierrez, George Wolfe and the New York Shakespeare Festival, Jim Too, Jimmy, Truman, Bruce, Ron.

And a special thanks to Tomie dePaola for his invaluable contribution to this play.

DOG OPERA was written with the help of a Mellon Foundation Grant.

~

ACT I

PETE and MADELINE are semireclining in aluminum chaises on a public beach, under a beach umbrella. They are wearing T-shirts, hats, sunglasses, and towels over their thighs. They are sharing a can of Diet Coke.

PETE: There's just one thing . . .
MADELINE: What?
PETE: One thing I'm worried about.
MADELINE: What?
PETE: Will guys think I'm a transsexual?
MADELINE: You're too hairy.
PETE: I could be in transition.
MADELINE: If you'd take off that towel—
PETE: And let the world see my thighs?
I don't think so.
MADELINE: *Your* thighs? Puh-leeze.
PETE: There's nothing wrong with your thighs.
MADELINE: If Jacques Cousteau were here, I'd be on PBS. Okay? (*Sees a guy.*) Oh man.
PETE: Where?
MADELINE: At three o'clock.
PETE: Now—wait a minute. Where is midnight?
MADELINE: Straight ahead.
PETE: And six is back here.
MADELINE: You're going to miss him.
PETE: Where?
MADELINE: I'm not pointing. Forget it.
PETE (*Spying the guy.*): Oh, wait a minute.
Blue Speedos?
MADELINE: Grey.
PETE: If you're quibbling about the color, how great can this guy be?
MADELINE: You missed him.
PETE (*Sees another guy.*): Whoa, doggies.
MADELINE: What is this? Jed Clampett cruises Jones Beach?
PETE: Lord have mercy.
MADELINE (*Sees this guy.*): Oh my.
PETE: Ohhhh. Ohhhhh. Mama.
MADELINE: A basket worthy of Carmen Miranda's head.
PETE: She'll have to fight me for him.
MADELINE: Buns.

PETE (*They take him in.*): Buns.

MADELINE: Gay.

PETE: Straight.
(*Reconsidering.*): Straight.

MADELINE: Gay.

PETE: No way.

MADELINE: Invite him over.
If I fall in love with him—he's gay.

PETE: If I fall in love with him—he's straight.
(*Weakly.*) Oh, sir? Sir? Can you come over here and ruin our lives?

MADELINE: Oh, please, it's been at least two weeks.

PETE: Oh my God.

MADELINE: What?

PETE: He's looking at us.

MADELINE: Oh jeez.

PETE: I'm going to take off my towel.

MADELINE: That should do it.

PETE: What's that supposed to mean?

MADELINE: Peter, take off the towel.

PETE takes his towel off—he's wearing a long pair of black bathing trunks.

MADELINE: Those *are* fetching.

PETE: He's coming over, Madeline!
Oh fuck.

MADELINE: Will you relax?

PETE: He's looking at me.

MADELINE: I knew he was gay. He's motioning. . . .

PETE: I've attracted a deaf-mute.
It'll be like *Children of a Lesser God.*
Oh my God! I'm Bill Hurt! (*To guy.*) What?
Oh no, I don't have any—sorry! I quit six months ago. (*PETE watches guy exit.*) But I'd be glad to make you one if you bring me the tobacco! (*Guy is gone.*) Or just bring me your seeds and

we'll grow it together.

Or if you have a gun, I'd be glad to shoot myself in the other foot. (PETE *sits down.*) I'm sure he appreciated the lecture on quitting smoking.

MADELINE: It wasn't a lecture.

It was a comment.

PETE: He was gay, Madeline.

And he almost talked to me until I turned into Bobby Bizarro.

MADELINE: Pete—he was straight.

PETE: How do you know?

MADELINE: If he were gay, he would have talked to me, too.

PETE: You're right.

I wasn't just rejected.

MADELINE: You weren't just rejected.

PETE: I was asked for a cigarette.

And I didn't have any.

MADELINE: That simple. (*Long beat.*) I was rejected.

He didn't even talk to me.

I don't know—maybe the towel makes me look fatter.

PETE: Take it off.

MADELINE: When pigs fly. (*Beat.*) When pigs fly, maybe I'll join the air force—at last, a suit that fits me.

PETE: Stop it.

I like that black thing you bought.

MADELINE: Which black thing? All my clothes are black.

PETE: The dressy suit thing.

MADELINE: Oh, my memorial outfit?

PETE: I guess so.

MADELINE: It's ten years old!

I bought it for . . . Barry.

PETE: Barry.

Barry's memorial.

That's an old suit.

MADELINE: Too old.

Burn it.
Take it out and burn it.

I need a new suit, Peter.

PETE: Me, too.
Hey! Hey, hey, hey!
What are we doin'?

MADELINE: We are cruisin'.
We are strategically placed just to the left of Field Six at Jones Beach, so the pickin's are great.

PETE: And the livin' is easy.

MADELINE: Straight men to the left of me.

PETE: Gay men to the right of me.

MADELINE: Into the valley of . . . *life*
Rode the six hundred.

PETE: And that's why there are no cute guys—
Six hundred hunky light brigade officers rode up—

MADELINE: And took the cute ones—(*Sees a guy.*)
—wait a minute. Nine o'clock. Approaching—

PETE: Now, where's nine again?

MADELINE: (*Showing him quickly.*) Noon. Three. Six. Nine.

PETE: (*Sees him.*) Very attractive black man?

MADELINE: Red speedos.

PETE: Oh my God.
Remind me to make an offering to the god of nylon.

MADELINE: All synthetic fibers aren't bad. (*They watch him.*)

PETE: Well, that made my afternoon.

MADELINE: Yeah. (*Still watching as he disappears down the beach.*)

PETE: Gay? Straight?

MADELINE: Beautiful.

(*end of scene*)

~

JACKIE, a young effeminate teenager, is waiting on a highway for a ride. It's a beautiful dusk evening—the sound of crickets. We see a few fireflies.

JACKIE: Crickets make that sound by rubbing their parts together —they're trying to get a date of some kind. They're also eating spiders as they do this.

It's a beautiful night.

Fireflies are mooning each other. They die in a few weeks. In the grass and trees, insect life is trying to overpopulate in between doing search and destroy attacks on each other. Once this whole state was a swamp and dinosaurs sloshed around. Now their decay could ignite a fire fifty feet high. Trees died to make those houses. And under all of this is a layer of dead Indians. If motel rooms didn't have cable, I wouldn't know any of this, and I'd be a lot happier. Everyone says I'm smart, and I shoulda stayed in school. Well, yeah. Where would I have lived, I wonder? I have some skills—I can put on a condom with my teeth, before the guy even realizes it's there.

Mostly, I jerk off to music of my choice. I take requests, but I will not do "People" by Barbra Streisand or anything of a religious nature. (*Looking down the street.*) Here they come— on their way home from work, in their big dark cars with the ample backseats. But I won't be getting in—even wrapped in latex. I have a date tonight. With somebody's husband— yours? (*Sees car pulling up.*) Oh my God. He brought the station wagon—with the kid's car seat still in the back. No graham cracker crumbs on this boy—we're getting a room! (*He waves to the driver and exits to get into the car.*)

(*end of scene*)

~

Soft, meditative music and ocean sound. MADELINE has her eyes closed and is wearing earphones. We are listening to what she hears.

WOMAN'S VOICE (*Soft, smooth.*):

Breathing doubt out,
Breathing hope in,
Don't stop breathing.
It feels good to relax and breathe.
Notice what you're thinking
And observe your thoughts
Without judging them
There's no such thing as a bad thought
Or a better thought
Thoughts are just thoughts,
Nothing more, nothing less.

As MADELINE*'s tape continues,* PETE *enters in a separate space. He is wearing a bathrobe and jockey shorts and nothing else. He crosses to an attractive little box, opens it and puts three unopened condoms in it and shuts the lid.*

All your thoughts are valuable
Because they give you useful information
And they help you to understand and accept
Your total self.
So even though your thoughts might be
Illogical, unreasonable or untrue,
They're just thoughts,
They're not actions.

PETE *picks up the phone and thinks about dialing.*

WOMAN'S VOICE:

Put aside your thoughts one by one
As your body relaxes
Take a mental vacation
Let your conscious mind ramble on and on
While your higher self takes over.

PETE watches as a man wearing only a pair of jockey shorts, earphones and a cassette player in the crotch of his shorts, crosses through, mopping the floor as he goes. This is STEVEN.

WOMAN'S VOICE:

Trust in the compassion of your higher self
And its wisdom
Listen to it.
You use food only to nourish your body
Food is not love
Love is love
Food is not a reward

MADELINE reaches for a bag of Oreos. She can't find then and begins to search with real energy. PETE dials the phone.

WOMAN'S VOICE:

A reward is emotional satisfaction
So reward yourself in positive, healthy ways
Because you deserve to be loved.

As the taped message continues, MADELINE finds the Oreos.

You are getting comfort and companionship
In healthy and constructive ways.

MADELINE puts an Oreo in her mouth—it is bliss. Phone rings. She turns off the cassette and picks up the phone receiver.

PETE: Are you alone?

MADELINE: Oh no, the L.A. Raiders are over here. They're fucking my brains out. Unfortunately, I'm in the other room, because, like all men on the planet, they only want me FOR MY MIND!

PETE: Since you're awake, anyway.

MADELINE: Of course I'm awake. I ran out of batteries for all my sex toys an hour ago.

PETE: Take some out of your cassette player.

MADELINE: Wrong size.

PETE: Remember—size doesn't matter.

MADELINE: It's been so long—do they come in different sizes? I forgot. Wait a minute—you had a date.

PETE: That was the rumor.

MADELINE: Oh no.

PETE: Oh yes.

MADELINE: So he canceled?

PETE: No. He came—arrived.
What does it mean when they clean your house?

MADELINE: In my case, it means they should be going out with *you*.

PETE: What would it mean in my case?
I thought I was dating my own kind.
I'm not straight. Evidently, I'm not gay because if I were I would be HAVING GAY SEX, RIGHT?!!! So what am I—a fucking amoeba? I mean, what am I—a fucking chromosome? What am I supposed to do, huh? Split in two discrete pieces, say "ah!" and then have a cigarette? And worry if I'm going to call myself the next day?
Wait a minute—Hazel, the celibate maid, is coming around again.

STEVEN *enters, carrying a bucket of water and a sponge, and humming to the cassette player.*

STEVEN (*Too loud because he can't hear.*) FOUND SOME MURPHY'S SOAP—GONNA DO THE WALLS. THIS PANELING IS FABULOUS. YOU SHOULDN'T NEGLECT IT.

STEVEN *putters around.*

MADELINE: Why is Hazel shouting? Does celibacy make you deaf? See, our mothers had it all wrong.

PETE: Why does every weird homo in the world want to date me?
MADELINE: I don't know, Peter.
You're too normal.
You're like the Statue of Liberty—"Give me your weird ones, your refugees from too much therapy. Send these, the retro queens who still think their mothers made them a homosexual, and are gathering wool so their mothers can make them another."
PETE: I lift my lamp and go door to door: "DATE ME, I'M HOPELESS!"
MADELINE: What happened?

STEVEN bends over to clean and the butt shot is too much for PETE to bear.

PETE: Uhhhh.
MADELINE: Are you all right?
PETE: I'm alive. (*Vincent Price arising from the grave.*) "I'm ALIVE!"
MADELINE: No nooky, then?
PETE: No. Nope on the nooky.
Wants to be friends.
Needs a friend. Wants a friend. Had too much meaningless sex! Worried about AIDS. Needs companionship. "GM wants to meet other GM for walks on the beach, long dinners and lots of talk"—in short, anything you can do with your MOTHER!
MADELINE: With *my* mother?
Only if you bring a walker.
And that rubber donut she's sat on since 1986.
And a bottle of Canadian Club.

(Beat.)

MADELINE: You still there?
PETE: I'm watching the floor show.

STEVEN: I FEEL SO AT HOME HERE, PAUL!!

PETE: Pete. My name's—MY NAME'S PETE!! PETER!

STEVEN: MAYBE LATER IN THE RELATIONSHIP!
I WANT TO REDISCOVER MY VIRGINITY!
HA! HA!
BUT IN THE MEANTIME, THIS APARTMENT IS GONNA BE *CLEAN!*

STEVEN goes back to cleaning.

PETE: I have to go now—I have to go open a vein.

MADELINE: Make sure it's his.
Wait. Did you actually get anywhere?

PETE: Nope.

MADELINE: Not even mutual pud pulling or anything?

PETE: Oh, you old romantic, you.

MADELINE: Well, "Masturbation" sounds like something we did in high school chemistry. "Now, students, carefully masturbate your pipettes and be certain you get none of it in your mouths."

PETE: Sister Mary Joseph was ahead of her time.

MADELINE: I can't stand it! Did you or didn't you?

PETE: I had that little problem again, but it had nothing to do with "Hazel's" telling me about his "vocation." (*Long pause.*) Aren't you going to say it happens to every man now and then?

MADELINE: How would I know? The entire fucking world could be impotent, and I wouldn't know the difference!

PETE: Don't say "impotent."

MADELINE: You're not, Pete. You are not. It's just a temporary thing. If you were faced with someone really hot who wasn't afraid, you know it would all be there.

PETE: I'm dying.

MADELINE: No, you're not. (*Pause.*)

PETE: All right.

MADELINE: 'Bye, Pete.

PETE: And don't eat the rest of those Oreos, Madeline. You know what chocolate does to you.

MADELINE: Yeah—makes me happy. (*Beat.*) All right.

PETE: Movies on Friday?

MADELINE: Right.

Your choice, God help me.

PETE: 'Bye, Maddy.

MADELINE: 'Bye.

They hang up. MADELINE *smiles and puts the Oreos away.*

STEVEN: I LOVE THIS SONG! I'M GOING TO PLAY IT AGAIN! (*He reaches into his jockey shorts and reverses the tape and then starts it again.*) GOD! I LOVE THIS SONG!!! (STEVEN *dances off.* PETER *lies back down in bed.*)

(*end of scene*)

~

BERNICE, MADELINE'*s mother, enters, walking with her walker, heading for her chair. It's a big recliner with a chairside cabinet on which rests a small refrigerator. She gets there, sits.*

BERNICE: Damn. (*She gets up slightly and takes a large rubber donut from her chair seat, rearranges it, and sits back down. She picks up her TV remote and flicks through the channels—stops at something.*)

BERNICE: Now, what in God's name is that? (*Flicks more—finds a disaster program like* Code 3. *She likes this litany of disaster, opens her refrigerator, takes out an already prepared highball and takes a taste. Then she takes out a bottle of Canadian Club and pours some on her drink, sips it, then really downs a slug of it.*)

BERNICE: Perfect. (*She turns up the volume on the disaster program, then turns it down.*) Shit.
I gotta go to the toilet. (*BERNICE gets up and walks off with her walker. Beat.*)
BERNICE (*Yells offstage.*): ACK! (*We hear a big thump.*)

(*end of scene*)

~

Celestial music. MADELINE is sitting next to an empty chair. PETE stands behind her. They are both bathed in white, listening to the music. When they talk, their voice-overs are a little off, so it seems they are in a dubbed movie.

MADELINE: This music . . .
PETE: So beautiful.
MADELINE: This is the most beautiful memorial—
PETE: —anyone could imagine.

You know why?
MADELINE: No.
PETE: It's because it's the last one. (*PETE starts to leave.*)
MADELINE: You mean, there's—
PETE: We're finally all dead. (*PETE is gone.*)
MADELINE (*Waking suddenly, terrified.*) Wha!? Pete!
MAN'S OFFSTAGE VOICE FROM PODIUM: . . . and the hospice people who were so wonderful to Joe and me.

MADELINE hopes no one saw that she was asleep, looks at her watch and then behind her, worried.

MAN'S OFFSTAGE VOICE FROM PODIUM (*cont'd*): Once the Catholic Church rejected me, I never looked back, but today, I'd like to offer a special silent prayer to all of the souls that I feel are around us—to thank them for their help because I know they're here, today, sharing our memories of Joe. We're all one community, the living and the dead, and I believe that all of our friends and lovers are still with us.

MADELINE *looks behind once more, then bows her head.* PETE *enters, breathless, and sits beside her.*

PETE: Sorry.
MADELINE: Thank God.
PETE: Tough one?
MADELINE: You're sweating.
PETE: I had to run for a cab. I told them I had to leave early. They knew I was coming here. And still George kept droning on and on.

Oh God, are we supposed to be praying? Shit.

Bows his head. We see the source of the offstage male voice. It is Joe's Lover.

JOE'S LOVER: Amen.
Joe's mother and I want to thank you all for coming. He wanted me to read this today, whenever today came. He kept this piece of paper by his bed. He'd found this saying in a book of Native American writings and copied it out for himself, so he could read it any time. Later, he had me read it to him. It's Arapaho. "Every time I go about pitying myself, I remember that I am being carried on great winds across the sky."

Good-bye, Joe.

A recording of "Pavane for a Dead Princess." MADELINE *and* PETE *sit there. After a beat, they wave weakly to someone they recognize. Then they see someone else and wave. They do this a bit more.*

MADELINE: You know, it just gets harder and harder to get out of these seats.

PETE: I still think Allen's was the best memorial in a long time.

MADELINE: This one was good—great music, since Joe was a musician, but not as many stories, you know—outrageous stories, like at Allen's.

PETE: Oh God, has it killed outrageous, too? Left us only outrage?

MADELINE: Joe was younger, that's all. Shorter life.

PETE: Uh-oh.

MADELINE: Uh-oh.

PETE: Right. Right. Right.

MADELINE: Out of here.

They get up to go.

PETE: You didn't know Bill? Or Joe's mom?

MADELINE: You mean, do we have to say anything to anyone?

PETE: Right.

MADELINE: We met Joe at the same time, didn't we? Through Don at that—a—

PETE: Through Kevin.

MADELINE: Oh God, Kevin. Of course.

They see someone else they know and wave. Upstage, a man appears, walking with those aluminum crutches that are braced with the forearm. He is sick, but looks okay—his clothes are big on him. This is Chris.

CHRIS: Peter?

PETE turns around, sees him.

PETE: Oh my God.

CHRIS: It's Chris.

PETE: Oh my God.
Hello. How— (*Stops himself.*)

CHRIS: I moved back months ago, but I didn't call you.

I couldn't stay in Texas. I hated it.
I should've called, but you know—I thought you'd still be pissed.

PETE: No. Not at all.
Well, I was, but . . .

CHRIS: Listen, I've still got your mother's afghan.
I'm living with Jerry. Olsen, you know.

PETE: Oh my God.

CHRIS: So, call me and come pick it up. Sometime. (*To MADELINE.*) You must be the famous Madeline?

MADELINE: Right. You must be the famous Chris.

CHRIS: Infamous—please. (*To PETE.*) Don't wait too long—asshole. (*CHRIS turns to go, has trouble with the crutches.*) Rugs are death with these things.

MADELINE: Let me help.

CHRIS: I got it.

He exits.

PETE: Jesus.

MADELINE: Peter?

PETE sits down.
(Long beat.)

PETE: Jesus. Chris.
Jesus.
Jesus.

MADELINE: Pete?

PETE: It's been four years since Chris.
I am negative.

MADELINE: I know that.

PETE: And, let's face it, with my love life—there's no threat.

MADELINE (*About PETE's health.*): You're sweating.

PETE: I ran for the cab. (*Gentle and adamant.*) I ran for the cab.

MADELINE: That's right. I forgot.
Sorry.
PETE: Let's get out of here. (*They exit quickly.*)

(*end of scene*)

~

JACKIE is in a motel room, watching the television. There's the sound of a shower running.

JACKIE: He has to get home, but I get to keep the room. I love it. A double all to myself. People make fun of motel rooms—say they all look alike, but it's only the nice ones that do. Crummy motel rooms are always different because no one has decorated them in a modern fashion, so they are stuck in whatever time they were built, so they're different. Ones built in the seventies have shag carpeting and fake wood beams and they're orange and brown, and sometimes they have flocked wallpaper. This one has carpeting on the wall, in a stripe between two fake wood beams. It's a decorative motif. (*Tries to change the channel.*) Fuck! This remote is fucked! (*Opens his bag and pours out lots of remotes. He tries them, one by one.*) No. No. No. Nope. Shit! (*One of the remotes works.*) Thank God.

You know how most remotes are in these bracket holder things that are bolted to the bedside tables in motels? It's because of me. (*Switches the channels as he talks.*) Now nice motels, like Budgetel, Days Inn, TraveLodge, they do all look alike—the rooms. But I love that. Because, when I walk into one, I feel as though I've just walked into an apartment of my own. I don't get many of those dates, but, when I do, I always take the miniature shampoo and conditioners and sometimes they have hand cream and good brands like Vaseline Intensive Care. You ever noticed shower caps? They come in all these different boxes—round ones, and big flat ones, and little narrow ones, all different, right? No, when you open one of these up, it's the same fucking shower cap. Always. If you find a different one, send it to me.

NATURE PROGRAM VO: . . . have evolved extravagant breeding plumage as sexual advertisements to attract their mates. Long white plume which this bird bears on its back in the mating and nesting season have long been used for adornment, but this beautiful plumage can only be acquired by killing the animal.

JACKIE: Those are egrets. They're very, very ancient birds. And they almost died out. But they're not gone yet. They're hanging in there.

NATURE PROGRAM VO: The delicately plumed Snowy Egret with its yellow feet, called "golden slippers," is beginning to repopulate Northern California where it originally suffered great losses to the plume trade.

(*end of scene*)

~

PETE *is in his bathrobe, holding some videotapes.*

PETE: "Send Me a Few Hard Men. Discipline and hard-core fun at a Marine boot camp."

Maybe Gomer Pyle will be in this one. (*Puts the tape in the VCR, settles back, fast forwards.*) (*In Gomer Pyle voice.*) "Sergeant Carter? Surprise, surprise, surprise!" (*About the movie.*) Still dressed? What can this be? Plot?

MALE VOICE 2: You wanted me, Sarge?

MALE VOICE 1: Yes, Private. You could say that.

PETE: These guys are great actors.

MALE VOICE 2: What do you want me to do, Sarge?

PETE: Hello? Sir John Gielgud?

MALE VOICE 1: I think we both know the answer to that one.

PETE: You're fired.

MALE VOICE 1: Down on your knees, soldier!

PETE (*Seeing the size of the actor's dick.*): You're definitely fired.
Sir John.

PETE *watches the videotape as the marching snare drum and groans take over. He tilts his head to the side, slowly, to see better.*
Phone rings. He picks up. Lights up on MADELINE *calling from her apartment.*

MADELINE: Hi.
PETE: Hi.
MADELINE: Whatcha doin'?
PETE: Watching a movie.
MADELINE: Oh great! What?
I thought I'd drop by.
PETE: Uhhhhhhhhm.
MADELINE: Somebody's there. Cool.
PETE (*Turns down the movie.*): No. Don't hang up.
MADELINE: What's the movie?
PETE: It's a—it's an educational film: an anthropological study of male bonding behavior among the inhabitants of a small military installation.
MADELINE: I'll let you go.
PETE: I'll turn it off.
MADELINE: No, Peter.
PETE: HOW CAN I DO ANYTHING KNOWING YOU KNOW WHAT I'M DOING?
MADELINE: Call me later. (*She hangs up.*)
PETE: Maddy! What if nothing happens again?

He turns the volume up again. We hear the moans and more frantic snare drums.

MALE VOICE 2: Do me, Daddy!
PETE: Yikes.

PETER *tries to relax and get into the movie again, hoping for arousal.*

MALE VOICE 2: Daddy. Daddy.
PETE: Stop with the dad stuff, for God's sake.

Back to MADELINE. She dials the phone. It is picked up by CHARLIE, a middle-aged man in a suit.

CHARLIE: Detective Szczepanek.
MADELINE: Bang.
CHARLIE: Maddy. Put that thing down. If I've told you once, I've told you a million times, a little girl like you can't handle those big guns.
MADELINE: I can hope, can't I?
CHARLIE: So what's the plan?
MADELINE: The Zen Palate.
CHARLIE: Oh God.
MADELINE: It's not *your* birthday. It's Peter's—your son.
CHARLIE: What's wrong with good old American food? Like in Chinatown, for God's sake?
MADELINE: Peter loves the Zen Palate.
CHARLIE: I'll eat before I come.
MADELINE: What are you going to get him?
CHARLIE: I'm having his grandfather's ring resized for him.
MADELINE: The twenty-year ring? God, isn't that an antique?
CHARLIE: Thanks.
MADELINE: No, I mean, really, Charlie. Your dad was in the NYPD when they were chasing Al Capone.
CHARLIE: That was Chicago! Jesus! Your generation has no memory!
MADELINE: I'm sorry—I'm not up on gangster history. If, however, you'd like to discuss the role of the patron in Renaissance art—
CHARLIE: Throw your education up to me—fine. Let me tell you something, Madeline Newell. Renaissance art will only tell you what you aren't because you are an American. And gangster history *is* American history. Your professors at NYU

didn't tell you that. And you know why? Because *that* is the truth.

MADELINE: Charlie? Take two Midol and call me in the morning. Or, better yet, take the whole fucking bottle and don't call me.

CHARLIE: Now, don't get mad, Maddy.

MADELINE: Why do you always say that?

CHARLIE: Because you always get mad, Zelda. (*Pause.*) Getting any?

MADELINE: Mr. Szczepanek—

CHARLIE: Giving any away?

MADELINE: Charlie, I'm hanging up now.

CHARLIE: Hey, I like our exchange of ideas, you know? The word "renaissance" never comes up here—hardly. I'll see you at the Zen Plate.

MADELINE: *Palate.*

CHARLIE hangs up.

MADELINE: Prick! He beat me to it! (*She slams down the phone.*) Next time I'm going to hang up on you when I say I will!

PETE (*Talking to his genitals*): I rented this movie for YOU! And I'm not renting any more unless you stay awake and WATCH them.

(*end of scene*)

~

MADELINE is dressed nicely and wearing sock puppets on her hands. One of the puppets has hair made from zippers. She speaks to an audience.

MADELINE: Okay, shall we—all right shall we—come on, shall we—let's let's let's—everybody, come on, come on—shall we—let's come on—NO, no no no nononononono— Kaiesha, Emma—watch that over there—that's a bad desk, bad desk, bad—don't sit—Jaime, move the desk, so no one

—Julian, there's water—that's the bad water place—they'll fix that someday, but now we have to—Dorcas and Cloud, sit on the right—Shona and Tyrone, move away from the window—the screen isn't really—yes, just come here now, now now now NOW. All right. Time for Madeline and Zipper Man.

ZIPPER MAN (*Puppet*): Whoa, Madeline, I got some fat rhymes today.

MADELINE (*Puppet*): Who you calling fat, Zip?

ZIPPER MAN (*Puppet*): No, Madeline. I'm not dissing you. These rhymes are dope. They from an old grandmama called Mother Goose.

MADELINE (*Puppet*): Well, lay them down upon us.

(*ZIPPER MAN raps the rhyme while MADELINE bops to it.*)

ZIPPER MAN (*Puppet*):

Humpty-Dumpty sat on a wall,
Humpty-Dumpty had a great fall,
All the king's horses
All the king's men
Couldn't put Humpty together again.

MADELINE (*Puppet*): Oh, man, poor Humpty dude.

MADELINE (*Person*; *answering a question, back to her own voice.*): What? No, Humpty just fell, Rosita—I'm sure he wasn't pushed. Tawanda?

No, he wasn't shot either. He just fell off the wall.

Kevin?

No, they didn't have snipers in those days and they didn't have cars to drive by in.

Sunil?

No, honey, they didn't have police, either. All the king's men were the police, and they tried to put him together—they really, really tried—they didn't just leave him there.

MADELINE (*Puppet*): Yo, Zip! This Mother Goose got some more rhymes?

ZIPPER MAN (*Puppet*):

Goosey, goosey, gander,

Whither does thou wander?
Upstairs and downstairs
And in my lady's chamber.

There I met an old man
Who wouldn't say his prayers;
I took him by the left leg,
And threw him down the stairs.

MADELINE (*Puppet*): You all like that one better! Madeline can tell!

MADELINE (*Person*): Hiroko? Why are you crying, honey? It's only a—

She did?!

Well, honey, I'm sure she didn't mean to hurt him, and I'm sorry you had to see that.

No, Mother Goose doesn't live in your building. This was written a long time ago, in another country.

Madeline and Zipper Man are out of rhymes for today, so this is the end of library period. Line up and meet your teacher in the hall. Bye-bye.

MADELINE (*Puppet*): Bye.

ZIPPER MAN (*Puppet*): Bye.

MADELINE (*Puppet*): Bye.

ZIPPER MAN (*Puppet*): Bye.

MADELINE (*Person*): Bye.

DAVID enters—a young male teacher with glasses.

DAVID: Madeline.

MADELINE: David. Big bomb.

DAVID: Not you, baby. (*To someone offstage.*) Be right there, Ted! (*He kisses her neck and feels her up.*)

You look beautiful in puppets.

You coming to the faculty meetings? I'll pick you up.

MADELINE: I'll need picking up by then.

DAVID: I'm your man. (*Kisses her on the forehead.*) Bye.

He exits. MADELINE *waves bye with one of her puppets because it's still on her hand. She notices the puppet, it attacks her throat, the other puppet pulls it off.* MADELINE *crosses to a pay telephone, takes puppets off, puts in a quarter, dials.* PETE *picks up.*

MADELINE: Is it sexual harassment when you want them to do it?

PETE: Oh, Maddy.

MADELINE: But they only do it in public, in front of other people, when you've got puppets on your hands?

PETE: Are you still at school?

MADELINE: Couldn't wait. And has it ever occurred to you how violent Mother Goose is? It's one little horror story after another.

PETE: What's left?

MADELINE: I tried Anansi the spider—they're afraid of bugs. Any story with rodents of any kind is definitely out. I'm looking for a fable involving a lost piece of asphalt looking for its pothole or the story of the brave little R train that thought it could huff and puff its way to Connecticut.

PETE: So what are you cooking for the showdown with David the neck kisser?

MADELINE: Some chicken thing with lots of wine. Or maybe we'll go to that Bojar place by the entrance to the Six?

PETE: More alone time—the better. Call me.

MADELINE: Nothing's going to happen, Peter.

PETE: You don't know that.

MADELINE: The man is a classic clit tease. He's all over me in public, in front of our friends. As soon as I get him alone, he won't touch me.

PETE: Use a condom.

MADELINE: For what? Party favors? Water balloons? Shall we blow them up and let them fly around the room?

PETE: Think positively.

MADELINE: I want him, Pete. It's been like this for months. He's got me almost obsessed, and we've never been alone.

PETE: Cook that chicken. Buy those condoms.

They hang up.

MADELINE: Even clit teases have to eat. (*Pause.*) Hope is lemon chicken with no garlic. (*She exits.*)

BERNICE *is lying on the floor. Her walker is nowhere to be seen.*

BERNICE: I've sifted through my life and I can't find a single reason why I should be lying here on my own bathroom floor while my sister Bea is happily married for the third time in San Diego. But, you know, I bet anything, I bet you fifty dollars that she will be nursing him in six months and spending her hard-earned dollars on a hefty nurse to lift him in and out of the bathtub. Men are such weaklings. How they got control of the world I don't know. It's because women have no guts and are afraid to make anybody mad because they hate to be alone. And how do most of them end up? Alone! Ow. Ow. 'Course what do I know, I'm lying on my own bathroom floor. If I wet myself, I swear I'm gonna roll over and drink every bottle of lye under this sink.

Don't you know that when they find me, some young prick is gonna say, "She's fallen, and she can't get up." Oh, the young. I'm so jealous of them. The beautiful are cruel and stupid—there's no doubt about it.

I'm glad I went to the mall and got a decent bathroom rug the last time. Bathrooms always remind me of confessionals. Not that our confessional was ever tiled. But I did feel sitting in there with the priest like we were on a two-holer—a kind of really nice one with walls to separate the sexes and a little grate to talk through, like they might of had in Venice. Although I suspect most people just went in the canals. Oh, we're a dirty bird, mankind. Dirty, dirty—(*Sees something.*)—I've got to tell Henreeka to do a better job on this floor, particularly around this bathtub.

It's strange I'm not in more pain. Maybe I've had a stroke. Oh God, I'll be a vegetable!

Wait a minute—I'm talking. Vegetables don't talk, old girl.

I'm dead. I just *think* I'm talking, and I'm actually—

HELLLLLP! HELLLLLLLLLLP! HELLLLLLPPP! (*She whistles.*) There's an echo. The dead don't make echos. HELLLLLLP GODDAMITT!!!

MADELINNNNNNNNNNNE!!!

(*end of scene*)

~

MADELINE is sitting with a glass of wine—she is eating the remains of something from a pot. Phone rings—she picks up.

PETE: Pretend I'm selling something and hang up on me if anything—
MADELINE: Hello, Peter.
PETE: No, really—just pretend—I—had to know, so—
MADELINE: I'm alone, Peter.
PETE: Oh.
MADELINE: But the chicken was good. We talked about it endlessly.
PETE: Oh God.
MADELINE: And the apartment. Loves my apartment. Has lots of personality—like me. I think personality in the female must be like saltpeter in the meat.
PETE: Maybe he's a closet case.
MADELINE: No, maybe I am. Maybe I'm a lesbian. Maybe I give off lesbian vibes that only men pick up. Like those whistles that only dogs can hear.
MADELINE: Do you have sexual fantasies about women?

MADELINE: No. But maybe it's so buried, Peter, that—wait a minute, I did have that crush on my Girl Scout counselor when I was eleven or so—

PETE: I don't know, Madeline. I knew when I was five or six.

MADELINE: Yeah, but you're always been precocious.

PETE: Yeah, Pete Szczepanek, the sexual prodigy. Burned out before he could get free of the nuns. And what good has it done me? I'm getting fucking desperate here. I'm about to encase myself in latex and go to the park. I need some infusion of . . . something. Sleaze may be the answer.

MADELINE: Be careful.

PETE: Rough trade.

MADELINE: Be careful.

PETE: Shut up!

MADELINE: I'm just—

PETE: I know.

MADELINE: Uh-oh—let me take this call. Maybe he's changed his mind.

PETE: Take it. 'Bye. (*PETE hangs up.*)

MADELINE (*Still on phone.*): Yes?

Yes.

You what?!

Is she all right?!

Oh my God.

Oh my God.

(*end of scene*)

~

JACKIE has his back to audience—he's putting some cream on his face.

JACKIE: Ow. Just a sec—(*He turns around, and we see that he has a black eye and facial contusions. He's looking in the mirror, putting on makeup.*)

I normally hate makeup. This is pimple cover-up. I don't think Clearasil ever imagined the uses it would be put to. This shit happens. Not from fag bashers—I'd be facedown in the river, floating out to sea. This shit happens from my dates now and again. This one was an accountant—goes to show you never know people. If the guy hitting you is gay it's not fag bashing. Is it?

I'll be all right. It's a lot worse than it looks. Reverse that.

(*end of scene*)

~

MADELINE and BERNICE are sitting in BERNICE's apartment. MADELINE's boredom borders on the supernatural. BERNICE has her feet up and is wearing a brace on one leg. She is listening to Jo Stafford sing "Shrimp boats is a comin' "—it repeats and repeats. They stare. BERNICE turns off the radio—she sees something out of the window. It's a plastic bag flying around.

BERNICE: Look at that! That's the same plastic bag that was flying around up here three hours ago!

MADELINE: YOU MEAN, BEFORE "SHRIMP BOATS" STARTED TO PLAY?

BERNICE: No, I'm serious. Isn't that something?

MADELINE: IT'S NOT THE SAME BAG.

BERNICE: Yes, it is.

MADELINE: NO, IT'S NOT!

BERNICE: Dammit, Madeline—I think I know my plastic bags when I see them.

MADELINE: IS IT YOUR PERSONAL PLASTIC BAG? HMMMMMMM?

BERNICE: It goddam is if it's flying around outside my balcony!

MADELINE: THAT PLASTIC YOU SAW OUTSIDE WAS FROM DUANE DRUGS! THIS PLASTIC BAG IS FROM A & S! AND THAT BALCONY IS NOT A BALCONY! IT IS A HIGH-DIVING BOARD FOR SUICIDES!!!!

BERNICE: You need to get out more. You need a boyfriend that's not a homo.

MADELINE: Pete is not my boyfriend, Mother. For Chrissake.

BERNICE: Well, you know that. And I know that. And Pete knows that. The rest of the world—I dunno.

MADELINE: TO HELL WITH THE REST OF THE WORLD.

BERNICE: You've got a bad attitude. You've stopped trying. I mean, look at your hair. What is that?

MADELINE: MOTHER, THE DYNEL WIG LOOK AND BIG HAIR WENT OUT DECADES AGO!

BERNICE: If Oprah can lose a hundred pounds, why can't you? And Tom Arnold lost a hundred and even that ex-wife of his lost some, too.

MADELINE: HER NAME IS ROSEANNE, MOTHER.

BERNICE: Well, whatever.

MADELINE: Her name is ROSEANNE, MOTHER. ROSEANNE, ROSEANNE, ROSEANNE!!!!

BERNICE: Are you a lesbian, honey? Because you could tell me if you were. And if you are, and I'm NOT saying you are. But IF you are, I'd think you'd be attracted to someone more, well, attractive, like that Cindy Crawford girl or that girl on *Cheers* who cries all the time. Now those are nice-looking women. No, Tom Arnold's ex-wife just can't take off that weight. Born fat. Died fat. Her curse. Hmmp. What were we talking about?

MADELINE: LIZZIE BORDEN.

BERNICE: Is she the one with the weight program where you buy the food?

MADELINE: NO, THAT IS JENNY CRAIG!

BERNICE: Well, what about that? Have you tried that? The food comes in plastic bags—*there* it is! See? That's my plastic bag! Now what does it say on it?

MADELINE: Macy's.

BERNICE: Huh. So that's what we've come to. A fine store like Macy's floating by on a plastic bag. That's your world, honey. So much trash in the sky. I'm sorry. Well, let's see what's on the radio.

MADELINE takes the radio and throws if off the balcony. BERNICE quietly turns on the lamp—it plays "Shrimp Boats is a Comin'." MADELINE throws the lamp off the balcony. BERNICE picks up a ballpoint pen and clicks it—"Shrimp Boats is a Comin' " comes out of it. MADELINE takes the pen and stamps on it.

BERNICE: Well, let's watch TV. Maybe Lawrence Welk is on.

BERNICE clicks the remote. We see Lawrence Welk.

LAWRENCE WELK:

Anda now for dat wunnerful song of da sea,
"Shrimp Boat Comin' In." A-one, a-two, a-tree—

Chorus of "Shrimp Boats is a Comin', their sails are in sight, shrimp boats is a comin', there's dancin' tonight."

MADELINE: Vodka still in the cupboard?

LAWRENCE WELK (*To MADELINE.*) Helpa yourself. (*MADELINE exists to get the vodka.*)

Light change. The National Anthem blares out of the television. MADELINE is drunk and dialing the phone. BERNICE is asleep in front of the television.

MADELINE: Be home. Be home. Be home.

It rings in PETE's apartment. Finally, the answering machine comes on.

PETE'S RECORDED VOICE: You have reached the answering machine of Pete Szczepanek. The poetry selection today is from Hart Crane:

There are no stars tonight
But those of memory
Yet how much room for memory there is
In the loose girdle of soft rain

We love you, Hart. Don't jump.

Sound of the beep. MADELINE *just hangs up the phone. She gets up and turns off the television and helps* BERNICE *up from the chair.*

MADELINE: Come on, Mom. Come on.
Here's your walker.
We'll stop at the potty.
BERNICE: I do not pee in a potty.
MADELINE: Toilet.
Come on.
BERNICE: Don't ever call it that.
MADELINE: Yes, Mom. (*They exit.*)

(*end of scene*)

~

PETE *is outside, trying to cruise. He crosses the stage and exits. After a beat, he crosses back, slowly, trying to watch someone. He stops and tries to look sexy. A man enters, crosses to him.*

MAN: Hi.
PETE: What? Oh! Yes! Hello! I was passing. I live—I live near here, and I was just—I always thought it was so adorable—"Gay Street." Have to live there. I wonder who . . . ? Lucky people, whoever. What a name! What's in a name?

MAN: Yeah. (*MAN exits.*)

PETE (*To the now absent MAN.*): It's the Prozac. I left my other personality at home. (*To himself.*) Oh yeah, I'm a funny, funny man.

(*PETE starts to exit one way, then changes his mind, then changes it again and exits.*)

(*end of scene*)

~

MADELINE is a little drunk and in a church, talking to a statue of the Virgin.

MADELINE: I know we haven't had a good relationship since that time in high school when, I felt, you really let me down. I guess I let you down, too. I just expected you to understand since you had been in the same position.

I waited in the backyard all night, on the terrace, and you never came, I never got a single feeling, no message, nothing—just the big cosmos, surrounded by a circle of orange from the lights off the avenue, just all that black sky with those holes of light staring back at me. I begin to feel like Sereta Lopez was right, that we were all just bugs inside a really big coffee can with a black plastic lid that some little mean white boy was keeping and he poked holes in the lid just to let us breathe a little and those holes let in light, and we thought they were stars.

So I had the abortion, Mary, and I never needed to use birth control again.

And Pete was the one who drove me there and back and talked to me while I lay in the backseat with a towel between my legs because fucking Ray—that's what we always called him after that—that was his generic name because that pretty much defined him—Fucking Ray wanted nothing to do with it since he was ashamed of knocking up a fat girl. And it was Pete who got me back into the house and sat up and drank with my mother who thought I was just brokenhearted over some guy which I was, but I was also mourning my womb which was pretty much a goner, too. And after that, Ray's Camaro had its headlights busted out about six times a year by an unknown vandal in various locations around the city until Fucking Ray got married and moved to Sparta. And Pete stopped carrying a hammer in his book bag.

As you can tell, I'm still pissed that I never heard from you.

You would not believe the world, Blessed Mother. And from whatever place you see it—those mountaintops in Yugoslavia, which doesn't exist anymore, by the way—from those tacos and potato chips and tree trunks that people see you in—from wherever—you must have noticed how really like the Last Days it is.

So I'm just here to let bygones be bygones, and to ask you to please protect Peter.

I forgive you, by the way, wherever you are. (*Looking up at the heavens.*) For God's sake, I know this is just a bunch of plaster here. (*MADELINE crosses herself and exits.*)

(*end of scene*)

~

PETE *is sitting in his bathrobe, watching television. He flicks between channels, absently, getting the usual snippets. Suddenly, he sees something and stops at a channel.*

PETE: Public Access—save me. Oh, let it be the woman on the organ that sings "Light My Fire."

TV VOICE: This is Randy. Not his real name. But neither was Joe in the fantasy before. But he likes the name "Randy," so that's what we'll call him. He's taken off those cowboy boots and is leaning back on the couch across from you. He just can't keep his hands away from his basket, he's so turned on by looking at you. Watch him rub himself while he's staring at you over his bandanna. He looks like an outlaw from a Western, like Paul Newman or Robert Redford in *Butch Cassidy and the Sundance Kid*. That's it, Randy—you're getting hard inside those worn "501s."

Let's have a little safe sex with Randy. Help him get out of those blue jeans—they can't be too comfortable. Yes, pull them off. I love smells. Put your nose into Randy's crotch, nuzzle him. Feel his balls under the cotton of his jockeys and smell that animal, hot smell of his groin. Now help him take those jockey shorts off. There. That's good. You're getting so hot now.

PETE (*Shouting at his crotch.*):
Anything goddam going on down there?! HUH?!
ANY SIGNS OF FUCKING *LIFE?!?*
HUH?!
BOYS??!!
ARE YOU AWAKE??!!

TV VOICE: You're getting so hot.

PETE tries to reposition himself and get into the mood.

TV VOICE: Soooooo hot.

Lights up on JACKIE, in jockey shorts and wearing a bandanna over his face.

TV VOICE: Now watch Randy take off those jockey shorts.

JACKIE doesn't move.

TV VOICE: Randy is a little shy and we love that.
He'll take them off now though.

JACKIE doesn't move.

TV VOICE: Randy. Butch. Sundance.
Take off the shorts for our closet case audience.
It's cable, Randy.
You can do what you want.
JACKIE: I'm waiting for my music.
TV VOICE: Aren't we all?

JACKIE makes a few dance moves. Stops.

JACKIE (*Pulls bandanna off his face.*): I need my music.
TV VOICE: WE'RE LIVE!!! THIS IS IT!! DO IT, SUNDANCE!!!
JACKIE (*To the camera.*): Help me.
PETE (*Sincere.*): Poor guy. (*PETE looks down at his crotch—an erection is starting.*)
JACKIE: Help me. I hate my life.
PETE: Randy.

JACKIE disappears from the television as the cable program replaces him with some file tape.

PETE: RANDY!! (*PETE goes to the phone and gets information.*)
PETE: Manhattan. . . . Gay Broadcasting System . . . No, it's a program. . . . Well, then, Channel 20-something . . . Public Access . . . I don't know!!! . . . Sorry. (*He hangs up.*) God. (*His erection is gone. He turns off the TV and sits in the dark.*)
PETE (*To his crotch.*):
No, no—don't get up.
I'll just sit here in the dark.

A moment later, on the street outside the TV studio. JACKIE is standing with his tape player—he's getting dressed and is still wearing the bandanna.

JACKIE (*To someone offstage.*):

You told me I was gonna dance!
You told me I was gonna get to dance on TV!!
In my jockey shorts—you specifically said—
What kind of faggot are you, faggot!! (*To someone else, on the street.*) What are you looking at?!
And who do you think *you* are, Halston? Ralph Lauren?
Jerks! Dick-face!! (*To everyone.*)
Stop looking at me!! I'm not a freak!! (*JACKIE runs off.*)

(*end of scene*)

~

MADELINE VO: Madeline's Dating Life: A Puppet Play.

Lights up on two sock puppets—MADELINE puppet and a MAN puppet. The MADELINE puppet plays all the WOMAN parts.

WOMAN: I really enjoyed dinner tonight.
MAN: That was a nice little place.
WOMAN: Yes, it was nice.
Do you want to come in for a cup of something?
MAN: Sure.

Puppets mime entering the "apartment."

MAN: Nice apartment.
WOMAN: Thanks.
MAN: Can we sit for a moment?
WOMAN: Sure.

Puppets try to fake sitting.

MAN: We've been going out for a while now.
WOMAN: A month. And I've really enjoyed it.

MAN: Maddy. You're a very nice woman. But I feel—it's just that I've been trying to get over a bad relationship and I just can't . . . What I really need is a friend, not a lover.
WOMAN: Fine.
MAN: I hope you're not upset.
WOMAN: No.
MAN: I just don't feel . . .
WOMAN: Fine.
MAN: . . . that way about you.
WOMAN: Fine.
MAN: I hope we can be—
WOMAN: Fine.
MAN: Let me tell you my entire life story.
WOMAN: Fine.

Puppets hold, then disappear, as puppets do. Lights remain on the "puppet stage."

MADELINE VO: Act Two.

Two sock puppets—MAN and WOMAN—appear. This time the MAN is different.

WOMAN: I really enjoyed dinner tonight.
MAN: That was a nice little place.
WOMAN: Yes, it was nice.
Do you want to come in for a cup of something?
MAN: Sure. (*Puppets enter.*) I feel so close to you, Maddy. (*He snuggles WOMAN close to him.*)
WOMAN: I'm glad.
MAN: I can really talk to you.
WOMAN: That's nice.
I can talk to you, too.
MAN: I'm so in love with your friend, Irene.
Oh Maddy, can you talk to her for me?
WOMAN: I'd rather shoot myself in the foot, thank you.

MAN: What?
WOMAN: I'll try, Jerry. Byeeeeeeee.

Puppets disappear.

MADELINE VO: Act Seven.

Two sock puppets appear—MAN and WOMAN. MAN is different again.

MAN: I really enjoyed dinner tonight. The chicken—
WOMAN: —was good, yes. You said.
MAN: Cute apartment—lots of—
WOMAN: —personality—thanks.
MAN: This upholstery—
WOMAN: Fine.
MAN: Woodwork—
WOMAN: Fine.
MAN: I just don't feel . . .
WOMAN: Fine.
MAN: . . . that way about you.
WOMAN: Fine.
MAN: I hope we can be—
WOMAN: Sign the book.
It's in alphabetical order.

MADELINE VO: Act Four Hundred and Thirty-Two.

MAN: Can we sit for a moment?
WOMAN: Sure.

Puppets try to fake sitting.

MAN: Madeline, you're wonderful woman.
I just don't feel that way about you.
But I value our friendship so much . . .

WOMAN *Puppet devours* MAN *Puppet, making terrible noises, pulling* PUPPET *off hand—with her mouth—and tossing it away.*

WOMAN (*Satisfied.*): Haaaaa.

MADELINE *Puppet disappears.*
Puppets disappear.

MADELINE VO: The miniseries.

*Two sock puppets appear—*MAN *and* WOMAN. *They are snuggling.*

MAN: I feel so close to you, Maddy. (MAN *snuggles closer to her.*) I could sit like this for hours. But I've got a date with this humpy German boy I met at the bar. (WOMAN *moves away.*) Didn't I tell you I was gay?

WOMAN (*Holding an International Coffee packet in her mouth.*): Fine. Vienna Mocha? (*Puppets disappear. Lights up on* MADELINE, *stirring a cup of International Coffee. She smells it, tastes it, then drinks, disconsolately.*)

(*end of scene*)

~

JACKIE *and* PETE *are together at a hotel.*

JACKIE: This is a nice hotel. (*Pause.*) You seem nervous again. Sure you don't have a wife or lover that's going to knock on that door?

PETE: Yes. I'm sure.

JACKIE: Maybe they're going to call?

PETE: No. No one's going to call. Or come through that door. Or any door that I'm on the other side of.

JACKIE: You've never been to a whore.
Before now, huh?

PETE: I don't go to whores.
I'm gay.
JACKIE: I meant gay whores.
PETE: You mean hustlers.
JACKIE: Now you're getting on some word power trip thing with me. How did this happen?
PETE: You're a hustler.
JACKIE: I call myself a whore.
PETE: That's a girl's name.
JACKIE: Mary, what's wrong?
PETE: "Mary?" You're too young to remember that.
JACKIE: So? It can't be mine?
PETE: We don't do that any more.
JACKIE: Who decided that?
It must've been in that newsletter I didn't get because I don't have an address.
PETE: We never use those names.
We're men.
JACKIE: Well, I'm not a hustler.
I don't try that hard.
I don't hustle anything and I don't do that stupid dance from the seventies.
I'm a whore.
It's an old and noble profession.
PETE: I'm sorry. I don't know what I'm doing.
Politics.
Help.
JACKIE: Can I ask you something?
PETE: Sure.
JACKIE: Something personal?
PETE: More personal than my winkie?
JACKIE: Cocks aren't personal. Eyes are. (*Pause.*).
In the old days, you know.
In the days before, you know—
PETE: AIDS.
JACKIE: Condoms.

Was it really great to take a man's naked cock in your mouth and have him thrust or whatever and not worry about the condom breaking and then when he came, you could taste him and just lie back and not throw anything away? (*Beat.*)

PETE: Yeah. It was really wonderful.

The head's very soft, you know.

And it feels good . . . against . . . your . . . tongue. (*Beat.*)

JACKIE: I thought so.

PETE: And you get all sticky with that clean smell of cum.

JACKIE: How does it taste?

PETE: You mean you never. . . ?

JACKIE: How old were you when you sucked your first cock?

PETE: Fourteen. 1968. Boy Scout Camp. Aptly named.

JACKIE: Why? Never mind.

When did you first start using condoms?

PETE: Six years ago.

JACKIE: Six years ago, I was ten. I saw this program about the Greeks. They did what they wanted. And they put it on pottery, too.

It was a golden age.

PETE: You're sixteen?!

JACKIE: No, twenty. I was exaggerating.

PETE: Twenty?!

JACKIE: All right—twenty-one!!

What are you worried about, anyway?! Like, they're going to bust you for me being jailbait? We're both jailbait! We're queer!!

PETE: Oh man.

JACKIE: Listen, we don't have to do anything.

There's this series on the Bible that I like where this fat British fruit takes you all over the Holy Land and tells you where the stories really come from.

I mean, you paid for the room.

Don't make me leave. I'll be quiet.

Okay? Okay, Paul?

PETE: My name's Pete.

JACKIE: Okay, Pete?

PETE: Come here.

JACKIE: With or without music?

PETE: Just come here.

JACKIE: I usually don't get too close. . . .

PETE: Me, either.

JACKIE: I'm a little scared.
Actually.

PETE: Me, too.
Come here.
Mary.

JACKIE: I'm Jackie.

PETE: Jackie. Jack.
(*Whispers.*)
Jack.

JACKIE goes to PETE—they kiss.

(*end of Act I*)

~

ACT II

CHARLIE is on the telephone, waiting for it to ring. MADELINE picks up at her apartment.

CHARLIE: Hello?

MADELINE: Hello?

CHARLIE: It's so weird. I didn't hear it ring.

MADELINE: Charlie?

CHARLIE: Yeah. How are you?

MADELINE: Fine.

CHARLIE: How's your mom?

MADELINE: Fine.
Thanks.

CHARLIE: You're still mad at me.

MADELINE: Oh, man!

CHARLIE: Listen, Madeline, I've accepted my son's sexuality. I can deal with young black men calling me a cracker and not blow, like some of my fellow . . . police persons. I can help defend abortion clinics because of the way I feel about rights and my job as a cop, even though you KNOW how I feel about abortion—

MADELINE: Yeah, that was Pete's birthday party two years ago.

CHARLIE: Right. I can deal with all sorts of immigrants who don't speak English or wish to when MY grandparents went to goddam night school to learn!

MADELINE: Charlie . . .

CHARLIE: I just want some acknowledgment of how far I've come and had to come.

MADELINE: OK.

CHARLIE: But I WILL NOT be fleeced by some rich . . . Japanese person . . . for a meal that consisted of what I KNOW cost them no more than fifteen cents, if that. I mean, Maddy, tell me the truth—that egg roll and that tiny little piece of bait —twenty bucks?????

MADELINE: It wasn't bait, I mean, fish. That was bean curd.

CHARLIE: Even worse!!

MADELINE: Charlie, you've lived in New York your whole life. Why do you get so angry?

CHARLIE: Because I've lived in New York my whole life! And you know I put up with much more than you and Peter. I'm on the streets, Zelda! And your generation—I'm sick to death of hearing about it. What about MY generation? Before we even got to your goddam part of this century, we had plenty of our own tragedies! The Depression, the War—a *world* war—and gangsters, not gangstas, like every two-bit rap song says.

MADELINE: Been listening to a bit of rap there in the station?

CHARLIE: There? Every—goddam—where!! It's shoved down my throat in this godforsaken city. Bass beats shaking the whole goddam block. Some Nissan Sentra with tinted windows rolling by, pounding out some beat that sounds like cannon fire. I *swear* I wish it was cannon fire sometimes, so I could reply in kind! AND I KNOW YOU'RE JUST WAITING FOR ME TO SAY IT!!!

MADELINE: What, Charlie?

CHARLIE: That word. You know.

MADELINE: No.

CHARLIE: You're just trying to make me say it, so I'll say it in the office and get someone on my ass.

MADELINE: "Gook?" "Faggot?"

CHARLIE: No, the "*N* word"!!

MADELINE: Oh, yeah—"no progress," "no hope," "no future," "Narmaggeddon."

CHARLIE: DON'T BLAME ME FOR THIS WORLD! I fought in World War II and now I'm fighting Street War III!

MADELINE: Wait a minute, wait a minute. You were in Korea.

CHARLIE: Whatever! The point is I'm still protecting Koreans, and Japanese, and Indonesians and Australians—

MADELINE: Australians? Australians don't need protecting.

CHARLIE: If they're in New York City, they do!!

MADELINE: Well, fine, Mr. Protector! Come to my school sometime and convince my kids they're being protected—alright? Convince LaWanda and Carlos and Ping and Fiona and Hiroko who saw a man thrown down her stairs by one of your police persons! The child can't make it through a simple nursery rhyme without crying!

CHARLIE: Well, that's not my fault!

MADELINE: Well, it's not my fault, either!

CHARLIE: Goddammit, Madeline! I'm trying to apologize.

MADELINE: This is an apology? Get out the dictionary and look the word up, Charlie. It starts with an A.

CHARLIE: Oh, there we go again!

MADELINE: Oh, not the college degree argument again, Charlie!

You were the one who helped me fill out all the forms! I used you as a reference! You loaned me the money for the overnight mail. I probably wouldn't have gotten into NYU if you hadn't nagged me into it. And that was three hundred years ago, anyway.

CHARLIE: I had nothing to do with that. It was your SAT scores, and you know it.

MADELINE: I always thought you were, you know, a little proud—

CHARLIE: I am, Maddy. Don't you ever forget it.

MADELINE: Why does everything with you seem like an argument that I lose? Why can't we be in the same room without fighting? It wasn't always like this. Gee, when I was a kid, you were just about my favorite person.

CHARLIE: That was then. You're a grown woman now. You're fifteen years older than Muriel was when she and I conceived Peter.

MADELINE: Oh great. Oh fucking great. That makes me feel like the oldest broad on the face of the earth.

CHARLIE: Maddy. You are not a broad. You're a . . . very . . . very . . .

Long Pause.

MADELINE: Charlie?
Did you nod off?

CHARLIE: Look—I'm very sorry about the other night at the restaurant—okay? And I wanted to tell you that to make up for the birthday arguments for the last two—

MADELINE: —three—

CHARLIE: —three years, I'm taking Pete on a vacation. And not one of those stupid tours. I planned it myself—I got a deal for late May.

MADELINE: That's really nice, Charlie.

CHARLIE: You don't want to go, do you?

MADELINE: I can't—you know that. I'm socked in until June. (*Beat.*) You're relieved, aren't you?

CHARLIE:

No. No, Maddy, I'm not.
'Bye, Zelda.

MADELINE: 'Bye.

They hang up. MADELINE *dials* PETE, *gets his answering machine.*

PETE VO: You're reached 555-4320. It's such a burden being clever. Leave a message.

MADELINE: Your father just called me. We must start a fund—he's going to need professional help soon. Or I will.

She hangs up.

(end of scene)

~

JACKIE *is lying down*

JACKIE: We've become friends now, so I can tell you. Ever since I was six years old, I have seen this . . . thing in the corners of whatever room I was sleeping in. I thought it was a spider, but it only had four legs, and it was white. Every year it seemed to get bigger, and then I noticed that it had a head and two of the legs were arms. One night I saw this movie on TV called *Close Encounters of the Third Kind* and I just wanted to scream but I couldn't move, 'cause out of the spaceship came this thing that looked just like the thing in my room only the thing in the movie was a kind of alien, just really, really, skinny and about twenty feet tall. The thing in my room isn't that tall, and I know it's not kindly. It stares at me and I know it's a human thing, but not a guy because of no cock, but not a girl—no pussy—in fact, nothing between its legs, like some weird-ass doll, with spider arms. I'm sixteen and this thing is still hanging around in the dark, looking at me, and I'm terrified to sleep some nights. Even in the Days Inn, I've seen it. And I hope it's not here now because I really, really need to sleep. I really do.

(end of scene)

~

At a bar. PETE *walks in, carrying his briefcase. He's come from a meeting.*

BRAD *(Very fey bar waiter.)*: Hello.
PETE: Where's the piano bar?
BRAD: We sold it.

RUBY *crosses to* BRAD. *He's an older transvestite, played by* MOTHER, *wearing a cowboy hat and carrying another.*

RUBY: Brad.
BRAD: No.
RUBY: Brad.
BRAD: I hate the fucking thing and I fucking won't wear it! All right? *(*RUBY *just stands there. offering the hat.)*
BRAD: We're in New York, not Wyoming, Ruby! I came to New York City to live in New York City! If I'd wanted to wear cowboy hats, I would have stayed at home!!
PETE: Where are you from?
BRAD: Indiana.
PETE: Do they wear cowboy hats in Indiana?
BRAD: Psychologically, yes.
PETE: Hello, Ruby.
RUBY: Hello, Peter.
PETE: Is that a new wig?
RUBY: Yes, it's fabulous, isn't it? My mother bought it for me. *(Takes off her cowboy hat.)* See? No hat hair. It bounces right back.
PETE: Is this a country-western night or something?

BRAD: Oh, you poor darling, you don't know, do you?

RUBY: (*Offering hat.*) Brad?

BRAD: NO! GODDAMMIT!!

RUBY (*Exiting.*): Mr. Joondee won't like it.

BRAD (*Under his breath.*): I don't give a fuck what Mr. Fucking Joondee fucking likes! (*To* PETE.) Peter, what's happening to the world? I came to New York to be a *faggot*, not a cowboy! And what is Ruby doing in a cowboy hat? He's been wearing his mother's clothes since he was four! They started shopping together when he was sixteen! He's worked his whole life to turn himself into an elegantly dressed woman! And now this!!

PETE: What happened?

BRAD: The Morocco has become a fucking country-western bar!! Queer bars have to have concepts to compete! Didn't you know? It's not enough to have a nice, relatively clean place with a piano bar, tufted stools and a lighted disco floor. Noooo! All the theatre posters? Kiss them good-bye! Judy? Marilyn? Bette Davis? Even that old Laurette Taylor billboard? Bye-bye! And what's worse is that our concept is passé but Mr. Joondee doesn't know that because he's still living in the fucking seventies!

PETE: But it still says "Morocco." And the tables and everything—

BRAD: It's all gonna go. (*Sits.*) I've got to sit down. (*About the decor to come.*) Okay. Striped pine furniture. Knotty pine paneling. Ever seen knotty pine? Lots of little eyes looking at you, all over the wall. Sawdust on the floor. Barrels here and there. Bales of hay? I mean, back to the barn, darling. It's gonna look like a bad prom in Bumfuck, Oklahoma! I wouldn't be surprised if Mr. Fucking Joondee doesn't send us a carton of cow patties that we can fling here and there for some of that *real* country feeling! I swear I'm going to go work at Splash —at least it'll be clean!

RUBY (*Offstage.*): Brad! (*Throws him the cowboy hat.* BRAD *picks it up and puts it on his head, stands up, defeated.*)

BRAD (*The speech Mr. Joondee wants him to say to each customer.*):

Howdy. Cow. Poke. Brad's my handle. What would you-all like to drink?

PETE: I'd like a white wine, please.

BRAD (*Tearful gratitude.*): Thank God for you, Peter!

BRAD exits. TIM enters, dressed in a cowboy hat, looking very cowboy.

TIM: Howdy.

PETE: Someone already took my order.

TIM (*Really coming on.*): Did they?
What did you order?

PETE: Beer.

TIM: Can I sit down?

PETE (*Voice getting too high.*): Yes. (*Correcting.*) Yeah.

TIM (*Sitting.*): So, you like cowboys?

PETE: Maybe.

BRAD (*Enters with two drinks*): Here's your white wine. (*To TIM.*) And your Perrier with a twist. (*Country-western music starts.*) It's the end of civilization as we know it, darlings.

BRAD exits.

TIM: Ever done the Texas Two-Step?

PETE: I don't know. Is it hard?

TIM: We'll just have to find that out, won't we?

TIM takes PETE by the hand and lifts him out of the chair, pulls him to him, shows him where the hands go for the dance.

PETE: Are you a real cowboy?

TIM: Under our clothes, we're all the same.

PETE: And some of us are even better than that.

TIM: There you go. You're getting it.

TIM dances with PETE. Light and music change—they are in PETER's apartment, having had sex right inside the door, on the rug. PETER is stunned and happy.

TIM (*Cowboy persona gone.*):
That was fabulous. It's better on the floor.
Nice apartment.
I think you left your keys in the door.
Hey, that rhymed.
Speak to me.
PETE: Things are good. I'm back.
TIM: Back from where?
PETE: The desert.
TIM: The desert?
PETE: It's just been a while.
TIM: You seemed pent up.
Why don't we get up off the floor?
PETE: Right.
TIM: Where's the loo?
I'll take the condoms. (*Kissing PETE as he takes his condom off.*)
PETE: It's right through there. (*TIM gets up and exits to the john.*)
PETE: Oh my God.
I'm happy. (*PETE gets up and goes to the phone, starts to pick it up, thinks. TIM reenters.*)
TIM: Can't get it to flush.
Who are you calling? Boy, you're over me quick.
PETE: No! I was just calling. Do you want to stay the night?
TIM: You were calling to cancel someone.
PETE: No. I have no one to cancel.
TIM (*A joke.*): Do you know what lesbians do on the second date?
PETE: No.
TIM: Move in together.
Do you know what gay men do on the second date?
PETE: No.
TIM: Stop having sex.
That won't be us, will it?

PETE: No way.
TIM: Okay—prove it. The second date starts now.
PETE: Come on.
TIM: This is such a nice apartment.
I have lesbian tendencies, you know.
PETE: Come on, cowboy. (*They exit to the bedroom. Phone rings.*)
PETE'S VOICE (*On answering machine.*): You have reached 555-4320. No poetry today. Leave message after beep. 'Bye.
MADELINE (*On phone.*): Pete? Boy, you must be one tired boy, if you're not home yet. Anyway, sorry I missed your call, if I did. I went back to the Zen Palate to pick up my camera? That I left because I got so mad at your father? Anyway, I ran into Hank, and, well, what can I say? He's baaaaaaack. (*High voice.*) Help.

She hangs up. PETE *reenters and looks at the telephone.*

PETE: Oh fuck.
TIM (*From offstage.*): Hey! Bronco Billy! What's goin' on!
PETE: Nothing. Be right there. (PETE *exits back into the bedroom.*)

(*end of scene*)

~

Two hand puppets—MAN *and* WOMAN. *The woman hand puppet is the* MADELINE *puppet. The* MAN *puppet should be wearing a Patriots hat and a jersey from another team.*

MAN: We can fuck just as soon as this football game is over with. (WOMAN *puppet reaches behind and comes up with an Oreo in her mouth.*)

Blackout. Lights up and a real man, HANK, *sitting on the couch, holding the TV remote—he is wearing a Patriots hat and a jersey. Next to him is* MADELINE, *eating an Oreo.*

HANK (*To the TV.*): Go, go, GO! You asshole! (*Hates the play.*) Oh man. (*To* MADELINE.) Did you see that? The safety was right there—he was right THERE! (*Back to the game.*)
Oh, I can't believe it—they're going to kick. NOOOOOOO!
Just run it—you're right there!
I can't watch. (*He does.*) FUUUUCK! (*He throws the remote down.*)
MADELINE (*Picking up the remote and trying to turn off the TV.*):
I can't seem to get it to work now.
There.

TV off.

HANK: Oh man. Fucking Patriots—why do I fall for it? (*To* MADELINE.)
What? Did you turn it off?
Give me that! Are you nuts? (*Grabs the remote and turns the TV back on.*)
This remote is fucked. (*Not taking his eyes off the TV, he reaches for* MADELINE*—she snuggles close—he gives her a peck, then drops her for the TV.*) I think the switch on your remote is faulty, Babe.
MADELINE: I've long suspected it.
HANK (*To the TV.*): Oh NO! Not again, you fucking dick. You dick!

Phone rings. MADELINE *picks it up. We see* PETE— *on the other end.*

PETE: Whatcha doin'?
MADELINE: Hank's here.
HANKS (*To the TV.*): Oooooo, that's it. That's it, baby.
PETE: Yikes! Sorry. (PETE *hangs up.*)
MADELINE: No! Don't hang up. (*She dials the phone.*)
HANK (*To the TV.*): Go, baby, go, go, go!

Yes! Yes! Yesssssss! (PETE *picks phone up.*)

I'm comin'! I'm comin'!

MADELINE: Don't hang up!

PETE: This is too weird for me.

HANK (*To the TV.*): I'm in there! Yes!

MADELINE: Peter—don't hang up, whatever you do, I want to—

HANK (*To the TV.*):

I'm in the pocket, baby! I'm there! I'm there!

YESSSSSSSSSS!

At last!!

You're beautiful. You're beautiful.

PETE: Madeline?

PETE: He's watching football.

PETE: *While* he's doing it?

MADELINE: No, instead of doing it.

HANK: Who you talking to, babe?

MADELINE: Peter.

HANK (*About a player on TV.*): No, not this fucking guy. (*To the telephone.*) Hey, Pete—how's it hanging?

PETE: Tell Hank I appreciate his interest in the position of my willie, and that I would inquire about the relative positioning of his at this moment, but I fear I would know the answer, making his reply redundant. (*This cracks* MADELINE *up.*)

MADELINE (*To* HANK.): Pete says hi.

HANK (*Not pleased at the laughter.*): Yea. (*Back to the game.*)

Oh man . . .

Go for it go for it go for it—FUCK MEEEEEE!

PETE: The ironic thing is that he doesn't mean it.

MADELINE: I know, it is a stupid relationship, but it is the only one I've got.

HANK: Halftime. (*To* MADELINE.)

Don't get off the phone—I'm going out for a couple of grinders. Bring you back a tuna? (*He kisses her.*)

Baby baby baby. Oooooo.

MADELINE: Yeah.

HANK exits.

PETE: What the fuck are you doing? Haven't we been down this road before?

MADELINE: Can't I have love?

PETE: He manipulates you. He turns you on a dime.

MADELINE: Do you even know where my fucking dime is?!

PETE: Madeline! (*It hurt.*)

Ooo. You got me there. (*Really long pause.*)

MADELINE and PETE:

It's just that—

No, you go—

No, I'll—

PETE: It's your life—you talk.

MADELINE: You're right, Peter. It is my life. You are also right about Hank—you were, as I recall, right the last time.

PETE: He does look great in Levis.

MADELINE: I know.

PETE: Don't get hurt.

MADELINE: Peter . . .

PETE: All right. Get hurt. Call me. Watch your butt.

MADELINE: I have to do something!

PETE: "I have to"? What is this—catechism class?

MADELINE: I want to. I'm tired of love with batteries. I'm tired of my own hand. Sometimes I feel like a puppeteer. (*Making her hand a person—à la Señor Wences, she talks to it.*)

"Was it good for you?" (*Hand speaks back.*) "Yes, it was!"

PETE: Did you just talk to your hand?

MADELINE: Yes, is that a bad sign?

PETE: No worse than any of the others.

MADELINE: I'll be all right.

PETE: You'll be all right.

MADELINE: God, we sound like a seminar.

PETE: Uh . . . I have a boyfriend—I think.

MADELINE: Oh my God.

PETE: Yes.

MADELINE: What's he like?

PETE: He's great, but it's still new—I don't want to jinx it.

MADELINE: You won't. Just be yourself. Bless you and him.

PETE: You're such a better person than I am.

MADELINE: Oh my God. Get a grip, Peter. Yo'ure turning into the Pillsbury Dough Boy. Look, Hank will be coming back any minute now. Call me tonight—no, don't call me tonight—hopefully, I'll be busy unless ESPN has captured Hank's attention again. I want to hear all about the guy—whatever you want to divulge—okay?

PETE: OK. 'Bye.

MADELINE: 'Bye.

They hang up.

MADELINE: Oh, Peter, why do you get to be in love?

HANK reenters.

MADELINE: You're back quick. Where are the sandwiches?

HANK: I had to come back to ask you: How come I never make you laugh like that?

MADELINE: Like what?

HANK: Like Peter does.

MADELINE: You do make me laugh, you do make me laugh. You make me laugh a lot—you're a very funny man—humor isn't everything. I mean, there's a lot of a relationship that has nothing to do with laughing, believe me. Believe me, laughter is not what you want, you know, you know, at the height of passion. I mean, you know, *irony* is the death of erotic feeling. They can't really exist in the same space, you know, Hank.

HANK: I'm a sex object.

MADELINE: No, you're not! Well, yeah, you are! You are a mighty sex object! Yeah.

HANK: You're using me.

MADELINE: I love you. I am hot for you. You are a wonderful man.

HANK: Two nuns walk into a bar.

MADELINE: Yeah.

HANK: And one says:

I can tell by your face that you won't think this is funny.

MADELINE: Of course I will.

HANK: No, that's what the nun said. (*MADELINE laughs.*) See? You laugh harder at fucking Pete just looking at you than you do at a joke from me.

MADELINE: Tell me a better joke, Hank, and I'll laugh more.

HANK: OK. A guy goes hunting, see? And he sees this huge bear and gets him in his sights and shoots him, and the bear falls down, dead. So the hunter is jubilant—man, he is so pleased with himself. He runs down to where the bear fell, and the damn bear is gone. Suddenly, he feels this tap on his shoulder and turns around and there's the bear—huge motherfucking grizzly. "Blow me," says the bear. So the hunter is afraid for his life and he makes himself do it. He sucks the bear off and the bear runs off and the hunter goes back to camp and barfs, but he is so mad, he's even more determined to get this bear. So the next day, he goes out and, sure enough, he sees the same bear rambling through the woods, so he gets him in his sights and *blam, blam, blam!* shoots him several times. The bear falls and the hunter runs there. But when he gets there, the damn bear is nowhere to be seen. And then, he feels that tap on his shoulder. He turns around and there's the bear, but this time, the bear says, "Turn around, and drop your pants." So the hunter does and the bear fucks him in the butt, nearly tearing him apart. The hunter drags himself back to camp and sits in a cold stream and thinks about revenge. The next day, the hunger goes out with his biggest gun. He looks for the bear all day, and, at about evening, he spies the bear at the stream. The hunter empties his gun into the bear, sees him fall, and runs down to finally get his prize. Sure enough, when he gets there, the bear is gone. Just as the hunter's about to give up, he feels this tap on his shoulder. He turns and, yes, it's the bear looking him right in the eye and saying, "You didn't come to hunt."

MADELINE *laughs a lot at this one.*

MADELINE: That is so funny, Hank. I love that.
HANK: It's a homo joke. I heard it from Pete a year ago.
MADELINE: Yeah, but delivery means a lot. (*She sits on his lap.*) And you, Hank, you deliver. (*He embraces her, but we see his face—he's not completely happy.*)
HANK: Yeah. Old Hank—the delivery man.

(*end of scene*)

~

PETE *and his father,* CHARLIE, *are on vacation. They are outside in the sun.* CHARLIE *isn't having a good time.*

PETE: Dad—
CHARLIE: I'm fine.
PETE: Dad—
CHARLIE (*About someone staring at him.*): Oh God.
PETE: Dad, it's very beautiful here. It's a very beautiful place. And history as long as your arm.
CHARLIE: Put your arms down. What are you doing with your arms. Good God, do you want somebody to come over?
PETE: Maybe. (CHARLIE *looks incredulously at* PETE.) Dad, you picked this vacation! Without ever consulting me! And I love it—I love *that*. That you picked it.
CHARLIE: I didn't know!
PETE: Of course you didn't.
Believe me, I know that.
CHARLIE: I mean, it's just that—you know, son—I've made my peace—no, that's wrong—I've, *long ago*, accepted Your—Your—

STAVROS *enters, smiles at them.*

STAVROS (*Greek accent.*): 'Ello. Don't fight. Love.

STAVROS exits.

CHARLIE (*To exiting STAVROS.*): Listen! This is my *son*!
PETE: Dad, just look at this architecture. Isn't it beautiful? Like a storybook.
CHARLIE: . . . Yeah . . .
PETE: I wonder what Mykonos means in Greek?
CHARLIE: I have an idea.
PETE: You know, sex is prurient to you.
CHARLIE: What do you mean? I loved sex with your mother.
PETE: Dad! Spare me.
CHARLIE: Aha. Gotcha.
PETE: What do you mean?
CHARLIE: My sex with your mother—WHICH CREATED YOU, I might add—is prurient to you. Whatever the hell "prurient" means.
PETE: It's not normal for children to enjoy hearing about the sex their parents have.
CHARLIE: Normal? (*Gestures to take in their surroundings.*)
PETE: Oh Dad, are we going to have this fucking fight again?
CHARLIE: Watch your mouth, Peter.

(*STAVROS reenters.*)

STAVROS: You still angry? Fight? Nooooo. Bad. Most bad. Island of love. Many hunks. You American hunks. Huh? (*To PETE.*) Older man—good. (*To CHARLIE.*)
Younger man—most good.
I have love: gone.
PETE: Oh, did he . . . die?
STAVROS: Die? I wish die. Prick left me. German prick. Why do I love people I hate? Greek way—love/hate—who knows? Slavery, love—better to fuck pillow. Your hand. Hand never leave

you. Hand never talk back. (PETE *laughs to himself.*) Why you laugh? Stavros funny?

PETE: No. It's— I was thinking of something. I—

STAVROS: What?

PETE: Just some—my friend Madeline talks to her hand. And it talks back.

CHARLIE: What?!

PETE (*To* CHARLIE.): Just one night we were talking on the phone, and Madeline cracked me up with talking to her hand—you had to be there, I guess.

STAVROS: You have funny sister?

PETE: No, Madeline is—Madeline—she's . . . my . . . friend.

STAVROS: You have girlfriend, too? (*To* CHARLIE.) You watch him.

CHARLIE: He's my son. (*To everyone in hearing distance.*) He's my SON!!!!

STAVROS: Americans. Who are you? Anybody know over there? You bring slaves over. Now they yell at you. Your women are—are wild—touch themselves and talk to hands. Indians used to love fight—(*Mimes arrow leaving bow.*)—now they dress like cowboy. What happened to cowboys? I loved them. Cowboys here, but not real. Don't know horse from mo-ped. From big dog with long hair they comb and comb and walk around—hate dogs. America all gone. New name—you need new name. Greece—always same. Thousands of years—the same.

(DALE *enters {played by actress who plays* MOTHER*}.*)

DALE: Excuse me, I'm with a tour over there, and I couldn't help overhearing. I know it's none of my business, but I'm from Duluth, and we'd like to say that America is not all gone, and our name is fine.

CHARLIE: Wow.

DALE: And if it wasn't for us confused Americans, who would buy your T-shirts, sir?

CHARLIE: Yes!

PETE: Yikes.

DALE: And I'm a little fuzzy on World War II, but I think we saved your butts.

PETE: Oh God.

CHARLIE: That's right!

STAVROS (*To PETE.*): You want get laid?

PETE: No! I mean, good lord! Dad—

CHARLIE (*To DALE.*): My name is Charles Szczepanek, and this is my son.

STAVROS: What?

DALE: Hello. I'm Dale Williamson. I'm from Duluth.

STAVROS exits.

CHARLIE: Peter.

Look, Ms. Williamson. Could I buy you a drink?

DALE: All right. Sure. (*To her crowd.*) Girls!

PETER: Look, Dad. I've got a headache.
I'm going to lie down—I'll see you at dinner. (*CHARLIE gives him a look.*) Dad. I Have a Headache. I also have Taste.
Excuse me, Mrs. Williamson—

DALE: Call me Dale.

PETER: Perhaps I'll see you later.

PETER exits.

DALE: Nice boy.

CHARLIE: Well, aren't you a breath of fresh air.

DALE: We're all going to this place on the dock—you want to come, Mr.—ah—

CHARLIE: Szczepanek. Call me Charlie.

DALE: Charlie.

CHARLIE: You got any Polish people in Duluth?
DALE: Oh, we've got everything in Duluth.

CHARLIE and DALE exit.

(end of scene)

~

Lights up on PETE, fumbling with his room key. STAVROS steps out of the darkness.

STAVROS: Peter.
PETE: Oh.
STAVROS: I'm sorry. I'm a fool.
PETE: My father—
STAVROS: Beautiful man.
Like you.
PETE: I resemble my mother, actually—they say.
STAVROS: Peter—
PETE: I have a lover.
STAVROS: What do you think life is? You find a place you like, someone you like, you say, not now, I be back, very beautiful, very perfect, not now, I be back, I be back this way, not this time, another time, this time not right, another time, I be back, I embrace you then, I kiss you then, I hold you then, not now, another time, I be back. But no, no one come back, ever. Greece here thousand of year. Stavros here thirty-five. No one come back. Ever. Now is only time. Now. Now, Peter who resemble his mother. Now.

STAVROS kisses PETER.

PETE: I—
STAVROS: Now.

(end of scene)

~

MADELINE is in a girl bar. An older woman, DORIS, walks by and cruises her, exits. MADELINE crosses to a stool and sits. Music starts, and MADELINE looks up and stares at some entertainment. It shocks and transfixes her. The music is quite erotic. She stares. DORIS comes up and gives MADELINE a glass of white wine.

DORIS: Yes, those are female go-go dancers. And, yes, this is a dyke bar. And, yes, that is a nice glass of Chablis. And I'm a nice dyke and—are you from Minneapolis or something?

MADELINE: Queens.

DORIS: Haven't been out in a while. I know how it feels. They're very young, aren't they? Lots and lots of tight little butts and upturned breasts. I mean the whole bar—not just the dancers. Now, check this out. (*Shouts to dancer we don't see.*) Sabrina!

Music is belly-dancing music.

DORIS: It's a real belly dance. (*MADELINE watches, mouth open.*)

MADELINE: She's wonderful.

DORIS: I know.

MADELINE: How does she do that?

DORIS: She started young. In her uncle's restaurant.

MADELINE: And he let her?

DORIS: He did more than that.

MADELINE: It's just so—it's just so—I mean, we're all women, and she's doing these movements.

DORIS: Thousands of years—only for men. Now for us.

MADELINE: I mean, it's so, I don't know—like watching yourself do—(*Another amazing movement from SABRINA.*) Now that's just bad for her back.

DORIS: It's so effective, though. Good lord.

MADELINE: But—but—

DORIS: Doris.

MADELINE: Doris, didn't we condemn all of this in the seventies or whenever, I mean, we're close to the same age, I think—

DORIS: Fifty.

MADELINE: Fifty? I don't believe that.
DORIS: Yes.
MADELINE: You look wonderful.
DORIS: Thanks.
MADELINE: I mean—
DORIS: Just "thanks."
MADELINE: It's just that—I don't know why I'm here.
DORIS: Oh God. Why me?
MADELINE: I'm sorry. I—
DORIS: Drink your wine.

Music ends and Sabrina's dance—offstage applause and whistles.

MADELINE: Are they whistling at her?
DORIS: No, the go-go dancers are coming back.
MADELINE: They're wearing—they have—
DORIS: Cocks, I know.
MADELINE: Why, Doris?
DORIS: Just think of it as another aspect of our mysterious sexuality, I mean, men have worn false breasts for hundreds of years—on television, prime time! In front of children, even. And male drag queens have tucked their genitals up so they can dress in tight Las Vegas Showgirl drag. Girls are wearing cocks, as part of their male drag gear.
MADELINE: But that one is in a little cocktail dress.
DORIS: I know. I have a little trouble . . .
MADELINE: It is erotic.
DORIS: That it is.
MADELINE: You explained it well.
DORIS: I'm trying to embrace it. I'm—I'm—I'm actually very old and trying to be Miranda about the whole thing: "O brave new world, that has such people in it." Of course, what does she know? She was living on an island with her weird father, a fairy, and a talking missing link who tried to rape her. In short, she could be my neighbor on West 54th Street.
MADELINE: Have you had dinner?

DORIS: I don't know.

MADELINE: I'm not really here because . . .
I'd understand, if you said . . .

DORIS: Uh-huh.

MADELINE: I just know a lot of good restaurants. I eat out a lot. (*Pause.*) I have no idea what I'm doing.

DORIS: Oh, I know that. (*Scans bar for another prospect, fails.*) Come on.

They exit.

(*end of scene*)

~

PETE *is running on the beach at Mykonos, looking for his father. It's night. The surf is pounding.*

PETE: Dad, dammit, where are you? DAD! DAD! Shit. Damn. What am I doing? He's a grown man. I'm a grown man. (*Looks at his watch.*) It's almost five o'clock in the morning! (*He stops to catch his breath and prays.*) Father, find my father. (*Beat.* CHARLIE *enters quietly. He's more than tipsy.*)

CHARLIE: Pete? Jeez.

PETE: Dad? Dad! (*He runs to him, but stops before he hugs him.*)

CHARLIE: What are you doing out here? You're not with that slimely Greek, are you?

PETE: Dad! Christ!

CHARLIE: You been walking? I been walking. (*Peering up the hill.*) That our hotel? Yay.
I knew that.

PETE: I was so worried when I realized I had no way to find you.

CHARLIE: Found.

PETE: How as Whatshername? Gail?

CHARLIE: Dale from Duluth.

PETE: How was she?

CHARLIE: Desperate.
She was a desperate woman.
She scared me.
Like standing on the edge of a well—your cock about the size of a Vienna sausage—knowing that you could fall in at any moment and no one would hear your screams. (*Suddenly unsteady.*) Oh man.

PETE: Dad—

CHARLIE: I'm gonna—I gonna—sit (*CHARLIE sort of falls and lies there.*) Peter, the stars. Come down. (*PETE lies down next to CHARLIE.*)

PETE: Beautiful.

CHARLIE: You know, I'm really lonely all the time. Lonely, lonely.

PETE: There's Sirius, Dad.

CHARLIE: Yeah. Sorry.

PETE: No, just look up there. The Dog Star.

CHARLIE: What's it for? Ugly girls to wish on?

PETE: Are you sure we're related?

CHARLIE: You are my son! That's not funny. (*Tries to sit up.*) Whoa. (*Lies back down, sees star.*) It's bright.

PETE: Are you sure you're looking at the right star?

CHARLIE: Oh, who cares?
I'm sorry, what's it for, Peter? Love?

PETE: No, just heat. Dad. And good harvest. And the rising of the Nile. That's what it's for.

CHARLIE: The Nile rises, the heat comes, and we chase after Duluth babes. Some star comes out, some river rises, and we make fools of ourselves. It's too beautiful here. Let's go back to New York. I need a body with multiple stab wounds. Help me. (*PETE helps his father stand.*)

CHARLIE: If your mother could see me now.

PETE: It's all right, Dad.

CHARLIE: If your mother could see me now.

PETE: Dad.

CHARLIE: If she could see me now, I'd be saved. You need somebody to watch you live.

PETE: Don't tell me that, Dad.
CHARLIE: Okeedoke. (*A confession.*) I love Madeline, son.
PETE: So do I, Dad. (*Pause.*)
CHARLIE: Right.

They exit.

(*end of scene*)

~

JACKIE is standing on a beach—we hear the surf.

JACKIE: I had a baby sister who was born to see the future—she was born veiled, you know. The thing around her face—the placenta. My mother is a Baptist, so she didn't want to say it out loud, in front of the doctor or anything. But she really did believe that it was a sign of future-seeing, and it is, from way back. Then the baby died in a few hours, having never even seen the sun, or a star. But I wonder, sometimes, if she really did see the future. In the few short hours she lived. And her little babiness couldn't take it—just couldn't take it.

An older man {played by the MOTHER actor} enters—more androgynous than male, dressed badly and smoking.

SANNY: Who you talking to?
JACKIE: No one.
SANNY: I heard you talking.
JACKIE: It was nothing.
SANNY: You don't want to tell me. You think I'm old and weird. That's all right. That's all right. I give you your space. It's a big old beach. I come here for years. I'm a little boy over there. I'm a big boy over there behind those rocks. I'm an old man here. Huh? Huh? How old do you think I am?
JACKIE: Forty-eight—?

SANNY: I'm sixty-two.

JACKIE: Wow.

SANNY: Sixty-two years old. I've seen a lot. You a fairy?

JACKIE: I'm waiting for my girlfriend.

SANNY: Uh-huh. I seen the burning of Wonderland. Hours it burned. Nothing left. Midgets, bearded ladies, dog-faced boys and girls scurrying out with no place to go. No home. That's why Manhattan is so weird. They spawned, you know. Their blood is in all of us. I seen them kill an elephant. Fifteen minutes it took—one lethal injection after another and she wouldn't die. That blood is on our hands, too. Now Coney Island is filled with niggers on welfare. You look like James Dean.

JACKIE: Who's that? Oh. Oh, the dead guy. (*Starts to go.*) Look—

SANNY: Don't go. What'd I say? Fairy? Nigger?
I'll be good. I'm from another generation—we don't know how to be polite, sometimes. Hey. You talk to nobody just fine—you can talk to me. I'm more fun than nobody out there.

JACKIE: OK.

SANNY: You an actor? You rehearsing?

JACKIE: No, I pretend there're people out there who watch me, and I talk to them.

SANNY: You a lonely boy. Like me.
Putting on a show, huh?

JACKIE: Sometimes.

SANNY: I live up there. My mother died. Come with me? I've got some hamburger I'm gonna fry.
I got a big screen TV.

JACKIE: You get cable?

SANNY: A hundred and two channels. Kids programs from Japan. Cooking in Egypt. Indian movies.

JACKIE: Nature programs?

SANNY: Every minute somewhere. Come on. (*SANNY reaches out his hand.*) Hey. (*JACKIE shakes his hand.*) Nice ring there.

JACKIE: NYPD. My dad gave it to me.
SANNY: I'd better take good care of you.

They exit.

(end of scene)

~

PETER is back from his trip—his suitcase is open. TIM and PETER have just made love.

TIM: Now, what else did you bring me?
PETER: I can't believe how happy I am now. Do you know how hard it is to be in some romantic place without you?

TIM reaches into PETER's suitcase, finds something.

PETER: Don't. That's for Maddy.
TIM: Can't I see?
PETER: It's wrapped.
TIM: Not well.
PETER: Don't. The wrapping is part of the funny story. Here's your big present.
TIM: But it's small. (*Opens it.*) Oooooo. Nice.
PETER: We can have it sized. It's lapis lazuli.
TIM: Thanks, baby. (*Kisses him.*) No funny story to go with this?
PETER: No . . .
I could make something up.
TIM: You called Maddy from the Detroit airport.
PETER: I had that layover—flight from Hell.
TIM: Why didn't you call me, Peter?
PETER: It was two A.M.!
TIM: I need more sleep than Madeline?
PETER: I've called Madeline at two A.M. so many times—God. (*Beat.*)

TIM: Peter. I am a gay man. I want a relationship with another gay man.

PETER: Well, you've got that.

TIM: You save things for her.

PETER: What? That gift? It's just a joke thing. What do you mean, I save "things" for Madeline?

TIM: You save little stories for her.
And little jokes.
And little things that you felt.
You call her at two A.M., for Chrissake!

PETER: Tim—

TIM: *I* want to hear about your flight from hell!
I can't tell you how many times you have said this to me, "I was telling Maddy this, and I realized how great that moussaka was." And *then* you tell *me* about it. I want to hear about the moussaka! I want the real raw moussaka story before it goes through her!

PETER: Timothy, you're jealous of Madeline.

TIM: Damn right! How can I compete with a twenty-five-year old relationship!

PETER: I love you.

TIM: You love her.

PETER: It's a different love.

TIM: You save things for her!

PETER: Here! Do you want the damn present I got for her?

TIM: Oh, that's not it, and you know it!

PETER: Tim, you are my lover.

TIM: Do you know what it's like to lie with someone in the dark, after you've made love, and realize that only part of them is really there? That, inside, they're are secretly thinking of something funny that happened, that they can't share with you because it's about you?

PETER: When have I ever done that? Told Madeline anything about our sex life, for Chrissakes?

TIM: Oh, it doesn't have to be about our sex life—it can be about anything. Because you've known each other so long, everything anyone can think of has some reference, some story from the past, some poem, some fragment of a memory. You have this entire life with Madeline. And she's not even an ex-wife that I have a chance of supplanting. Nooooo. She's still here—right smack-dab in the center of your life, still "Maddy," with both hands on this enormous, unchangeable, rock-solid relationship of yours. Do you know why you haven't gotten a lover before now? You never really needed one. You just needed to get laid. You are in a celibate marriage with Madeline. The "marriage of true minds" already happened when you were sixteen.

PETER: Fourteen.

TIM: Jesus! Who can compete with that? Well, I *need* a marriage. In these fucking awful times, I need a marriage of true minds.

Beat.

PETER: Wow, Tim.

TIM: Right.

PETER: I can't give up my friendship with Madeline. I . . .

TIM: Just stop saving things for her. Save things for *me.*

PETER opens MADELINE's present, shows it to TIM.

PETER: It's a box of Greek tampons.

TIM: Oh man.

Just what I always wanted. (*They laugh weakly.*) Look, I'm sorry. (*TIM kisses PETER.*) I'm going to take a shower. Then I'll take you out to eat some real American food—sushi.

TIM exits. Sound of a shower. The phone rings and PETER looks at it, but lets the answering machine pick it up.

ANSWERING MACHINE (PETER VO): You have reached 555-4320. I'm not back from my vacation, but Tim is here and can take a message for me, so leave it after the beep. Frank O'Hara will return with a new poetry selection soon.

Beep sounds. MADELINE*'s voice comes through on the answering machine.* PETER *just looks at the phone, but doesn't pick it up.*

MADELINE'S VO (*Through the answering machine.*): Hello? Peter, where the fuck are you??!!! Life sucks!!!! I loved your phone call from Detroit, but WHERE ARE YOU?????!!! Tim, you needn't answer this hysterical message. Give Pete my love when you talk to him. This is Madeline and she's MAAAAD! I can't believe you're not home yet. Are you there? Are you there? Peter????? OK. 'Bye. 'Byeeeeeeeeee. God, I am so not funny without you. 'Bye.

She hangs up. PETER *puts his head in his hands.*

(*end of scene*)

~

DORIS *and* MADELINE *are at* MADELINE*'s apartment.* DORIS *is popping some Tums.*

MADELINE: I liked this Afghani place where we ate tonight better than that Thai place we went last week, didn't you? Although Thai food is easier to digest, I guess. Now there's a Venezuelan place near—well, I'm not sure, but I'll find out for next week. So what do you want to watch on TV tonight? Did you notice that guy at the door when I was getting my mail? I swear he was staring at us. But I could be just—is that a new shirt? I didn't notice before—

DORIS: Madeline—

MADELINE: It's good on you, the shirt. I mean—

DORIS: Just "thanks."

MADELINE: Where do you want to go next Thursday or Wednesday, it could be. It doesn't have to be Venezuelan, and Pete can come with us, then—you've got to meet him—you two—

DORIS: Madeline—

MADELINE: Or maybe on the weekend.

DORIS: Madeline!

MADELINE: . . . yeah . . . ?

DORIS: You're a really nice woman, but—

MADELINE: Uh-oh.

DORIS: I don't think you feel "that way" about me.

MADELINE: Uh-oh.

DORIS: Look, darling. I'm too old to do therapy on someone, and I've got plenty of friends. I hate to be crass, but I need to get laid sometime. If I can't, I'm spending tonight with my VCR and a pint of Cherries Garcia.

MADELINE: Oh.

DORIS: I'm sorry.

MADELINE: Okay.

DORIS: You're really nice.

MADELINE: Okay.

DORIS: 'Bye.

MADELINE: Okay. (*DORIS exits.*) Fine.

(*end of scene*)

~

PETE *is doing his woodwork with Murphy's Soap. He pauses and stares for a beat or two, then starts cleaning again. The phone rings.*

PETE'S VO (*On answering machine.*): This is 555-4320. Leave a message for Peter. Please DO NOT leave messages for Tim here—he can be reached at his old number. Thanks.

CHARLIE: (*On the phone, leaving a message on the answering machine.*) Pete? This is your dad.
Pete? Call me.

PETE (*Picks up the phone.*): Dad?

CHARLIE: Peter.

PETE: What's wrong?

CHARLIE: Pete, did you lose your grandfather's NYPD ring?

PETE: Uh—

CHARLIE: Did you get ripped off?

PETE: No, Dad. I gave it to someone. Oh God. I'm sorry, Dad. I'm so sorry. It's not that it didn't mean anything to me. It meant so much I gave it to—(*Beat.* PETE *realizes.*) How did you find it?

CHARLIE: Son—

PETE: Oh God. Someone picked him up for hustling.

CHARLIE: No, son.

PETE: Oh God—what hospital?

CHARLIE: St. Vincent's. Peter?

PETE: What happened?

CHARLIE: Someone beat him up, and it's not good.

PETE: No! No!!!!!

CHARLIE: What do you want me to do?

PETE: What do I want you to do?!!

CHARLIE: TELL ME AND I'LL GODDAM DO IT!

PETE hangs up the phone and sits down. MAC, another police detective, enters.

MAC: Got an ID?

CHARLIE: Yes.

MAC— palms the ring into CHARLIE's hand. PETE exits quickly, putting on his jacket.)

MAC: It's not evidence. No reason for the hospital to see it.

MAC pats CHARLIE on the back and exits.

CHARLIE (*Looking at the ring.*): Dad.

CHARLIE exits.

(*end of scene*)

~

PETE stands in the elevator at St. Vincent's. He's gripping his wadded up jacket—he has seen JACKIE. Next to him is another gay man and a woman friend, mirror of PETE and MADELINE. They are holding a bouquet of roses and some other hospital gift.

PETE (*To himself.*): I've been here so many times. (*Realizes he's spoken out loud.*) Sorry.
WOMAN: Don't be sorry. Just saw you in ICU?

PETE nods "yes."

WOMAN: We've got another stop.
MAN (*Gives PETE a flower.*): It's a rose.

Doors open—MAN and WOMAN step out.

MAN: Why did you let me say that?
WOMAN: That? It was nice.
MAN: "It's a rose." "I'm a dork."
WOMAN: It was *nice*. I'm sure he thought it was nice.
MAN: And he was attractive, too.

They are gone. PETE leaves the elevator the other way and crosses outside. He pulls his collar up and exits.

(*end of scene*)

~

MADELINE and PETE are at his apartment. It's raining outside. He enters with the rose in a little vase—it's wilted.

PETE: It's been in my care for twenty-four hours and look at it.
MADELINE: Put an aspirin in the water.
PETE: You think it has a headache?
MADELINE: A migraine. PMS. Don't give it a gun.

PETE: Sorry about the rain.
No beach.

MADELINE: That's all right. I just feel like staying in. It's been a helluva year.

PETE: Have *you* heard from my father?

MADELINE: No.

(*He drinks from the Coke.*)

MADELINE: Should *I* call him?

PETE: No. I'll give him some breathing space.

He puts the Coke down. MADELINE *reaches for the Diet Coke to drink from, but* PETE *picks it up again.*

MADELINE: What? Do you have a cold? No biggie. (PETE *won't give her the can and she gets a little scared.*)
Give me the can, Pete.
Give me the can, Peter.
No.
No.
No.

Long beat.

MADELINE: It's not carried in saliva.

PETE: I read something—saliva's on the list.

MADELINE: No, Peter, no. No. No, no, no, no, no, no, noooooooo.

PETE: I'm just Positive. It's no further than that.

Long beat.

MADELINE: No.

PETE: If I take care of myself . . .

MADELINE: Looks like you already failed there!
I'M NOT GONNA SAY I'M SORRY I SAID THAT.

HOW COULD YOU SURVIVE TEN YEARS AND THEN FUCK UP??!!!!! YOU WERE *SAFE*, YOU WERE *SAFE, GODDAMMIT!!!* YOU SURVIVED TEN YEARS! YOU SURVIVED EVERYBODY! GOOD-BYE, BARRY! GOOD-BYE, KEVIN! AND ALLEN AND RON AND DAVID AND JERRY. AND SHAWN. AND BOB. AND STEW-ART. AND JOE. We saw everyone of them go! You and me. We sat in those awful pews and then chairs and then theatres and listened to the handful of stories and the shreds of our friend's lives and managed to get up and go on and live, and you were still safe and I thanked God every day that you were safe and I'm a goddam atheist and you know it!! And all those years when you were going to Fire Island, to those parties with your, as you call it, nonmacho body and your overdeveloped sense of taste, and not getting laid and spending all your time talking to some too-old queen in the kitchen while everyone is outside fucking madly in the sand, and I kept worrying that you weren't getting a date and it was not fair—Well, ever since this FUCKING plague hit, I have been more and more grateful that you have that "nonmacho" body because nearly every single person from those days is GONE, Peter! Dead, Peter.

And you're going to leave me in this stupid world to be wise or something. And I'll be an old lady and make my peace and thought I had a good life or whatever you say to the living to make them feel better, and I will have found some way to be happy some of the time, but it will all be without you. How in the FUCK am I supposed to live without YOU??!!

PETER: I don't know how I got it.

I was always very careful.

Tim is negative.

MADELINE: Does Tim know?

PETER: Yeah.

MADELINE: What did he say?

PETER: He said, "How are you gonna tell Madeline?"

MADELINE: I'm not crying anymore.

I'm so sorry about . . . the yelling, Peter. I'm so sorry. I'm so sorry. I'm so sorry. I'm so sorry.

PETER: It's all right.

MADELINE: I'm only thinking of myself.

When you really, really, really, really dread something, and it comes—

Oh, Peter, our lives—your life.

PETER: We always wanted to have lives like in a novel.

MADELINE: Yeah, but by Noël Coward, not . . . Tolstoy.

PETER: Kafka.

MADELINE: It's not carried in saliva. GMHC says it's not carried in saliva.

PETER: Do you want to chance it?

He offers her the Diet Coke—she doesn't take it. He puts the Coke can down. They both stare at it.

(end of scene)

~

An Arapaho man, very beautiful, is flying and holding JACKIE *from behind. There's the sound of wind and the faint regular beep from a heart monitor.*

ARAPAHO (*Singing to himself an Arapaho song and bit of country-western.*) (*Something whizzes by.*) Uh-oh—time string. Jackie?

JACKIE (*Waking up a bit.*): Uh?

ARAPAHO: Awake?

JACKIE: I— . . . yeah.

ARAPAHO: How do you feel?

JACKIE: Better. Good. Very light.
I could be flying.
ARAPAHO: Uh-huh.
JACKIE: Where's the IV? (*Looking at his arm, feeling his nose.*) Where are the tubes? (*Seeing down, a little alarmed.*)
Whoa! We're up in the air!
Way up!!
ARAPAHO: Don't be afraid. You're with me.

JACKIE reaches back and feels ARAPAHO's thigh.

JACKIE: 'Kay.
ARAPAHO: You're with me.
JACKIE (*About the earth.*): It's so beautiful. It's blue down there—like a picture from—I can see my feet.
ARAPAHO: I know.
JACKIE: I'm hurt real bad. Some pervert beat the shit out of me. They don't think I'll—

ARAPAHO doesn't say anything. JACKIE finally understands what's happened.

JACKIE: Oh.
Oh man, I hope they figure out how to call my mother.
I don't have any ID.
MOMMA! IT'S ALL RIGHT!!!
And Pete—his ring. I hope he gets it back.
PEEEEETE!!! MOMMA!!!! EARRRRRTH!!!

Sorrow to hyperventilation to the death rattle to the last breathing out. The beep turns to a solid sound and fades away. JACKIE's breathing out becomes the sound of the wind.

ARAPAHO: There. Jackie?
JACKIE: Yes.
ARAPAHO: Wanna go back as someone else?

JACKIE: No.
ARAPAHO: Babies being born every minute.
They need good souls.

JACKIE leans forward like he's tempted to fall down into a new body on earth.

JACKIE (*Changes his mind.*): No. I've seen enough of the world.

JACKIE turns around until he's facing ARAPAHO. Let me just look at you.

They embrace as they fly.

THE STAND-IN

Keith Curran

For My Parents
And for Richard—Again and Always

THE STAND-IN was originally produced by Naked Angels; Toni Kotite, Artistic Director.

Characters

To be performed by seven men and three women

Men:

LESTER PERRY
HAL BRADBOB
GORDON FUENTE
CODY WILLOW
CORBIN TOTTLES
GUS
KEVIN FLANDERS
WALTER WILLIAMS
HARRY
BOB
ROD
GREG ROEBUCK
JESUS MORALES
TOM
SPARKY
HEDGEHOG
DOORSTOP (SPARKY)
RUFFY THE CLOWN
MICHAEL ROLLINSTOCK
DAN PERRY
ARCHER PIPPINS
LEROY
CHESTER CYNTHIONI
ROCKO POOL
HILTON
MAN 1
MAN 2
ELMER'S VOICE
PAUL'S VOICE
REPORTER 1
CREWPERSON

Women:

FESTA LONGO
BICKY LOOP
LINDA
DEBBIE PLAGENT
EDITH
ULA KESSLE
BETTY
FIONA
ASHLY
DEEDEE PERRY
GILDA
PAULA TODSON
WOMAN 1
REPORTER 2

~

ACT I

Lights up. We are on a television sound stage. HAL BRADBOB *and* BICKY LOOP *enter and take their places behind a news desk. A crew person, wearing headphones, enters downstage. He counts down with his fingers.*

CREW PERSON: In Five—Four—Three—Two . . .

The crew person indicates "one" and exits. We hear the theme song to a network television entertainment program. Lights come up behind HAL *and* BICKY. *They chat animatedly in silhouette. Lights up full on* HAL *and* BICKY *as they turn to the "camera," laughing.*

BICKY: I'm Bicky Loop.
HAL: And I'm Hal Bradbob.
BICKY: And welcome to this edition of "Entertainment Incessantly."
HAL: First up: "Gay in Hollywood." No one would talk to us. Bicky?
BICKY: Thanks, Hal. Pam Severenson, of the recently canceled long-

running series *The Seventeen Of Us,* is in a play . . . somewhere. Hal?

HAL: A play, Bicky, is a movie that happens right in front of you.

BICKY: Interesting. (*Pause*) Hal?

HAL: Thanks, Bicky. Ex Hot Soap Stud Lester Perry has made the move from short-lived network series to original Made-For-Cable *movies*. He has snagged the title role in the Lifeline Network's *You're Out—The Gilbert Feldstein Story.*

BICKY: I understand, Hal, that Ex Hot Soap Stud Lester Perry will have to learn how to tango and how to be a homosexual person.

HAL: That's right, Bicky. The Lifeline Network has hired a professional tango dancer to work with Ex Hot Soap Stud Lester Perry.

BICKY: Have they hired a professional homosexual person?

HAL: Oh, I suppose at *some* point. If not, Bicky, we'd be doing a report on homosexual protesters holding signs and chanting annoying things that rhyme out in front of the Lifeline Network's corporate offices.

BICKY: Would we?

HAL (*Pause*): Celebrating birthdays today . . .

Tango music starts. LESTER PERRY *and* GORDON FUENTE, *both wearing tuxedos, tango onstage. The desk, along with* BICKY *and* HAL, *goes off. Lights change. We are in* LESTER'*s New York apartment.* LESTER *and* GORDON *continue the dance. It is precise, tightly choreographed—strong, masculine—almost dangerous. The dance ends with* GORDON *pulling* LESTER *into a dramatic pose.* LESTER *immediately breaks the pose and exits to the kitchen.* GORDON *holds the pose.*

GORDON: Lester?

LESTER'S VOICE: Gordon?

GORDON: Why are you in a different room?

LESTER'S VOICE: The music ended.

GORDON: *La music se ha terminado, pero el baile continua.* "The music has ended, the dance has not." Get out here, fella.

LESTER *hurries back into the living room, puts down his beer and joins* GORDON, *resuming his part of the pose, but looking away.*

Look at me. Meet my gaze.

LESTER: Right, right, right, right, right! *Absolutely.* Sorry, man. Okay . . .

LESTER *looks at* GORDON *for one second then breaks the pose, going for his beer.*

GORDON (*Muttering*): *Quiero hacerti muerta, o quiero hacer muchas problemas . . .*

LESTER: If I could just get the *steps* right first!

GORDON: The steps are there.

LESTER: You are *so* just saying that.

GORDON: *The steps are there, Lester.*

LESTER: It's just that darned middle section. It's . . .

GORDON: Threatening.

LESTER: Or . . .

GORDON: Incriminating.

LESTER: I just keep worrying that I'll knock over a *lamp.*

GORDON: Or that someone will come *in.* You *are* playing a gay person in this movie, right?

LESTER: And I have no problem with that.

GORDON: I'm sure I speak for all my gay brothers and sisters when I say how very much I appreciate your problemlessness.

LESTER: You got it.

GORDON: Now, the steps are only one aspect of the dance, Lester. There's also passion, sensuality, being in the same room. I know how hard trust can be for us "guy" people. Following. Being led. The implications of "backwards."

Throughout the next lines, GORDON, *using* LESTER *as almost a life-size doll, acts out what he is describing.*

But when you take your partner's hand it isn't just a pose, Lester, it's a promise of intimacy, an exchange of temperature, of desire. Your hand on his back isn't a mere grasping of the steering wheel, it's a coming together, a measuring of resistance. And when at last you start to move . . .

They start to dance.

. . . taking your partner with you—what you're really engaging in is a culturally sanctioned public display of choreographed but nonetheless spontaneous *feelings. Sensaciones.* These feelings—these steps—are the result of centuries of tradition, yes, but they're influenced in the moment by a tightening of the hand, an arch of the back, a glance, an expression, an intake of breath. . . .

LESTER: So, a beer?

LESTER lurches into the kitchen.

GORDON: I'm going to start killing people.

GORDON collects his things.

LESTER'S VOICE (*Laughing*):

Oh, now! Gordon, come on! This is hard for me! But I'm trying, Gordo! I am really trying so hard. I am. Really, Gordo . . . So . . .

GORDON:

This is hard for *you?* My name isn't "Gordo." No one's name is "Gordo."

LESTER'S VOICE: . . . really, what can I get you? A beer? Some cereal?

GORDON: I should get going, anyway. I'm really late. Some *cereal?*

LESTER'S VOICE: Just to thank you, pal, for coming over so last minute.

GORDON: Snap and I'm here, Lester. Anytime. Anywhere. Any reason. (*Pause*) I mean it. I'm being serious. (*He's said too much.*) Oops.

LESTER, oblivious, returns from the kitchen with GORDON'S beer.

So . . . Excellent tux, fella! Thanks. God, look the hell at *us!* Where are *you* headed?

LESTER: That movie premiere. *Dawn Of Destruction.*

GORDON: Oh, right. Cool. Robots and shit. Sounds excellent.

The intercom buzzes. LESTER pushes the button.

LESTER: Yes?

FESTA'S VOICE: LET—ME—IN!

LESTER: Come on up.

He buzzes her in.

GORDON: Your date sounds eager.

LESTER: She *does,* doesn't she? But it's not a date, really. It's an appointment. Her publicist set it up. We've never met. She's "Dawn." She destructs. In the movie tonight.

GORDON: Festa Longo! I know her. *Of* her.

LESTER: But, Gordon, just *tell* me that you can be there when we film the first tango. *Tell* me that, Gordo, please.

GORDON: Wish I could, fella, but you'll be fine. *Ahora yo pienzo con mi corazon.* Okay? The steps are there. They are. *Go beyond them.*

There's a knock at the door. LESTER opens it. FESTA LONGO, late twenties, stands in the doorway, striking a dramatic pose, smoking a cigarette. She is wearing a very minimal, rather startling, evening dress. LESTER offers his hand.

FESTA: Careful. We were doing publicity shots this afternoon and I'm still in character. I had to fight the impulse to scale the exterior wall of your brownstone.

GORDON: I'm loving this.

LESTER: I'm Lester. Great to meet you, Festa. You look . . . amazing. Whoa . . . *Oh,* this is Gordon Fuente, my personal tango instructor.

FESTA: That's a new one.

GORDON: You're "Dawn."

FESTA: Despairingly enough.

GORDON: Excellent meeting you, Festa.

FESTA: Do people have drugs anymore? Does anyone on either side of me have drugs? No way I'm getting through this premiere lucid.

LESTER: Beer?

GORDON: Cereal?

FESTA (*To Lester*): You.

LESTER: Comin' right up, lovely lady.

LESTER exits for the beer. FESTA and GORDON individually react to the "lovely lady" usage, then check each other out, circling. FESTA sits.

GORDON: I've heard that you used to be a man.

LESTER'S VOICE: GORDON!

FESTA: Look, if that's the *worst* thing they have to say about me.

LESTER'S VOICE: Oh, my God, GORDON!

FESTA: Gordon, is it? Hi. I've heard that, too. That I used to be a man named Carl and was unkindly dealt with in high school.

GORDON: A wealthy Arab paid for your tits.

FESTA: Who else? But tell me, tango person, do I still have my penis?

GORDON: You kept it awhile, movie person—waffling, unsure—but then a wealthy Arab removed it.

FESTA: Himself?

GORDON: Or something.

GORDON AND FESTA (*Shivering at the thought*): *EeeeOoooRrrrGggg!*

LESTER returns with FESTA's beer.

LESTER: I can't even believe I'm even hearing this.
FESTA: *Believe,* lad.
GORDON: Es la *ver*dad. So, Festa—cool meeting you.
FESTA: *Carl,* please.
GORDON: Carl. And, hey, Lester—I'm there with you tomorrow in my heart, okay? And anytime you need me, just . . . I'm here. (*To Festa*) I'm here for Lester, Carl.
FESTA: I'm getting that.
GORDON: All Lester has to do is call. Anytime. Anywhere. Any reason. I mean it. I'm being literal. (*To himself*) Oops. (*Laughing—escaping*) Adios!

GORDON exits.

FESTA: Cute. Gordon. And very much in love.
LESTER: Huh? *Oh,* no. He's just, you know . . . kind.
FESTA: And *you* are *really* pretty.

LESTER, embarrassed, smiling, looks away.

So, what's the worst thing they have to say about *you?*
LESTER: That I can't act.
FESTA: Monsters. You should know, by the way, that you are about to spend an excruciating night at the cinema with none other than the next Ida Lupino.
LESTER: Who?
FESTA: I mean, I play a homicidal cyborg in this approximation of a movie, right? I vaporize public transportation. Bio-metal-alloy suction cups sprout from the palms of my hands. I scale windowless industrial complexes using only my *teeth*—and I'm the next Ida Lupino. Must be her later films. You're not the next James Dean, are you?
LESTER: Montgomery Clift.
FESTA: Wise. There are hundreds of the Next James Deans. You

trip over them at the A&P—it's like we're surrounded. Was Montgomery Clift you or your publicist?

LESTER: I don't have a publicist.

FESTA: Sorry?

LESTER: It just seems stupid to hire someone whose job is to get people to bother me on the street.

FESTA: You're fucking with me, aren't you. I just signed one on. A publicist. Babs Goldberg-Rosenburg. She's frightening to me. We had lunch today and the first thing she asked me was if I'd ever been raped.

LESTER: *What?*

FESTA: She said she wanted to know my background. I used to think that meant what I'd *done,* but apparently in this very scary moment in cultural time, it means what's been done *to* me. She actually had a list in front of her, scratching off each possibility as she went along. Had I ever been raped. Had I ever been sexually harassed. Had I ever been to a recovery clinic. Had I ever had an abortion. Had I ever been abused—preferably by a family member. By the time she got all the way down to whether or not I'd ever fought my way back from a time-consuming series of exploratory dental procedures, *sparks* were coming out of her eyes. Her nostrils were billowing thick, black smoke. She said: "Festa, dear, how do you expect me to get you on the covers of magazines if you don't give me anything to WORK WITH?"

LESTER: I was . . . mugged.

FESTA: A star is born. (*Pause*) Gay?

LESTER: Wh . . . ?

FESTA: In the parlance of the Image Makers, "The Next Montgomery Clift" is code for "Gay."

LESTER: Oh, my God. You're kidding. Wow. Okay. (*Pause*) No.

FESTA (*Enjoying this*): Tango with me, let's see. "Ida Lupino" is code for "Aggressive."

LESTER: Well, pretty lady, I don't know. I . . . (*FESTA takes LESTER's arms in tango position.*) Or, okay, "Ida." Now, the tango . . . No one necessarily follows or—as I understand it, I'm new at this, I'm a pupil—leads. What happens happens as you go. It's almost like a . . . fight.

FESTA: Ding.

Music starts. They do an approximation of a tango, with FESTA *most assuredly leading. They tango offstage. Lights change.* LESTER *immediately returns, tangoing with* CODY WILLOW. CODY WILLOW *is the next James Dean.* We're on the set of You're Out—The Gilbert Feldstein Story. *The camera is rolling.* LESTER *and* CODY *end the dance, sriking a pose on the last note of music.*

CODY: I am very clumsy, Gilbert. But you are very good.

LESTER: You are very good at this, Marty. You are.

CODY: Well, Gilbert—coming from a professional . . .

LESTER: It is just a hobby, despite all the trophies.

CODY: You dance very sexily, Gilbert, as well. And I am serious.

LESTER: And I am finding myself hoping that you are planning to do something about that, Marty.

CODY: And you are finding yourself hoping that I am planning to do something about how sexily you dance, Gilbert? Well, now that you mention it, Gilbert, what I am planning to do is . . .

CODY *goes to kiss* LESTER. CORBIN *enters with* LINDA, GUS, *and* EDITH.

CORBIN (*British accent*): And . . . *hold.* Hold it there. (CODY *and* LESTER *freeze.*) We're still rolling. Kevin! Where is that Stand-In? *Kevin?*

KEVIN *enters. He is* LESTER's *height, build, wears a wig that looks like* LESTER's *hair, and is wearing an identical tuxedo.*

KEVIN: Sorry.

LESTER *steps back from* CODY. CODY *freezes in position.* KEVIN *takes* LESTER's *place with* CODY.

CORBIN: And . . . *action.*
CODY: ". . . *this.*"

CODY leans in and kisses KEVIN. Then CODY slides seductively down KEVIN'S body.

CODY (*Muttering*): This is bullshit.
CORBIN: *Cut!*
CODY: This is *bullshit!* Who *is* this guy? This guy in the Lester Wig and the Lester Outfit Dickhead?
CORBIN: You knew this was how we were handling this, Cody.
CODY: "Handling" this? *Blow* me, Corbin. I mean, okay, I'm doing this scene. This piece of shit scene—with Lester—with Lester as Gilbert. There's a *scene* here—a *fucked* one—but, okay, I took the gig. I'm playing Marty. Marty is hot for Gilbert. We're gonna *do* it, man! It's gonna be fucking *amazing,* right? And I move in to kiss the man that I love—the man of my fucking dreams—and there's this Pod-Person-Switched-At-Birth-Abducted-By-Aliens-Fucking-*STEPFORD* person staring back at me! And I'm like: "WHAT? Who are . . . ? Oh, my *God!* WHAT HAVE YOU DONE WITH GILBERT!
CORBIN (*Weary of this*): Just *kiss* him, Cody . . .
CODY: *Kiss* him? I'll suck his *dick,* man! If it was in the script—if it *meant* something—if all of a sudden we were in the fourteenth dimension and one *word* of this fucking Written-By-A-Can-Of-Diet-Coke script even vaguely *resembled* something that might maybe even *happen* on an inhabited fucking *planet,* I'd suck his dick and *enjoy it!*
CORBIN (*To Someone*): Hi, I used to direct.
CODY: Lester? Lester, man? What's your problem, man?
LESTER: You're kidding me, right?
CODY: No, man. I want to know what your problem is.
LESTER (*Pause—smiling*): I don't kiss guys. It's not . . . something I do. (*Pause*) Sorry, pal.
CODY: Wait, wait, wait. You never kissed a man before?
LESTER: Nope.

CODY: I'm straight, man, too, and I have. Biff Longacre. Cal State. Freshman year. Corbin?

CORBIN: Where to begin?

CODY: Got it. Mr. Stand-In?

KEVIN: The first? Danny Spectre. Fourth Grade.

CODY: Gus?

GUS: Richard Jessup, Queens Community College.

CODY: Linda?

LINDA: I'm comin' up blank.

CODY: So, look, Mr. Ex-Hot-Soap-Stud-Used-To-Have-A-Series-Took-This-Movie-To-Prove-That-You-Can-Act-*Maybe,* fess up. You kissed a man *some*time. Fess up.

KEVIN: Climb off, Cody.

CODY: It speaks!

KEVIN: It bites, buddy. Just climb off.

A silence.

CORBIN: Five! Take five!

We hear the theme music to a morning TV talk show. Lights change. LESTER, CODY, KEVIN, CORBIN, GUS, *and* LINDA *exit. We see three men on chairs, today's guests on the show.* WALTER WILLIAMS, *the host, stands with his microphone stage left.* DEBBIE PLAGENT, *the host, stands with her microphone stage right.*

DEBBIE: Thanks for joining me. Today on the *Debbie Plagent Show,* we'll be talking to America's hottest Soap Opera Studs!

The audience, all women, scream.

WALTER: Welcome to The Gay Cable Network, access channel 73. I'm Walter Williams. Tonight on *Out And About* we'll be talking to America's Hottest Gay Porn Stars!

Three technicians sort of clap.

DEBBIE: Let me introduce my guests. Harry Smith who plays Arch Wainwright on *Love Is For Giving.*

The women scream.

Bob Silver who plays Brake Deveraux on *The Lean And The Clueless.*

The women scream.

WALTER: And Rod Swayzee whose most recent film is *Asshole Buddies In The Persian Gulf.*

The technicians sort of clap.

DEBBIE: Now, I know all the ladies out there want to know everything about your personal lives. (*The women scream.*) Harry?

HARRY: Well, Debbie, as you know, working on a daytime drama is very demanding and I don't really have time for a personal life.

The women sigh.

DEBBIE: Bob?

BOB: Well, Debbie, as you know, working on a daytime drama is very demanding and I don't really have time for a personal life.

The women sigh.

WALTER: Rod?

ROD: Well, Walter, as you know, after having a twelve-inch dildo up your butt ten hours a day, all you want to do is watch television.

The technicians sort of clap.

WALTER: Don't I know *that*. Let's get a bit juicy, shall we? I want you to tell us all about your first sexual experience. Rod?

ROD: My first sexual experience was with a priest.

WALTER: Bob?

BOB: Priest.

WALTER: Harry?

HARRY: It was with a priest, Walter.

The women scream.

DEBBIE: Wait a minute. Your first sexual experience was with your *baby-sitter?*

HARRY: That's right, Debbie.

DEBBIE: Bob?

BOB: Baby-sitter.

DEBBIE: Rod?

ROD: It was with my baby-sitter, Debbie.

WALTER: A pattern is forming.

DEBBIE: I sense a trend.

WALTER AND DEBBIE: This is so *fabulous!*

WALTER: Wait, let me ask some of my staff. Elmer?

ELMER'S VOICE: It was with a priest, Walter.

WALTER: Paul?

PAUL'S VOICE: *Priest!*

WALTER: Paul? You're Jewish.

PAUL'S VOICE: I guess they *find* us!

We hear tango music. LESTER *and* CODY *tango onstage as* DEBBIE, WALTER, *and their guests exit. We're in* LESTER'*s dressing room on the set. The music, now coming out of a tape player, finishes.* LESTER *and* CODY *stand a millisecond, holding each other's gaze. Then, uncomfortable,* LESTER *steps away, turning off the tape player. . . .*

CODY: I *SUCK* at this, man! I fuckin' BLOW MYSELF at this!

LESTER: You are *so* doing better, Cody, come on.

CODY: For someone not supplied with a instructor. But, hey, listen up. *I am keeping the God damn motherfuckin' sideburns, man!*

They elaborately and violently high-five.

LESTER: *Hey!*

CODY: Corbin had to *eat* it, man, eat it *all,* 'cause I have this whole fourteen page past-history-thing that inevitable-ises Marty's sideburns. The sideburns *work* for Marty. They work *hard,* man.

LESTER: They work *hard,* man.

CODY: *Man!* (*Pause—he looks at Lester*) So, what's up with your man Gilbert?

LESTER: Oh. Well, man, I can't say that I've paid all that much—not to mention fourteen pages' worth of attention—to my *own* past history.

CODY: "The unexamined life," man, yeah, it's goin' around. *My* take on Gilbert—reaching into the *void*—is that he went through some major shit—maybe with some *guy*. Some *fuck*. Some *psycho,* man.

LESTER: Absolutely.

CODY: And I think I, Marty, love you, Gilbert, because of your eyes. Because I can never get a really good look at them. Your eyes. You hide them from me. You look away, man. And I *love* that. It *moves* me, man. (*Pause*) And Gilbert loves Marty because . . . ?

LESTER: It says so.

CODY: It says so.

LESTER: Yeah.

CODY: Gilbert loves Marty because it *says* so?

LESTER: In the script.

CODY: I know it fucking *says* so, man, but . . . I'm playing Marty a lot more complex and particular and layered and interesting than what's in the fucking *script!*

LESTER: I know *that,* man, I just . . .

CODY: Stop, man. *Stop.*

LESTER, *who isn't doing anything, freezes.*

What *is* it? *Look* at me, man! What's Gilbert love?

LESTER: Oh. Uh . . .

CODY: I got pretty teeth, a strong jaw, my chest is buffed, my legs are tree trunks and I got a big dick—what'll it *be,* man?

LESTER: Oh. Okay. All right, uh . . . Well, if I, *ohhhh,* have to—because of your question—say *something* . . . *man* . . . I'd say . . . in *particular* is what you're asking? Okay—say . . . Alright, let's just see. Uh . . . Okay. Uh . . . Yes. Hmmmmmmm. Your—*Marty's*—masculineness. His—*your*—*his*—masculine-whatever-ality. (*Pause*) Is what it is.

CODY: The fact that I'm a man. Gilbert, a *homosexual,* loves Marty because he's . . . a man. *All* men are *men,* man!

LESTER: But . . .

CODY: What, I'm not *special* to you, man? I'm just *there* with a *dick?* Fuck *you,* man.

LESTER: Your lips, okay?

CODY: Oh, just pull something out of the fucking *air,* man, right? Don't do me any *favors,* man.

There's a knock at the door. LESTER *goes and opens it.*

LESTER: Oh! Uh . . . Just a . . . Oh, my . . . *Greg!*

GREG: I gotta talk to you, Les. *Now.*

LESTER: Come in, man, come in, you . . .

GREG, *midthirties, enters. He and* LESTER *do a quick and violent hugging-backslapping thing.*

GREG: You been getting my messages, or *what?*

LESTER: I have, Greg, but . . . *Oh,* this is Cody Willow.

GREG: Real name, man?

CODY: Changed it, man.

LESTER: Greg and I met while working on a beer commercial together two years ago and we still say hi and talk when we run into each other every couple of months.

CODY: I'm gettin' chills. So, Lester? Over the next few days, man, talk to some friends, some family, some *therapist*—then reach into your blackened soul and see if you can up with an explanation for why you so obviously fucking *hate* me.

CODY exits.

LESTER: Greg, sit, you . . . And, hey! How's that terrific Lucy?

GREG: Leave the movie.

LESTER: I'm sorry, a beer? Some pudding?

GREG: *Leave the movie, Les.* Artistic differences, exhaustion, *whatever.* I know the script. They offered me a part. The guy who lip-synchs to Minnie Ripperton while jumping off the Verrazano Bridge. The script's a joke, Les! That role, your role. What the hell are you *doing?*

LESTER: Working, I think, aren't I? Taking an opportunity, I think. This movie's a chance to . . . Oh, well, you know, not carry a *movie,* but . . . Oh, well, you know, not build a *career,* but . . . Oh, well, you know, not necessarily *succeed,* but . . .

GREG: Les, I know you just kind of lope along dealing with whatever happens to fall off the truck in front of you . . .

LESTER: No, I don't.

GREG: But Gilbert Feldstein doesn't even have *AIDS!*

LESTER: Right.

GREG: Your character has AIDS you win an Emmy. Assured nomination, anyway, probable win. You get to play noble. Anguished. You get to cough. Lose weight. Have trouble standing while crying at the injustice of it all while making sad yet life-affirming wisecracks while hugging your finally-accepting parents who are played by respected older actors with Broadway credits. You come to terms, you move on, but you die anyway. It's *safe.* You play a gay character with no gay characteristics aside from a reassuringly brief life span.

LESTER: What? No one's going to think . . . at *all,* that *I'm* . . .

GREG: But people could think that *I'm* gay?

LESTER: You? Come on, man, *no!*

GREG: Well, they *do!* Remember the last movie I did? *Fatal Confession?* I played that small part—the priest? My phone stopped ringing.

LESTER: You're saying you played a gay role and it ruined your career?

GREG: You got it.

LESTER: Greg, you can't *act*. I'm really sorry, but you're awful. You say so yourself. All the time.

GREG: I say it so I'll be corrected.

LESTER: Oh.

GREG: *And since when has being able to act had anything to do with having a career?* I don't mean a *DeNiro* career. I mean a Tony *Curtis* career. Not everyone can be riveting, Les. Not everyone can do accents and mesmerize and look totally unrecognizable every ten minutes. *You* can't. Actors like you and me, Les—we're handsome. We have charm. Sincerity. Nice butts. We play *ourselves*—so we gotta be real careful. Now I can't even *get* a commercial or a lousy soap or even a *play*. I'm history.

LESTER: But . . .

GREG: And I'm not saying this, but you haven't been serious about a woman in the entire time I've sort of known you.

LESTER: You know how demanding it is being an actor. I just don't have time for a personal life. *Not that I don't . . . "ya* know."

GREG: And I'm not saying this, but you dress nice and you sing. You started in musicals, right? In the *chorus?*

LESTER: Baritone, man.

GREG: Just tell me that you're at least dating someone.

LESTER: Well, actually, Greg, I have been seeing rather a lot of Festa Longo.

GREG: FESTA LONGO USED TO BE A MAN, MAN!

We hear the highly dramatic theme music to a sleazy tabloid TV show. LESTER and GREG exit as lights change. JESUS MORALES, the host, enters sitting on his desk.

JESUS: Welcome to *Now It Can Be Bludgeoned.* Me: Jesus Morales. Today: "Careers In Ruins." Item: Greg Roebuck. Actor. Handsome. Gym membership. Bad with accents. Sincere. Nice butt. Many believed he was the next Tony Curtis. *What happened? Fatal Confession.* Roll the clip.

Lights up on GREG and TOM in a locker room. TOM is in underwear and GREG is wearing a priest's exercise vestments. They're surrounded by golf equipment. Underscoring plays.

GREG: "Well, Kip. Two under par."
TOM: "I was j-j-just lucky. You sure play golf good for a p-p-priest."
GREG: "I get a lot of help from my boss."

GREG points up to heaven. They laugh.

TOM: "G-G-Good joke, F-F-Father."
GREG: "Kip? Your shoulders look tight."
TOM: "R-r-r-r-r-really, F-Father?"

GREG starts rubbing TOM's shoulders.

GREG: "For the love of God, Kip—your shoulder muscles are like bands of steel that have been bent into the shape of shoulder muscles."
TOM: "G-G-G-G-Gosh, F-F-F-F-F-F-F-Father."

GREG leans over and very gently kisses TOM. He then raises one hand over TOM's back. The hand contains a knife. Fade to black.

JESUS: Item: Actors. Lockers. Homosexuals. Kisses. Christians. Knives. Golf Equipment. Joining us from a trailer park in upstate New York: Greg Roebuck! (*A light comes up on GREG.*) Good of you to join us, Greg.
GREG: My pleasure, Jesus.

JESUS: *Hey-soos.*

GREG: "Hey-soos," sorry.

JESUS: Item: A growing career. Off Broadway. Commercials. *Circus Of The Stars. What—happened?*

GREG: Well, I'm hardly the first actor to suffer a career crisis as a result of playing a homosexual role.

JESUS: But after watching that clip, Greg, the strongest impression I come away with is that you can't act. Item: There were homosexual protesters holding signs and chanting annoying things that rhymed outside the movie theatres showing *Fatal Confession.*

GREG: The protestors were afraid that after seeing the movie, people might assume that all homosexuals play golf.

JESUS: There were also protesters from the Association For The Fair Representation Of Stutterers.

GREG: Well, I guess the stutterers were tired of seeing themselves portrayed in movies and on television as people who sometimes have difficulty speaking clearly.

JESUS: Item: Before *Fatal Confession* came out you were a confirmed bachelor. Just after its release you got married in a hurry, and your children are, I believe, your wife's children from a previous marriage. Why the sudden rush to suddenly acquire a sudden wife and suddenly all of a sudden have a family?

GREG: *Christ . . .*

JESUS: *"Hey-soos".*

Dramatic theme music plays as JESUS *and* GREG *exit. Lights change. Soft music plays. We are in* LESTER*'s bedroom.* LESTER *is in bed, very pleased with himself. We hear* FESTA*'s voice from the bathroom.*

FESTA'S VOICE: Jesus, really? Your first time was with your *baby-sitter?*

LESTER: Absolutely. Tiffy Winnick from up the block. She was really . . . kind.

FESTA'S VOICE: "Kind"?

LESTER: Yeah. Friendly.

FESTA'S VOICE: "Kind . . ."

LESTER: Understanding. Reassuring. You know—kind. (*Pause*) She had big tits.

FESTA steps just outside the bathroom door wearing LESTER's robe. She is brushing her wet hair.

FESTA: *My* first sexual experience was with my best girlfriend, Irma Lunch. We lit candles and drank wine and listened to "Jacques Brel Is Alive And Well And Living in Paris" dressed all in black with very straight hair—awash in all that French-Belgian bleakness. We kissed and it felt like good-bye. (*Pause*) Y'ello? I've just dropped an actual adolescent lesbic experience right in your presumably expanding lap . . .

LESTER: Oh. Right. Sorry. "Oooooooooh . . ."

FESTA: Probably not nearly "kind" enough a story for you. So—cyborg sex. Talk to me.

LESTER: It was . . . intense. Really very *so* amazing.

FESTA: An accomplishment, what with the requisite technological aspect—all this recent latex. And am I alone in thinking that "Nonoxynal 9" sounds like one of those troubling George Lucas creations that contains a perspiring British dwarf? Well, whatever, lad—sex with you was a refreshing change.

LESTER: From?

FESTA: I'm auditioning a lot right now. And every role I go up for involves being penetrated at knifepoint. I scream my head off all day long with a poorly dressed assistant casting director trying to pry my legs apart.

FESTA sits on the bed, offering LESTER the brush. He takes it.

Rape victims, hookers, killer lesbians-that-nonetheless-fuck-men. I've auditioned for killer lesbians-that-nonetheless-fuck-men, now that I mention it, three times this month alone. Dithering movie people. They cover their asses with red ribbons at award shows, then lack the temerity to make a movie with lesbians who happen not to be homicidal, or gay men who, when presented with flowers and a vase, have no idea what to do next.

FESTA *looks at* LESTER *who is just sitting there with the brush.*

FESTA: I'm not asking you to redden my ass with it, Lester. Brush. It makes me feel young and clean and taken care of and . . . "something." (*Pause*) *BRUSH!* (LESTER *starts overawkwardly brushing her hair.*) Very good, Lester. You've got the knack.

LESTER: I do *not.*

FESTA: So—how are things on the set of *your* homosexual little movie?

LESTER: They're still calling it *You're Out—The Gilbert Feldstein Story.* . . .

FESTA: Shudder. Who is Gilbert Feldstein and why should I give a shit?

LESTER: He was an umpire. A professional umpire.

FESTA: A Jewish professional umpire. A gay, Jewish professional umpire.

LESTER: He also danced the tango competitively.

FESTA (*Dumbstruck*): Akh . . .

LESTER: At least he didn't arrange flowers or brush . . . *style* hair.

FESTA: The pendulum can swing too far the other way. And here I thought I was flirting with incredulity by playing a character who makes whirring noises when she walks. Apropos of nothing, I didn't used to be a man.

LESTER: Darn!

FESTA: *Fuck* you.

LESTER: I was so afraid I'd slip and call you "Carl."

FESTA: Don't think it didn't occur to me that that was the appeal. I *did,* however used to be named Nancy Reagan. AHHHHHHH! I *told* you! Do you hate me? Are you mortified? It was my birth name, I swear to Christ, Nancy Reagan, my *God.* It's amazing I got up in the morning.

LESTER: Yeah.

FESTA: When I was Nancy Reagan . . . God, I was so shy. So touched by every kindness. Even aside from the name and its wracking implications, I was just a blur. A smudge on the mirror. No fingerprints. Then I changed my name to Festa Longo—a Ouija Board was involved, *all right?*—but when I created Festa, edges appeared. Angles. I sent Festa out into the world to do all the things I couldn't do as Nancy. Nancy stayed home. With Ronnie. I *swear* that was the name of our dog. It's almost *eerie.*

LESTER: I don't send myself named something other than what I'm named out into the world to do all the things I can't do as what my name is.

FESTA: Sure you do. And it's exhausting, isn't it? I mean, Festa Longo may well be fearless and opinionated and sexual and impressive, but Festa Longo *also* makes *whirring noises* when she walks. On *and* off the screen. There's a mechanical aspect, isn't there? A calculation. With little Nancy banging away at the inside of my forehead trying to get out.

LESTER: I think I'm feeling . . . sleepy.

FESTA: I've bored you. I "Nancied" there for a moment, didn't I? Gotta watch that.

FESTA gets off the bed, heading for the bathroom.

LESTER: Really? No. You don't have to go. *Really?* Darn. This is the best part. The part I do best.

FESTA: The falling asleep part is the part you do best? I actually believe you mean that, lad, and I am intrigued, but I have to put on Festa's face and leave here looking gorgeous and satiated. Babs Goldberg-Rosenburg, my harrowing publicist, has alerted the media—anonymously, of course—that Festa "Dawn" Longo will be stumbling out from this address after a torrid evening with Lester "Gilbert Feldstein" Perry. I apologize for falling into step with this publicity yah-yah, but Babs can look so pitiful, blood streaming out of her eyes—fuck me, I acquiesced. Tomorrow night? Same time, place, activity? Nancy will stay at home. And maybe we'll even do what you do best. (LESTER *looks away, embarrassed.*) I love that you look away.

FESTA *goes into the bathroom.* SPARKY's *voice comes from the bathroom.*

SPARKY'S VOICE (*Valley-dude-ish*): Whoa, really? Your first time was with a *priest?*

LESTER: You about done in there? 'Cause . . .

SPARKY'S VOICE: My first time wasn't with a priest, but it *was* in, like, a church—in the confessional—two birds with one stone, right?

SPARKY *steps out of the bathroom wearing* LESTER's *robe. He sings the "Nah-nah-nah-nah" section from* HAMMER's *"Can't Touch This."*

"Nah-nah-nah-nah—nah-nah—Nah-Nah . . ."

Indicating that LESTER *finish the phrase.*

LESTER (*Going along*): . . . "Can't Touch This."

SPARKY: *AGAIN!*

SPARKY *jumps on* LESTER, *kissing his chest.*

LESTER: Oh, now no. *No.* It's time to go, Sparky. I mean it. *Sparky!*

SPARKY: But guess what, Kevin? Kevin, guess. *You* are a majorly cute dude.

LESTER: Just . . . *go.*

SPARKY (*Reacting as if shot*): Ouch! Zing! Blam! *Aarghaargh!* (SPARKY *lies "dead" across* LESTER's *body.* LESTER *keeps his hands at an awkward distance.*) Revive me.

LESTER: *What?*

SPARKY: Revive me. CPR. "The Kiss Of Life."

LESTER: I haven't . . . taken the classes.

SPARKY: My fuckin' luck. (*Sitting up*) *AGAIN!* (*SPARKY kisses LESTER's chest*)

LESTER: Absolutely not. Absolutely maybe. Absolutely. No! Just no, Sparky. Up. Up! (*Laughing*) *Up*, Sparky! (*SPARKY acts like a dog. Barking, scratching, panting.*) *Beg,* Sparky! *Beg,* Sparky!! *Sparky—beg!*

SPARKY (*Abruptly kneeling in prayer*): *Please,* Kevin? By the way, I know your name isn't at *all* Kevin.

LESTER: Wait, what do you . . .

SPARKY: Well, Lester, I mean that your name's Lester, Lester. I watch TV. You're Lester Perry, dude! You were on *Love Is For Giving* and that sitcom, *The 35 Of Us*. And you were on that commercial. What was it for? Cars?

LESTER: Wafers for people with lactose intolerance.

SPARKY: Exactly.

LESTER: I *so* needed the money.

SPARKY: Don't gotta tell me about needin' the money. And you were *way* cute as that "Oh, I just wish I could eat ice cream" person.

LESTER: *Anyhoo,* Sparky, I think you should be just running along.

SPARKY: Tell me about the movie you're doing that you're doing. What's it about? TELL ME!

LESTER: It's—CALM DOWN, PAL—It's . . . about a homosexual, Jewish professional umpire who danced the tango competitively.

SPARKY: Cable, right?

LESTER: Absolutely.

SPARKY: MORE!

LESTER: Look, you . . . The guy I play, Gilbert Feldstein, came out during the 1975 World Series. He kissed the catcher.

SPARKY: He kissed him through that baseball catcher's wire-mesh face thing?

LESTER: I am *so* hoping the catcher took off the mask first. I'll see. *Kevin* will see. My stand-in. He . . . But Gilbert Feldstein was . . . very masculine, really. But, you know what, Sparky? I'm thinking that it may have been a huge mistake. Taking the . . . *doing* the . . . movie. Sometimes I just don't *think.* And there ya have it. There ya have it, my fine young fellow, you really should just go. (*Caressing Sparky's skin, tentatively*) God, you feel good. Being touched this way. By my hand. Your skin is so . . . *dry.* Wait. I don't mean dry as in "A bad skin thing resulting from lack of care," I just mean dry as in . . . clean. Clean and amazing and real good and wonderful and . . . papery. Oh, DEAR! I . . . (*Laughing way too hard*) That was certainly STUPID! *"Papery!"* I just *said* it! That stupid *papery* word! *Gosh, gosh, begosh, right?* (*Recovering*) Now you know, Sparky, why I don't ever just ever even *say* things. . . . Oh, just *honestly!* (*Pause*) I don't actually feel like I'm inhabiting my body at this time. My stomach is . . . How does that song go? "There's a somebody I'm . . . Something to be . . . lah-dah dee dee . . ." (*Pause—then really touching Sparky*) Oh, *my*, you little bucko! This muscle on your upper arm here. I found it earlier and there it . . . still it. (*Doing a drag queen "snap"—badly*) "Girl!" Or "Whatever!" Or . . . "Help! Help!" you know? *"Heeelllp!"* (*Pause—closing his eyes*) Oh, my sweet man . . . Oh, God . . . I mean . . . if only it could stop. If only we could stop. Stop moving so fast so slowly. (*Tears in his eyes*) I'm so tired. So really, really tired. If everything could just . . . stay. Stay. Like this. Here. Like this. With us. Like this. Ohhhhhh . . . Ohhhhhhh . . . please . . .

SPARKY *is looking at* LESTER*'s face, very close.* LESTER *opens his eyes then looks away.*

What? What did I say?

SPARKY: I love that you look away. No, it's like . . . you're *really* pretty.

LESTER (*Sadly*): Oh. That. Do you . . . ever forget who you are? Who you're supposed to be?

SPARKY: Totally. Mostly when people call me Gordon. You called me Gordon two times when you came. And jeez, Lester, did you ever

COME! "Ah . . . AH . . . AHHHHH . . . Gordon . . . AHHHHH . . . GORDON . . . AHHRRGGHHAARRGGHH!"

LESTER: Oh, now, I, you, honestly, if, just . . . !

SPARKY: So, who's this, like, Gordon? Your boyfriend?

LESTER: *What?* Come on . . . man! *No*. He's not . . . Are you saying I'm . . . He's just the guy who taught me the steps. Gordon, that's all. Just "Gordo, the tango guy!" But . . . you know what, pal? I am *so* feeling sleepy.

SPARKY: My name's not Sparky. It's, like, *Andrew*.

LESTER: Fine. I'm just not good at the falling asleep with people part. I can't close my eyes with someone there.

SPARKY: Andrew Sparkowski-Martinez. OUCH! I use, like, "Brad" when a guy wants an Undergrad-Social-Sciences-Major-Couldn't-Get-A-Scholarship type, and Sparky when a guy—you—wants a Disadvantaged-Straight-Boy-Just-Doing-It-For-The-Money. I never use Andrew. Except in living. (*Pause, looking at Lester's stricken face*) Oh! Wait. Apologies, dude. *You* wanted the "I'm-Not-A-Hooker-But-Here's-Two-Hundred-Dollars-For-Cabfare" scenario. Sorry, babe. It's been a long day. So—"Could I have Two Hundred Dollars for a cab please?"

LESTER: Look, it's . . . I can't *do* this. . . .

SPARKY: Or I'll stay. Like this. Here. With us. Like this. You make way special love to me, Kevin—*Lester*.

SPARKY has moved in to kiss LESTER—LESTER pulls away.

LESTER: Andrew—*Sparky,* I . . . I'm not . . . Lester. I'm not who I am, okay? As far as you're concerned. And I . . . I DON'T FUCKING WANT YOU HERE!

SPARKY: "Anymore." (*SPARKY gets off the bed.*) How'd you, like, *find* me, anyway? What disguises were involved. What *steps?* (*Pause*) I don't know who this dude Gordon is, but he's got his work cut out. You're cold. . . . "Kevin." Brrrrrr.

SPARKY exits into bathroom. CODY enters from the bathroom, also wearing only a robe. CODY drops the robe, unembarrassed, and gets into bed with LESTER.

CODY: "Look at you. You are cold."
LESTER: "Are you cold?"
CODY: "I am fine now that I am with you in the bed that is yours."
LESTER: "I cannot believe that you are with me in the bed that is mine."
CODY: "Oh, Gilbert. You feel . . ."

LESTER turns over. CODY runs his hand down LESTER's back.

CORBIN'S VOICE: And . . . HOLD. Hold it there. (*CORBIN enters followed by GUS, LINDA, and EDITH.*) Hold it there. And . . . Kevin? Kevin? Still filming. *Kevin?*

KEVIN enters wearing only a robe.

KEVIN: Sorry. Hi, Cody.
CODY: Yo.

LESTER gets out of bed wearing pants, shoes and socks. He puts on a robe. EDITH holds the bedclothes in place. KEVIN takes off the robe and gets into bed with CODY, taking LESTER's place. CODY puts his hand on KEVIN's back.

CORBIN: And . . . action.
CODY: ". . . so good."
CORBIN: And stop sound. Still filming. Cody, move your hand to his buttocks. Yes. Gently. With some longing. Now slip the bedclothes off the buttocks. *Yes,* Cody. "It's the first time." Kevin, good for you. Tight. Tight shot. Move in tight. We have that? Sufficient uncoverage? And . . . hold. Lester?

CODY freezes. EDITH holds the bedclothes. KEVIN gets out of bed putting on his robe. LESTER takes off his robe, gets back in bed and lies on his stomach.

Cover Lester's trousers, Edith. Close shot. And *action.*

LESTER: "That feels good."

CODY: "You are telling *me.*"

LESTER: "Hold me. Just hold me."

CODY lies on his back. LESTER gets on top of him. CODY's arms are outstretched awkwardly.

CORBIN: And . . . *hold.* Hold. Kevin? *Kevin?* Still rolling.

EDITH holds the bedclothes, CODY freezes his arms, as KEVIN takes LESTER's place on top of CODY.

And . . . action. And grinding and rubbing. And "God, how good it feels." Delight, Kevin. Delight we can see in your *back.* Cody, run your hands down . . . slowly . . . and show us the top of Lester's—Kevin's—*Gilbert's*—pert and downy yet delightfully firm buttocks.

CODY: Aren't you gettin' any, Corbin?

CORBIN: More work for me in post—and—insertion! (*KEVIN and CODY start grinding furiously.*)

And fireworks and bombs going off and the Bells Of Saint Mary's and whatever *else* one hears, it's been so *long,* and it's wonderful. It's love, actually, we can see that now. It's religion. It's rutting of an almost Italian intensity. And . . . *sound* . . . and *Kevin* . . . (*KEVIN throws his head back.*) . . . and *Lester!*

LESTER: "Ah . . . AH . . . Ahhhhh . . . OHHHHH . . . AARRGGHHAARRGGHH!"

CORBIN: And . . . *HOLD!* Stop sound!

LESTER takes KEVIN's place on top of CODY.

CODY: Lester.
LESTER: Hi.
CORBIN: And . . . sound. And . . . *action.*

LESTER rolls off CODY onto his back. They groan with pleasure.

LESTER: "That was great."
CODY: "I'll say. It was almost like being in a heaven of some kind."
LESTER: "I never knew it could be like this."
CODY: "So . . . you are an umpire?"
LESTER: "Sports fan, Marty?"
CODY: "You bet, Gilbert. I am *now.* As well as a fan of Liza Minnelli."
KEVIN: Save me . . .

During next lines, LESTER starts really feeling what he's saying. CODY, surprised, goes with it, matching LESTER's sincerity and passion. CORBIN, amazed, calls silently for a tighter shot. LESTER, lost in the moment, notices none of this.

LESTER: "And let's not forget that homosexuality is just like heterosexuality except it's just different in certain ways but the same. Oh, Marty. I just want to be with a guy. A masculine guy like other guys that I could love with no shame at all. With no having to hide anymore. Or pretend. I'm so tired, Marty. So tired of pretending. I just want to be who I am. Is that too much to ask?"
CORBIN: "*No,* man."
LESTER: "But could you love someone the way everyone else loves someone and could that someone you love the way everyone else loves someone be someone a lot like me?"
CODY: "Oh, yeah."
LESTER: "Could you be staying? Like this? Here? With me? Like this?"
CODY: "*Definitely,* man."
LESTER: "Thank you. Ohhhhh . . . Ohhhhh . . . Thank you."

CODY: "I love you, Gilbert."
LESTER: "I love you."

They kiss. It lasts a couple of seconds, then LESTER *snaps out of it, pulling back, freaking out.*

Hey, you . . . ! You . . . *wait,* wait, I . . . Kevin? *Kevin?*
CODY: (*Trying to stay in the moment*): Whoa, whoa, no, Lester, man, stay with me, stay with me . . .
LESTER: You . . . what are you . . . ?

LESTER, *horrified, jumps out of bed.*

CODY: *Don't break it, man!*
LESTER: What the *hell* do you think you're *doing?*
CORBIN: *CUT!*

LESTER:

I mean, *shit,* Corbin! What *was* that? I mean, Kevin is here for a Goddamned reason, right? I mean, you're supposed to yell "CUT! CUT!" Why the hell didn't you just yell "CUT" then!

CORBIN:

It was going quite well, Lester, I . . . don't you think? The words you were saying started to sound almost human. But I . . . I'm sorry. I am truly sorry.

CODY:

Oh, man, you were GREAT! You were fuckin' *amazing*, man! It felt so *REAL,* man! It was *really happening!* I was seeing you! Really *loving* you, man!

CODY *approaches* LESTER.

LESTER: *Don't you . . .*

CODY: It was *working,* man! It was fucking amazing!

LESTER: It was not even at all even "working," Cody, and just up *yours*. So *there. Okay?* You have been playing around with me from day *one*, and I have had it up to *here! All* of you! All fucking *all* of you! Behind my *back!* I *hear* you—do you even *know* that? I am *here*, for the love of Pete, *aren't* I? Right *here?* In this *area?* Does everybody think I'm just a big, damned, fucking *stupid person*? Just get *off* me—off my *back*—and stop . . . *stop looking at me.* I DON'T UNDERSTAND WHY EVERYONE ALWAYS HAS TO BE LOOKING AT ME!

KEVIN (*Long pause*): Lester? Buddy?

CODY: *Whoa . . .*

LESTER (*Suddenly quite humiliated*): Oh. I'm sorry. I . . . Okay, so . . . I took this part I'm . . . playing, because no one, I mean, makes movies, showing . . . homosexual personages that are . . . or that it maybe even said something . . .

CODY: . . . about umpires. Something about umpires that's never been said before.

LESTER: Yes! I mean . . . Maybe . . .

CODY: The un*told* homosexual tangoing professional Jewish umpire with more than one *butt* story.

LESTER (*Laughing*): All right, all right . . .

LESTER grabs CODY's face and kisses him.

All right? All right? (*To the others*) *All right?*

The technicians sort of clap.

CODY: Oh, wait! Listen up, guys! Here's a good one: *Foul Balls—The Story Of A Gay Umpire.* (*Everyone laughs*) Or, no, wait, wait: A queer umpire about to get fucked—"Safe! Safe! Safe!"

Everyone but KEVIN laughs.

KEVIN: Don't go there, buddy.

CODY: Come *on,* man! What else? A fag umpire about to get fucked: "Just *slide* on in. Just *slide* on in. Just . . ." Right?

Some laughter. KEVIN *exits.*

CODY (*cont.*): Hey, Kevin? Where ya goin'? You kiss much better than Lester! Though for a first time, Lester . . . "first time" my *butt.*

KEVIN *returns shoving* CODY.

KEVIN (*Furious, shaking*): Where do you think you are? *Where the fuck do you think you are?* What, you think you're *safe* here? Are you *safe* here? ARE YOU FUCKING SAFE HERE, CODY? (KEVIN *offers his shaking hand to* CODY) God . . . Look at my . . . God . . . *damn* it . . . (CODY, *confused, takes* KEVIN'S *hand*) Hi. *Hi.*

CODY: Hi . . .

KEVIN: Hi. I'm the gay-queer-*fag* who's been dry-humping you for the better part of the week. *Very* dry, by the way. I *work* here. Every day. Where the holy fuck do you think you *are?*

CODY (*Suddenly crying*): Oh, man . . . Oh, man . . . It goes real deep. I'm sorry, man. I'm so sorry.

KEVIN: Cody, it's . . .

CODY: *Hit* me, man. (KEVIN *perfunctorily hits* CODY. CODY *hugs him*) Thanks, man.

CORBIN: Take five. Take a *long* five.

Everyone leaves except KEVIN *and* LESTER.

KEVIN: I'm your Stand-In. So I said something. This *once,* okay?

KEVIN *takes a few steps, then turns back.*

Are *you* safe here, Lester?

KEVIN *exits. We hear the theme music to a TV talk show.* LESTER *exits. Lights change. We are on the set of the* Ula Kessle Show. ULA *enters.*

ULA: Welcome back to the *Ula Kessle Show*. For those of you just joining us, today we'll be talking to male homosexual prostitutes. Good stuff. Keep in mind that all my guests' names have been changed to protect their identities. Let's welcome them, shall we? Male homosexual prostitute number one . . . (*Looking at a notecard in her hand*) . . . Hedgehog!

Applause. A man enters. He has a black rectangle covering his eyes.

Male homosexual prostitute number two . . . Doorstop!

Applause. DOORSTOP *enters holding a piece of opaque glass in front of his face. He stands beside* HEDGEHOG.

And male homosexual prostitute number three . . . Ruffy The Clown!

Applause. RUFFY *enters dressed like a clown. He stands beside* DOORSTOP. ULA *indicates the chairs.*

Prostitutes?

They sit.

I'm sure we have a lot of questions.

A woman in the audience raises her hand. ULA *goes to her.*

Yes?

WOMAN 1: Hi, Ula. Love the show. Watch every day. Have no life. First I would like to commend your guests for coming forward to tell their stories that I'm sure will really help all of us who were seduced by a priest and ran away from home and went to New York and were picked up in a bus station by people who eventually turned out to be pimps. I have a question. Uh . . . Hedgehog, is it?

ULA: Hedgehog, yes.

WOMAN 1: Hedgehog. Have you accepted Jesus Christ as your personal savior?

HEDGEHOG: No.

WOMAN 1: Doorstop?

DOORSTOP: No.

WOMAN 1: Ruffy The Clown?

RUFFY: No.

WOMAN 1: Thank you.

She sits. A man raises his hand. ULA *runs to him.*

ULA: Yes?

MAN 1: God created Adam and Eve not Adam and Steve.

ULA: What's your *point?*

MAN 1: Thank you.

He sits. Another man raises his hand. ULA *runs to him.*

MAN 2: Why aren't your guests using their real names on the show today?

ULA: Good question. Hedgehog?

HEDGEHOG: To avoid arrest.

ULA: Ruffy The Clown?

RUFFY: To protect my parents, Bobo and Zeppy.

ULA: Doorstop? (*Pause*) Doorstop? Footrest? Table Lamp? Help me here.

Doorstop lowers the glass. We see that he is really SPARKY.

DOORSTOP (SPARKY): My name is, like, Andrew. Andrew Sparkowski-Martinez. I'll accept Jesus Christ the day after he accepts me. Maybe. God didn't create Adam and Eve—it's a *story,* people! My name is Andrew. Andrew Sparkowski-Martinez. I'm writing a book. Be afraid.

Lights change. Music plays. ULA *and her guests exit.* LESTER *and* FESTA *enter. Lights up. We are in* LESTER*'s dressing room on the set.*

FESTA: Sit. (*LESTER, confused, sits.*) For the few—is it even *weeks?* —that we've been . . . "doing this" . . . you've intrigued me, Lester. You have. But I've been intrigued primarily, I think, by the answers I myself have come up with to all my own questions about you. You have contributed so little to my perception of you that I have no idea how to react to the fact that, mere heartbeats ago, you asked me to *marry you.*

LESTER *starts to speak.*

Pull back, little fella, just let me *at* it, okay? Now . . . Most of all, Lester, I want to . . . touch you. No, *look* at you. Even now, with nothing but confusion on your face, I'm pulled *in.* *Poems* are written about a face like that! Love sonnets! Page after page. *Look* at you! To see joy on that heroic face. To *inspire* something—*anything*—that would flash across those eyes. To be responsible for altering those heroic features. I mean, the few times I succeeded, however temporarily, in chiseling away at that visage—that monument to . . . *"God's work done well"*—I felt so *powerful.* So *proud.* So . . . *accomplished.* (*Pause*) No.

LESTER: I don't . . . I don't know what to . . . Just being in the same *room* can be so *dangerous,* and I . . . The sun goes down, or comes *up*, and this feeling happens. This awful *thing*. More and more all the time. It goes away, but it comes back. Like it knows where I *am.* I thought that this thing, this feeling, that when it saw you, how strong you are, how beautiful you are . . . that it would . . .

FESTA (*Pause*): We never fell asleep. The thing you do best. We missed it.

LESTER: Stay with me. Be with me. Marry me, Festa. Please.

There's a knock on the door. BETTY, *Lester's mousy new publicist, sticks her head in.*

BETTY: How's my timing?

BETTY *rushes in with* MICHAEL *and* ASHLY. MICHAEL *has a knapsack,* ASHLY *has a camera and a light meter.* LESTER, *tears in his eyes, turns away.*

I've told them it's your birthday, Lester, they've promised to be nice. (*To Michael and Ashly*) This is Festa Longo. Note her presence.

MICHAEL: *Dawn Of Destruction.*

ASHLY: Go girl.

BETTY: Michael and Ashly—*Entertainment Monthly* magazine.

FESTA: 'Bye, Lester.

FESTA *exits.* ASHLY *takes light readings, etc.*

BETTY: Now, Michael, *Entertainment Monthly* has always been nice to my little people. That's why you're here. To be nice. And Ashly? Hello. Lester's right side is more gruff and Robert Mitchum-y and theatening, his left side is more sensitive and Monty Clift-y and "Awwww . . ." You decide but go with Mitchum, all right? For me? And Michael? Good to see you. I'll be just outside. Any heavy artillery and I'm right back in here chewing on your scrotal sack. Have fun!

BETTY *exits.*

MICHAEL: Lester, so nice of you to agree to an interview. I know how demanding it is being an actor.

LESTER: Huh? Oh, it's my pleasure, Michael, Ashly. I don't actually have anything to actually even *say,* but . . . Oh, I'm sorry, a beer? Some pork? Kabob?

MICHAEL: Uh . . . no. Thanks. (*MICHAEL puts a small tape recorder on the table.*) Okay? Now . . . this movie.

ASHLY starts taking LESTER's picture.

LESTER: I am *so* enjoying working on it. This movie.

MICHAEL: I read the script. It's . . . *swill* . . . isn't it?

LESTER: Oh. Well. Michael, Ashly, no. I'm enjoying . . .

MICHAEL: I understand you had a personal tango instructor.

LESTER: Yes! Gordon Fuente. Amazing guy. A real pal. Very . . . kind. And the actors on the movie are amazing. Corbin Tottles, our director, is amazing. *Very* from England. And . . . you know what, Michael, Ashly? It's almost as if we've become sort of like a family.

MICHAEL (*Feigning incredulity*): No!

LESTER: Absolutely.

MICHAEL: Is Lester Perry your real name?

LESTER: Absolutely.

MICHAEL (*Pause*): You seem . . . I don't know. Are you comfortable, Lester?

LESTER: Sure. Absolutely. Yeah, man. I mean, I've *done* interviews . . .

MICHAEL: —and I've read every one of them. Place of birth, Cedar Falls, Iowa. Standard childhood with Dan and DeeDee, a forklift operator and a forklift operator's cook. Indiana University . . .

LESTER: Right.

MICHAEL: Voice major . . .

LESTER: Right.

MICHAEL: And "Cynthia" was that special college sweetheart. Always mentioned.

LESTER: Amazing girl. Cynthia. Ashly, do you think you have enough pictures?

ASHLY: No.

MICHAEL: You graduated, you moved to New York, you did some commercials, you sang in the *chorus*. . . .

LESTER: Baritone, man.

MICHAEL: You have quite a number of female fans as a result of your television . . . activity. "Lactose intolerance?" Well, let's hear it for *intolerance,* anyway.

LESTER: Absolutely.

MICHAEL: Favorite color.

LESTER: Absolutely.

MICHAEL: What is your favorite color?

LESTER: Oh! Right! Right! Uh . . . blue?

MICHAEL: You don't sound sure.

LESTER: I can't remember what I said.

MICHAEL: When?

LESTER: In my other interviews.

MICHAEL: This isn't a quiz.

LESTER: It feels like a quiz. Ashly?

MICHAEL: Our sources tell us that you aren't doing your own kissing.

LESTER: Absolutely not . . . Not me, man! I just . . . Not that I . . .

MICHAEL: Sorry, was it blue?

LESTER: What? *Oh.* Uh, blue. Right.

MICHAEL: Millions of people will be reading this.

LESTER: I'm almost certain. My palms are sweating.

MICHAEL: Why?

LESTER: No reason, man.

MICHAEL: My God, you are *hating* this.

LESTER: Yes, but . . .

MICHAEL: Why?

LESTER: You know.

MICHAEL: I don't.

LESTER: What?

MICHAEL: Know. (*Pause*) Every time our eyes meet you look away. I mean, you act—we look.

LESTER: When I'm acting no one is looking at *me*.

MICHAEL: Oh, *that*. I want you to look at something, Lester.

LESTER: No prob.

MICHAEL puts a photograph on the table.

MICHAEL: Andrew Sparkowski-Martinez. A known hustler. He was on a talk show recently—he's writing a book—and we got that picture of him coming out of your brownstone—your single-dwelling brownstone—two weeks ago—3:00 in the morning. We were there to get a picture of Festa Longo. Her publicist, Babs, tipped us off—anonymously, of course—so there we were, in the bushes, waiting. But then—out came "Sparky." I'll bet we were there on the wrong night.

LESTER (*Very thrown*): Absolutely.

MICHAEL: We talked to him, Lester.

LESTER: I don't think—look at my palms—that I'm getting this. *Entertainment Monthly* magazine?

MICHAEL: "*QT*." *Queer Times*. We lied. We had to.

LESTER: But . . .

MICHAEL: We also tracked down Cynthia, your college sweetheart. His name, it seems, is Chester Cynthioni. You studied voice together at IU. He's a member of Queer Nation now and we got our hands on some pretty interesting pictures of the two of you.

LESTER: He was, you know . . . friendly, kind, just *joking* all the time, he . . . *How the hell is that little jokester these days, man?*

MICHAEL: He's in Washington right now, I believe, holding signs and chanting annoying things that rhyme while lying down in traffic.

LESTER: I knew him. I mean, Michael, Ashly, I *knew* him, but . . .

MICHAEL: Was that weird? "Lester and Chester"?

LESTER: He wasn't . . . We never—*wait!* Didn't you get a picture of Festa on maybe another different night coming out of . . . *She was just here!*

MICHAEL: Festa Longo used to be a man. Carl Reagan.

LESTER: *Nancy* Reagan. She created Festa to . . . to stand in for her in the world. To do all the things that she—Nancy Reagan—couldn't. Nancy stayed home. (*Desperately laughing*) With *Ronnie!*

MICHAEL: Look, Lester—we'd rather you came out on your own. By yourself. We want to give you the opportunity to be proud. To be a hero to millions of queer men and women. Lester, just *talk* to us . . .

LESTER: Hey, you know what? I don't even understand this using by people these days of the word "queer." It . . .

ASHLY: I'm not comfortable with it either, Lester.

LESTER: It . . . that WORD! I mean, *Gosh,* you know? *Doesn't* it, Ashly? It really so *does*—and I . . . And even "gay" is kind of hard, and I'm gay, you . . . *oh.*

Slowly, MICHAEL *reaches out and switches off the tape recorder.*

MICHAEL: "Oh."

LESTER: But so I can't. Oh, dear, I can't *do* anything—anything here anymore. And stop taking my *picture,* Ashly, *please!*

ASHLY: Okay, Lester.

LESTER: Michael?

MICHAEL: Lester?

LESTER: Can you do this? I'm sorry, but can you do this? You can't *do* this, can you?

MICHAEL: *Clearly* you don't read our magazine.

LESTER: OK. OK, I think . . . you should leave now.

MICHAEL: We have your confession—acknowledgment—on tape, Lester. Actually, I don't think we could have done a thing without it. Thanks.

LESTER: GET OUT!

MICHAEL and ASHLY go to the door.

MICHAEL: I'm not sorry about this, Lester. We can't hide anymore. There aren't enough of us left. But, look—maybe you're closer to being ready than you think. I think you are. Closer. For what it's worth. (*Pause*) Call us. We'll turn this whole thing into a celebration. (*Pause*)

The article will be on the newsstands in about two weeks. Everywhere. But, hey, look on the bright side. Your first cover.

ASHLY: Happy birthday.

MICHAEL and ASHLY exit.

LESTER: And . . . hold. Kevin? Kevin? *Kevin?*

We hear a tango as lights fade to:
—Blackout

(*end of Act I*)

~

Act II

Lights up. We are simultaneously on four sound stages. BICKY LOOP *enters and sits at her* Entertainment Incessantly *desk,* WALTER WILLIAMS *enters and sits on his* "Out and About" *stool, network news anchor* ARCHER PIPPINS *enters and sits at his anchor desk and* JESUS MORALES *enters and sits on a corner of his desk. A crew person, wearing headphones, enters downstage and counts down with his fingers.*

CREW PERSON: In Five—Four—Three—Two . . .

The crew person indicates "One" and exits. We hear the overlapping theme songs from four TV tabloid, entertainment, and news programs. Lights come up behind BICKY, WALTER, JESUS, *and* ARCHER *as they arrange papers, chat with unseen co-hosts, etc., in silhouette. As lights come up full, they all turn to the camera, smiling.*

BICKY: I'm Bicky Loop . . .

WALTER: I'm Walter Williams . . .

JESUS: Me: Jesus Morales . . .

ARCHER: I'm Archer Pippins, and welcome to World News Of The Moment. Our top story tonight:

Simultaneously, as graphics of the LESTER PERRY *cover of* Queer Times *appears over their heads:*

BICKY: Lester Perry, Lester Perry, Lester Perry, Lester Perry, Lester Perry, Lester Perry, Lester Perry, Lester Perry.

WALTER (*Scolding*): Lester, Lester, Lester! Lester, Lester, Lester, Lester, Lester! Lester, Lester, Lester, Lester, Lester!

JESUS: Perry, Lester Perry, Lester Perry, Lester Perry, Lester Perry, Lester Perry, Lester Perry, Lester Perry, Lester.

ARCHER: Lester Perry, Lester Perry, Lester Perry, Lester Perry, Lester Perry, Lester Perry, Lester Perry, Lester Perry.

Lights to black. BICKY *and* WALTER *exit,* BICKY *with her desk and stool. Lights up on* JESUS.

JESUS: My staff tried to perfunctorily contact Lester, but since his people would not return our phone call, we had no choice but to send two highly respected investigative journalists to go through Lester's trash.

JESUS *gets two boxes and places them on his desk. One box is labeled "Gay," the other is labeled "Not."*

"Gay"—"Not." (JESUS *takes something out of the "Not" box.*) The remains of a Hungry Man Salisbury Steak Dinner.

He takes something out of the "Gay" box.

The remains of a Squid Ink pasta with an olive-caper rémoulade.

He alternates between the two boxes.

A copy of *Dead Men Don't Reiterate* by Elmore Leonard—a copy of *Martha Stewart Living*. A ticket stub to a Yankees home game—a ticket stub to a Saturday matinee of *Sunset Boulevard*. *You* decide!

Lights off JESUS *as he exits with the boxes and the stool. Lights up on* ARCHER.

ARCHER: Other allegations against Lester Perry include allegations that he forged his mother's name on his report cards, once said something that could be construed as marginally insensitive and that he has a small birthmark that resembles the ruby slippers worn by Judy Garland in *The Wizard of Oz* on the lower left quadrant of his alleged right buttock.

Blackout. We hear ULA KESSLE*'s theme song as she enters down stage.*

ULA: Welcome back to the *Ula Kessle Show,* my first guest today, via satellite, is recently outed Ex Hot Soap Stud Lester Perry's college "roommate"—activist, tenor and sodomite, Chester Cynthioni.

Lights up on CHESTER. *He wears many ribbons, pins, and slogans.*

I understand, Chester, that you've been holding signs and chanting annoying things that rhyme for a number of years now.

CHESTER: I'm an activist, Ula. Is that collar real fur?

ULA: More importantly, Chester, does Lester *really* have a birthmark that resembles the red shoes worn by Judy Garland in *The Wizard Of Oz* on the lower left quadrant of his alleged right buttock?

Blackout. ULA *and* CHESTER *exit as lights come up on* ARCHER.

ARCHER: Activist, tenor and sodomite, Chester Cynthioni, reached while holding signs and chanting annoying things that rhyme in front of the Gloria Redding Cosmetics factory in Boca Raton, Florida, alleges that, while Mr. Perry *does* have a small birthmark on the lower left quadrant of his alleged right buttock, it more *closely* resembles the ballet slippers worn by Vicki Page in the 1947 film *The Red Shoes.*

Lights go to black on ARCHER *as* ULA *returns.*

ULA: I'm sure we must have lots of questions.

A man in the audience raises a hand, ULA *goes to him.*

Yes?

MAN 1: Have you accepted Jesus Christ as your personal savior?

ULA: *Me?*

MAN 1: No, your guest.

ULA: 'Cause I was gonna *say* . . .

Blackout. ULA *and* CHESTER *exit as lights come up full on* ARCHER.

ARCHER: It *is* worth noting, however, that Chester and Lester were roommates in college, and *I* certainly recall looking at my college roommate's buttocks with a certain regularity. Even a certain longing. The way the sun would make a golden halo of the all-but-invisible hair on T.J.'s bubblelike mounds of Socrates.

Lights off ARCHER. *Up on* ULA *and* CHESTER.

ULA: Chester? *Have* you acepted Jesus Blah, Blah, Blah?

CHESTER: No, Ula. But I *have* accepted that the slaughter of helpless animals in the name of creating unnecessary and, in your case, ineffective fashion accessories, is an abomination even in what may well be a Godless universe. Are those shoes real leather?

ULA: You can't see my shoes. You're on satellite. Go 'way now!

Blackout. ULA *and* CHESTER *exit as lights come up on* ARCHER*'s news desk.* ARCHER*'s desk is now occupied by another reporter.*

REPORTER 1: . . . and finally tonight: "Vacationing" news anchor Archer Pippins has denied allegations that he once had a deep homosexual obsession with his college roommate, T.J.

Lights off ARCHER, *tight spot up on* ULA. *Her theme plays softly.*

ULA: Tomorrow, on the *Ula Kessle Show,* we'll be talking to Lester Perry's elementary schoolteacher, two of Lester's Cedar Falls neighbors, a lesbian mother who used to baby-sit Lester, Lester's childhood priest—who will be talking to us from his cell at the Gracefall Rehabilitation Center—twin strippers who feel that, in certain light, they rather *look* like Lester, and three people *named* Lester who used to work in the Adult Entertainment Industry until involvement in a neoreligious cult resulted in a frightening maze of eating disorders that encouraged them to finally accept a rather large person named *Gabe* as their personal savior.

We hear a chaos of themes, sound bites, etc., as ULA *exits. Lights change. We are in* LESTER*'s apartment.* LESTER *is there with* FIONA, *his agent. We hear* BETTY, *his publicist, calling from offstage.*

BETTY'S VOICE: But, I mean, as Lester's publicist, it's my job description to know!

FIONA: Stop flogging yourself, Betty.

BETTY *enters from the kitchen, crying, carrying a beer for* LESTER *and a cup of tea for* FIONA.

BETTY: I mean, *all* of *Entertainment Monthly*'s reporters are gay, but they're more "Summer Sweaters in the Hamptons" gay. Michael and that lumbering photographer show up looking like disaffected NYU students with majors in New Wave French Cinema and I usher them right *in!*

FIONA: Stop nailing yourself to a cross, Betty.

BETTY: Our denials *have* been picked up? Hello? Everywhere? I mean, I have actors Lester's never worked with declaring his frenzied heterosexuality on publicity junkets for movies Lester isn't even *in*. It's the *least* I can do—I'm an *idiot!*

FIONA: Stop tying yourself to a chair in a third world prison and beating your ankles with rubber tubing, Betty.

LESTER: I just want to say—*again*—that I don't understand why we don't just get a lawyer. It's . . .

FIONA: Lester, our drooling infant, you sue and they really rake you over the coals. But look, we've discredited little "Sparky," thank Buddha. It was almost too easy.

LESTER: But, we have to hurry more. Go faster. Every day this is so worse and I don't know how much more of me I can *take!*

FIONA: Will you let us do what we do, baby? Thank you. (*Back to Betty*) So, looking up Lester's college chum, Chester Cynthioni, was a trip, I'm telling you. He's an activist, thank Allah, way out on the fringes of even the *gay* community. He boos himself at rallies. And even though he had those pictures of Lester sitting on his lap at a kegger sipping what may well be a somewhat incriminating glass of white wine, the general impression we'll be creating is that he'd dynamite an occupied daycare center if he thought it would further his "cause."

LESTER: That's . . . No, I mean, that's good, discrediting him, great, whatever, please, *absolutely,* fuck him, who cares, but . . . It's part of what's so weird. Back then he, Chester, was a—and I'm sorry, but I imagine he still *is*—a kind person. I was . . . not.

FIONA: *Impression,* Lester, our puling toddler.

LESTER: Right, right, right, right, right . . .

FIONA: The *reality* is that you plowed a tenor in college, rented people named Sparky and, with a tape recorder mere inches from your mouth, you adamantly declared: ". . . even gay is kind of hard, and I'm gay. You . . . Oh."

BETTY (*Sobbing*): Hi? Hello? And it's all my fault.

FIONA: Stop aiming a firefighter's hose at your own midsection and spraying yourself down the street and into a metal fence, Betty. What we'll say is that the tape was tampered with. What Lester *really* said was: "Stop pushing so hard. I'm not gay. You . . . *Go*."

LESTER: That will work? It's . . .

BETTY: *Queer Times* presented "a" Lester Perry, so what *we* do is send out another one!

FIONA: People won't know which Lester is the real Lester, Lester. And when people are confused they grasp at the reassuring.

BETTY: That God is in her heaven, America is the best damned country in the world . . .

FIONA: . . . and all the really cute actors are heterosexual.

BETTY: It'll wash, Lester.

FIONA: It always has.

BETTY: Do you need help finding a girlfriend, Lester? I represent any number of terrified lesbians.

FIONA: Get a girlfriend, Lester. Do it now.

BETTY: Call me.

FIONA: By the way, Lester—have you had an HIV test? If we get this past the Great Unwashed Public and you turn up sick, we'll *all* look pretty silly. (*Pause*) God, listen to me.

BETTY: What one turns into.

BETTY AND FIONA (*Pause—then cheerily back to business*): So . . . !

We hear tango music. Lights change. BETTY *exits.* FIONA *remains.* CORBIN *enters with* CODY, KEVIN *and* GUS. *Someone wheels on a huge cake that is in the shape of a baseball diamond, a tango dancer made of frosting at home plate. We are at the screening party for* You're Out—The Gilbert Feldstein Story. *Everyone has drinks.*

CORBIN: Lester! Where have you been hiding yourself and what *did* you think of our final product? I can take it. Fib.

LESTER: Oh, uh . . . I felt it was finished. Corbin? Tell me something. Why did you offer me the part?

CORBIN: Ah. Well, Lester, I did not offer you the part because of any perceived effeminancy, if that's what you're asking. I did not "sense" anything that made me think you might be homosexual. If I had, I would not have offered you the part. I offered you the part, Lester, because of the way you *look*. Why did you take it?

LESTER: I figured you offered me the part because of the way I look and figured the way I look, at least, was something I could do well.

CORBIN: You're a decent actor, Lester, and you looked the way you look very convincingly, I assure you. Your current scandal will only help with the ratings, and your discomfort with certain aspects of the role will contribute only to putting the whole tired controversy behind you. Ultimately you will be guilty of nothing more complicated than being naive enough to take on a nonterminal homosexual role. You may even be touted for bravery. Don't despair, dear, embroiled Lester. The pretty are attacked, yes—but the pretty are also forgiven. Forgiven everything. Get drunk with me.

LESTER: No, I'm . . .

CORBIN: As you wish.

KEVIN comes over as CORBIN heads to the bar.

Kevin—*bravo.*

LESTER: Kevin! Hey, pal. So, *this* is what you look like. As you.

KEVIN: No one knows who I am. Security keeps throwing me out.

LESTER: Was this fun for you at all?

KEVIN: I had to kiss Cody and show my ass, but at least I didn't have to say any of those lines.

LESTER: What's up next for you?

KEVIN: I'm in the next Joe Harper vehicle. I play a close-up of Joe getting a B-12 shot. Well, there are heroes and there are heroes' asses.

LESTER: Your time will come. You're good. I'll bet you really are.

KEVIN: Lester? Do you have friends?

LESTER: What? Oh, uh . . . yeah. Sure. Absolutely.

KEVIN: 'Cause if you ever need to talk . . . I'm not hitting on you. I'm not my type. (*Pause*) I just keep picturing you all alone in the dark in a little rowboat in the middle of an ocean. I feel like . . . waving.

CODY enters.

CODY: *My two men!*

KEVIN: Let me know, buddy.

CODY come over. BICKY LOOP from Entertainment Incessantly *enters, followed by HILTON, her cameraman.*

BICKY: *Cody Willow!*

CODY: Oh, no. Oh, fuck, no. (*BICKY comes over.*) Bicky Loop, you dried up old slag.

BICKY: Lick me, Cody. Hilton, let's get one of those tired "Oh, we're having so much fun at the screening party" shots.

HILTON turns on the camera. Its light illuminates BICKY and the three men. LESTER gets quite suddenly butch, confident and cheerful.

Hi, talent! How are you enjoying the party?

LESTER: We're having a great time, Bicky. It was a long shoot and we've all become, well, sort of like a family.

BICKY: I can't use anyone else saying that ever.

CODY: Bickster, this is Kevin Flanders. He played the role of Lester's sexuality. Well, Gilbert's sexuality. I didn't have a stunt double, but since Lester had *NEVER KISSED A MAN BEFORE,* he used Kevin.

KEVIN: Nice to meet you, Bicky. My lover, Ted, and I watch your show all the time.

BICKY: Why are you telling me this? Why is he telling me this?

KEVIN: I've never been interviewed before.

BICKY: You aren't being interviewed *now*. Lester . . .

KEVIN: But I guess I always thought that if I ever *was* interviewed, I'd make sure to acknowledge the fact that I'm queer, and that Ted and I have been lovers for five years, and though it's not always a day at the beach, we fight sometimes over the lamest things, like all couples, but we are generally very happy together. (*Pause*) Ted and I. (*Pause*) Who are queer. (*Pause*) Thank you.

BICKY: If indeed you watch my show—*Gregor,* is it?

KEVIN: Kevin.

BICKY: Kevin. If indeed you and your little friend watch my show, you must know that we do *denials* of homosexuality, *allegations* of homosexuality. We don't even have a *graphic* prepared for *declarations* of homosexuality. Who *are* you?

KEVIN: I'm Lester's stand-in.

BICKY waves her hand and HILTON turns off the camera's light.

BICKY: Take your butt to the bar, Gregor. Cody, step into my orifice. Lester? Man of the moment? *Stay. Stay.*

BICKY secures CODY in a corner as LESTER crosses, running into GORDON, his tango instructor.

GORDON: Hey, there you are! Movie star!

LESTER: Oh! Oh, Gordon! *Gordo,* you . . .

GORDON hugs LESTER. LESTER, surprised, reacts by slapping the hell out of GORDON's back.

GORDON (*Laughing*): Ouch!

LESTER takes a large step back from GORDON, looking around.

LESTER: Sorry. It's . . .

GORDON: No, it's . . . Hi. You . . .

LESTER: A drink? Some cake? You . . . I'll be right . . .

LESTER goes to the bar. GORDON gets a piece of cake. HILTON turns the bright light on BICKY and CODY.

BICKY: All right. Let's talk movie. I understand that the character you play in *You're Out—The Gilbert Feldstein Story* doesn't have AIDS.

CODY: No one in the movie has AIDS.

BICKY: I'm confused, Cody. Aren't there a number of gay characters in the movie?

BICKY: Yup.

BICKY: And *none* of the characters in the movie has AIDS? Interesting.

LESTER returns with GORDON's drink. BICKY continues to interview CODY silently.

LESTER: Here you go. It's . . .

GORDON: Oh. Thanks. You . . .

LESTER: So, did you . . . what? I'm sorry, you . . .

GORDON (*Starting on Lester's "I'm"*): No, I was just going to say that I liked the movie. I stood in the back. People were pacing. It was cool. Finish your sentence.

LESTER: I didn't have one, really. A complete one.

GORDON: I got your legs.

LESTER: You . . . ?

GORDON: My piece of cake. I got the tango dancer's legs. I'm assuming they're yours.

LESTER: Right!

GORDON: But this guy in the back of the screening room? He was freaking out, trying to get the protesters outside on the street to shut up. They were banging their signs on the exit door.

LESTER: Is that what that was?

GORDON: I don't know what that guy's problem was. *I* think "We're Gay—Hey, Hey—And We'll Never Go Away" was kind of a cool underscoring. (*Pause*) Have you actually looked in my eyes yet? Come on—"Meet my gaze."

LESTER: "Can I just get the steps right first?"

GORDON: "The steps are there." (*Pause*) I've missed you.

LESTER: Yeah . . . well . . . Did you . . . happen to . . . see the . . . article?

GORDON: I have it taped to the mirror in my studio, are you kidding me?

LESTER: Well, don't worry about it, we got it covered. No prob.

GORDON: Cool.

LESTER: There's just so much *about* me now, but . . . (*Pause*) I don't even know who that person *is,* but . . . (*Pause*) All these *strangers*. My first grade teacher and my baby-sitter and my priest are all on TV, all saying I really didn't make that much of an impression back then, which is *so* fun to hear, Gordon—*Gordo*—let me tell you, but did the second tango—if you could even *hear* it over all that . . . I mean, Kevin, my stand-in, *he* didn't do any of my dancing, but sometimes it looked more like him than *me!* And *Chester!* And *enrollment* might pick up after the movie's on—Chester on *TV,* for the love of Pete! But enrollment at your thing, about *fur,* which would be *so* amazing. And I just sort of do little dance steps in the dining room and fifteen minutes later, I'm like: *"I forgot to turn on the radio!"* I'm telling *you* this, of *all* the people I try not to think about, and I'm always alone—like being alone *means* something now! Not even making an *impression!* "We're Gay—Hey, Hey—La-la-la-la-la!" *THAT* must have been annoying.

GORDON (*Pause*): Let's go.

LESTER: No, I'm here. It's what I'm doing now. I'm here and I'm over this and I'm better and I'm indignant.

GORDON: You're messed up, Lester. You are a messed-up man. And you're afraid and you're baffled and you're unsure of the next step and you find me really attractive.

LESTER: Absolutely.

LESTER looks away.

GORDON: None of that, fella. Look at me. Meet my gaze. (*Pause*) Hi. (*Pause*) Hi. (*Pause*) You break my heart. (*Pause*) Hi.

LESTER: Hi.

GORDON: Let's go. I want to touch you someplace.

LESTER: That would . . .

CODY: Thank YOU, Bickster. You are to journalism what the International House Of Pancakes is to journalism.

BICKY: Eat me, Cody.

CODY: Never, you lush, Harpy, Detroyer of Culture.

BICKY: Chew me. Barkeep?

BICKY goes to the bar. CODY joins LESTER and GORDON.

CODY: Lester, man, I'm outta here. Can I steal Lester a minute?

GORDON: Give him back.

CODY takes LESTER aside.

CODY: I always thought that if I ever was mugged I'd fight back like a motherfucker, man. Pretend I was a nutcase. Freak the dickheads out. I was mugged last week. This one little putz with maybe a knife. I burst out bawling and talked like a girl and pissed my pants and begged. But the worst part, man? I can't go back. I can't go back and do it over. The bitch, man, is that I'm stuck for the rest of my life with how I reacted the one time it's gonna happen.

CODY looks at LESTER, then throws his arms around him.

See ya, man.

CODY exits. LESTER returns to GORDON.

LESTER: Do you really want to get out of here? Because I so—with *you*—want to get out of here.

FESTA LONGO enters.

BICKY: *FESTA LONGO!*

FESTA: Oh, no. Oh, fuck, no. (*Seeing Lester*) *Lester,* you . . . (*Seeing Gordon—pleased*) Oh! (*Back to Lester*) Anyway, I'm here. Your cryptic little message was a prong to the psyche, but I'm here. What's so imperative you're ringing up old flames?

LESTER: Oh. Right. You're here . . . because I . . .

BICKY comes over followed by HILTON.

BICKY: FESTA FUCKING LONGO!

FESTA: Bicky Loop, you lurking parasite.

BICKY: Mount me, Festa. Hilton?

HILTON turns on the blinding light. BICKY sees GORDON.

Hello. Are you someone I should give two shits about?

GORDON (*Laughing*): Nope.

LESTER: Bicky, this is . . . Gordon Fuente. He taught me the tango.

BICKY: Go away, Feliciano. Festa, take Feliciano's place.

FESTA: Ask Gordon a question.

BICKY: What?

FESTA: Ask Gordon a question, or you don't get a word out of me.

BICKY (*To Gordon*): Where ya from?

GORDON: Queens.

BICKY (*To Festa*): *All right?*

FESTA: Stick around, Gordon. Bicky's going to buy you a drink.

GORDON: No, no, no, I'll just . . .

LESTER: Okay. You . . . go. Just . . . Gordo, good. *Go.* Away. Okay, pal?

GORDON: Oh. Uh . . . cool. Cool. (*Pause*) The music has ended, the dance has not. Okay, fella? See ya, Carl.

FESTA: Gordon, you don't have to . . .

GORDON exits.

BICKY: And . . . Festa Longo! Don't you look scrumptious.

FESTA: G'won.

BICKY: And, Lester? I know of actors who have been destroyed by allegations similar to those leveled against you, and yet here you are, all bunnies and balloons. How much of the credit goes to Festa?

LESTER: A . . . lot.

BICKY: Oh? What's the copy on the two?

LESTER: We're . . . close.

BICKY: My sources, Lester, your agent and publicist, tell me that you two may very well be *engaged.*

LESTER: Well, Bicky, all I can say is that your sources are . . . correct.

BICKY: Yay! Yay, me! Bag it, drag it home, and *nail it to the wall!*

The tango music comes up louder. Lights change. FESTA *looks at* LESTER, *he looks away. The others exit. Lights up. We are in* LESTER'*s apartment.*

FESTA: Well, Lester . . . congratulations. You did it. Problem solved. And what a brilliant idea—all of a sudden getting *engaged.* Who would ever think of *that* as a response to rumored homosexuality?

LESTER: When people are going through your trash, Festa, maybe you start throwing things out for them. Maybe you start contributing to what they're going to find.

FESTA: People who were merely wondering will now be *laughing.*

LESTER: And I'll be hearing them! They'll *call* me. Half the messages on my machine are of people just laughing—passing the receiver back and forth, listening to my voice. So, *I* listen to my voice, my message, and I have to think that maybe there *is* something funny. So I record it again—over and over—

lowering my voice, eliminating words with *S*s. I'm even worried about what the music in the background *says* about me.

FESTA: Who isn't?

LESTER: And I see people on TV—*gay* people, I guess—"homosexuals"—in movies and on TV and on the street—and I get so *embarrassesd*. For *them*. All of a sudden everything they do is all about *me,* and I want them to *stop* designing the world's clothes and arranging its flowers and decorating its rooms and choreographing its dances and having a "knack" for brushing its God-damned hair!

FESTA: A sense of fun and an inkling of which colors go together are strange things to be embarrassed about, Lester, but every group has its embarrassments. Think what I, as a *woman,* have to answer for. *Phyllis Shlafly*. The popularity of New Age composer *Yanni*. And what if you were straight? *War* comes to mind. Newt Gingrich. Those men that go out in the woods with drums and cry while hugging naked, hairy tax consultants who haven't urinated recently. And what if you were black? *Al Sharpton*. Give me a *break*. Actually, "Gimme A Break" would be something you'd have to atone for. Consider yourself lucky that all you have to answer for is track lighting, the Village People, and the occasional all-male production of *Anything Goes*.

LESTER: You see? Do you *see* now? I'm being a . . . "gay" now, right? And I'm standing here with a woman I used to . . . or something, and we're talking about the Village People!

FESTA: I'm still back at that "woman I used to . . . or something" part.

LESTER: Do I look different? Am I changing right in front of my eyes into some other person? Some other *species?* I mean, what am I expected to *do* now? March down the street *chanting* things? Am I angry now all of a sudden. Am I *oppressed* now? Am I *proud* now? Am I expected to be *proud* now? Proud of *what?* I mean, *look* at them, Festa! Every trip to the corner deli's a parade. Every bizarre way of dressing, acting, making love—*Anything Goes,* right? Swishing down the street, for the love of Pete—hugging, kissing, shoving it in your *face!* Holding signs—banging on the exits—holding *hands*—making everyone *look*. Dancing around in big faggot groups—chanting and rhyming like fucking *idiots,* lisping away! Lisping about justice and blame and pride and hate—and they *look* at you. Like they *know*. And you just want to *stop* them. *Stop* them from being so *sure*—so *different*—so not the *same*. Like being different is some kind of *accomplishment*. It's a lot harder to be the *same,* Festa, *believe* me—and I am not at all *proud*. Not of *them*. Not for *that*.

FESTA: I see. (*Pause*) I'm afraid, sometimes, of what I might be. But what I might *not* be *really* keeps me up at night. (*Pause*) I should go. Those photographers outside in the bushes have lives, too. Children who miss them. Dinner waiting. (*Pause*) Who were you picturing when we fucked? Who did you see when you closed your eyes?

LESTER: Gordon, my tango instructor.

FESTA: This is acceptable to me. Picture Gordon, Lester. He might be gentle. He might, at last, be "kind." Then again, he might well be proud—and that, as we now know, would be unacceptable to you.

LESTER: Can you stay?

FESTA: No. I can't. I am sad to be among you.

FESTA exits. LESTER, lost, lies down on the couch. A moment passes. Lights shift. We hear a bloodcurdling scream from offstage. Then laughter. DAN and DEEDEE, LESTER's parents, enter from the bedroom.

DEEDEE: Oh, Lessie! Your bedroom is such fun I love that chair that looks like a hand.

DAN: Your mother pretended it goosed her.

LESTER: Everyone does.

DEEDEE: An entire bedroom with nothing but a bed . . . and a hand. *I* know, Dan! Those old curtains from our den! You remember, with the corn? The stalks of corn? They're just sitting in a box somewhere.

DAN: They're sitting in a box somewhere, DeeDee, for a damn good reason. They're awful.

DEEDEE (*Howling with laughter*): They *are,* aren't they, Dan? Just *awful!* Even then, what *was* I thinking? Well, it's your apartment, Lessie, and if it takes you a while to turn it into a home . . .

DAN: Lester, sit down. Your mother and I would like to talk to you.

LESTER (*To himself*): Oh, no . . .

Everyone sits.

DEEDEE: As you know, Lessie, we read that article in *Queer Times* magazine.

DAN: We were surprised that where you put your mister was such a large part of the story, but we read every word.

DEEDEE: As well as those advertisements for phone sex, gay Bed and Breakfasts and Windjammer Cruises.

DAN: We were pleased that, should you indeed be gay, you'll have plenty of things to do with your spare time.

DEEDEE: I apologize if we're being flip with you, Lessie, but we've just never been very excitable, and we see little call to get all upset this far down the road.

DAN: That's what we wanted to say, Lester, and we've said it well.

DEEDEE (*Pause.*): This is where we hoped *you'd* say something.

LESTER: I . . . but you . . . But I . . .

DEEDEE: Oh, *Lessie.* You must have thought we'd be destroyed by this. But we talked about that—had a little family conference—and though we considered *acting* destroyed by this so you wouldn't be thrown, we agreed that it was best to present ourselves as we really are. We aren't your twenty-five-year-old parents anymore. Or your thirty-five-year-old parents. Or even your forty-five-year-old parents. We've had a very interesting life since you moved out, Lessie, and we agreed, your father and I, to *tell* you about that sometime. But for the moment, Lessie, please try and forget about those frightened, judgmental . . .

DAN: . . . small-minded . . .

DEEDEE: . . . small-minded—thank you, Dan—parents we used to be.

DAN: We know it won't be easy, son.

DEEDEE: But we'd like you to accept us as we really are. We can't change for you, Lessie.

LESTER: I . . . But you . . .

DEEDEE: Oh, Lessie—*Plus ça change!* You remember, Dan, how hard it was to get little Lessie to tell us even about what he did that day in *school?* So shy and cute and frustrating.

DAN: We knew you were gay even then, Lester. We talked about it, your mother and I, one day in Calcutta. I knew you were gay when you were fifteen. Your mother claims five. When did *you* know you were gay, son?

LESTER: You went to *Calcutta?*

DEEDEE: *Tip* of the iceberg.

DAN: It was actually on another trip—was it the Galápagos?—the sea turtles?—that we met our lesbians.

DEEDEE: We call them "our" lesbians—they chose the same tour package.

DAN: We told them we thought we had a gay son.

DEEDEE: And they were *beside* themselves!

LESTER: I can't believe this.

DAN: Talk to us, Lester. We're your parents.

LESTER: Oh, you are *not.*

DAN: All right, then, we'll just ask some God-damn questions.

DEEDEE: It's always been the only way, Dan.

DAN: Are you seeing anyone special, Lester?

LESTER: Wait. Okay. You mean . . . ?

DAN: We remember that nice young fellow from college—he was mentioned in the article—Chester Cynthioni.

DEEDEE: Wasn't he nice, Dan? And such a sweet singing voice.

DAN: You said you and Chester were just friends and that you were dating that attractive young girl we had dinner with, Cathy. You must have thought we were idiots.

DEEDEE: Chester was attractive, Lessie.

DAN: Even *more* attractive, we thought.

DEEDEE: He had those haunting eyes and that effeminate charm and that "swimmer's build" mentioned so often in those *Queer Times* personal ads.

DAN: *You* are an attractive man, Lester. You have your mother's good looks.

DEEDEE (*Blushing wildly*): Oh, *you!* We were on the Yucatán Peninsula recently, and your father was *incorrigible.*

DAN: You're a damned handsome woman, DeeDee.

DEEDEE: And after twenty-six years of marriage.

DAN: It only gets better. Which is why we want you to find love in your life, Lester. Fall in love, damn it.

LESTER: But . . . you know how hard it is being an actor. I really don't have *time* for a personal life.

DEEDEE: Oh, how much time does it take, Lessie—falling in love? It took your father and me fifteen minutes.

DAN: Gosh, gosh, begosh, DeeDee, don't badger the boy.

DEEDEE: Well, it just breaks my heart, Dan. Look at him. Look at your son. So lost and alone, no blood in his cheeks.

DAN: And speaking of health, Lester, we'd like to give you these.

DAN *takes a chain of condoms out of his pocket.*

DEEDEE: Left over from Egypt.

DAN: There are only so many hours in a day.

LESTER: I . . . Mom . . . Dad . . . I don't . . . I mean, *gosh,* I *have* protection.

DEEDEE: Oh, we know you're protected, Lessie.

DAN: If anything, *too* protected. Always have been.

DEEDEE: We just thought it would be cute to give you condoms.

DAN: And we think it was.

DEEDEE: And should you ever get sick, Lessie, we're here for you.

DAN: We love you, Lester.

DEEDEE: You're our son.

DAN: Although we talked about it, your mother and I, and we

agreed that even if you were someone else's son, we'd love you anyway.

LESTER: I . . . I love you . . . too.

The buzzer buzzes.

DEEDEE: Oh, Dan—maybe *this* is someone!

LESTER pushes the door buzzer.

LESTER: Oh, no. I forgot. Oh, no. I have an appointment. Now. Great. It . . .

There's a knock on the door. LESTER *opens it.* MICHAEL, *the reporter from* Queer Times, *is there.*

Hello, Michael. You are *so* on time. These are my *parents*. (*Pause*) Mom? Dad? This is Michael Rollinstock. He wrote the . . . article.

DEEDEE: DeeDee, please. And this is Dan.

DAN: Pleased to meet you, young man. Now, our lesbians, Heather and Duffy, tell us that a gay person's decision to come out, on his or her own time, is the most important event in the life of a gay or lesbian person.

DEEDEE: You robbed Lessie of that event, Michael.

DAN: For that we can never forgive you.

DEEDEE: *Ever*. Well, so nice to *meet* you, Michael! Lessie? We'll be by at eight tomorrow to fetch you for breakfast. Michael is welcome if he can control himself and come to respect other people's feelings and if you come to tolerate him and he doesn't have plans.

LESTER: You really don't have to stay in a hotel. I have plenty of room.

DAN: We don't want to stay with you, Lester.

DEEDEE: *That's* what it is. We shared a home with you for eighteen years. There's a limit.

DAN: Good-bye, son. Try and think of things to say at breakfast tomorrow.

DEEDEE: Sometimes it helps if you go over it in your head.

DAN and DEEDEE hug LESTER, then go out into the hall.

We'll see you at eight. Dress casual.

As LESTER closes the door, DEEDEE points at MICHAEL and mouths the words "he's cute." DAN gives the "thumbs up" sign. LESTER closes the door.

LESTER (*Pause*): My parents think you're cute. My *parents* think you're *cute!* Wow . . . Where were they? My parents. *Those* parents, when I really . . .

MICHAEL: Am I correct in assuming I'm here so you can show me that you're a real person who bleeds when pricked?

LESTER: Look, you can go. I wish I . . . hadn't even called you.

MICHAEL: Really?

LESTER: Yeah, because . . . You know what? It's over. There hasn't been anything about me in *days,* thank Allah, and . . . this is going to *so* sound weird, Michael, but . . . some good even came out of it, you know?

MICHAEL: No. I don't.

LESTER: I've gotten a lot of stuff off my chest . . .

MICHAEL: Yeah?

LESTER: A *lot* of stuff. And people are being so *supportive* . . .

MICHAEL: "You really find out who your *friends* are, don't you?"

LESTER: You *do,* you . . .

MICHAEL: "And, and, *and . . ."!* Advance word on your "movie" is *great!*

LESTER: *Is* it? I . . .

MICHAEL: You are being "touted," Lester.

LESTER: I . . .

MICHAEL: Your performance as Gilbert Feldstein? One word, Lester. One word: "Brave."

LESTER: No.

MICHAEL: *Yes.*

LESTER (*Pause*): I'm *sorry,* I should be offering you something. A beer? Some soup?

MICHAEL: Some soup.

LESTER (*Caught*): Oh. Really? I have . . . split pea. It's . . . with ham.

MICHAEL: "Mmmmmm, ham!"

LESTER: Okay. I'll just . . .

LESTER exits to kitchen.

LESTER'S VOICE: I just want to go on with my . . . *quietly* on with my *life,* you know?

MICHAEL: Oh, I know.

The phone rings.

LESTER'S VOICE: *Damn it! Christ!* For the love of . . . *Shit!* I just let the . . . Gosh damn . . .

The machine picks up.

LESTER'S VOICE (*Machine*): "Hi. This is 555-8097. Please leave a message at the . . . sound of the tone."

We hear the tone.

CHESTER'S VOICE: Hi, Lester. It's Cynthia. (*Laughing*) It's Chester! Hi! A voice from your checkered past! It was hellish getting your number. I want you to give me a call. And don't worry, I still don't love you at all. And, hey "The Battle Hymn of the Republic"? Sure, it's *effective* . . .

LESTER returns, giving MICHAEL his soup. MICHAEL starts eating.

Oh, my number is . . . (*Exaggerating his Ses to make a point*) Five-Five-Five-Sssssssssssix-Five-Sssssssssseven-Ssssssssssssix.) (*Laughing*) Okay? And look—I understand a lot of people are watching you right now. Watching you sleep, taking your pulse, looking at you. Don't look away, Lester. Not this time. Okay? Talk to me. 'Bye.

The machine turns off.

MICHAEL: Your *S*es are fine, by the way.

LESTER (*Pause*): Than*k*. You can go. After you have your soup.

MICHAEL (*Pause*): You are feeling pretty good about yourself, aren't you?

LESTER: Look . . .

MICHAEL: Hey, I *also* heard that your engagement to Festa Longo is . . .

LESTER: That's *my* business, please.

MICHAEL: How you use people is your business, but how I use people is up for discussion. I *know* what this is—I recognize the birth cries of a "weekend fag" when I hear them—and I will *not* allow what I did to be your "bridge" to a pragmatic, half-assed, lifelong "adjustment." You're just *renovating* your closet, aren't you? Expanding the square footage to better accommodate the private *parties* you'll be throwing in there. "Boys everywhere, not a man in sight." Steel reinforced doors, twelve-foot walls, barbed wire, plugged-up keyhole, so no one can see through, over, under, *in*." People are *dying* out *here*, Lester, I hate to ruin how fabulous you feel spread out by your *pool* . . .

LESTER: I *know* what's going on. I . . .

MICHAEL: What's "going on," Lester, is "ongoing" because of terrified little shits like you who hide what they are in order to fully partake of the benefits of a society that, should it know what you really are, would have nothing for you but *contempt*.

LESTER: *SO, DON'T TELL THEM! DON'T TELL THEM, MICHAEL! CHRIST!* I didn't know if I'd ever work again, if I'd have a home anymore, if I'd ever get away from them, from *everyone, always looking at me!* I used to have some idea what they were seeing—I used to be *responsible* for what they saw —but you really fucked with that, Michael, and *who the hell are you? (Pause)* You want to know who *I* am? Okay. Here it is. I'm *pretty*. I'm *pretty,* Michael. I'm pretty, I'm lucky, I go where I'm told and my favorite color is *blue*. I don't rock the boat, Michael. I'm not even *in* the boat!

MICHAEL: *The troops are advancing, Lester.* And who's going to stop them when most of *our* troops are Piss-ass little fucks like you hiding away in designer bomb shelters waiting for it all to pass? It's not going to *pass,* Lester. And it's *us.* It's our *fault.* You and me. Our "people." No one has any idea who we are. *We* have no idea who we are! We *choose* invisibility. And then we get all surprised when our cries for justice are met with institutional apathy—when there's no response to our muffled voices. And we have no *right*. We're *theoretical,* Lester. And it's breaking me. All of *you*. All the gays and dykes and fags and lesbians and homosexuals and queers I carry on my *back*—and I am sick to *death* of standing in for you—for your theoretical ass. You're *winning,* Lester. There's *more* of you. And I'm sick of it.

LESTER: You might not believe it, Michael, but I'm sick of it, too.

MICHAEL: Not sick enough. (*Pause*) You aren't important, Lester. You don't matter. Your survival—your economic, career, emotional survival . . . Every year has its casualties. (*Pause*) Good soup. (*Pause*) On top of everything else—no, in the *middle,* maybe, of everything else—it would be so amazing to have a . . . God-*damn* movie star. Just one. I know there are plenty of gay movie stars—*plenty*—I'm just tired of waiting until they die and their biographies come out to find out who the fuck they *are*. I want one *now*. One totally cute movie star we *know* is gay because he *told* us. Because he and his boyfriend, the . . . fucking Republican Congressman, are planning a June wedding.

LESTER: Wow . . .

MICHAEL: Of course, he would ultimately *leave* the congressman, tired of life on the Hill, and move in with *me*.

LESTER: I might have something to say about that.

MICHAEL: But we could go to see our movie star—Oh, let's call him "Mel"—and we could go see Mel in his latest stupid car-chase-on-another-planet movie, and Mel would be . . .

LESTER: On a *stakeout*. With *cold coffee*.

MICHAEL (*Pause*): Okay . . . And Mel would turn to his partner . . .

LESTER: Tom.

MICHAEL (*Slight pause*): Tom . . . And Mel would say: "You know, Dylan . . ." "Dylan" is the name of Tom's character. That okay with you, Lester?

LESTER: Absolutely.

MICHAEL: And Mel would say: "You know, Dylan—we have a lot in common, even aside from our homosexuality, and you have the dreamiest blue eyes." And Mel would kiss Tom and they'd renovate a carriage house together in Vermont. They'd . . . dance off together into the sunset like Fred and Ginger. Fred and . . . Doug.

LESTER: "Fred and *Doug*"? Yikes!

MICHAEL: And we could go home after that moronic, wonderful movie—*"Yikes"?*—and we could go home after that movie and fantasize about Mel and Tom without having to come up with some elaborate, fraternity "Gee, if only I could get him drunk" scenario. I want an uncomplicated fantasy, Lester—in the middle, maybe, of everything else. (*Pause*) What do *you* want, Lester?

LESTER: I want to go to the movies.

MICHAEL: Have you ever been in love?

LESTER: Yes. Once. Ago. He—*he*—watched me when I slept. He put his hand . . . here . . . to make sure I was still breathing. And I think I am. Again. With a very . . . with *another* . . . kind man. He's a . . . dancer.

MICHAEL: Way to go. (*Pause*) What *I* want—*all* I want, Lester—is a hero.

LESTER: Me, too. (*Pause*) *Me?* Come on, Michael. I don't even think I have the potential. But there are heroic people . . .

MICHAEL: No one cares about the real heroes, Lester. I'm not even sure *I* do. We care, for some reason, about *you*. About *cute* people. (*Pause*) Let me interview you again. Come clean with me. I'll just ask the questions and, against my better journalistic integrity, I'll print your actual responses word for word.

LESTER (*Long pause*): I'm not the one.

MICHAEL (*Long pause*): Oh, well. Thanks for the soup. (*Pause*) I hope that when you're finally sick enough of hiding you won't be too sick to do anything about it.

LESTER: Do I deserve that, Michael? Is that fair?

MICHAEL: Fuck fair.

MICHAEL exits. LESTER stands a minute, lost. The phone rings. The machine picks up.

LESTER'S VOICE: "Hi. Thiſ *is* 555-8097. Pleaſe leave a meſſage at the . . . ſound of the tone."

We hear the tone.

GORDON'S VOICE: "Hi, it's Gordon. Bummer, you're not there. And, hey, give yourself a break with those *S's,* fella. And, what, are you marching off to *war?* Did I say it was Gordon? Gordon Fuente? Damn, I wish you were there. Well . . . you have my number. And I have yours, so . . . Come on. Do the next step, Lester, okay? 'Bye."

The machine turns off. LESTER stands, staring at the phone. This holds. He goes and picks up FESTA's ashtray and MICHAEL's bowl of soup. He looks at them, puts them down, paces, then picks them up again, unsure of the next step. Then we hear, loudly, the bombastic showbiz theme song to a television awards show accompanied by applause. Lights change as LESTER exits. GILDA LILY and ROCKO POOL, dressed to the nines, enter and step up to a Plexiglas podium. They are both wearing many colored ribbons.

As the music and applause fades we hear voices chanting, "We're gay, hey-hey, and we'll never go away!"

ROCKO: We're back!
GILDA: I'm Gilda Lily.
ROCKO: And I'm Rocko Pool.
GILDA: And right now we're waiting for those homosexual protesters who are holding signs and chanting annoying things that rhyme to be dragged from the hall.

We hear a scuffle as the chanting dies off.

Better. On to the next award. The nominees for Best Actress In A Made For Cable Movie Based On An Idea Stolen From A Recently Successful Hollywood Film are . . .
ROCKO: Tammy Robbins for *Fatal Desire—The Victimization of Emily.*
GILDA: Hester Burton for *Fatal Infatuation—The Victimization of Amy.*
ROCKO: Paula Todson for *Fatal Preoccupation—The Victimization of Debbie.*
GILDA: And Jane Valley for *Fatal Error—The Victimization of* Jim.

ROCKO opens the envelope.

ROCKO: And the winner is . . . Paula Todson for *Fatal Preoccupation—The Victimization of Debbie!*

Applause, music. PAULA comes onstage. She kisses ROCKO and GILDA and takes the award.

PAULA: This is such a shock! I didn't think *my* victimization had a sufficient number of crying scenes and bruises. I'd like to thank Corbin Tottles, who directed every film in this category—and most of all, I want to thank Doris Blodky—the "Debbie" of the title—whose strength and courage in fighting her way back from a time-consuming series of exploratory gynecological procedures was the inspiration for this very self-important film. Doris! This is for me!

Applause. PAULA *exits.* GILDA *and* ROCKO *return to the podium.*

GILDA: I loved that movie.
ROCKO: Missed it.
GILDA: The nominees for Best Actor In A Made For Cable Movie Based On An Idea *Not* Stolen From A Recently Successful Hollywood Film are . . .
ROCKO: Jeb Harris for *You're Dead—The Elmer Billings Story.*
GILDA: Satchel Bennet for *You're Fatal—The Phillip Oster Story.*
ROCKO: Lester Perry for *You're Out—The Gilbert Feldstein Story.*
GILDA: And Joshua Parker for *I Don't Get It Either—The Steve Guttenburg Story.*

GILDA *opens the envelope.*

And the winner is . . . I'd just like to take this opportunity to express my concern for the homeless . . . Lester Perry for *You're Out—The Gilbert Feldstein Story!*

Applause. The orchestra plays tango music. LESTER *comes on-stage in his tuxedo. He kisses* GILDA, *shakes* ROCKO*'s hand and takes the award.*

LESTER: Oh, *no,* I'm . . . I'm really . . . "Yikes"! Uh . . . I'd like to thank our director, Corbin Tottles. Uh . . . Gelb Waxman, who wrote a . . . script. I'd like to thank Cody Willow for . . . something . . . *man.* Thanks also to my stand-in, Kevin Flanders, a wonderful actor I sent out to do the things I . . . didn't. Couldn't. And Skip Oomahtah who played the catcher I kissed. Kevin kissed. I want, also, to thank my Mom and Dad who are really . . . amazing all of a sudden. And, uh . . . Festa Longo. Festa, I hope you're watching this because so much has been, *is* . . . I just . . . As a result of . . . looking at . . . I . . . (*Pause, looking at the award*) I wonder why you're really giving me this.

The orchestra starts playing LESTER*'s exit music.*

Oh, and Gordon Fuente! He taught me . . . (*Hearing the music, looking down at the conductor*) Was that eleven seconds *already?* Wow. Okay, uh . . . 'bye! Thank you!

LESTER *starts to exit, then returns to the podium.*

But, just let me—please—thank Gordon. Gordon Fuente. He . . . taught me the steps. Gordo? *Gordon?*

The orchestra stops playing.

I know you're here—I avoided you in the lobby—and I just want to say thank you, and . . . I'm trying to do the next step, but . . . it's hard when there's no one to *follow!* (*Pause*) Everyone is *so* looking at me.

ROCKO *makes his way to the podium, taking* LESTER*'s arm.*

ROCKO: Lester Perry, Ladies and Gentlemen!

The orchestra plays, the audience sort of applauds.

LESTER: I'm fine. Just let me . . . Step *back,* man.

ROCKO *backs off, "fake laughing," and exits with* GILDA*. The orchestra stops playing. In the silence,* LESTER *feels all eyes on him.*

And Michael. Michael, who wrote the . . . I can't believe I'm thanking *him,* but . . .

The orchestra starts playing.

(*Looking down*) SHUT UP!

The orchestra stops playing. LESTER *stands a moment,* looking away, *breathing. Then, suddenly, he relaxes. He looks back.*

I'm gay. (*Pause*) "Hey-hey." (*Trying out different ways of saying it*) *I'm* gay. I'm *gay*. Even gay is kind of hard and I'm gay you *oh*. (*Laughing*) No, I'm gay, I'm gay. God, is *that* all I am? (*Pause*) Is that *all* I am? (*Pause*) I think I've always known that I have very little in common with the person who's been living my life. His favorite color is blue. My favorite color . . . I have no idea what my favorite color is! Or what kind of *music* I like. What I'm attracted to in a person. What I find *funny*. Wait, I'm sorry, I *know* what I find attractive in a person, that is *so* not a problem, at *all,* "Hi, Gordon," but . . . I wonder what I'll *say* now? What *else* I'll say? I wonder what my voice will sound like now that I've taken my name back from that person who looked just enough like me to fool everyone. Even me. (*Leaning into the microphone*)

My name . . . is Mrs. Norman Maine. (*Laughing hysterically, then collecting himself*)

I'm not sure what's going to happen now. This may be the last you hear of me, the last you see of me, I don't know. But, I do know one thing. (*Pause—smiling*) From now on . . . I do all my own kissing.

LESTER *smiles. This holds. Then, softly, we hear a tango. A rich, vibrant, triumphant tango. It gets louder . . . louder . . . as the lights narrow to just a spot on* LESTER. *The music reaches full, celebratory volume. The light focuses now on just* LESTER'*s face. We see his beaming, jubilant and, yes, heroic smile. The music blasts its last jubilant note as lights bump to . . .*

Blackout

The music is over. The dance, needless to say, is not.

LONELY PLANET

Steven Dietz

This play was written for, and is dedicated to,
Michael Winters and Larry Ballard.

LONELY PLANET received its premiere at Northlight Theatre (Russell Vandenbroucke, Artistic Director), in Evanston, Illinois, on January 20, 1993. It was directed by Steven Dietz; the set design was by James Dardenne; the costume design was by Gayland Spalding; the lighting design was by Rita Pietraszek; the sound design was by David Zerlin and the stage manager was Patty Lyons. The cast was as follows:

JODY . . . . William Brown
CARL . . . . Phil Ridarelli

LONELY PLANET was produced by A Contemporary Theatre (Jeff Steitzer, Artistic Director) in Seattle, Washington, on July 8, 1993. It was directed by Steven Dietz; the set design was by Scott Weldin; the costume design was by Carolyn Keim; the lighting design was by Rick Paulsen; the dramaturg was Steven E. Alter and the stage manager was Craig Weindling. The cast was as follows:

JODY . . . . Michael Winters
CARL . . . . Laurence Ballard

LONELY PLANET was produced by The Barrow Group (Seth Barrish, Artistic Director), in New York City, in February 1994. This production was subsequently produced by Circle Repertory Company, in New York City, in June of 1995. It was directed by Leonard

Foglia; the set design was by Michael McGarty; the costume design was by Markas Henry; the lighting design was by Howard Werner; the sound design was by One Dream and the stage manager was Deborah Heimann. The cast was as follows:

JODY . . . . Mark Shannon
CARL . . . . Denis O'Hare

Acknowledgments

The author wishes to thank Kevin Kling, Jim Stowell, the Playwrights' Center in Minneapolis and Susan Booth for their contributions to the development of this play.

And, a special note of gratitude for TXT, who gave me my first Peters Projection Map—and thereby made this play possible.

Author's note

The following was written for the original production of the play at Northlight Theatre, Evanston, Illinois.

LEAVING SOME TRACES

> To hope for better times must not be a feeling,
> but an *action* in the present.
>
> —*Vincent Van Gogh*

My parents taught me that an act of kindness is its own reward. That took a while to sink in. Over time, I have begun to appreciate the depth of their wisdom. I thought of this recently while doing research for a new play I'm writing about Joyce Cheeka, a young Squaxon Indian girl growing up in the Pacific Northwest in the twenties. One phrase from the teachings of her elders keeps coming up again and again: *be useful.*

In the midst of a world that is too big and too fast, a world where information rules like a dictator and news travels like a virus, it is easy to be overcome by the hopelessness of the world and the helplessness of we, its keepers. What impact can we hope to have? What traces will we leave behind?

History, I believe, is not the story of grand acts and masterpieces. History, instead, is the inexorable accumulation of tiny events—footsteps and glances, hands in soil, broken promises, bursts of laughter, weapons and wounds, hands touching hair, the art of conversation, the rage of loss. Historians may focus on the famous, familiar names—but history itself is made, day after day, by all those whose names are never known, all those who never made a proclamation or held an office, all those who were handed a place on earth and quietly made a life out of it.

So, what do we affect during our lifetime? What, ultimately, is our legacy? I believe, in most cases, our legacy is our friends. We write our history onto them, and they walk with us through our days like time capsules, filled with our mutual past, the fragments of our hearts and minds. Our friends get our uncensored questions and our yet-to-be-reasoned opinions. Our friends grant us the chance to make our grand, embarrassing, contradictory pronouncements about the world. They get the very best, and are stuck with the absolute worst, we have to offer. Our friends get our rough drafts. Over time, they both open our eyes and break our hearts.

Emerson wrote "Make yourself necessary to someone." In a chaotic world, friendship is the most elegant, the most lasting way to be *useful*. We are, each of us, a living testament to our friends' compassion and tolerance, humor and wisdom, patience and grit. Friendship, not technology, is the only thing capable of showing us the enormity of the world.

> For the world is not to be narrowed till it will go into the understanding (which has been done hitherto), but the understanding is to be expanded and opened till it can take in the image of the world.
>
> —FRANCIS BACON

Welcome to Jody's Maps. We're glad you're here.

STEVEN DIETZ
December 1992
Evanston, Illinois

We will leave some traces, for we are people and not cities.
—Ionesco, *The Chairs*

Characters

JODY, a man in his forties.
CARL, a man in his early thirties.

Time

The present.

Place

Jody's Maps, a small map store on the oldest street in an American city.

~

ACT I

SCENE I

In a shaft of light we see a simple, wooden chair. Nothing else. JODY *stands, looking at the chair for a long time. Then, he looks at the audience.*

JODY: One day I saw a chair here. I had no idea where it had come from. I looked at it. I sat in it. (*He sits, pause.*) A chair. Nothing else. (*Lights expand to reveal the store: Jody's Maps. There are numerous maps on the walls, globes on pedestals, travel books in wooden cases, rolled-up maps poking out of bins. A small counter with an old, vintage cash register. A map table with drawers. A watercooler. A front door which contains several small windowpanes. Featured *prominently is a huge photo of planet Earth as seen from space. Morning. A sign hanging in the window tells customers that the store is "Closed."* CARL *enters, quickly. He stops and stands in the center of the room.*)

CARL: Can I just say this? Can I just say this one thing?

JODY: Certainly.

CARL: Everyone is boring. How did this happen? *When* did this happen? At some imperceptible moment everyone became absolutely shuffle-your-feet, stare-out-the-window *boring.* I try, okay? I do my part. I strike things up. I toss out words to grease the conversation. But these people, these people at the bus or the market or the newsstand, these people bore me. Not just a little. They bore me a lot. I'm sure they all came from good families, but over time they've lost what small part of them was ever of interest to anyone. They are even sort of hard to *see.*

JODY: Carl?

CARL: Yes?

JODY: Where did this chair come from?

CARL: I know. I've read the books. I can imagine people in their underwear. That helps, for a while. Then their underwear starts to bore me. So, I imagine them without their underwear, and then their embarrassment bores me. So, I imagine them in my underwear and that's moderately exciting, until they roll over, drop ashes on my pillow and say "I heard this joke at the cash machine today. You're gonna love it. It'll kill you." And they're right. It does. The yawn begins in my groin and stops at their eyes. I watch shadows fill the room like a cancer.

JODY: Carl—

CARL: So, finally, I try to imagine these people as someone else and soon *that* person bores me, and I imagine that person as someone else and *they* bore me, and so on and so on until I've imagined them all into something so small and distant and insignificant that there is nothing left but me standing alone at the bus, alone at the market, alone at the newsstand—reading an article about the tidal wave of boredom that is sweeping the nation. And, naturally, the article bores me. All I'm saying is this: Don't step out your door in the morning until you've thought of something interesting to say.

JODY: Carl, let me ask you something—

CARL: Not now, Jody. I've got things to do. (*CARL exits. Silence. JODY rises from the chair and moves to the counter. He presses a key on the old cash register and the cash drawer opens. From the drawer he takes a wrapped toothpick. Closes the drawer. Unwraps the toothpick. Stands in his shop. Stares at the huge photo of planet Earth. Picks at his teeth with pleasure. It's a lovely, quiet morning. CARL enters, calmly.*) I'm much better now. Thanks. Any good dreams?

JODY: Not now, Carl.

CARL: Your sign says you're closed. Are you closed?

JODY: No, Carl. I'm open. (*JODY moves to the sign in the door.*)

CARL: You should turn in. You should adjust it to reflect accuracy. This is twice now, Jody. This is twice I've noticed this. (*JODY turns the sign to read "Open."*)

JODY: There.

CARL: You asked about the chair.

JODY: I did.

CARL: A good chair, isn't it? A strong chair.

JODY: I don't need a chair, Carl. This shop is getting too small as it is.

CARL: A person could sit in it.

JODY: You know me, Carl. I am perpetually fighting clutter.

CARL: A person could peruse a map. A person could plan a trip, an adventure—

JODY: Carl?

CARL: Yes.

JODY: We need to play our game.

CARL: What game is that, Jody?

JODY: Our game, Carl. The game we play.

CARL: Names of child stars who were miserable in later life?

JODY: No.

CARL: A different game?

JODY: Yes.

CARL: Oh. (*Silence.*)

JODY: Well? (*Silence.*)

CARL: The game where we tell the truth.

JODY: Yes.

CARL: Okay. (*Silence.*)

JODY: Well? (*Silence.*)

CARL: Jody?

JODY: What?

CARL: I can't play our game, yet. I'd prefer to lie a little longer.

JODY: That's your choice, Carl.

CARL: I got the chair at an auction.

JODY: Did you?

CARL: Yes. I did very well. I got it for a song.

JODY: That's wonderful.

CARL: Yes. You should have come with. You'd have loved it.

JODY: Maybe next time.

CARL: You need to get out more.

JODY: So you've told me. Anything else?

CARL: Actually, I found it. Stroke of luck. I was walking to the newsstand—and there it was, abandoned, just lying in the alley. So, now it's mine, Jody—ours.

JODY: I see.

CARL: A good chair, isn't it?

JODY: Yes.

CARL: Did you sit in it?

JODY: Yes, I did.

CARL: Good.

JODY: Anything else?

CARL: Any good dreams?

JODY: Carl.

CARL: What?

JODY: Anything *else?* (*Silence.*)

CARL: No, I think that's all for now. (*JODY stares at him.*)

JODY: OK. (*CARL sits and watches JODY, expectantly.*) I am a fireman. (*CARL smiles.*) Well, not really. What happened was I had bought this fireman's shirt—dark blue, you know, with the patch, the real McCoy—I had bought this shirt at a second hand store—some childhood dream come home to roost, something, who knows, but anyway—now I'm wearing it. I am walking down the street, wearing my fireman's shirt, and a tragedy strikes. I'm not sure what the tragedy is, actually. The dream never lets me see the actual tragedy. What I do see, though, is all these people rushing up to me for help. They need me to do CPR. They need me to dash into burning buildings. They need me to climb ladders and haul babies out of smoke. And I keep saying: "Look, it's just a *shirt*. I bought it secondhand. You've got the wrong person." But they are relentless. They demand I help them. They won't take no for an answer. And I just keep saying: "You've got the wrong person. I'm not a fireman. I own a map store. I don't have any of the skills that you—" (*Stops.*)

CARL: What?

JODY: I just remembered something.

CARL: What?

JODY: You are there.

CARL: I am?

JODY: Yes. And I say: "Tell them, Carl. Tell them I'm not a fireman. Tell them I can't save them."

CARL: And what do I do?

JODY: You hand me a ladder and say: "Jody, don't let us down."

CARL: I was kidding, Jody. I was just—

JODY: No one is kidding in dreams. No one is just casually chatting.

CARL: So, what do you do?

JODY: I climb the ladder toward the fire, my ax in my hand. I hear their screams in my ears. I feel the heat on my face. (*Pause.*) Then, I wake up.

CARL: Thank God.

JODY: You were no help, Carl.

CARL: I'm sorry.

JODY: And I don't need a chair.

CARL: Fine. I'll take it home with me.

JODY: Good.

CARL: What time is it?

JODY: Nine-fifteen.

CARL: Oh, my God. (*Rushes to the door.*) I'm late, Jody. I had an eight-thirty meeting and I totally—oh, God. I'll see you, Jody. I'll call you later— (*CARL is gone. JODY, unfazed, goes to the watercooler. Draws a paper cup of water. He stands in his shop, drinking water and watching the door. He looks at his watch, smiles. Then, he moves to the door and opens it—just as CARL reenters.*)

JODY: Hello, Carl.

CARL: Jody.

JODY: Meeting go well?

CARL: I was lying, Jody.

JODY: I know that.

CARL: I wanted to dash out and leave the chair behind.

JODY: I know that.

CARL: But I've rethought things.

JODY: You have? (*CARL sets the chair down in front of JODY.*)

CARL: Happy Birthday, Jody! (*Hugs him.*) You're a great friend and though it's hard to shop for the man who has everything, I saw this—(*Indicates the chair.*)—and, well—

JODY: Thank you, Carl.

CARL: So, you'll take it?

JODY: Yes.

CARL: You'll take the chair?

JODY: Yes.

CARL: It's not really your birthday, is it?

JODY: No, Carl.

CARL: Thank God, I don't have a thing to give you.

JODY: I'll take the chair, Carl.

CARL: Great.

JODY: Are you happy now?

CARL: I'm happy, take my picture.

JODY (*Takes chair.*): I'm going to Goodwill tomorrow. I'll take it with me. Someone will put it to good use.

CARL (*Grabs chair back from Jody.*): Actually, truth be told, I bought it for my apartment.

JODY: You live in a shoe box, Carl. You've got no room for—

CARL: I'm knocking out a wall. This chair will be stunning. It will be the missing link in my—you know—my decorating—

JODY: Your decorating what?

CARL: My—

JODY: Yes?

CARL: *Scheme.* My decorating *scheme.*

JODY: Can we play our game now, Carl?

CARL (*Sharp.*) I don't want it taken to Goodwill. I've got to go. (*CARL picks up the chair.*)

JODY: Where are you going?

CARL: I HAVE PLANTS TO WATER. Have a good day, Jody. Hope business picks up.

JODY: Carl—

CARL: 'Bye. (*CARL leaves, taking the chair with him. JODY stares at the door for a moment, then turns and talks to the audience.*)

JODY: This is the way things go with Carl. I've probably known him as long as anyone. He was one of my first customers here. Browsed for two hours and then went home with the Caribbean. Since then, he's been a fixture. Depending on which day you ask him, what Carl does for a living is either water plants for corporations, work as an art restorer at the museum, run an auto glass shop, write for a disreputable tabloid, or work as a bartender. He has the energy of eight and the patience of none. You can never pin him down. Carl is a constant reminder of what I love about maps: they are *fixed objects.* They have been called "surrogates of space." They attempt to make order and reduce our reliance on hypotheses. They are a picture of what's known. (*CARL tiptoes in, still carrying the chair.*)

CARL: Am I interrupting?

JODY: No.

CARL: Bobby's dead, Jody. (*Pause.*) The memorial is Thursday. (*CARL walks into the room and sets the chair down. He looks up at JODY.*) Jody.

JODY (*Soft.*) What?

CARL: Don't let us down.

SCENE 2

Noon. The store is "Open." Three dozen chairs of all varieties have been placed around the room. For a long while, we stare at the room. Then, we hear voices.

VOICE OF CARL (*From behind the map table.*): I AM THE BASTARD SON OF RICHARD NIXON, AND I SHALL RULE THE WORLD!

VOICE OF JODY (*From behind the counter.*): ADVANCE THEN, IF YOU DARE! (*JODY and CARL leap up from their hiding places and scream: AAAHHH! They race toward each other at the center of the room. They each hold long, rolled-up maps wrapped in plastic—and they are in the midst of a playfully vicious duel, using their maps as swords. The following lines happen during the fighting.*)

JODY: Your lies have gone too far, they have jeopardized our fair kingdom, and it is the will of the citizenry that you must die!

CARL: I bow not to your authority. I hear not your cries. History shall be my judge and jury! I recognize only the Opinion Polls of the Most High.

JODY: Renounce it all, oh foundling son of a most derelict tape-worm! You must this day renounce it all!

CARL: Never, I say! Never!

JODY: You must renounce your rutting father and his rotting legacy!

CARL: 'Tis a hero of whom you speak! Father Dick is a man of destiny, and 'tis I will fan the fire and fervor of his famous flame forever! (*A standoff.*)

JODY: Fie, then, bastard boy. Prepare to meet thy maker.

CARL: And at whose hand shall this appeasement be enacted?

JODY: Why by my very hand, and this noble— (*Checks the end of the map/sword.*) Australian weapon of death!

CARL: The gods laugh at thy piteous, pixiesh posturing. (*CARL spits.*

JODY spits back. CARL spits. JODY spits back.) For 'tis I, knave, who hold the weapon which shall open thy torso and send thy wretched soul to hell's gaping maw.

JODY: And pray, what weapon is that, sir?

CARL (*Under his breath.*): Just a second. (*He, too, reads the label on the end of his map/sword.*) Aha!

JODY: What, sir? Do tell thy weapon's name. (*Pause, then CARL holds the map/sword high, triumphantly.*)

CARL: CHINA! (*More dueling. Ad-libs. Some swords/maps may be dropped, and others picked up from the bins in the store. Finally, JODY is without a sword and is lying back over the counter. CARL is ready to finish him off. Under his breath.*) Beg for mercy.

JODY (*Also under his breath.*): What?

CARL (*Under his breath.*): Beg for *mercy.*

JODY (*Full voice.*): I beg of you, sir, MERCY.

CARL: Beg not to me, quivering cur. Beg thy pagan gods to speed thy fate. (*Lifts map/sword high over his head.*) Let history note whom here was smote:

> T'was the rightful heir of Dick Nixon
> who did thy unworthy banner of flesh unfurl,
> and with one great longitudinal thrust
> did send thee from this world—

As CARL begins his final thrust, the phone rings.) Shit. (*JODY hands the phone to CARL.*) For thee.

CARL: What news?

JODY: I know not.

CARL (*Into phone.*): Yes? (*JODY crosses the room to get a drink of water. He also picks up some of the strewn maps. CARL turns upstage with the phone, so we do not hear his conversation. After a moment, he hangs up the phone and heads for the door.*)

JODY: What is it, Carl?

CARL: I'm wanted at the museum. There is art to be restored.

JODY: I see. (*CARL gets to the door.*) What kind of art?

CARL (*Stops.*) Pardon?

JODY: What kind of art, Carl? What kind of art is in need of restoring today? (*Silence.*)

CARL: Umm . . .

JODY: Yes?

CARL: *Old* art. Some very . . . old art needs restoring today.

JODY: Which art, Carl? American, European, African? The Gauguin, the Rauschenberg, the Hopper? What kind of—

CARL: The Hopper. It's the Hopper, Jody.

JODY: Which Hopper?

CARL: The one of his mother.

JODY: That's not Hopper, Carl.

CARL: No, of course not. The other one. The one, we've seen it together, Jody, the one with the clown and the general and the worker and the society couple. And the lanterns.

JODY: "Soir Bleu."

CARL: Yes, you see. And the woman with the cheeks, the rouged cheeks, red like meat, standing behind them all, looking down on them. "Soir Bleu."

JODY: Blue Night.

CARL: Yes.

JODY: And it is being restored?

CARL: Most definitely.

JODY: I see. (*CARL starts off again.*) What is being done?

CARL (*Stops.*) The clown is, his, uh, face is falling. It is falling, sinking down into his costume. His white face. We must lift it up.

JODY: Lift it up?

CARL: Yes. And the woman, she is, uh, cracking. Her, uh, red cheeks are cracking and there is, uh, another woman, another woman behind her who is peeking through—and we can't have this, Jody, it would be wrong, it would be criminal, to allow this other woman, this *painted-over woman* to get back into the picture. We must keep her out. She does not belong.

JODY: Who is this other woman?

CARL: We don't know her name, Jody. We don't know everything.

JODY: How do you know she doesn't belong?

CARL: Because she is *behind the paint*. She is trying to butt in, trying to crash the painting because she is the one with the answer to the riddle.

JODY: What riddle?

CARL: The riddle of the painting. Who are these people, why are they gathered? Who is the woman, who is she there to see, to whom is she about to speak?

JODY: And the woman behind the painting knows these things?

CARL: This and more. She's clever, Jody. She sleeps with her eyes open and always knows where you're parked. We must cover her back up. She must not give the answers.

JODY: Why, Carl?

CARL: Because, the painting *is* the questions. That's what it *is*. Without that, it's just cloth that's giving a frame a job.

JODY: I see.

CARL: I hoped you would.

JODY: You're not going to restore art, are you, Carl?

CARL (*Direct.*): No.

JODY: You're on your way to get more chairs.

CARL: Three of them. *(Silence. JODY stands. During the following he takes a few chairs which are in the middle of the room—and adds them to stacks in the corners of the room.)* Is it still all right for me to store them here, Jody? This is the largest room I know of. You know I'd keep them at my place, you know that—but it's so tiny and there's, well, there's just no—(*Pause.*) Are they in the way, Jody?

JODY: *Yes.*

CARL: Be honest with me.

JODY: More honest than yes?

CARL: I don't think you—

JODY: They are *terribly* in the way. They block aisles. Customers trip over them. The first few were fine, Carl, they really were, but this is too much now. They are horribly, disastrously IN THE WAY. (*Pause.*) Is that clear?

CARL: Yes.

JODY: Good.

CARL: I'm glad we can be direct.

JODY: *Get rid of them, Carl. (Silence.* CARL *turns and looks at the chairs. Then, he turns back to* JODY.)

CARL: I'd known Bobby since I was five. It was the first day of kindergarten and I was playing on the swings before the first bell rang. A kid I'd never seen before walked up and started swinging right next to me. When the bell rang, we stopped swinging and started for the door. He grabbed the hood of my coat and said "What's your name?" I said Carl. He said "I'm Bobby." I said hi. He said "You want to be best friends?" I said okay. Then we went inside and became best friends for twenty-five years.

I think everything good is attained through simplicity. I think that's why when you're all fucked up they say you have a complex. (*Silence.* CARL *goes to the door. Opens it.*)

JODY: I'll see you tomorrow, Carl.

CARL: You will. (CARL *leaves,* JODY *goes to the closed door and stares out the glass. Then, he pulls the shade closed. He locks the door. He turns the sign from "Open" to "Closed." He turns to the audience. As* JODY *speaks, the lights in the room gradually shift from noon . . . to dusk . . . to night.*)

JODY: Any talk of maps ultimately comes around to one very specific, lingering issue: The Greenland Problem. (*He indicates a large Mercator Projection World Map on the wall.*)

Now, you may not know this, but Greenland is actually about the size of Mexico. However, on the well-known Mercator projection map—the one hanging in front of your classrooms in grade school—Greenland appears to be roughly the size of South America and twice the size of China. Clearly a world power to be reckoned with, if it were, you know, habitable.

The Mercator map also shows most of the earth's landmass to be in what we consider the "north," when, in fact, the "south" is more than double the size of the north. Scandinavia seems to dwarf India, though India is three times as large. And the old Soviet states appear to be twice the size of the entire African continent. In reality they are smaller. Smaller by, oh, about four million square miles.

A map maker takes a messy round world and puts it neat and flat on the wall in front of you. And to do this, a mapmaker must decide which distortions, which faulty perceptions he can live with—to achieve a map which suits his purposes. He must commit to viewing it from only one angle.

The Mercator map, developed in Germany in 1569, was a great aid to navigators since, for the first time, all lines of longitude ran perpendicular to the equator—or straight up to the top of the map—rather than converging toward the poles. This meant that all the lines of longitude and latitude intersected at right angles—and this meant that, for the *first time,* a sailor could draw a straight line between two fixed points on the map and steer a constant course between them. The map had accounted for the curve of the earth—the sailor did not have to.

To accomplish this, Mercator had to accept a distortion: the parallel lines of latitude would have to be spaced progressively further apart as they moved away from the equator. This, in turn, would progressively distort the sizes and shapes of landmasses—from zero distortion at the equator, to absolute distortion at the poles . . . the Greenland Problem.

Mercator was a brilliant man. He freed the art of cartography from superstition, from the weight of medieval misconceptions. And his map revolutionized global navigation. He never intended it as a tool to teach the sizes and shapes of countries. He never intended to make Greenland a global behemoth. (*He points at Mercator map.*)

But, nearly four hundred and fifty years after Mercator, we still think the earth looks like this. It doesn't. It never has. But we've come to accept the distortion as fact. We've learned to see the world from this angle.

I like this map. I sell this map. I don't warn people when

they buy it that, like any good newspaper, it contains a few lies. And I've grown accustomed, when I feel the tug of a perplexed child on my sleeve, to turn and patiently say: "No, it's not really that big."

Maybe it's comforting to us because we, too, have our blind spots. We, too, have things on the periphery of our lives that we distort—in order to best focus on the things in front of us. In order to best navigate through our days.

Sometimes, though, these things on the periphery, these things that we do not understand, these *faraway* things grow to massive proportions—threatening to dwarf our tiny, ordered, known world. And when they get big enough, we are forced to see them for what they are.

People I know are dying.

This is my Greenland Problem. (*It is now dark outside. Someone tries to open the front door and discovers it is locked. Another try. Then, knocking. A pause. Then, more knocking, pounding. And still more.* JODY *stands in the room, motionless. Knocking and pounding continues. Finally, silence.* JODY *takes a deep breath. Closes his eyes. He moves to a switch and turns off the lights in the room. He sits. Silence. Phone rings.* JODY *keeps his eyes closed. Phone keeps ringing. Finally,* JODY *relents. He goes to the phone and answers it.*)

Jody's Maps. (*Silence.* JODY *brings the phone away from his head and stares at it. Then he hangs it up and walks to the front door. He opens the door.* CARL *stands in the doorway, holding a cordless phone to his ear. Next to him is a chair he has brought.*) What is it, Carl?

CARL: Do you know what time it is, Jody?

JODY: It's seven forty-five.

CARL: Are you closing early?

JODY: Am I—no, I'm—Carl, what do you—

CARL: It's Friday night.

JODY: I know that.

CARL: You're open till nine on Fridays.

JODY: I know that, Carl.

CARL: The sign says "Closed." The door is locked. The lights are off. (*JODY abruptly turns the sign around, and turns on the lights in the room.*)

JODY: There. (*CARL hands JODY his daily mail. JODY grabs it from him, goes to the cash register, opens it, and looks for a way to stay busy. CARL brings the chair into the room, takes off his coat, looks around.*)

CARL: Did you have a good day?

JODY: Mm-hmm.

CARL: People are buying maps. That's good. They're still interested in things. What's water and what's land. Things like that. (*Silence. JODY keeps busy at the register. CARL walks up and stares at the Mercator map.*) Hey, Jody. I have a question.

JODY: No. It's not really that big. (*Silence.*)

CARL: It looks bigger than South America.

JODY: It's not.

CARL: Too bad. Think if it was. Think of all the coffee they could produce. (*JODY just stares at him. Carl grabs a travel map from a display case. He sits in the most recent chair, peruses his map. Silence. Finally, JODY relents and talks to him.*)

JODY: And how about you?

CARL: Me?

JODY: How was your day?

CARL: I don't want to disturb you, Jody. You do your work. I'm contemplating Chad.

JODY: You're not disturbing me. I'm just finishing up. How was your day?

CARL: Really?

JODY: Yes. (*Silence.*)

CARL: Well, things at the paper are crazy.

JODY (*After a moment.*): Really?

CARL: Yes. Just *crazy*. No one understands, Jody. They really don't. There are all these so-called "reputable" journalists who walk around bitching and moaning how hard it is to cover the news. How *taxing* it is to look around and put into inverted pyramid form something that happened. I should be so lucky, Jody.

Do you think I can get away with just typing up stuff that happened? Please. When you write for a tabloid, you have to *create* the news. And believe me, *that* is taxing.

Many's the day I wished I could walk out my door, see a little fire across the street, go to work and type it up: "A little fire happened yesterday across the street." How sweet, how simple. But that little fire is not a story at my paper unless an elderly woman with a foreign accent was washing dishes, and she looks down at the white plate she is scrubbing, and there, there on the white plate she is holding is the face of Jesus, Jesus himself, all beatific and covered with suds—and the face of Jesus speaks to her. The face of Jesus says: "Drop. The. Plate." And the woman is frozen with fear. And again, Jesus says: "Drop. The. Plate." And the woman speaks. The woman says: "It's part of a *set*." Jesus stands firm. "If you want to be with me in heaven, you will drop. The. Plate." The woman is shaking with fear. She tries to explain that it was a wedding gift some forty years ago from an uncle who suffered from polio and died a pauper—but Jesus doesn't give an inch. It's as though he's gone back and read the Old Testament. "I'll give you one more chance," he says, "then I'll have the fire of hell consume your soul." The woman, tears streaming down her face, tries to quickly submerge him under the soapy water—but the water is gone. The sink is gone. Only the plate, and the face, remain. She stares at him, trembling. He says: "Well?" She has a realization. This is not Jesus. This is not her Lord and Savior. This is an *impostor*. This is the spirit of Satan entering the world through her dishware. She looks the plate squarely in the face and says: "I renounce you."

Within seconds, she's toast. So is the building.

The firemen do not find the slightest trace of her. But there, in the midst of the smoking rubble, the dinner plate shines white and pristine. And burned into it forever is the image of the woman's final, hideous expression. The last face she made before she became a china pattern.

My paper can run a story like that. (*JODY stares in disbelief. CARL returns to his tavel map.*)

JODY: Carl?

CARL: Yes?

JODY: How do you figure this story gets to the reporter?

CARL: What do you mean?

JODY: I mean, she was alone in the room, and now she's dead. So, who witnessed this? Who reported it?

CARL: Her goldfish.

JODY: Her—

CARL: Jody, make an *effort*. Her goldfish survived the fire and channeled the woman's voice into my tape recorder.

JODY: I see.

CARL: News is hard, Jody. (*Closes his map.*) So, what's the verdict?

JODY: Hmm?

CARL: How'd you do today? Make any money?

JODY: Well, I wouldn't say it was—

CARL: There was no money in the drawer, Jody. I saw that.

JODY: It was slow.

CARL: Did you close up again?

JODY: Carl, this is none of your—

CARL: I'm just asking. I'm just wondering if you *forgot* to keep the shop open. If you forgot to sell things to people today. This is your livelihood, Jody. This is what pays off your plastic.

JODY: I was out today. I took some time off. I went out.

CARL: Where?

JODY: *Where?*

CARL: Yes, where?

JODY: Where, like there are places I shouldn't have gone? Where, like I need your okay before I go?

CARL: Name one place. Name one thing you did.

JODY: No.

CARL: Fine.

JODY: Carl—

CARL: No. That's fine. Let's change the subject. Let's talk about Chad.

JODY: I don't have to tell you where I go, Carl. and I don't have to make things up about my day like you do.

CARL: I don't make things up.

JODY: You don't.

CARL: No. I lie.

JODY: There's a difference?

CARL: There certainly is.

JODY: Do tell.

CARL: If I made it up, that would imply that I wished I was doing it. That I wished I wrote for a tabloid, or restored art or worked at the auto glass shop, or all the rest of it. But I don't wish to do those things.

JODY: Then why do you tell me you do?

CARL: You have to get out, Jody. You weren't out today. I know. Because *I* was out. I was out there driving a rented truck around this neighborhood, packing things, opening and closing doors, going in and out, Jody.

JODY: That's enough. Let's just—

CARL: I was in people's homes today, Jody. I was walking through rooms. This is our *neighborhood*, Jody. You can't hide from it. You can't just—

JODY: Carl—

CARL: You can't just *deny* it.

JODY: I'm going home, Carl. It's been a long day. I'll see you tomorrow. (*CARL does not move.*) You can go ahead. I've got to close up.

CARL: I'll wait.

JODY: You don't have to.

CARL: I'll wait.

JODY: I'll talk to you tomorrow, Carl. (*CARL goes to the door and throws it open.*)

CARL: I'm waiting for you to leave. I want to watch you walk out this door.

JODY: For God's sake— (*JODY is putting his mail and a few other items in a small shoulder bag.*)

CARL: I want to see you go home.

JODY: Don't push this, Carl. I'm warning you.

CARL: You certainly are. You've been warning me for some time, but I've been slow to see it. Ordering in food. The sofa in the back room. Seldom a change of clothes. You've been warning me all right. (*JODY grabs his coat, and his shoulder bag. He moves toward the door, then stops, staring at CARL.*)

JODY: You're in my way. (*CARL backs away from the door and stares at JODY.*)

CARL: Go ahead. (*Pause.*) There's nothing in your way. (*Longer pause.*) Why don't you go?

JODY: I want you to leave, Carl. (*Silence. Standoff. Then, CARL leaves. JODY stares at the open door for a moment, then moves to the water-cooler. He begins to fill a cup with water, as—CARL bursts back through the door, carrying several chairs. JODY startled, drops the cup of water.*)

CARL (*Moving, talking in a flurry.*): This is fine, Jody. If you won't go out, I'll bring things to you. I'll let you see what you're missing—(*And CARL is out the door again. JODY stares at the chairs. He starts after CARL, but stops.*)

JODY: Carl. CARL. I DON'T WANT ANY MORE OF YOUR CHAIRS. (*Pause.*) DO YOU HEAR ME? (*CARL is back in—hauling several more chairs, including a wooden rocking chair, with effort.*)

CARL: No, I don't hear you. I don't hear you at all—

JODY (*Overlapping.*): Carl—

CARL: What are you saying, Jody? I can't understand a word you're saying—(*He sets one of the chairs at JODY's feet—and is gone.*)

JODY: GODDAMMIT, Carl—(*JODY picks up one of the chairs, in frustration—as though he were about to hurl it across the room—phone rings. JODY is frozen. He drops the chair. He looks at the ringing phone. He moves to the door and begins to slam it shut, but—CARL arrives before he gets the door fully shut. CARL is dragging eight or ten chairs that have been lashed together with rope. He hauls them to the center of the room.*)

CARL: Phone's ringing, Jody. Someone wants to talk to you—

JODY (*Overlapping.*): Enough, Carl. Enough of this game of yours. I don't care if you—

CARL: What game is that, Jody? I'm playing no *game* here. I went out and got these things— (*And* CARL *is gone,* JODY *calls after him, stumbling over chairs on his way to the door.*)

JODY: I'M LOCKING THIS DOOR, CARL. I DON'T WANT YOU HERE. DO YOU UNDERSTAND ME? I DON'T WANT YOU HERE. (*The phone is still ringing.* JODY *slams the door shut and locks it. Then, he stumbles over the pile of chairs toward the phone, and answers it.*) Jody's Maps. (*Pause.*) Who? (*A pane of glass in the door is smashed with a chair leg.*) NO, CARL IS NOT HERE. (JODY *slams down the phone, as* CARL *reaches through the shattered glass and unlocks the door. He throws open the door and brings in another chair.*)

CARL: That's about it for today, Jody. I'm sure there'll be more in a few days. Who was on the phone?

JODY: Get out of here.

CARL: Bobby's dead, Jody.

JODY: I don't give a *fuck* that Bobby's dead. Do you hear me, Carl? I don't give a fuck.

CARL: And José. And Michael. And Doug. And Anita—

JODY (*Overlapping.*): I know this—

CARL: And Vince and Jackie and Richard and—

JODY: I know this, Carl.

CARL: Do you? I've buried thirty people in six months, Jody. It's gotten to the point where I go to the memorial services to see who's still *alive.*

JODY: I said I KNOW THIS.

CARL: I don't think you do. I don't think you see any of it, anymore.

JODY: What do you want me to do? You want me to march up and down the street shouting MY FRIENDS ARE DYING AND LOOK HOW MUCH I CARE? That does *nothing*, Carl. Do you hear me? *Nothing.*

CARL: Jody, you don't—

JODY: THAT BRINGS *NO ONE* BACK. THAT CHANGES *NOTHING.*

CARL: It would change you.

JODY: *Carl?*

CARL: *What?*

JODY: Make someone else your mission. (*JODY slams the door shut. Long silence.*)

CARL (*Softer.*): Do you recognize these chairs?

JODY: Some of them. (*Silence.*) Not that rocker. (*Silence.*)

CARL: *Phillip. (Silence.)*

JODY: Phillip Carter?

CARL: Phillip Taylor. (*Silence. He touches the back of the last chair he brought in.*) This was Phillip Carter's. (*Silence. CARL sits in the chair and stares front as he speaks.*) I volunteer. I go help move these people—these people's things—out of their homes. And I can't stand the chairs. I can't stand all the empty chairs. Sitting alone in rooms. On the sidewalk outside. Or in the middle of a trimmed green lawn, waiting to be auctioned off to the highest bidder. All these chairs, draped with empty clothes.

JODY (*Soft.*): What does this *do*, Carl? Does it do something?

CARL: It does for me. This is the thing, Jody: I'm just trying to value my life enough to not throw it into traffic. In the midst of this fucking disease, I'm just trying to find the *worth* of me. And I've stopped trying to find it in grand acts, in major accomplishments. I'm looking for it now in every dish I wash. I'm looking for worth in the way I greet the mailman, the way I make a pot of tea, a letter I actually *write* instead of just *intend.*

Because I don't get much done, Jody. I really don't. I know people who get things done with their days. I admire and despise them. They put their heads on pillows at night and something in their life is actually *different* than it was when they woke up. Those people are mutants to me.

Me—I plan, I plod and I fall short. And if I shorten my plans, I fall still shorter. And if I widen my scope, if I take the long view of *the thing we are living in,* the enormity of it devours me. I see headlines that haunt and silence me. I hear people talk about some Famous Man or Unsuspecting Woman or Innocent Child who got sick—and *yes,* that is *tragic* . . .

. . . But this culture can't just *grieve that life*—they have to place it *above* the others. They have to remind us that *these* people did not deserve it. They didn't do anything *wrong*. They're just normal people. Unlike those *deviants* who got what they *deserved*—these people's death is *wrong*. This Neanderthal Puritanism *chokes at me*. It clouds my perspective, and it robs me of my irony. And I need my irony. These days it is standard equipment. It is the penicillin of modern thought. Without my irony, I am just bones that talk. I am just a marksman looking for a bell tower. (*Silence. Softer, now.*)

This is who I am now, Jody. These are my three A.M. thoughts. These are the things that make me spend all morning making the bed not just well, but *perfectly*. (*Long silence. Finally,* JODY *moves to the chair he dropped to the ground. He looks down at it. Lifts it. Holds it. Then, stands it upright in the room. After a moment, he walks slowly to the front door. He opens the door. He peers out.* CARL *turns and watches him.* JODY *stands motionless, looking out the door for a long time. Finally, he turns back to* CARL.)

JODY (*Standing in the doorway.*): I am a boxer. Well, not really a boxer. What happened is that I'd always liked those shorts, those Everlast shorts, and I saw a pair at a thrift store and I bought them. And one day I'm wearing them, and suddenly a cheering crowd of people is all around me, and they are walking me to this ring. This brightly lit ring.

CARL: In Las Vegas?

JODY: The dream didn't tell me. It didn't tell me where it was.

CARL: I love Las Vegas.

JODY: And I try to tell them that they have the wrong man, that I'm not really a boxer at all, I just happened to buy these shorts at—but they don't listen. I am their champion.

I'm sitting on a stool in the corner, and an old man is rubbing my shoulders and talking in my ear, and other people are putting mouthpieces in me and oil on my face. And I feel so . . . confident. I can't quite see my opponent across the ring, but I feel so sure, so cocky. The old man is telling me about my jabs, my footwork, my use of the ring. He's telling me about all of it and I am ready.

A bell rings.

I stand up and step forward.

And this is the thing: they will train you, they will teach you to hit, they will teach you to move—but they never tell you about the fear. Nothing the people in your corner can tell you will prepare you for the fear.

There is a huge man in that ring and he plans to omit you. (*Silence.*)

I look back to my corner and— (*Stops.*)

CARL: What? what happens?

JODY: I just remembered something.

CARL: What?

JODY: You are there.

CARL: I am?

JODY: Yes.

CARL: What do I do?

JODY: I ask you for water. I say: "Carl, please, I need some water."

CARL: And I give you some.

JODY: No.

CARL: Sorry.

JODY: You just shove me back into the center of the ring. I tell you I don't want to go, I try to leave the ring to get some water—but you have shoved me back into the center. I can feel my opponent's breath on my face as he circles me. And my arms are so heavy, I'm trying to lift them but they are solid lead, they are hanging at my sides, just *hanging there*—and I'm trying to lift them, lift them in front of my face, I'm trying to lift them to protect myself— (*JODY stops. He turns and looks outside the door. After a moment, he closes the door. He walks into the room and sits in a chair. He stares front. Silence. CARL stares at him, then looks over at the watercooler. CARL goes to the watercooler and fills a small cup with water. He brings the water to JODY. JODY takes the cup, without looking at CARL. Simply.*) The phone was for you, Carl.

CARL: Thank you.

JODY: Someone has more chairs. (*Silence.*)

CARL: I'll stop by tomorrow. (*CARL goes to he door. He turns the sign from "Open" to "Closed." He leaves, closing the door behind him. He reaches through the broken pane and locks the bolt from the inside. Then, he is gone. JODY stares front. He lifts the cup of water to his mouth and drinks. Lights fade to black.*)

(*end of act one*)

~

ACT II

SCENE I

The room is cluttered with chairs. Everywhere. In some places they are stacked to the ceiling. A few, small pathways provide access to the front door, the watercooler, the cash register. The broken windowpane has been boarded up. Morning. The store is "Closed." Jody sits in a large, old-time barber chair. A towel covers his neck and shoulders. He is half-reading a book. Carl stands behind JODY, giving him a haircut.

JODY: Umm—

CARL: It—it—it—

JODY: It was umm—umm—

CARL: It—it—it—

JODY: I'll never forget it—it was umm—

CARL (*Pointing to the tip of his tongue as he speaks.*): It's here—it's right here—I can almost taste it—

JODY: It was—umm—oh, for heaven's sake—it was—

CARL: Umm—

JODY: You remember, Carl—we all read it—

CARL: Mm-hmm—

JODY: We sat up late, all of us, night after night, talking about it—

CARL: Mm-hmm—

JODY: Arguing, debating its pros and cons—

CARL: Mm-hmm—

JODY: Each and every one of us read it—but I can't—

CARL: I can't either—

JODY: Was it—?

CARL: Hmm?

JODY: No.

CARL: Well—

JODY: Umm—

CARL: I can see the cover—

JODY: I can, too—

CARL: I am reading the cover—

JODY: I'm with you, Carl—

CARL: And the cover says—

JODY: It—it—it—

CARL: It's says, umm—

JODY: It's—it's—it's—

CARL: Gone.

JODY: Dammit.

CARL: Sorry, Jody.

JODY: *It was the book that changed our lives.*

CARL: Right.

JODY: But what was the *name* of it? (*Silence. CARL stops cutting JODY's hair. They both think.*)

CARL: Oh, well. (*CARL resumes cutting.*)

JODY: We remember the wrong things. We remember the combination to our high school gym locker, we forget the name of the woman who taught us to swim. We remember the capitals of states and forget our parent's birthdays. Our friend's middle names. I can recite the periodic table of the elements, but I don't remember the name of the café I was sitting in when I realized I'd fallen in love. (*Pause.*) Isn't that odd, Carl?

CARL: What kind of café was it? I can check the yellow pages—

JODY: No. I'm sure it's long gone. I just mean, shouldn't we remember those things?

CARL: Like the book that changed our lives?

JODY: Exactly.

CARL: It'll come to you, Jody. Be patient. (*Silence. The haircut continues.*) What are you reading now?

JODY: Ionesco. *The Chairs.* Do you know it?

CARL: Is that the one with the hippos in it?

JODY: No. An old man and woman fill a room with chairs, in expectation of an orator who they trust will "bequeath their message to the world," who will "radiate upon posterity the light of their minds."

CARL: Tall order. What happens?

JODY: Well, once the Orator arrives, the old man and woman throw themselves out the window and fall to their deaths.

CARL: That's tragic.

JODY: Yes.

CARL: But, at least they *get out,* Jody.

JODY: Don't start, Carl.

CARL: So, then what? What does the Orator say?

JODY: He mumbles incoherently. He says nothing.

CARL: And then?

JODY: It's over. (*Long silence. JODY closes the book. CARL clips hair.*)

CARL: Jody?

JODY: Hmm?

CARL: What happens to the chairs?

JODY: Carl, that's not the point.

CARL: Do you know, though? Do you know what happens to all of them?

JODY (*After a moment.*): No. I don't.

CARL: Maybe the Orator moves in and takes care of them. Maybe he turns the place into a museum and people come and—

JODY (*Firm.*): Carl. That is not what happens.

CARL: You don't know.

JODY: Yes, I do. It *ends*. That's what happens. It ends.

CARL: But those chairs *belong to someone.* Someone has to deal with them afterwards.

JODY: There is no afterwards. Nothing happens afterwards because it is over. It has ended.

JODY: But the Orator is STILL THERE. He didn't LEAVE. He didn't JUMP OUT THE WINDOW. HE'S STILL THERE. HE HAS NOT ENDED.

JODY: It's a STORY, Carl.

CARL (*Pause.*): I knew you'd say that. It's a story. It's not real. That's always how these arguments end. Ultimately, everyone falls back on fiction. (*JODY offers the book to CARL.*)

JODY: Here, Carl. Read it yourself. Maybe that will help. (*CARL takes the book. He hands JODY a hand-mirror.*)

CARL: Okay. You're done. You're ready for a night on the town. (*JODY checks out his haircut in the mirror as CARL removes the towel and puts the scissors away.*)

JODY: It's—

CARL: What?

JODY: Well, it's—

CARL: What?

JODY: It's *subtle*, Carl.

CARL: You know me.

JODY (*Looks in mirror, pause.*): Thank you. (*Silence. JODY continues to examine his hair in the mirror.*)

CARL: *What?*

JODY: I usually go down to Water Street. I usually have it cut down there. I'm just used to how they— (*CARL grabs the mirror away from JODY.*)

CARL: Go, then. (*Silence. CARL heads for the door.*) I'm turning the sign, Jody.

JODY: I'm not ready, Carl.

CARL: It's ten-thirty. You should be open.

JODY: It's a mess in here. I need to straighten. There's clutter. There's more than clutter. There's *bulk*.

CARL: All I want to do is turn the sign. It doesn't mean someone will come. Perhaps, today, there is not one person who needs a map.

JODY: Someone does, Carl. I'm certain.

CARL: Perhaps not today. I just want to turn the sign.

JODY: And if someone comes in, what then?

CARL: You'll say hello. You'll answer a question. You'll send them home with Scotland or Chad.

JODY: I don't know, Carl—

CARL: If it goes badly, if it's too hard, you can, well—

JODY: What? I can what?

CARL: You can throw yourself out the window.

JODY: There are chairs in the way.

CARL: I think you'll be fine. (*CARL goes to the sign, takes hold of it, turns back to JODY.*) Jody? (*JODY nods, reluctantly. CARL turns the sign to announce the store is "Open."*) There. (*JODY stands and goes to the cash register for a toothpick to gnaw on. CARL gets a small broom and dustpan—or an electric Dustbuster—from behind the counter.*)

JODY: Don't you have to work today, Carl?

CARL: I called the shop. They don't need me till later.

JODY: The shop?

CARL: The auto glass shop.

JODY: Oh.

CARL: It was a quiet night for thuggery. There is not much glass to be replaced. (*CARL is finished sweeping up the hair in a matter of seconds.*) There we go.

JODY: Not much hair, Carl.

CARL: I was selective. (*Phone rings.*) Tell them I'm on my way. (*CARL gets his coat as JODY answers the phone.*)

JODY (*Into phone.*): He's on his way. Yes. Good-bye. (*CARL starts for the door. JODY hangs up the phone.*) Carl—

CARL: I've got to go. (*CARL starts out the door.*)

JODY: What else have I forgotten, Carl?

CARL (*Stops.*): *What?*

JODY: I've forgotten the name of that book that changed our lives. I've forgotten the name of that café. What *else* have I forgotten? What else do I think I know that I really *don't?*

CARL (*Quickly.*): Ed's Café. Rita's Café. Old Timer's Café. Half Moon Café. Joe and Bob's Café—

JODY: No. Carl. Forget the café.

CARL: I never knew it. You're the one that—

JODY: We don't know our minds, Carl. We don't get a printout. Nothing in our minds warns us it's going. It just goes. And something else follows. And our last thought is left to turn out the lights.

CARL: LOOK, if you don't like your haircut, just SAY IT.

JODY: Close the door, Carl.

CARL: They're waiting for—

JODY: Please. (*Silence.* CARL *closes the door.*) You've been a good friend to me, Carl. Even when I've wanted to kill you. You're like the little brother I never wanted to have.

CARL: Thank you.

JODY: But, I don't *know you,* Carl. I don't really know you. When you go home to your apartment at night, and you close the door behind you—I have no idea what you do. (*Pause.*) What chair you sit in. What song you hum. (*Pause.*) I think about that a lot, Carl.

CARL (*After a moment.*): Well, the chair part is easy. I only have one chair. It's a classic 1950s kitchen chair, silver with a bright turquoise seat.

JODY: That was a figure of speech, Carl—

CARL: You've seen it, haven't you, Jody? You've seen my turquoise kitchen chair?

JODY: Yes.

CARL: It's a collector's item. The turquoise seat is actually—

JODY: Carl.

CARL: What?

JODY: We don't know people.

CARL: It's a mystery, Jody. Like people who knowingly buy jackets with fringe on them. It's an absolute mystery.

JODY: I'm talking about our friends. Who are really our friends? We don't know.

CARL: Do this: Pack up and move on two days' notice. See who helps you. *Those* are your friends.

JODY: You're missing the—

CARL: I answered this ad. It said: Are you interested in a cruelty-free relationship? (Well, I think, there's a first time for everything.) So, I make plans to meet this man at the park. We have agreed upon a time and a bench. Then, we have made plans to have a quiet cup of coffee. I go to the park. I like the park. I like to walk around the lake and look at the babies and dogs. I sit on the bench with my expectations. I am expecting a man who is just plain no-debate handsome. Someone who could pull off one of those black turtleneck *Hamlet*s. The man approaches. My expectations are nowhere in sight. He is one of those men who honestly believes he can iron his shirt by tucking it in. And his breath. It was not just bad, it was *ancient*. I'm telling you, Jody, something had crawled down in there and *died*. He didn't need mouthwash, he needed *archaeology*.

JODY: So, what happened?

CARL: Nothing happened. We didn't even get as far as the coffee. He bored me to tears for ten minutes and I left. I saw him a week later, and he avoided me like I was carrying a clipboard at an airport.

JODY: But, what is your *point?*

CARL: Yesterday that man took his car and mowed down twenty people at a sidewalk café. (*Pause.*) A reporter asked him why. (*Pause.*) He said: I just couldn't look at them anymore. (*Silence. JODY stares at him, still waiting for the point.*) Maybe it's better not to know. (*CARL starts for the door.*)

JODY: We trick ourselves. (*CARL stops.*) We add up our time with someone, we arrive at a number of hours or days or years, and we check that number against a chart on the wall. And the chart on the wall says: If you've spent X number of years with so-and-so, you must know them well. I no longer believe the chart on the wall.

CARL: Give me an example.

JODY: WHAT DO YOU DO FOR A LIVING? There's an example.

CARL: I've told you.

JODY: You've told me many things.

CARL: I do many things. (*Opens door.*) They're waiting for me, Jody—

JODY: You tell lies.

CARL: Yes.

JODY: You create occupations.

CARL: Yes.

JODY: Why?

CARL: For the same reason I create you, Jody, (*Pause.*) So, I have something to hold onto. I don't know what chair *you* sit in, Jody. I don't know what song *you* hum—though, I suspect it's something pretty dated and embarrassing—I don't know much about you, either, except that you love your store and your maps and lately you will not leave, you *will not go out there.* (*Pause.*) So, I create you. I create the part of you that does stuff while I'm not around. (*Pause.*) That's what people do, Jody. That's the closest they get to knowing each other. (*Silence.*)

JODY: Can we play our game, Carl?

CARL: The game where we tell the truth?

JODY: Yes.

CARL: Sure. (*JODY stands and approaches CARL.*)

JODY: I have to go out, Carl.

CARL (*Soft.*) I know.

JODY: I have to be tested. (*Silence.*)

CARL: You've been tested. (*Pause.*) Every six months for the past few years.

JODY: No. (*Pause.*) No.

CARL: You've told me you—

JODY: *No.* (*Silence.*)

CARL: I'll go with you.

JODY: Can you find someone who'll come here? Someone who'll come here and test me here?

JODY: I'll try, Jody. I'll make some calls.

JODY: Thank you. (*Phone rings.*)

CARL: Tell them I've left. Say I've left. (*CARL goes. JODY answers the phone.*)

JODY (*Into phone.*) Jody's Maps. (*Pause.*) Yes. He left. He'll be right there. (*JODY hangs up the phone. He looks around his shop. He *points to a spot on a large map or standing globe. He turns to the audience.*) When I was a teenager, I pumped gas in the middle of Montana. A little station alone in the Big Sky Country. Sign out front: "Next Gas, Two Hundred Miles." That's where I learned my geography. Folks'd pull up and say "How far is it to such-and-such? Can I make such-and-such by nightfall? And what about so-and-so—is that straight north of here?" At the end of every day I tried in vain to wash the diesel off my hands. And then I'd sit down with my father's atlas, open it up . . . and see how many lies I'd told people that day. (*Music begins softly: Intro and first verse of a song such as Bob Dylan's "I Shall Be Released," sung by Joe Cocker.*) I haven't forgotten that. (*Music builds.*)

SCENE II

More chairs. Evening. The store is "Closed."

JODY *sits in a chair, sewing a button onto a shirt. As he sews, he hums a song such as the Joe Cocker version of Bob Dylan's "I Shall Be Released."*

After a moment, a key opens the front door, and CARL *enters.* CARL *carries three chairs, a sack of food from the deli, and a small plastic bag.*

CARL: Ask me where I've been. Go on, just ask me.

JODY: Where've you been, Carl?

CARL: I've been out not smoking, not drinking and not getting laid. I've been out there watching my step and not doing anything, *anything* in the least bit reckless or spontaneous. I've been out there acting like I'm not out there. *God,* life is grand.

JODY: What's to eat?

CARL: Not dessert. Not sugar. Not caffeine. Not cholesterol. (*Opens the sack, lifts food out.*) It's . . . BLAND SOUP AND BREAD.

JODY: Again?

CARL: Yes, again. (CARL *removes a second container of soup from the sack, as well as two plastic spoons.*)

JODY: Makes me want to pour whiskey on a steak and smoke it.

CARL: Now, now, Jody. At this point in the century, we know better. We are no longer hunter-gatherers. We are browser-nibblers.

JODY: Did you get butter?

CARL: *Please,* Jody. (*CARL removes three large white candles from the plastic bag, sets them on a surface and lights them, during the following.*) You know what happened just before the dinosaurs went extinct?

JODY: No, Carl.

CARL: They changed diets. Think about it.

JODY: Is that true?

CARL: It's what I tell my students at the University. (*JODY stares at him. They settle down into two of the newest chairs and begin eating.*)

JODY: You asked them, Carl? You did?

CARL: I told you I did.

JODY: I want to be sure.

CARL: I spent all week on the phone with them. They don't make exceptions. I tried, Jody. But they won't come here and give you your test. You have to go there.

JODY: And the other places?

CARL: I called all of them. (*Stands.*) Here. I'll get the phone book. You can call them yourself.

JODY: Sit down, Carl. I believe you.

CARL: It's five blocks, Jody. It's a lovely walk. You'll like it. (*JODY stares at him.*) Okay. You'll hate it. Maybe you'll get hit by a car. Would that cheer you up?

JODY: Eat your soup. (*CARL sits and resumes eating.*)

CARL: They're good people. I've been there twice.

JODY: When were you there last?

CARL: About six months ago.

JODY: You're due to go again, aren't you?

JODY: As a precaution, yes.

JODY: Come with me.

CARL: No.

JODY: But you have to go, anyway.

CARL: I'm going next week. You're going on your own. Deal with it. (*Pause.*) They close at eight tonight.

JODY: I know.

CARL: I know you know. (*CARL stares at him.*)

JODY: I'm GOING, Carl. I'm GOING TONIGHT. Are you happy?

CARL: I'm happy, take my picture. (*Silence.*)

JODY: Did you work today?

CARL: I can't talk about it.

JODY: Why?

CARL: It's scandalous.

JODY: The tabloid?

CARL: No. The glass shop.

JODY (*After a moment.*): What can be scandalous about an auto glass shop? (*Silence.*)

CARL: Well. Okay. But what I'm about to say can't leave this room.

JODY: Don't worry.

CARL (*Pause.*): The man who runs the shop—I'll call him Mr. R—has been having some tough financial times. So . . . Mr. R enlists the help of his delinquent son—whom I'll call Tad. Tad, it seems, has been very, very bad. So . . . father and son strike a deal. Mr. R will refrain from sending Tad to a military academy, if Tad and his little delinquent friends will do Mr. R a favor. So, last night, Tad was bad. He and his little friends take a 3 A.M. joyride through several neighborhoods, smashing every car window they find. Before calling it a night, they sever the phone cables of the competing auto glass stores. The next day, Mr. R's business has grown twenty-fold.

JODY: How can they get away with that?

CARL: Mr. H.

JODY: Who?

CARL: The chief of police.

JODY: You're kidding.

CARL: You didn't hear it from me.

JODY: That's amazing, Carl.

CARL: I'm telling you, Jody, there's some heavy hitters working down at that shop. Guys with connections that'd curl your toes.

JODY: You sure can pick 'em.

CARL: There's a man installs windshields down there who used to be a *municipal worker* in Dallas.

JODY: So?

CARL: Jody, this guy *mowed the Grassy Knoll.* (*Pause.*) That's all I can say about it. (*CARL gathers up his empty food containers and throws them away. He watches JODY. JODY continues sewing the button on his shirt. He hums, as before.*) It's seven-thirty.

JODY: I know that.

CARL: You want help with your shirt?

JODY: No.

CARL: They close at eight.

JODY: I *know that*, Carl. (*Silence, JODY sews. CARL gathers up JODY's food container and throws it away.*) If I don't make it, I'll go tomorrow.

CARL: They're closed tomorrow.

JODY: Monday, then. (*Silence. CARL stares at him. JODY sews. CARL blows out the candles—and, after doing so, his eyes land on a large map on one of the walls. He stares at the map.*)

CARL: Weird. (*Pause.*) Weird.

JODY: What's that?

CARL: This map. (*Pause.*) Weird.

JODY: You've seen that before.

CARL: Not really. I never really noticed.

JODY: That's the Peter's Projection map. It's an equal area map.

CARL: A what?

JODY: It lets you accurately compare the sizes of all the countries.

CARL: But, the shapes are weird.

JODY: That's because the projection is—

CARL: It's like Salvador Dalí took some continents and melted them.

JODY: They're as accurate as the shapes on the Mercator map. You're just used to the other.

CARL: So, these are the real sizes?

JODY: Yes.

CARL: So, Chad is bigger than the entire American west coast?

JODY: Yes, it is.

CARL: Go, Chad.

JODY: And the equator is in the center of the map, instead of relegating the southern hemisphere to the bottom third.

CARL: I don't know, Jody.

JODY: What?

CARL: The people in Greenland must be pissed.

JODY: This map solves the Greenland problem. I envy them that.

JODY: Yeah. But, everything looks weird.

JODY: It's a trade-off, Carl. It bends your preconceptions to achieve accuracy.

CARL (*Directly to* JODY.) It tells us what we need to know.

JODY: Exactly. (*Silence. Then,* JODY *resumes sewing.*)

CARL: Jody?

JODY: Hmm?

CARL: You've been done sewing that button for a while. You can stop now. (JODY *looks at* CARL. *Then, he stops sewing. He bites the end of the thread. He holds the shirt, tightly.* CARL *moves very close to* JODY. *He looks at him. Silence. Carl reaches into his pocket and slowly pulls out a Mounds candy bar. He smiles.*)

JODY (*Smiles.*): Guilty pleasures.

CARL: The only kind worth having. (CARL *sits near* JODY. *Gives him half the Mounds bar, keeps the other half for himself.*) Cheers. (*They "toast" and then delicately bite into their candy. It is naughty and delicious. They moan with delight.*)

JODY: Oh.

CARL: Mm-hmm.

JODY: It is so . . . (*With delight.*) *bad for us.*

CARL: That's today's view. Tomorrow's research may reveal the opposite. Someday this may be part of a healthy, balanced diet.

JODY: God, I hope not. (*Takes a bite, savors it.*) I like it just the way it is. (*They eat.*)

CARL: I know you're scared, Jody. (*Silence.*) The not knowing is worse. Being left alone with your imagination is worse. (*Silence.*)

JODY: Nobody can just be "sick," anymore. Sometimes I can barely remember that "sick" used to mean you had a cold, or the flu. Now, you ask how someone is. You're told they're "sick." And you know exactly what that means. (*Long silence.*) Look at this place, Carl.

CARL (*Soft.*) I know.

JODY: It's obscene. And every minute you're hauling chairs in here, there are people out there making the world a safer place to live. They are out there fighting *language* that is obscene, *pictures* that are obscene, *movies* that are obscene. We should be so lucky. Imagine if our safety depended on protecting our children from *words,* from *ideas,* from *pictures of people's bodies.* Imagine if those things were our great plague. (*Pause.*) We should be so fucking lucky. (*Silence,* JODY *stands and puts the shirt on. After a moment, he stares at the front door, then stands, motionless.* CARL *fills the silence.*)

CARL: Hey, Jody.

JODY: Hmm?

CARL: What was that song?

JODY: Which?

CARL: The one you've been humming.

JODY (*Pause, smiles a bit.*): Mr. Dylan's "I Shall be Released," as interpreted by Mr. Joe Cocker. (*Pause.*) Everyone has one song that can never be turned up too loud. That's mine.

CARL: I never knew that. (JODY *gets his shoulder bag and coat.*) I guess I expected something more—

JODY: What?

CARL: I don't know. Something more . . . Sinatra-ey.

JODY: Carl. Please. (JODY *puts on his jacket, then stands, staring at the door. After a moment,* CARL *again fills the silence.*)

CARL: Hey, Jody?

JODY: Hmm?

CARL: Do you have a copy of it here?

JODY: No.

CARL: Not anywhere?

JODY: It's at home. (*JODY opens the door. He stands in the doorway, staring out, motionless. Again, after a long moment, CARL speaks.*)

CARL: Jody?

JODY (*Gently.*): Carl. You have to shut up, now.

CARL: I was going to get you some water. You want some? (*JODY looks at CARL, then nods. CARL gets two cups of water, brings one to JODY. They drink their water.*) I'll keep one eye on things, here. (*Pause.*) I've never run a map store before.

JODY: It was just a matter of time. (*They are standing under the huge photo of planet Earth. Jody looks up at it as he sips his water.*)

CARL: It'll be okay, Jody. (*Silence.*)

JODY: The astronauts of Apollo 17 took this photo. It's become the definitive image of our planet. They may have taken it with the intent of showing the grandeur, the enormity of the earth. But, they captured something else, instead. Humility. (*Quietly, reverently.*) From the Latin: *humus.* Meaning: earth. They captured a planet, small and alone, surrounded by enormous darkness. (*Silence. They sip their water.*)

CARL (*Soft.*): Hey, Jody.

JODY: Hmm?

CARL: You know what's great about us?

JODY (*Smiles.*): No, Carl. What's great about us?

CARL: We never fell in love. (*Pause.*) All these years, all that's happened. We never did.

JODY: No. We never did. (*Silence.*)

CARL: And I'm glad, you know, because the thing is, the thing about meeting people is this: lovers are easy, *friends* are hard. The right combination of small talk and clothing will land you a lover. Friends, though, are a mystery.

JODY: Jackets with fringe.

CARL: Exactly. (*Silence.*) Why do you think that is, Jody?

JODY: Hmm?

CARL: That we never fell in love.

JODY: You're a nuthead, Carl.

CARL: Yeah, but at least I'm not a map-geek. (*Silence. They smile. They sip water.*) Let's never do. No matter *what*. Okay?

JODY: Okay. (*Silence.*)

CARL: Do you have the address?

JODY: Yes. (*JODY throws away his paper cup, picks up his bag. Stops.*) Wait for me, Carl?

CARL: I'm not going anywhere. And when you're finished, we'll kick up our heels. We'll put on Joe Cocker, get drunk, tell lies and make promises we can't keep. It'll be *great*. (*Silence. JODY smiles.*)

JODY: I'll see you later, Carl.

CARL: You will. (*JODY leaves the store, closing the door behind him. CARL watches him go. Silence. Then, CARL goes to his coat and gets a stack of envelopes. He also gets some sheets of stamps. He sits in the room and begins to affix stamps to the numerous envelopes. As he does so, he begins talking to the audience. As CARL speaks, the lights in the room gradually shift from evening . . . to dawn . . . to morning.*)

Here's something I've thought about: Why aren't there stamps for the things you *don't* want to mail?

I have a stack of bills here. I am mailing them to organizations that have been badgering me, threatening me to give them their money or else. I've tried to reason with them, but although their commercials depict them as companies with big hearts—I have found them to have big hearts of *ice*. So, I succumb to their threats and prepare to mail them their blood money.

And now it's time for the stamp. And what kind of stamps do I attach to these things I don't want to mail? Little *flowers. Birds.* Cuddly animals and smiling poets. I attach stamps that say *love,* and *peace,* and *joy*.

This sends the wrong message.

I want stamps that say: HERE'S YOUR FUCKING MONEY, NOW SHUT UP. I want stamps with pictures of raw sewage and Mussolini. I want skull-and-crossbone stamps that have warnings from the Surgeon General. (He looks at one of the stamps he is about to affix.)

I've had it with giving flowers to the wrong people. (*He affixes the stamp. Stops. Silence.*)

A life is such a lot of paperwork. I do what I can. I try to keep the stacks of bills and claims and counterclaims from reaching mythic proportions. But, I fall short. (*He holds up the stack of envelopes.*)

None of these people had time to finish their paperwork.

Robert was too busy restoring art. The tabloid that Jeremy wrote for refused to pay his health costs. Eric watered the corporation's plants but couldn't get a loan from them. Bridget had her tenure denied by the University. And Frankin . . . Franklin just threw 'em all away. If it had a picture window, he threw it in the trash with all the other broken windows, then he cranked up his radio and installed another windshield.

They say fame is when a lot of people you've never met celebrate your death. None of these people were famous. Like most of the people taken by this disease, we in the general public murdered them twice. First, by romanticizing them. Glamorizing their grief. And, then by ignoring them.

My friend, Hank, worked for the police department. He dusted crime scenes for fingerprints. He loved his job (except for the paperwork, he said). And he was good at it.

When a cop is killed in the line of duty, the entire force turns out for the funeral. Speeches are made. The anger is channeled into ceremony.

When Hank died, there was no one. The "official" line was that since Hank did not die in the line of duty, a ceremony would not be appropriate. I called one of his co-workers and got the "unofficial" line: "If we'd gone, it'd look like we approved of what he *did*." (*He affixes the final stamp.*) The paperwork is all that's left. The unfinished business. (*The front door opens and* JODY *enters. He wears a fresh change of clothes.*)

JODY: Hello, Carl.

CARL: Hello, stranger.

JODY: You've forgotten the sign. (JODY *turns the sign to read "Open."*) It's nine o'clock, Carl. We're supposed to be open.

CARL: Sorry, Jody. I was catching up on paperwork.

JODY (*Smiles.*): I hope you didn't forget the sign all week.

CARL: No, I didn't. I didn't sell a lot of maps, though. Fewer people than I thought shared my interest in Chad. And people seemed to think the shop was sort of—

JODY: What?

CARL: Cluttered. I told them you'd be back today. I told them you'd taken the week off. (*Silence.*) How was it?

JODY: The test?

CARL: The week. Out there. (*Silence.*)

JODY: They drew the blood from my arm. And I left. And I walked home. (*Pause.*) The long way. (*Pause.*) Past everything that was familiar. Past everything that had a memory attached to it. I walked every day like that. And as I walked, I remembered.

CARL: The name of the book?

JODY: Not yet. But I'll get it. I had a week where I believed I could remember everything. (*Pause.*) I'm glad you made me go out, Carl. (*Silence.*)

CARL: When do you get your results?

JODY: Today.

CARL: In person?

JODY: No. I can call. (*Silence. Then,* CARL *puts his envelopes in his coat and prepares to leave.*)

CARL: Well, I'll let you get settled in here. Maybe you'll have better luck than me at selling those weird-shaped maps.

JODY: They're accurate, Carl. They tell us what we need to know. (CARL *stares at him.* JODY *walks to the counter and looks at the phone.* CARL *starts to leave, quietly.*) Carl. (CARL *stops.*) Stay with me. (CARL *tosses his coat on a chair.* JODY *takes a card out of his wallet, sits behind the counter, and is about to dial a number written on the card. He stops. Silence.*) How 'bout you? How was your week?

CARL: It was busy. There was a theft at the museum.

JODY: Did they take the Hopper?

CARL: The what?

JODY: The one you restored?

CARL: I have no idea, Jody. That's not my job. I go in, I dust for fingerprints, I run 'em through the computer. Prints talk, Jody. Prints talk and they never lie.

JODY: Imagine that. (*Silence.* JODY *looks at the card in front of him.*)

CARL: Hey. Did you rem—

JODY (*Smiles.*): Archie's. Archie's Café. It came to me last night. (*Silence.* JODY *dials a number written on the card.* CARL *has a seat.* JODY *speaks into the phone.*) Yes, I'm calling for my test results. (*Reads a number off the card.*) 1 5 7 2 2 dash 7 6 dash 8 3. (*An* extremely *long silence, as* JODY *waits for the results.*) Jody. (*Pause.*) Yes, I'll hold. (*Another* still longer *silence. Finally . . .*) Yes, I'm here. (*Pause, he waits, then says simply.*) Thank you. (*Pause, begins to hang up, stops.*) What? Oh, that was a question I had when I—you can disregard— (*Stops.*) I didn't know that. Thank you. (*He hangs up the phone.* CARL *stares at him.*) It's negative. (*Silence.*)

CARL (*Soft.*): It's negative.

JODY (*Also soft.*) Yes. (JODY *moves away from the counter, slowly. He looks around the room.* CARL *stands, watching him. Then* JODY *moves to* CARL. *They embrace. As they release each other,* JODY *says . . .*) And you know what else, Carl?

CARL (*Smiling.*): What?

JODY: If I need another test some day, and I'm unable to leave my home—they'll send someone here.

CARL: They *said* that?

JODY: You knew that, Carl.

CARL (*Pause.*): Yes. I knew that. (*Jody stands in the middle of the room.*) How does it feel? (*Silence.*)

JODY: I was talking to a man in the waiting room, before I went in. He was paging through a magazine, waiting for a friend who was being tested. This man told me he came to this city in 1980, planning to be wild and live out all the fantasies he'd harbored for so long. But, instead, right away, he met someone and fell in love. They were together for eight years. This man closed his magazine and looked up at me. "Falling in love," he said, "saved my life." (*Phone rings.* CARL *stares at* JODY, *then heads for the door.*)

CARL: Tell them I'm on my way. (*Music: "I Shall Be Released"—verse two.*)

SCENE 3

In a shaft of light we see a 1950s silver kitchen chair, with a turquoise seat. Nothing else.

JODY stands, looking at the chair for a long time. Then, he looks at the audience.

JODY: One night, a few months later, I saw a chair here. (*Pause.*) I looked at it. I sat in it. (*He sits, pause.*) A chair. Nothing else. (*Lights expand to reveal the store. Night. The store is "Open." The room remains cluttered with chairs. JODY sits in the chair, staring front, for a long time. Phone rings. He looks at the phone, then goes to it. He answers it.*) Yes? (*He looks at the front door. He sets the phone aside, goes quickly to the door, and opens it. CARL, wearing a long black coat, stands in the doorway, holding his cordless phone to his ear.*)

CARL: Your sign says you're open. Are you open?

JODY: Yes.

CARL: Can we talk, Jody?

JODY: Sure.

CARL: Can we talk on the phone?

JODY: On the—?

CARL: I wanted to call and talk to you on the phone, but I didn't want to be alone, so I came over. (*Silence. CARL gestures to JODY's phone. JODY stares at him, then goes to his phone and picks it up. Standing behind his counter, JODY speaks on his phone.*)

JODY: How's this?

CARL: Good. (*Pause.*) It's bright in here, Jody. Can I light these?

JODY: Sure. (*CARL lights the large white candles, which are just beneath the huge photo of planet Earth. Then, he turns off the lights in the room.*)

CARL: Good, yes?

JODY: Yes. (*In silence,* CARL *walks to the furthest corner of the room away from* JODY. *He crouches there, amid the stacks of chairs. From this point till noted at the end, the men speak only into their telephones.*) What did you want to talk about, Carl? (*Silence.*) What did you do today? Was there art to be restored, was there—

CARL: No. All the art's been restored, all the broken glass has been fixed. Things are in order, Jody. (*Silence. The room darkens.*) Did you find my chair, Jody?

JODY: I did.

CARL: It's a good chair, don't you think? Sturdy.

JODY: Yes.

CARL: A person could sit in it. A person could peruse a map. Plan a trip.

JODY: It's a good chair, Carl. (*Silence.*)

CARL: "We will leave some traces, for we are people and not cities."

JODY (*Smiles a bit.*) Ionesco. You read it.

CARL: I liked that line. (*Silence.*) Will you keep my chair, Jody?

JODY: I will.

CARL: That would make me happy.

JODY: Good.

CARL (*Soft.*) I'm happy, take my picture. (*Silence. The room darkens.*) Hey, Jody?

JODY: Yes?

CARL: Any good dreams? (*Silence.*)

JODY (*Not into the phone.*) Carl—

CARL: *Please*, Jody. (*Silence. The room darkens.* JODY *lifts the phone to his head and speaks.*)

JODY: I am . . . at a concert. Outdoors. And on the way to this concert, I've stopped at a thrift store and bought a big black turtleneck and a black leather jacket, and thick, black sunglasses.

CARL: Fringe, Jody?

JODY: On the jacket?

CARL: Yes.

JODY: No, Carl.

CARL: Good.

JODY: And I'm standing there, looking up at the moon, waiting for the band to come on—and suddenly a group of people is ushering me backstage. They're introducing me to the rest of my band, there are sound and light guys running around with headphones and cables—and I'm trying to tell them: I think you have the *wrong person.* This is not my band. I'm not a singer. I just bought these clothes at a thrift store and—the next thing I know, I'm at center stage. A spotlight hits me in the eyes. The band launches into the song.

CARL: What song, Jody?

JODY: My favorite song, Carl. And my band is looking at me and waiting for me to sing. I close my eyes. I hear the crowd screaming. I hear the music rumbling under me. I open my mouth . . . *and I am singing that song, Carl.* I am singing that song like Joe Cocker. I am doing Mr. Dylan proud. And the crowd is— (*Stops.*)

CARL: What?

JODY: I just remembered something.

CARL: What?

JODY: You are there.

CARL: I am?

JODY: Yes, you are. You are standing right next to me, Carl. You've been to the same thrift store.

CARL: Do I look okay?

JODY: You look great. And we are *singing*, Carl.

CARL: I'm singing, too?

JODY: The band is shaking the rafters behind us, the crowd is shouting and swaying. And we are together, Carl. We are together. And we are singing. (*Long silence.* CARL *puts his phone inside his coat. He sits, staring front. Jody hangs up his phone, quietly.*)

CARL: Jody?

JODY: Hmm?

CARL: Can I stay here tonight?

JODY: Of course you can.

CARL: Thanks. (*Silence. Music: The final verse and chorus of "I Shall Be Released" begins, very softly.* JODY *looks at* CARL. *Then, he stands, puts on his coat, and moves to the door. He turns the sign to read "Closed." He pulls the shade. He turns back to Carl, indicating the lit candles.)*

JODY: Carl?

CARL: Hmm?

JODY: Should I—

CARL: Yes. (*Music builds.* JODY *walks to the candles. He takes a long look at the photo of planet Earth. He blows out the candles.* JODY *opens the door, looks back at* CARL. *In the musical break prior to the final phrase of the song,* JODY *speaks.)*

JODY: I'll see you in the morning, Carl.

CARL: You will. (JODY *leaves, closing the door behind him. As the song ends, lights fade to black on* CARL.)

AT THE ROOT

A PLAY IN ONE ACT

Linda Eisenstein

AT THE ROOT was first presented by LEND International in its Celebrate Lesbian Plays! Festival at the Courtyard Theatre in New York City, in June, 1994. Director: Jean Parker.

WOMAN . . . . Jean Parker

Character:

WOMAN Late thirties. She wears jeans, a T-shirt with a witty feminist slogan, boots, one earring (or several nonmatching earrings), no makeup. Artsy-butch.

~

A WOMAN *in her late thirties sits with her finger in her mouth, absently circling her tongue as she carefully pronounces words.*

Lullaby . . . Language . . . Lover . . .

She looks up.

When the doctor first approached me and said there was a chance for him, a new experimental procedure, a transplant, and that I was the likely donor, my very first reaction was: Jesus Christ this is typical, how they always expect the mother to be the one to sacrifice—I can almost hear them revving up the Mother Machine, violins and all, and honey, no way, no how, not this time, not this gal, this is bullshit, his father's got one, too, take his. (*Pause.*) "But you see, Ms. Green," says the doctor—"we did a tissue typing." (*She nods, as though reacting, throughout the following.*) Ahhh. "Your ex-husband's doesn't match, his would be rejected." Ahhh. I see. "It's you or nobody." Ahhh. I see. And the next thought I had was: Fuck, no! You're on your own, kid . . . you'll just have to learn to live without one, you're not getting mine. I mean, c'mon, he wouldn't want it anyway, it's just too grotesque, too Freudian, neither of us wants to end up with our faces blazing across the cover of the *Enquirer:* "Boy wakes up with Mother's tongue in his mouth."

She shudders.

I mean, wouldn't he constantly be thinking about all the places it's been?

She slowly runs her index finger around the circumference of her tongue, in a circle. Throughout her speech, she will go back to this behavior many times, unconsciously.

Ever since then, I've been obsessed with it. My tongue. I can't stop touching it, playing with it. At night I find myself stroking it, I'm in a constant state of arousal. It feels . . . huge, huge and fleshy and wet and growing in my mouth, sometimes hard, sometimes velvety soft, liquid, languid, language, love, oh God, all the things I couldn't say or do or feel if it were gone. Do you know how many nerve endings there are in the tongue? As many as in the head of a penis. But the penis doesn't have tastebuds.

And you know how men sometimes give their penis its own name, almost like it's a separate person? I swear, sometimes my tongue is so completely . . . Other, it doesn't even feel like part of me. It has its own ideas: what it wants to say—what it wants to taste—where it wants to push its way into. You know how your mother used to say, "Your eyes are bigger than your stomach?" Wrong. All that hunger? (*Tapping the tip of her tongue*) It's right here.

That grotesque . . . request, that wasn't framed as a request, just as a theoretical "possibility": the obscene assumption, that thanks to new scientific breakthroughs, because I COULD give up my tongue to my child, my male child, I of course SHOULD—it's fucked up everyone I know. Everyone who hears it becomes infected in some way. My support group has completely gone to pieces, of course. People are enraged, upset, divided, struck at the very root. Oh, it's raised some very ugly questions. For instance: If it were my daughter who were losing her tongue to this hideous cancer, and not my son, would I, would they feel differently? Or here's another good one: to lose your tongue—you can call it reverse sexism if you want to, but think about it. To lose your tongue: doesn't it somehow seem like less of a loss for a man?

And yet. And yet . . . nowadays I have trouble swallowing. Our sex life is of course nil at this point. I can't even be kissed without immediately dissolving into sobs. Oh, Mara has been great, don't get me wrong. She's been incredibly loving and supportive—so far—but it's got to be wearing her down. She's been like a fortress, a bulwark, standing there between me and everyone else's flapping tongues, repeating that it's my decision, that I'll do what I have to, and everyone else should just butt out.

When I wake up, sometimes a dozen times a night, from my nightmares—and they're of epic proportions, they make Edvard Munch look like Disney—Mara holds me until I shudder back to sleep. And when I hole up in the other bedroom, as I do more frequently, she doesn't intrude. She knows, I'm sure, what I'm doing in there, my new . . . vice. (*Her finger encircles her tongue again.*) Yesterday I went to the hospital. Oh, yes, I go every day. I *am* his mother. Every day. Especially now. Ever since I said no, I've been particularly determined not to avoid him. It's been like a penance. Anyway.

He was in bed, groggy, propped up with pillows. The

operation was over, and his was gone, now, all but that little stump way in the back of the throat, the part they hadn't had to cut away, the part that still lets him swallow his food. I had brought him a book, and I was trying very hard not to cry, trying desperately hard not to explode, from all the guilt, and the anger, and the pain, and the fear of what I'd see in his eyes—and he looked up—and said, very carefully— (*Imitating, not using her tongue, as though it's gone.*)

"Hi, Ma"—ironic, isn't it, that those are words you can still form, even without a tongue, and the moment was so supremely goofy, like those athletes grinning and waving into the TV cameras before they pour onto the gladiatorial field—"Hi, Ma".

And I ran out of the room, my tongue heavy in my mouth, running down the corridors saying lullaby languid language love and I found the doctor and I said . . . could I . . . could we . . . maybe you wouldn't have to take it all? Maybe you could split it down the middle? Could there be enough for two, two small ones? And I tried to remember my biology, where were the tastebuds laid out, would one of us get the sweet and the other the bitter, or could we share that too? We shouldn't have to live with it one way or the other. . . .

And I could taste my tears and I thought . . . that it wouldn't be all bad, for my son's new tongue to taste some of the things I've tasted. Like a new Teresias, he could taste both woman, and man, lap up his new language, we'd both prophesy with our new tongues, thin and sharp as rapiers, and sing our songs, and lick our ice cream cones and our lovers' curves—languidly—split to the root. (*She traces again the circumference of her tongue.*)

My surgery's tomorrow. I keep having the weirdest thoughts. Will my new smaller tongue fit in better? Will it find its way into more places? Or will I still feel its original dimensions, like a phantom limb? Mara says I'll probably be able to talk twice as much, twice as fast. She's buying earplugs. (*She smiles, then begins to whisper words to herself while she slowly caresses and encircles the tip of her tongue again, as the lights go down.*)

BRAVE SMILES . . . ANOTHER LESBIAN TRAGEDY

The Five Lesbian Brothers
(Maureen Angelos, Babs Davy, Dominique Dibbell, Peg Healey, Lisa Kron)

BRAVE SMILES . . . ANOTHER LESBIAN TRAGEDY was first presented at the WOW Café in New York City in January 1992 under the direction of Kate Stafford. Sets and costumes were designed by Susan Young, lighting was by Joni Wong. The stage manager was Jimmy Eckerle.

Cast

MAUREEN ANGELOS . . . . . . Thalia, Martha, Reporter No. 1
BABS DAVY . . . . Millicent, Miss Gateau, parisienne maitre'd
DOMINIQUE DIBBELL . . . . . . Will, Frau von Pussenheimer, Reporter No. 2, Audrey
PEG HEALEY . . . . Babe, Miss Phillips, the wounded soldier, Shirley, The Bum
LISA KRON . . . . Damwell Maxwell & the Baroness
and introducing NIPPER as herself

Act I

The Tilue-Pussenheimer Academy, somewhere in Europe, *c.* 1920

—a brief intermission—

~

Act II

Scene 1—The Grand Ballroom of the Hôtel Goldene Gewölbe, Vienna, *c.* 1939
Scene 2—New York Harbor, *c.* 1943
Scene 3—the cockpit of the Grand Dame, a few weeks later
Scene 4—a gay parisienne nightclub, *c.* 1946
Scene 5—a Broadway theater, *c.* 1956
Scene 6—a mission on the Bowery, *c.* 1959
Scene 7—Sing Sing Prison, October 12, 1959, 7:12 A.M.
Scene 8—a book signing at Rizzoli in NYC, *c.* 1969
Scene 9—Southampton, later that day
Scene 10—Southampton, two years later.

> God help all children as they move into a time of life they do not understand and must struggle through with precepts they have picked from the garbage cans of older people, clinging with the passion of the lost to odds and ends that will mess them up for all time, or hating the trash so much they will waste their future on hatred.
>
> —*Lillian Hellman*
> Pentimento

Authors' Note

Comedy is tragedy speeded up. Somebody said it, not us, but we took it to heart. Having grown up amidst the dismal imagery of lesbian life in the seventies, we decided to accept our fate as doomed pathetic inverts with abnormal hypothalamuses, embrace the misery that was inevitably in store for us and write a play about it. *Brave Smiles . . . another lesbian tragedy* is the product of our busy beaver effort to shine the light of comedy into the dark corners of lesbian unhappiness and despair. With tongues firmly in cheeks, we marched through the canon of lesbian literature, film, myth, and image and took with us whatever caught our eyes, while at the same time giving voice to the reality of tragedy in our sometimes sad lives. It's not easy to be a dyke, but it can be awfully funny.

Brave Smiles was first produced at the WOW Café and the Brothers would like to thank first and foremost all of the WOW girls whose devotion and love of performance has made WOW the chaotic institution that brought us together under one roof and first produced this show. For their invaluable support on subsequent productions the Brothers would like to thank Downtown Art Company, One Dream, New York Theatre Workshop, Theatre Rhinoceros, DiverseWorks, Fresh Dish, Highways, Alice B. Theatre, Dr. Gail Freund, Amy Meadow, Diana Arecco, Jamie Leo, Billy Swindler and Tom Judson and the Brave Smiles Orchestra. A most extra-special thanks to Kate Stafford, Susan Young, and our manager, Sama Blackwell.

Brave Smiles is lovingly dedicated to our good friend, Jimmy Eckerle, the bravest smiler.

~

ACT I

SCENE 1—MIKE'S FUNERAL

Scene: The grounds of the Tilue-Pussenheimer Academy. Dawn. Lights fade up slowly. Millicent is at the head of Mike's grave, facing the audience. The five girls stand in a semicircle facing the audience, heads bowed. Martha wears all black.

MILLICENT: We offer up all our work this day to the memory of Mike, who fought so hard to survive despite the cruel blows of a hatchet wielded by Dick Moorehead, groundskeeper and a misguided heathen—

WILL: And a low-down dog!

MILLICENT: Yes, and unenlightened about the sanctity of all life and limb—

BABE: Especially the head.

MILLICENT: Yes, which is necessary for mammals if they are to conduct themselves in a spiritual way.

DAMWELL *starts to leave,* BABE *stops her. The girls all gasp and exclaim.*

DAMWELL: Sorry. I thought she was finished.

WILL: Go on, Millicent.

MILLICENT: So now we commend your soul, Mike, to heaven above or to that watery grave in the well from which you emerged.

BABE: Fear not, Mike, you will be reunited with your beloved head in the great beyond or below . . . we're not sure which.

WILL: Mike, you gave us many weeks of loyal service as pet of the school, mascot and general chum to all the girls.

MILLICENT: We'll keep you in our prayers. Please keep us in your prayers and put some good words in for us poor little orphan girls here at the Academy. We're not really that bad and we did try to put your head back on. We're sorry about it being separated from your beautiful domed body by Dick, but that's Dick. (*Girls assent.*) Would anyone else care to say a few words?

DAMWELL: Maybe Martha would like to say something.

WILL: Shut up, Damwell!

DAMWELL: What? Everyone knows Martha's a dummy.

WILL (*Shoves* DAMWELL.): She's a deaf-mute and brighter than you'll ever be!

MARTHA runs off. WILL chases her calling "Martha! Martha wait!"

DAMWELL: They make a perfect couple.

MILLICENT: Have you no feelings, Damwell? Really. At Mike's funeral . . .

DAMWELL: Mike is a turtle! And we're all sixteen and practically adults although no one would guess it from the way you carry on. Come on, Babe. (*BABE doesn't move.*) Babe! I'll see you later at play practice. (*DAMWELL exits. Will enters.*)

BABE: I—I just think I ought to say something.

WILL: Amen.

BABE: Yes. Amen. And, well, sorry about Damwell.

MILLICENT: Where's Martha?

WILL: In the root cellar. It's okay. She likes it there. That Damwell really galls me.

MILLICENT: Don't let her get to you, Will. Her sense of humor is her armor against cruelty and sadness in this world.

WILL: Yeah, that and the million dollars she inherited ought to give her pretty good protection.

MILLICENT: I believe that money won't be hers until she's twenty-one.

BABE: Damwell's okay. She doesn't mean to hurt anyone.

WILL: She doesn't try to get at you the way she does with me, Babe.

MILLICENT: Maybe Damwell likes you, Will. I mean really likes you.

WILL (*Spitting in the dirt.*): Curse the day! Take that spell away!

BABE: She said she liked me.

MILLICENT: I'm sure she does, Babe.

BABE: I'm late for kitchen duty. (*Runs off.*)

WILL *remains with* MILLICENT. *There is an awkward silence.*

MILLICENT: It's okay. Go to Martha. I don't mind being alone.

WILL *smiles. Kisses* MILLICENT *gently on the forehead. Runs off.*

MILLICENT: Dear God, wherever and whoever you are, please help Martha in all her sadness. Will is trying for her so hard. We all want so much to tranform people like they will see and understand that little, hard, green, lesson about life—that you have to accept and love yourself.

MILLICENT— TAKES OUT HER GUITAR AND SINGS. MISS PHILLIPS appears, smoking a Tiparillo, while MILLICENT *sings her song.*

MILLICENT: *Oh, a turtle dies*
and a young girl cries
and the world is changed forever.

When the death knell rings
Oh, the grief! It brings
both turtle and girl together

Turtles are free (2 times.)
Turtles are free

Oh, a turtle's life
Is a hard, hard life—

MISS PHILLIPS clears her throat.

Oh, Miss Phillips!

MISS PHILLIPS: Don't let me stop you. It's a lovely song.

MILLICENT: It's nothing compared to the poetry you read to us in class.

MISS PHILLIPS: One day you'll be as great as Sappho. But you must work at it. Here—(*Hands MILLICENT a napkin.*)—you missed your breakfast.

MILLICENT: Oh! I must get to breakfast. Frau von Pussenheimer will be—

MISS PHILLIPS: I explained to her that you weren't feeling well.

MILLICENT: But I'm—oh, Miss Phillips . . .

MISS PHILLIPS: Millicent, I need your help.

MILLICENT: Why . . . anything.

MISS PHILLIPS: There's a new girl arriving next week. I want you to be kind to her. She'll need a friend. And try to—well, I know you girls have rules about new girls but Thalia may be in for more difficulty than the rest of us, and it is our moral duty to help her.

MILLICENT: Thalia . . . I'll do what I can.

MISS PHILLIPS: Good. Eat your breakfast. And don't be late for your French lesson.

MISS PHILLIPS exits.

MILLICENT (*Opening the napkin.*): Oh, Miss Phillips! A sugar donut!

Blackout.

SCENE 2—PLAY PRACTICE

Scene: BABE *duels with* FRAU VON PUSSENHEIMER *while* DAMWELL *and* MILLICENT *look on.* PUSSENHEIMER *attacks ferociously until she has backed* BABE *into a corner and then flings the foil from* BABE*'s hand.* BABE*'s hand has been cut.*

FV.P: Nonsense. It's a slight flesh wound. I'm very disappointed in you, Babe. Romeo is supposed to win the fight.

DAMWELL: Yeah, Babe.

MILLICENT: Frau Von Pussenheimer, couldn't we just *act* like she wins the fight?

FV.P *wheels around to face* MILLICENT whipping her foil through the air

FV.P: Good stage fighting is essential to good theater!

DAMWELL: Shouldn't we practice the scene where I'm a snowy dove showing over crows? After all—isn't Will supposed to be in the fighting scene?

The girls gasp in unison at DAMWELL*'s faux pas.*

FV.P: Where is Wilhelmina?

The girls all sputter different explanations.

FV.P: Never mind. She'll be deal with later. Millicent—bring the gear to the equipment shed and return at once. No dilly-dallying under the trees. (FV.P *goes to* DAMWELL *and gets uncomfortably close.*) Now, Damwell. You wish to be a snowy dove trooping with crows, do you? Tell me, have you ever attempted a stage kiss?

DAMWELL: Actually . . . Babe and I have been practicing . . . every night . . . I think we . . .

FV.P: Don't be silly. You and Babe are merely girls. You have no idea how a man might kiss a woman. Whereas, I, although I remain an honest woman, have had some experience which might benefit you.

DAMWELL and BABE look ill at the prospect of kissing FV.P.

DAMWELL: Oh but . . . I doubt Romeo kisses anything like Professor Pye. (*BABE and DAMWELL gasp.*) Oh, Frau von Pussenheimer, I'm so sorry . . .

FV.P (*Smiling a crazy smile.*): It's quite all right girls. I suppose it's only natural you should talk of such things among yourselves. I have taken no offense. Although you'd be surprised at the professor's passion. Why, I must confess, it takes everything I have to resist Herr . . . Peter.

DAMWELL: His first name's Peter? What does he look . . .

FV.P (*Becoming quite unfriendly.*): That's enough of that. Soon you will know all of my secrets, and we can't have that, can we?

MILLICENT (*From offstage.*): Frau von Pussenheimer! Babe! Come quick. It's Thalia! The new girl!!

BABE runs off. FV.P indicates that she is to walk not run. Then she nods to DAMWELL to go as well. They meet MILLICENT as she enters with THALIA who is disheveled.

MILLICENT: I found her out by the river, near the shed.

FV.P: Well, her coat is certainly a mess.

THALIA: It's not my fault. I was attacked!

DAMWELL (*Thinking it's the coolest thing ever.*): Attacked?!

THALIA: Yes. I arrived in Schlongbahd on the 12:35 train from Vienna. I'm supposed to look for a Ludmilla von Pussenheimer at the Tilue-Pussenheimer Academy.

FV.P: Well, you've found us. (*FV.P approaches THALIA, the girls scatter.*) But we weren't expecting you until next week.

THALIA: My mother wanted me to leave sooner than planned—

BABE & MILLICENT: You have a mother!

DAMWELL: You were attacked!

THALIA: When no one met me at the train I set off to find you on my own. Just past the crossroads by the tall hedges—a band of wild boys jumped out at me.

DAMWELL: You were beaten up by a wild band of boys?

THALIA: They didn't beat me—exactly.

FV.P: What did happen. Exactly.

THALIA: Their leader said: "We just want to talk to you. You have such pretty black hair." They stood around me. They all laughed. That awful boy walked right up to me and said, "Are you afraid of boys?" "No," I said. "You're not afraid of us?" he asked again. "Why should I be? You're just boys."

MILLICENT: How brave . . .

THALIA: And then . . . then . . .

FV.P: What happened?

THALIA: Then he said: "Then you wouldn't mind if we tried to kiss you?" "Well," I said, I knew I shouldn't. But I didn't want them thinking I was afraid of them. "Then you'd let me kiss you?" And he did. But softly. Not like you would expect from such a rough boy. I began to cry. Then they pushed me into the mud and rubbed it in my hair. And they ran off laughing. They weren't boys. They weren't boys at all. They were horrible beasts!

FV.P: Filthy boys! No better than pigs!! Remember that, girls. Boys are pigs. Filthy and disgusting!

DAMWELL, BABE, & MILLICENT (*Reciting their lesson.*): Filthy, and disgusting!

FV.P (*Trying to soothe* THALIA.): There, there, girl. Damwell, bring Thalia to the dormer in the east wing. Babe, fetch Miss Gateau to tend to her there. (*They exit.*) Millicent, remain with me a moment.

MILLICENT: Yes, Frau von Pussenheimer?

FV.P: Chocolate, Millicent? (*Tempts her with a giant chocolate bar.*) How did you know that Thalia was to be a new student here?

MILLICENT: I don't know, Frau von Pussenheimer. I guess . . . I guess she must have told me so.

FV.P: I see. You found her facedown in a puddle and she told you her name was Thalia and she was to be a new student here?

MILLICENT: Yes. I'm sure now that she told me.

FV.P: Very well.

Awkward pause.

MILLICENT: Am I excused?

FV.P: Well now, Millicent, that is between you and your God, isn't it?

MILLICENT: Pardon?

FV.P: You see, Millicent, little girls who lie seldom become saints, they invariably end up burning in eternal hell. That will be all.

MILLICENT scurries out.

SCENE 3—DAMWELL & THALIA CROSS

Scene: Main Hall. DAMWELL is taking THALIA to her room.

DAMWELL: Well, there's a girl who moos at night. But hopefully you won't be put next to her.

THALIA: Such grand halls. Just like mother said. But, why are they so dark?

DAMWELL: Things aren't what they used to be. But you'll find that out soon enough. I'm sure if my mother had known what a hellhole this would turn into she never would have sent me here but . . . well . . . did you hear about the *Lusitania*?

SCENE 4—MISS GATEAU IN THE KITCHEN

Scene: Kitchen. MISS GATEAU *is cooking and sipping from a bottle of champagne.* FV.P *sneaks up behind her and whacks her on the butt with a wooden spoon.*

FV.P (*Playfully.*): I'm very mad at you, Miss Gateau. You made a soufflé and it fell. Bad, bad girl. (*Goes to whack her again.*)

MISS GATEAU: Forget it, Ludmilla. I'm not in the mood.

FV.P (*Not so playful anymore.*): What are you hiding from me? Sometimes I wonder if you are to be trusted—

MISS GATEAU: Me? Whatever—don't be silly!

FV.P: I am never silly, Colette. You would do well to remember that. You will come to see me in my room later tonight?

MISS GATEAU: Not tonight. I am busy.

FV.P: You are, teaching one of the students a French lesson?

MISS GATEAU: No.

FV.P: Then you are, perhaps, washing your hair?

MISS GATEAU: No.

FV.P: You're going to see Dick.

MISS GATEAU: Yes. Yes, I am. What of it?

FV.P: Tell me, this Dick—he is a tender lover to you?

MISS GATEAU: He is my beau!

FV.P: I am your beau! I am your beau! And your doctor! And your mother! And your father!

MISS GATEAU: I am someone else's daughter, Ludmilla. I have a mother already. See? (*She shows her locket.*) You cannot possess me like you possess the girls. I am a woman. I am not so naive and fresh for the picking as a herd of fifteen-year-olds! If I wish to have a beau, I'll have a beau. Besides, it's for the best.

FV.P: That thing. That killer of turtles! He is not your lover. Your diversion. Your *barbe*, perhaps. But not your lover. (*Kisses* GATEAU *deeply.*) Now. I have lubricated you for your date . . . (MISS GATEAU *slaps* FV.P.)

LUDMILLA *notices* BABE *in the doorway.*

FV.P: How long have you been standing there, dumb ox?

MISS GATEAU: Babe is on kitchen duty, Frau von Pussenheimer.

FV.P: Don't let her near the kitchen knives, Miss Gateau, the girl is clumsy with a blade. We don't want her cutting her precious hands off. And wash these hands before you touch anything. They're filthy. Carry on, Miss Gateau. (*She exits.*)

BABE: I wish I weren't so clumsy.

MISS GATEAU: Yes, well. Wishes are funny. I used to wish I were my Aunt Elizabeth who used to get into the broom closet and grunt.

BABE: Really?

MISS GATEAU: Oh my, yes. She used to tell me, "Beware of Tiparillo-smoking women. They will always surprise you."

BABE: What did she mean by that?

MISS GATEAU: Ha! She said, "Never trust a man in a hat."

BABE: But that's ridiculous, all men wear hats!

MISS GATEAU: *Exactement!* (*Swallows a glass of champagne, pours another.*) Let me tell you a little something about us French. Once we open a bottle of champagne, we must drink it all at once *parce que* it's all downhill from there. (*She swallows another glass.*) *Vive la France!* Get the beans.

BABE: I wish I could speak French like you.

MISS GATEAU: Oh, *merde.*

BABE: Maird!

MISS GATEAU: No, no, no. (*Drawing it out.*) *Merde.*

BABE: Mairrrrd.

MISS GATEAU: No, no, no. Here, try this. Take a sip of this.

BABE: But that's champagne.

MISS GATEAU: *Oui.* It will help you to speak the French. Take a small sip. Don't swallow! Now, say, *merde.*

BABE (*Gargling.*): Merrrrde.

MISS GATEAU: *Très bien!* (*They hug.*)

SCENE 5—SMOKING CLUB

Scene: The basement where the girls have their secret club. BABE *and* WILL *play cards.* DAMWELL *sneaks up on them.*

DAMWELL (*Imitating* FV.P.): Come, come! Where are your brave smiles?! Remember girls, smile unt za vurld smiles bock! (. . . . . WILL *and* BABE *ignore her.*) What are we waiting for?

BABE & WILL: Millicent.

DAMWELL: Oh hell, she doesn't even inhale. Come on, pass out the goods. (WILL *lights a Tiparillo, and they pass it around.*) What a day it's been. We've got so much to talk about.

BABE: I know! I heard Frau von Pussenheimer talking with Miss Gateau about Professor Pye—

DAMWELL: Oh that! That's old news. His first name's Peter, by the way, which information I got straight from the horseface's mouth just as she was about to try to plant one on me.

BABE: I know. I was there.

DAMWELL: But I'm talking about the new girl. Will, you missed rehearsal, for which I'm sure you'll get skinned alive by the way, even though I tried to cover for you, so you haven't seen her yet. But she was attacked by—hey. Don't you even want to hear about her?

BABE: Will and I had to get Martha out of the root cellar again.

DAMWELL: Oh. Sorry.

WILL: Shut up, Damwell.

DAMWELL: Really I am. I don't think she's ever been this bad.

MILLICENT (*Offstage.*): Code of honor, sisters in sin! Open the doors and let us in!

DAMWELL: You can cut the secret club crap, Millicent. I think we're a little old for that.

MILLICENT (*Enters with* THALIA.): Hi! Sorry we're late.

DAMWELL: What do mean we? What's she doing here?

MILLICENT: Thalia, this is Damwell.

THALIA: I know Damwell. You brought me to my room.

MILLICENT: And this is Babe.

THALIA: You fetched Miss Gateau for me.

MILLICENT: And this is Will.

THALIA (*A little stunned.*): Oh . . . Oh . . .

WILL: She's not supposed to be here. No offense, but this is a secret club. Members only.

MILLICENT: Want a Tiparillo?

WILL grabs a Tiparillo back from MILLICENT.

DAMWELL: Will's right. Members only. No offense, Thalia. But you would have to be initiated first.

THALIA (*Leaving.*): Sure. I understand.

DAMWELL (*Grabbing THALIA.*): Wait! You want to join us, don't you?

MILLICENT: Of course she does. All you have to do is take the secret oath. It's nothing. Just repeat after me—

DAMWELL: This special circumstances calls for special measures. Since Thalia has already seen our secret place, and she already knows we smoke, the oath alone isn't enough. She must pass the test.

MILLICENT: What test?

DAMWELL: *The Test.* The test of spirit, brains and loyalty. Everyone come here. Thalia, stay there.

WILL: This is stupid, Damwell. You said yourself we're too old for this.

DAMWELL: Will? What's wrong with you? You're always first in line for a little fun.

BABE: Maybe Will's right, Damwell. Why don't we just let her join the club?

DAMWELL: We're not gonna hurt her, we're just gonna have a little fun, that's all. It's not like we get a new girl our age everyday.

MILLICENT: We can't do anything to hurt her. I promised.

DAMWELL: Oh, some secret club! Why don't we just invite all the fourteen-year-olds over for a smoke. Now. I've got an idea. Babe, get the old wool blanket. We're going to do the desert survival test.

MILLICENT: Oooohhh!

DAMWELL: Come on. It's a fair test, and no one gets hurt.

MILLICENT: Okay . . . (*They all go over to* THALIA, *surrounding her.*) Okay. It's agreed. If you pass a simple survival test, you can be in our club.

THALIA: Well . . .

DAMWELL: Otherwise we can't let her out alive.

MILLICENT: Damwell!

DAMWELL: It was a joke!

WILL: She's just kidding. It is a simple test, really.

THALIA: Okay then.

DAMWELL: All right. This is a test to see how strong you are mentally and spiritually. Because once you take the oath, we have to be able to rely on you to keep the law of silence about the club—even if Von Pussenheimer herself tortures you. Now sit over there. (THALIA *sits on crate.*)

MILLICENT: Don't be afraid.

THALIA: I'm not afraid.

DAMWELL: Good. Now we're gonna put the blanket over you. And so it begins. Imagine, Thalia, that you're in the desert. It's 150 degrees in the shade—if there was any shade, which there's not. You're burning up with heat. You're parched (*cough, cough*) with thirst. There's only one thing you can do in this circumstance to make yourself feel better and that's if you take something off. What are you going to take off, Thalia?

THALIA: What?

DAMWELL: You're hot. It's a million degrees out. You're boiling up. Take something off (*There's movement.*) Did you take something off?

THALIA: Yes.

DAMWELL: Well, what is it? (THALIA *pushes her shoes out from under the blanket.*) Good, Thalia. Now, it's hours later and even hotter than before. Don't you think you should take something else off? (THALIA*'s socks come out from under the blanket.*) You're being a bit conservative here, Thalia. Because now, now it's high noon and the sun is beating down on you . . . Beating down on you so hard that blisters are starting to form all over your body . . . pus-ey, bloody, blisters. And as the wind blows the blisters break and sand mixes with the pus and the blood. Don't you think you should take something else off? What would really cool you down? (*THALIA's frock comes out.*) Good, Thalia. That feels better. Now you're walking over hills of sand, miles and miles of sand as far as the eye can see . . . Oh! Look, Thalia! In the distance, a little pond and some palm trees. Run for it Thalia! Run for it! You're almost there, you can taste the water . . . Oh, no! It's a mirage! What a cruel circumstance! You'd better take something else off. (*THALIA's underpants come out. BABE picks them up. DAMWELL grabs them and takes a sniff.*) Good, Thalia, good. (*BABE, hurt and alarmed, grabs them back. MILLICENT tries to comfort her.*) What can you take off now?

THALIA: Nothing.

DAMWELL: Nothing?

MILLICENT: Think, Thalia! Think!

DAMWELL (*Grabbing MILLICENT to make her be quiet.*): That's right, Thalia, think. Surely there's something else you can take off.

THALIA: No there's nothing. Nothing's left.

DAMWELL: Oh, but there is, Thalia! Why are you in the middle of the boiling-hot desert wearing a wool blanket over your head? (*DAMWELL rips off the blanket to expose THALIA. WILL rushes toward her and covers her with the blanket.*) Will! We're supposed to see her naked!

WILL: That's enough, Damwell. It's not funny.

THALIA: You're all sick. All of you! And you're the worst. (*To WILL.*) How can you even pretend to be kind after you tricked me and threw me down in the mud. I should have known the minute I saw you here there would be trouble.

MILLICENT: Will, that was you?

WILL: We didn't know it was her. We thought she was some rich girl from town.

THALIA: So that makes it all right to torture people?

MILLICENT: Will!

WILL: We were just having some fun! We were playing field hockey and—

THALIA: And you decided to terrorize me! Torturing a person for no other reason than she is a Jew.

DAMWELL: A Jew?

MILLICENT, WILL and BABE speak together.

MILLICENT: Thalia! Gosh! We didn't know you were a Jew.

WILL: Geez, I'm sorry Thalia.

BABE: I never saw a Jew before.

MILLICENT: When I joined the club they made me wear my underwear outside my stockings for a whole week. I remember now how terrified I was, but looking back it seemed all in good fun. Please forgive us, Thalia.

DAMWELL: Are you really a Jew?

THALIA: Yes, I am. And proud of it, too.

DAMWELL: Well, then. (*Tense pause.*) You're my first Jewish friend, ever.

THALIA: So? Have I passed your initiation?

WILL (*Takes her pen knife.*) Come on everyone. (*WILL cuts all the girls' thumbs, THALIA's last. All put thumbs together in circle. WILL says each line of the oath, the other girls repeat it.*)

I swear by this blood oath
To always and forever
Until each and every one of us is completely dead
Be a true and honorable blood sister
And never to part.
So say we one, so say we all.

Each kisses her own thumb, then puts it to the lips of the girl on her right. They sing.

Ohhhh . . . who's the bravest smiler
At Tilue-Pussenheimer
It's Thalia, it's Thalia, it's Thal. . . .
She's a great big doll . . .
But we love her anyway . . .

SCENE 6—HERR PYE

Scene: The grounds of the academy. Afternoon. MILLICENT *flails herself with a switch.*

MISS PHILLIPS: Millicent!

MILLICENT: Yes, Miss Phillips.

MISS PHILLIPS: What are you doing?

MILLICENT: My heart is wicked and full of impure thoughts.

MISS PHILLIPS: What thoughts, Millicent?

MILLICENT: Bad, nasty things. Things about Frau von Pussenheimer.

MISS PHILLIPS: Frau von Pussenheimer?

MILLICENT: Yes. She and Professor Pye.

MISS PHILLIPS: *Professor* Pye?

MILLICENT: Professor Peter Pye.

MISS PHILLIPS: Peter Pye is . . . no professor, I assure you.

MILLICENT: Oh. Not a professor? But then how would one address him?

MISS PHILLIPS: As you would address any man of German extraction, I suppose. Herr Peter, or, if you like, Herr Pye. Millicent, why such concern with Frau von Pussenheimer's friend?

MILLICENT: I don't know, Miss Phillips. Frau von P. talks about him, little comments here and there about her and her Herr Pye. And they roll over and over in my mind. What if I had a Herr Pye? What horrible things would I do? (*She begins to beat herself again.*) Filthy! Dirty!

MISS PHILLIPS: Millicent, please stop.

MILLICENT (*Throwing her arms around* MISS PHILLIPS.): Oh, Miss Phillips! You're my favorite teacher. Is that wretched of me?

MISS PHILLIPS: Caring for someone is never wretched. It often feels wretched, of course, but intellectually we must remember that loving is good.

MILLICENT: Oh, Miss Phillips. What an exquisite thing to say. I must write it in my diary.

MISS PHILLIPS: I have a better idea. Here. (*Removing the necklace of tears.*)

MILLICENT: Your necklace! Oh no. It's so beautiful and I am so plain, so poor and so orphaned, and so full of nasty, nasty thoughts.

MISS PHILLIPS: You remind me of myself when I was a girl. This necklace was a gift from a teacher of mine as a matter of fact. Her name was Frau von Pussenheimer. Seventeen years ago she and I had a talk right here in this very garden when she discovered me wearing a hair shirt. She gave me this necklace. It is a necklace of tears, Millicent. Another bead is added every time crushing disappointment comes your way. When Frau von Pussenheimer gave it to me it held but a single bead. And now . . . well, my beloved teacher is a raving lunatic with a drinking problem, and the necklace is yours. Perhaps some day you will pass it on as well, my beautiful student with the nasty, nasty thoughts.

MISS PHILLIPS kisses MILLICENT on the forehead.

Lights fade out.

SCENE 7—BRAVE SMILES

Scene: The main hall. MILLICENT, DAMWELL, and THALIA are in a choral arrangement with FRAU VON PUSSENHEIMER conducting. They sing "Brave Smiles."

Brave Smiles
Try to hold your chin high
Brave Smiles
Shoulders straight and don't cry

Life is hard
It may be so
It all depends on you
A brave smile
Can help to pull you through

FV.P: Beautiful . . . that was very beautiful, girls. (*Gazing at portrait of Frau Tilue on horseback which hangs on the wall.*) Frau Tilue would have been very proud of you. Frau Tilue loves you, girls. You are her sponges. Her sad, beautiful little sponges soaking up the knowledge. Now, I want to see clean hands for dinner! Understood? (*She exits.*)

DAMWELL: What did I tell you? "Brave Smiles" again. This is real trouble. She's even been hitting the sauce.

THALIA: She didn't seem drunk to me.

DAMWELL: Any time she starts talking about Tilue it's a sure bet. The question is: How far into the label is she?

THALIA: What do you mean?

MILLICENT: She means she wonders how much liquor Frau von Pussenheimer has taken.

BABE rushes in, breathless.

DAMWELL: Babe! Where's Will?

BABE: Shhh. I'll explain later.

DAMWELL: Great. Now it's curtains for all of us.

FV.P (*Entering.*): Line up. Present hands. (*The girls present their hands. FV.P moves along the line, inspecting them.*) Good, Millicent. Very good, Thalia. Damwell. Babe! Your nails are a filthy mess. I want them scrubbed do you hear me? Scrub them until they are raw and maybe then you may return to the supper table.

BABE: Yes, ma'am. (*Scurries off.*)

FV.P: How you girls expect to be fed when all day long you are digging in the dirt like little doggies is a mystery to me. Anyway, tonight for after dinner Miss Gateau has prepared a special treat in honor of the new girl. Tell me, Thalia, do you like hamantaschen?

THALIA: A hamantaschen? For me?

FV.P: Yes, that's right. (*Gets bowls and spoons from offstage and hands them out. BABE enters.*) I hope you girls appreciate our Miss Gateau. She is a woman of extraordinary talents. Hmmmm. Much better, Babe. Now. You may begin eating. And remember: I want no slurping. (*DAMWELL slurps her soup. FV.P turns and, thinking it's nothing, turns away. DAMWELL slurps again. FV.P catches her.*)

BABE: Damwell, quit it.

DAMWELL: What?! I can't help it.

FV.P: Is the soup to your taste, Damwell?

DAMWELL: Lovely, Frau von Pussenheimer.

FV.P: Perhaps it's too much to ask you to enjoy your meal in silence?

DAMWELL: No, ma'am. (*DAMWELL is smiling. It's a nervous reaction that she cannot control.*)

FV.P: Perhaps you would like to share your amusement with the rest of us.

DAMWELL: Pardon?

FV.P: What is it that you find so funny?

DAMWELL: Nothing.

Now all the girls are snickering and trying to suppress their laughter.

FV.P: Babe?

BABE: Yes, ma'am.

FV.P: Where is Wilhelmina?

BABE: Who?

FV.P: That's not funny. Where is she? What's going on?

DAMWELL: I—I think she was helping Dick Moorehead mend the fence. I think that's what she said. He needed help and Will was the only one strong enough—

FV.P: Liar! Will is not with Dick Moorehead! Where is she? Speak one or you will all suffer! Millicent?

MILLICENT: I don't know, ma'am. I haven't seen Will since before—

FV.P: Ha! I already know you're a liar. Babe?

BABE: I haven't seen her since—

FV.P: Liars! Liars! All of you! Hiding something from me. Conspiring behind Frau von Pussenheimer's back. Perhaps you are you trying to play a practical joke on Frau von Pussenheimer. Is that it? Perhaps you have pinned a humorous message to the back of my frock! (*Twists around, trying to see her own back.*) After all I've done for you. This is how you show your gratefulness? Well, I won't have it! Go to your rooms! Go!

The girls rush out. FV.P *is left alone with the portrait of* F. TILUE. *She talks to it.*

FV.P: Oh, Emmeline. Why have you leaved me? They used to love me, the girls. They used to vie for my attention. Why, just a look from me would be all a girl could ever hope for or dream of. Now they are lost to me. Someone is stealing them away. Yes. Someone is usurping me. Trouble has come to live at the academy . . . and I know just how to root it out.

SCENE 8—NIGHT TALK

Scene: The bedroom. Nighttime. From offstage a girl moos.

DAMWELL: There goes that horrible mooing girl. (*Girls moos again.*) Girl! I'll give you twenty cents if you stop that mooing. (*Another moo.*) Babe.

BABE: What, Damwell?

DAMWELL: I can't sleep. That girl is mooing again. I need you to rub on me or I'll never sleep.

BABE: I can't.

DAMWELL: I'll give you three dollars if you come rub on me.

BABE: I'm all bloody again. It already happened. I don't know why I'm bloody again?

DAMWELL: You dunce! It happens every month.

BABE: Every month! You didn't tell me that. What about the match tomorrow?

DAMWELL: Well, you can't play. And I don't think you should wash either.

MILLICENT: She has to do something. If her sheets are bloody she'll catch it from Frau von Pussenheimer.

BABE: What will I do?

WILL: Hold it in.

DAMWELL: You'll have to sleep in the washroom.

BABE: But I'll be so cold.

DAMWELL: Do you want to catch it from Frau von Pussenheimer?

(*BABE exits. THALIA is crying.*)

DAMWELL: Shhh! New girl! Shhh!

WILL: Leave her alone, Damwell. She's an orphan.

DAMWELL: I've got news for you. We're all orphans. Besides, I heard she's got parents.

MILLICENT: I have two parents. (*DAMWELL and WILL groan.*) I do so. I have a mother and dad, and we live on Strawberry Lane in the village of Hootsville. When I grow up, I'm going to run an orphanage made of toast. Warm, buttery toast. So at night, when you feel like crying, you can take a nibble.

DAMWELL: Silly. If you took a bite of toast every time you were hungry or sad you'd weigh in at twelve stone.

THALIA continues to cry.

DAMWELL: Girl, stop that crying. I'll give you twenty cents if you stop that crying. Be sensible. All your people are sensible. That's what our maid used to say. That's why your people have pots of money.

WILL: Damwell, you're an oaf. You're the rich one.

DAMWELL: Oh! You're right. (*She laughs and laughs.*)

MILLICENT: Damwell! Can't you be quieter? What if Pussenheimer hears you?

DAMWELL: What if she does? Why, if she came in here right now, I'd say, "I'm so sorry to bother you, Ludmilla. But Wilhelmina was just telling us of how often she dreams of kissing you."

WILL: Damn you, Damwell!

WILL jumps on DAMWELL. They start wrestling around.

MILLICENT: Stop it, you two! What if Pussenheimer hears you and comes in instead of Miss Phillips! (*They quiet down immediately.*)

THALIA: Who is Miss Phillips?

DAMWELL: You haven't met Miss Phillips?

Speaking at the same time.

MILLICENT: She's is our guardian angel.

WILL: She's beautiful.

DAMWELL: She's heavenly. When she looks at you directly in your eyes you could just faint and die from it. (*MILLICENT and WILL assent.*)

MILLICENT: You'll see.

WILL: She comes to tuck us in each night.

DAMWELL: And sometimes, when the mood strikes her, she gives us each a little kiss.

All three girls sigh. There is a pause.

MILLICENT: Will, tell us a story.

WILL: One night, I slipped away from the school. A truck drove by and I hopped on the back. I dozed. I dreamt of the ocean and a night full of stars. An old sailor man found me. He said, "Hey boy, come here." He felt in my pants. He didn't find what he was looking for and said, "damn." He shoved me. I fell out of the back and ran. Later I became a star in Paris.

THALIA: That's not true!

WILL: It is!

MILLICENT: She's coming.

All the girls scurry into their proper beds.

MISS PHILLIPS: Good evening, girls.

GIRLS: Good evening, Miss Phillips.

MISS PHILLIPS: (Kissing each girl on the forehead as she goes.): Goodnight, Damwell. Will, sleep tight. Millicent, don't let the bedbugs bite. Little Thalia. Welcome to the academy. (MISS PHILLIPS *and* THALIA *have a long, deep kiss.*) I'll see you in the morning, girls. (MISS PHILLIPS *exits. The girls swoon.*)

SCENE 9—SLEEPING GIRLS

Silent scene with DAMWELL, MILLICENT, *and* THALIA *all feeling each other up in their sleep.*

SCENE 10—PHILLIPS V. FV.P

Scene: FV.P*'s office.*

MISS PHILLIPS: It's awfully late. Is this business?

FV.P: What else would it be? It's my sad duty to tell you, Miss Phillips, that you are dismissed.

MISS PHILLIPS: Dismissed? But why?

FV.P: You disagree with the Tilue-Pussenheimer method. You're subverting me in the classroom and on the athletic fields.

MISS PHILLIPS: Frau von Pussenheimer, girls must have a little kind attention once in a while.

FV.P: It's a dangerous world. A world made for men and not women. We can't allow the girls to leave here with their hearts so wide open and trusting. They'll be walking targets.

MISS PHILLIPS: But you're so hard on them.

FV.P: How do you propose to maintain order?

MISS PHILLIPS: With love.

FV.P: That's manipulative. Miss Phillips, you've been out in the world. I don't have to tell you what kind of options there are out there for girls.

MISS PHILLIPS: But there are, Frau von Pussenheimer. There are places—nightclubs, writing circles—

FV.P: You are idealistic. And yet here you are. Back in the wet, echoey halls of Tilue-Pussenheimer Academy.

MISS PHILLIPS: Yes.

FV.P: As I recall, you were all too eager to leave the Academy when you turned seventeen. As I recall, you wouldn't accept the gift I tried to give you.

MISS PHILLIPS: I didn't want your stupid hairbrush! I didn't want anything from you. You used me. You played me like the grand piano in the commissary. Night after night from the time I was old enough to notice your eyes. Don't you know it nearly killed me? Made me insane?

FV.P: My point exactly. Forgive me. I was young then. I have come upon my method through much trial and error. Greta, you have until noon tomorrow.

MISS PHILLIPS: Ludmilla, please, the girls need me . . .

They are interrupted by the girls crying out "Martha" offstage.

MISS PHILLIPS: Martha!

They exit.

Blackout.

SCENE II—MARTHA'S DEAD

Scene: The stage is in semidarkness. The girls hold candles and wander, calling, "Martha."

ALL GIRLS: Martha! Martha!

THALIA: Martha! Please come quickly. Frau von Pussenheimer will be very upset if we are not in our beds. Martha, please!

MILLICENT: I saw the look in her eye. It gave me such a fright. So cold. She didn't even see me.

THALIA: I think I heard something.

DAMWELL & MILLICENT: Where?

THALIA: Behind the chest.

BABE: Ohhhh.

DAMWELL: Now what is it?

BABE: I'm still hungry, and now I'm cold.

DAMWELL: I can't believe you're complaining at a time like this. We've got to find Martha.

ALL GIRLS TOGETHER: Martha!

The girls come downstage, facing the audience. The following lines should be slightly overlapping.

MILLICENT: The water runs cool and dark and full of those weeds—

DAMWELL: I was sitting in the attic when the bells rang—

MILLICENT: Long, dark weeds, don't want to get tangled—

DAMWELL: I ran down the stairs as quickly as I could; just in time to see Dick at the edge of the grass with Babe and Millicent close behind—

MILLICENT: Next to a big warm rock I saw a foot. No one had to tell me it was Martha's—

BABE: I swam fast and I called Frau von Pussenheimer—

DAMWELL: He held you in his arms as if he didn't quite know how to hold you. As though carrying some dread message of some awful mistake—

MILLICENT: All white and puffy-looking, sickly yellow through the water—

BABE: I had a big duckweed caught in my hair. Frau von Pussenheimer was mad 'cause I was swimming in the river alone but she was crying too about Martha—

MILLICENT: "Clambering to hang, an envious sliver broke—"

DAMWELL: He put you on the dining room table. Will standing there all wet and trembling. Frau von Pussenheimer let us sit there and look at you while we waited for the coroner to come—

BABE: She was caught in those woods like a puppy in a science room aquarium—

DAMWELL: I'd never seen you before without that crease in your forehead. You even wore it in your sleep. I'd never seen you sleep so peacefully.

WILL: In my heart I have already left. I am in it, Martha. Your leaving has pitched me right into the whole mess—

MILLICENT: Everyone must pray. Everyone must pray tonight. Everyone must pray for Martha's soul.

They blow out their candles.

SCENE 12—WILL LEAVES

Scene: THALIA *comes upon* WILL *in the root cellar, preparing to leave.*

THALIA: Will!

WILL: Get out of here!

THALIA: They're looking all over for you! We all thought you were dead, too!

WILL: I wish I were. Get out, damn you!

THALIA: What are you doing?

WILL: What does it look like?

THALIA: You mean, you're going? Dressed like that?

WILL: Yes! Now get out! And you better not tell anyone you saw me down here!

THALIA: You're a bully! You've been nothing but a bully since I met you!

WILL: Sorry.

THALIA: I'll help you, if you want.

WILL: I don't need any help. I been out there before. I know my way around.

THALIA: You can't go like that. I mean, you want them to think you're a boy, don't you?

WILL: Why? I think I look like a boy pretty good.

THALIA: It's . . . your hair. Wait here. I'll find a scissors.

WILL: No. Here. (*She produces her penknife.*) Cut it off. Cut it all off. I don't want it. I want to be somebody else. I'm gonna leave this place and never look back. Never.

THALIA: You won't miss your friends?

WILL: What? Who?

THALIA: Damwell. Millicent. Babe.

WILL: They're all right . . . I'm just different, that's all. I can't explain it. I belong out on the road where nobody knows me. I like people looking at me and they don't know who I am.

THALIA: There. You look good like this.

WILL: What're you gonna do?

THALIA: I don't know. I guess I'll just stay here. I'm not as tough as you.

WILL: Yeah. Well, I'll see you down the road, I guess.

THALIA: I guess. Good luck. You'd better go. The sun's coming up. You'd better go.

WILL: Thalia?

THALIA: Yeah?

WILL: Tell the others . . . tell them I said good-bye.

THALIA: I will. Run.

WILL: Thalia?

THALIA: Yes? (*WILL kisses her.*)

WILL: For good luck.

THALIA: For good luck. (*WILL leaves.*) Good luck, Will. (*She puts her fingers to her lips remembering the kiss.*)

Lights slowly fade on THALIA holding ponytail.

SCENE 13—FV.P'S FAREWELL

Scene: FV.P's office.

FV.P: Oh this rage! Where can it go? Where can it go in these damp walls? I only wanted to shelter you. To keep you from the drooling men. And now I see that I cannot. They seep in through the cracks in the door. And now all my girls are leaving me. Beautiful Martha. Bold young Will. I've failed. Of course, I never could have succeeded. I cannot create a planet of women. Where there is no pain to little girls and only excessive pleasure for their growing bodies. Failing this, what is there for me? (*She prepares her noose.*) I will never turn to them. I will never concede. That would be to die over and over again one million times. It is better to die but once. Good-bye. Good-bye my tender young buds, soon to be gorgeous flowers. May you protect yourselves better than I have. (*She hurls noose over a roof beam.*)

Blackout.

SCENE 14—MISS PHILLIPS'S FAREWELL

Scene: The main hall. MISS PHILLIPS *prepares to go.* DAMWELL *and* MILLICENT *protest and whimper.* THALIA *carries her trunk.*

MISS PHILLIPS: Come now. Strong hearts. Brave smiles everyone.

MILLICENT: Miss Phillips, don't go. Don't leave us.

MISS PHILLIPS: Oh, girls, I must. You can't see it now, but there's a whole world out there waiting for you. I hope I have given you the tools you need to fashion it to your hearts' desires. Come. We must make an end to it. (MISS PHILLIPS *kisses* MILLICENT *and* DAMWELL *on the forehead, then she and* THALIA *have another deep kiss.* MISS PHILLIPS *exits. Offstage she is heard knocking on* FV.P*'s door. No answer. She knocks again.*) Frau von Pussenheimer? (*We hear her knock several times. Trying the locked door. Frantically trying to get the door open.*) Ludmilla? Ludmilla! (*She screams and comes staggering in, collapsing into the girls' arms.*)

Girls. I'm afraid I have some bad news . . . and some good news.

Blackout.

(*end of Act I*)

~

ACT II

SCENE 1—DAMWELL'S WEDDING

Scene: The grand ballroom of the Hôtel Goldene Gewölbe, Vienna, c. 1939. It is DAMWELL*'s wedding. Wedding music subsides into conversation and music of a reception.* BABE, MILLICENT, *and* THALIA *are center stage.* DAMWELL *stands away from them, in her wedding dress.*

DAMWELL: Thalia! Babe! Millicent! (*They turn and see* DAMWELL. *They wave.*) Well, we're on our way! Jean Pierre is waiting. (*Horn honks.*) Just a minute, Jean Pierre! There's just one more thing—catch! (*She throws her bouquet. No one makes a move to catch it. They exchange looks.* DAMWELL *retrieves the bouquet.*) Oh, well. Maybe I wasn't close enough. Let's try again. Ready? Catch! (*She throws it a second time, they each take a step back.* DAMWELL *nervously giggles. Retrieves the bouquet again.*) Come on, Millicent. I'm trying to do you a favor. You're not the prettiest of girls. (DAMWELL *throws bouquet toward an insulted* MILLICENT, *who doesn't move a muscle.*) Come on, Babe. For an old school friend. You'll help me out, won't you? (BABE *doesn't catch it either.*) Thalia will help me, won't you, Thalia? Come on. It's a tradition in my country. Catch it! (DAMWELL *hurls the bouquet at* THALIA. THALIA *dodges it.* DAMWELL *chases her around the stage, throwing the bouquet.*) What'd you all come just to eat the free food?! Catch it!

SCENE 2—THE DISEMBARKATION

Scene: New York Harbor, c. 1943. BABE *with her companion, the* BARONESS, *has just arrived from overseas and is giving a press conference.*

REPORTER: Babe! Babe! Was Nina Rostova any match for you on the green?

BABE: Nina's a wonderful friend and she gave me a run for my money!

REPORTER: Babe! Speaking of money, we understand you did pretty well today!

BABE: Well let's just say it beats making soap at the orphanage!

REPORTER: What about Wimbledon, Babe? Any predictions on how you'll—

BABE: First things first, fellas. I gotta rest up for the Olympics tomorrow!

REPORTER: Hey, Babe! Who's your pretty friend?

BABE (*The BARONESS and BABE exchange a look.*): Uh . . . that's it for now, fellas.

BARONESS (*Holding BABE's dog, NIPPER.*): Come along, Babe.

MILLICENT: Excuse me. Excuse me.

BARONESS: No more questions. She is tired.

MILLICENT: I just want an autograph.

BARONESS: I said she is tired.

BABE: S'all right, Ginka. One autograph ain't gonna kill me. Who shall I make it out to, doll?

MILLICENT: To Millicent.

BABE: Millicent! (*To the BARONESS.*) Aw, look! It's my old pal, Millicent, from T-Puss!

BARONESS: Pleased, I'm sure.

BABE: Millicent, this is my trusty companion, Nipper.

MILLICENT (*Talking to BARONESS.*): Why hello, Nipper.

BABE: How the heck are you, for God's sake! I haven't seen you since Damwell's wedding. Too bad about the divorce. Say, Millicent, you don't look so hot. I guess the world's not ready for a musical genius like yourself, huh?

REPORTER: Actually, I'm pursuing a different career now, Babe. May I have a word with you, privately?

BABE: Sure, sure. Skunkers, do you mind? I'll only be a minute.

BARONESS: Well, all right. But make it quick. We have a train to catch in the morning. (*She makes kissing noises until BABE kisses her and exits.*)

BABE: Of course my darling one. Women! So what's happening, Millicent? You look like a death sandwich warmed over.

MILLICENT: No thanks. I wanted to see you Babe. You're doing quite well for yourself, aren't you?

BABE: Isn't it grand? I've got all the money in the world. I travel like a king. The whole world adores me and best of all, I'm not a klutz anymore. (*BABE accidentally slams MILLICENT with MILLICENT's autograph book.*) At least not on the playing field.

MILLICENT: You've grown up. Your great big hands and feet finally match your body a little. I'm so proud, Babe.

BABE: I never could've done it without all the girls at T-Puss. Especially you, Millicent. You were always the kindest and the most patient. All my success—I owe it to you.

MILLICENT: Then you wouldn't mind paying back a little of that patience and understanding?

BABE: Millicent, you name it.

MILLICENT: The world is changing very fast, Babe. Innocent people are going to be hurt. I've been trying to help these people in whatever way I can. But these are times that call for sacrifice. As Miss Phillips said to me—before the consumption took her on to heaven—she said, the world needs to be tended like a garden, and that I should be like a garden tender. And sometimes to be a garden tender you can't worry about yourself, you can only worry about the garden. She said this to me and she gave me the necklace of tears. Do you understand?

BABE: I guess so.

MILLICENT: Good. You're going to the Olympic Games in Stockholm, yes?

BABE: You bet. I'm entered in rowing, dressage, and gymnastics.

MILLICENT: I wondered if you would take a package for me to a friend. I'd rather not tell you anything more except that there's a chance you'll be caught and almost certainly be killed. Please think about it Babe, would you? For an old school chum?

BABES nods her head, nervously. Lights out.

SCENE 3—BABE ON A PLANE

Scene: The cockpit of the Grand Dame, *a few weeks later.* BABE *flies the plane with* NIPPER *(a puppet) at her side.*

BABE: Well, Nipper . . . looks like it's just you and me and the Axis. I always feel calm up here Nips, don't you? Dropping that package for my old pal, Millicent, sure made me feel young again. Like I have something to give the world. Like my days back at T-Puss on the hockey field. I could've done anything and now I have. I've done something real for the first time in my life, Nips. Oh sure, I know. I made folks happy when I broke the land speed record; gave them all something to cheer about. But it was always so empty, Nipper. Heck. I don't have to tell you that. You were with me all the way in Death Valley, you know how I felt about it. Yeah Nipper—I don't know where all this is headed, but when that pine lid comes down they're gonna say that Deirdre "Babe" O'Hanlon did something for humanity. Aw, don't cry Nipper. I hate it when you get all emotional. . . .

Dog whimpers.

Nipper? What is it, girl? (*Dog barks.*) Package? (*Barks again.*) What other package? (*Barks out of control.*) Okay. Don't get so excited. Bring it up here, we'll see what it is. (*Dog ducks into cockpit.*) I'm sure it's not that important—(*Dog reappears with bomb in her mouth.*) NUTS! Nipper! That's a bomb. Okay, Nips—drop it. (*NIPPER refuses.*) Nipper, drop the balley. (*Dog refuses again.*) I'm not playin' here, Nipper, DROP IT! NIPPER! (*Lights out as we hear the plane going down. Explosion.*)

SCENE 4—VIN'S PLACE

Scene: On the street, outside a gay parisienne nightclub—Vin Marconi's, c.1946.

THALIA: This dirty street. Why are we always relegated to the filthiest street in the most abhorrent part of town? I feel lost. I hope I got the directions correctly. I think she said Rue de la Quare. But I cannot be sure. Something has pulled me here. The same thing that has pulled me my whole life—through the interrogation and over the Alps on foot. What is it? A smile? A promise from someone long ago forgotten? Of happiness? That someday I will rest in a pair of strong arms holding me? I delude myself. I hope and my hopes are dashed.

Knocks on door. Peephole opens.

PIERRE: *Qu'est-ce que vous voulez?*
THALIA: I'm sure the baguette is stale . . .

Door opens.

PIERRE: Ah! *Bienvenue, mademoiselle.* Right this way.

Drumroll.

PIERRE: *Merci, mes dames et mes dames. Et maintenant,* I bring to you the most wonderful, the one and only, Vin Marconi!

Applause.

WILL (*Appearing in drag as* VIN MARCONI *sings.*):

I've always loved the girls
I don't know why, I don't know why
I want to kiss the girls
And not the guys, no, not the guys

This puzzled me when I was younger
And, oh, how I did wonder
How could I appease this burning hunger?

And then I met her
I shan't forget her
She told me she could love me so I let her.
And how our love did grow
She taught me all I know.
Hand in hand along the Seine
Proving to me I was a lesbian.

But long it could not last
She loved me deep
She loved me fast
I awoke one morning to find her gone
I had to find a reason to go on.

And then I met them
I shan't forget them
I loved them one and all
When I could get them
In a vast parade of stars
We were so young, the world was ours.
We were so gay, in every way
Carousing with the flotsam and the jetsam.

But how the years roll cruelly by,
With countless loves and countless sad good-byes
The mirror tells me truthfully, I've grown
I plan to live my later years alone

And then I saw you
How I adore you
When you fix your hair
I want to do it for you.
Is this true love at last?
How I'm afraid to ask.

My knees are weak
I cannot speak

I took the stage
Blood's boiling rage

Is this true love
Or is it just old age?

Applause. WILL *exits, reenters with champagne bottle and two glasses.*

WILL: Hello. May I join you? I only sing in that accent. I'm Vin Marconi.

THALIA: I know.

WILL: Who are you?

THALIA: I'm not sure. I think I'm starting to remember. Your song was very . . . amusing.

WILL: I'm afraid I'm an awful coward. I can never say just what I mean.

THALIA: What do you mean?

WILL: Shall we have a drink? Champagne.

THALIA: This is my first time.

WILL: At a nightclub?

THALIA: At this particular kind of nightclub. Where I've been, they don't have these kind of clubs. It's hard enough just to survive, let alone have a little fun. Paris is a great relief.

WILL: Times are hard all over—for everybody. I hate being careful. Tonight, to hell with being careful!

THALIA: I'll drink to that. Vin Marconi. That's an unusual name.

WILL: It's not mine, but in a way it is. You see, years back I was in the war. I disguised myself as a man and drove an ambulance. I saw a lot of action. One time, during some pretty heavy shelling, I ran into a young soldier. He was hurt pretty bad . . .

Flashback. Sound of bombing and gunfire. WILL *and soldier smack into each other downstage.*

WILL: Hey, fella, you're hurt pretty bad. I'll go get a medic. . . .

VIN: Forget it, kid, those krauts got us pinned down pretty good.

WILL: But you're bleeding, I'm just an ambulance driver—

VIN: Listen, kid. I'm just about to buy the farm and I need ya here with me. There's just something about you, kid, you remind me of a friend of mine. I got his picture. Want to see it?

WILL: Sure.

VIN (*Pulls out dog tags.*): He's real sweet-looking, ain't he? Fellas woulda give me the business if they knew his picture was in there. Harold. Not Harry neither. Harold. Ain't that a sophisticated name? Don't know what he ever saw in a bum like me.

WILL: I'm sure he loves you very much.

VIN: You keep it, kid. Keep the whole thing.

WILL: But you're not gonna die! I'm going to help you!

VIN: You're a real pal, kid. A good fella. Just sit quiet with me. Until the fighting stops. (*Dies.*)

WILL: No! Hold on! Don't die! Come on, pal . . . don't die. I don't even know your name. (*Looks at tags.*) Vin Marconi . . . (*Crosses back to table.*) So you see, I figure it was the least I could do for him.

THALIA: What a terrible story. Sometimes it feels like this whole world's gone crazy. Sometimes I feel crazy. I don't feel crazy tonight. You make me feel so calm, a little excited too. I feel as if you're reading me like a book, Vin Marconi.

WILL: I know you. I knew you from the very first moment I saw you—so frightened but not showing it. I talked a good game, but I never coulda made it out that cellar window if you hadn't pushed me.

THALIA: Will.

WILL: That's right, Thalia.

THALIA: I knew there was some reason—

WILL: I've been waiting for you, Thalia. Since that cold, gray morning ten years ago. Your smile, your courage. I never could've left Tilue-Pussenheimer without them. I never could've have left behind the memory of Martha.

THALIA: Oh, Will. You loved her.

WILL: Yes. But now I love you. Relax. I don't expect you to fall into my arms. After all these years and so much water under the—

THALIA interrupts her with a kiss.

THALIA: I do love you. I've always loved you.

WILL: Then Paris is ours! There's been so much sorrow, so much suffering in our short lives. It's all over now, my darling. There will be no more crack of Frau von P's boot horn to frighten us. No more kisses stolen in the hayloft. No more words unspoken. Our love will parade down the streets of Paris! I will write you poems on the front page of *Le Monde*! I will marry you in Notre Dame! I will sing your name every night, my darling!

THALIA: Yes, Will. Let's begin at once. I was so tired. And now I see what has tired me—the hiding, the lies, the fear of being found out. When I was crossing the Alps, my feet frozen in my cheap cardboard shoes, there were so many moments when all I wanted was to lie down and pull the snow over me like a blanket of death, and sleep. Something, the smallest, most quiet voice urged me onward. Onward, I think, to you.

They go to kiss.

PIERRE (*Offstage.*): Vin! You must sign for the linen!

WILL: The mundane world comes crashing in. I won't be but a moment my angel! (*Exits.*)

THALIA: To feel the air in my lungs. To take a drink of champagne and not be afraid to let it go to my head. Why not? The champagne tastes divine!

Sound of truck backing up. Screams and exclamations are heard offstage. Crashing noises. PIERRE drags WILL's mangled body halfway onstage.

PIERRE: She's been run over by the delivery truck! She is dead!

THALIA: No. No. It cannot be! Will, my love, my heart, my soul. Will, please don't leave me again. I can't bear it. Choke me! Choke me! Oh! This life of sorrows! This life of never-ending sorrows! (*Stumbles to table, picks up bottle.*) To your health! (*Drinks.*)

Blackout.

SCENE 5—CHILDREN'S HOUR

Scene: A Broadway theater, c. 1956. Rehearsal for a production of a play directed by DAMWELL MAXWELL. *The sound of rain comes up in the dark. Lights come up on a chair, center, where* SHARON *sits, forlorn.* BERTHA *stands just downstage left, looking out into the audience. The actors hold the script losely in their hands. They are just about off book.*

BERTHA: Where's Guy gone off to?

SHARON (*As if awakening from a dream.*): Pardon?

BERTHA: Guy. His car just pulled away. Dinner's almost ready.

SHARON: He won't be joining us.

BERTHA: Not another emergency, I hope. He's too good. Always taking care of everyone else, never a worry for himself.

SHARON: Hmmmmm.

BERTHA: I'll keep his supper warm. He'll need a good, warm meal when he gets back.

SHARON (*In a sudden burst of anguish.*): Oh, Guy!

BERTHA (*Quickly, walks to* SHARON.): What is it, Sharon? Is something wrong?

SHARON: Everything is wrong.

BERTHA: Was it something I said? Something I did?

SHARON: No, Bertha.

BERTHA: What then? (*No answer.*) What? Tell me, Sharon. What?

SHARON: It's not you, Bertha. It's Guy. He thought that you and I . . . Oh, I can't say it. It's all so dirty and filthy.

BERTHA: But I thought he knew. He *knew* it was all a lie. How could he believe that we—

SHARON: He doesn't know what to believe anymore. Do you?

BERTHA: It's all my fault.

SHARON: Oh, Bertha. Don't talk like that.

BERTHA: It is me, isn't it? All this talk. All this trouble. All because of me.

SHARON: Bertha, that's not true.

BERTHA: You're a good friend, Sharon. A loving friend. You and Guy are made for each other. Always looking out for other people, never a thought for yourselves. I want you to be together. I've always wanted it. Go to him now. I'm sure it's not too late.

SHARON: What's done is done. There's no changing it.

BERTHA: It's no use going on like this. I'll pack my bags. I can be out of here first thing tomorrow. I've been so selfish. Now I see it. Don't worry, Sharon. I won't stand in your way.

SHARON: Bertha! What are you talking about?

BERTHA: Don't you see?

SHARON: See what? I *can't* see it. I *refuse* to see it. Why should we let a nasty little lie come between us? If you leave, I'm going with you.

BERTHA: But that only makes it worse. People will think it's really true.

SHARON: Who cares anymore what people think?

BERTHA: Besides, there isn't anywhere for us to go. This lie will follow us to the ends of the earth. In every city, every town, we'll be ridiculed and scorned.

SHARON: There must be someplace where people can sort lies from the truth.

BERTHA: No. There's no escaping this. Not for me. Save yourself, Sharon.

SHARON: Nonsense. You're talking nonsense. (*She approaches BERTHA.*)

BERTHA: No! Don't touch me.

SHARON (*Stopping dead in her tracks.*): Bertha, please. Surely you and

I know the difference between an innocent touch and an illicit act.

BERTHA: Do we?

SHARON: Don't talk crazy. Of course we do.

BERTHA: A little girl tells a lie. Why does she tell a lie? She says she saw something. But what did she see? There's nothing to see. Unless she sees something we're not seeing.

SHARON: What can you be saying?

BERTHA (*Finally breaking down.*): Oh, God! Strike me down now! Take me before I can sin anymore! Even while we've been talking I can't stop thinking about how much I love you. I am what they say. Cursed and wretched. An abomination. More filthy and dirty than you could ever imagine.

SHARON (*Running to* BERTHA *and taking her in her arms.* BERTHA *is too overcome with grief and shame to resist.*): Bertha. Bertha, please. Stop it. (BERTHA *looks up to* SHARON *as* SHARON *gently caresses* BERTHA*'s face.*) I can't believe these things I'm hearing.

BERTHA: Believe it. It's all true. Finally, we come to the horrible truth.

AUDREY (*Looking at the script.*): It's not so horrible. Now that I think about it, it sounds pretty good. Come on, baby. Rub me. Rub on me, baby. Let me be a prostrate worshipper in your grotto of love. Oh yeah. Hump me, you . . . you . . . lascivious Jezebel. Over just a little. Oh, yeah. My . . . my tittie. Hump me 'til I climax! (AUDREY *stares at her script, incredulous.*) Is this right?

SHIRLEY (*Showing* AUDREY *in the script.*): I think it's "grotto of *moist* love."

AUDREY: Did Lillian write this?

DAMWELL: People! People! People! Audrey. Shirley. What is the problem here? We had some momentum going. Now let's take it back to "Rub on me, baby." Okay? And . . . lights up.

AUDREY: Damwell, this is not Lillian's writing.

DAMWELL: I don't know what to tell you, Audrey. That's what she gave me.

AUDREY: But this is your handwriting. You've crossed out all of her lines and written in lines of your own.

DAMWELL: Okay. Okay. Just between the three of us, I'm helping her out. She was shitfaced when she wrote this—it's crap. I'm just perking it up a little. No one needs to be the wiser.

AUDREY: But you're changing the whole intention! Sharon never would have said these things.

SHIRLEY: That's right, Miss Maxwell. Didn't Lillian say the whole point of the story was about how lies can hurt people? I mean, they're not really inverts.

AUDREY: Oh, I never would have agreed to play an invert.

DAMWELL: Is there a doctor in the house? Emergency! Audrey needs the pole removed from her butt! Audrey needs a polectomy!

AUDREY: That's it! I quit! I'm going to call that nice Capote man and tell him I'm available for that breakfast movie! (*AUDREY storms off.*)

DAMWELL: What? You afraid you're gonna catch something from Shirley?

SHIRLEY: Ooooh! Take another Seconal why don't you! (*Also storms off.*)

DAMWELL (*Calling after her.*): You'll be back!

SHIRLEY (*From offstage.*): Not in this lifetime, lady!

DAMWELL: Fine. Fine. I don't need you. You actor-types! Writer-types! I don't need any of you. You're forgetting who my father is! Senator Maxwell, that's who! Huh! Reds! Reds and alcoholics, the lot of you. (*Taking out pills and eating them.*) Right! Like I'm the only muffdiver in this crowd. I'll name names, y'know! I'll sing like a bird! They're right! There's a scourge upon the land! You can't blame me. Can't blame me for talking. There's a scourge upon the land. There's a scourge . . . Isn't there?

Blackout.

SCENE 6—THE MISSION

Scene: A mission on the Bowery, c. 1959

MILLICENT (*Cutting a large carrot into a soup pot. She sings to herself to the tune of her song for the dead turtle.*):

> *When an aviator dies*
> *And a pretty, young resistance fighter cries*
> *And the world is changed forever*

Oh, Babe. How could I ever have sent you off to such a wretched death? I don't deserve the cup of watery pea soup I eat daily. I am wretched. Horrible. I don't deserve my miserable cot.

THALIA (*Enters singing drunkenly to the tune of* VIN*'s cabaret song.*): And then I met her. And then I met her. And then I met her and I met her and I met her. All right I'm here. What do I do now? Confess? I confess. I confess everything.

MILLICENT (*Still working over her pot.*): This is not a church. It's a mission. You may speak to God here if you like. All we ask is that you leave the evil alcohol devil outside.

THALIA: Millicent?

MILLICENT: Yes . . .

THALIA: Hahahahaha!

MILLICENT: What's so funny?

THALIA: Do the words Tilue-Pussenheimer mean anything to you?

MILLICENT: Oh my God. Here, why don't you lie down on this cot—

THALIA: Oooooh! Who's the bravest smiler! At Tilue-Pussenheimer! It's me, it's me, it's me! I'm a filthy drunk!

MILLICENT: Thalia, please!

THALIA: Funny, isn't it. Ol' von P always said, don't pick on Thalia. At least Thalia will never become a stinking drunk. Her people never become stinking drunks. Proved the old bitch wrong, I guess. You're a brave smiler, aren'tcha?

THALIA *collapses.*

Blackout.

Lights up. A banner reading "three days later" is held up from offstage.

MILLICENT: Oh, Lord. Why have you sent her here? I came here to serve my penance, Lord! For my sins and my evil thoughts! Remember? I asked you to keep me far, far away from women—with their fleshy calves and shapely hips and . . . Oh, Lord, I'm trouble, don't you see? Trouble with a capital T! Please God, I feel bad saying this, but, please let her be in a coma and never wake up.

THALIA: Oh, my head!

MILLICENT: Oh, God! There is no God!

THALIA: Millicent! How long have I been asleep?

MILLICENT: About three days. You certainly slept like the dead. Well, g'bye now!

THALIA: Can't I stay with you a moment? I don't feel quite right. . . .

MILLICENT: I think it'd be better if you just went on your way. I've got a lot of hungry bums to feed, you see, and . . .

THALIA: Forgive me, Millicent.

MILLICENT: You? Forgive you? Why, how silly. I'm the one who should ask for forgiveness really—

THALIA: I was drunk.

MILLICENT: Yes, a little.

THALIA: When I was sleeping sometimes I awoke to see you looking down at me—caring for me—your eyes so blue and full of light. Millicent, you are an angel—

MILLICENT: I wasn't staring at you! Now, really, I think you should be going.

THALIA: Your necklace. It's so beautiful. Where did you get it?

MILLICENT: You don't want to know. (*The necklace has increased in size.*)

THALIA: I do. It's lovely.

MILLICENT: Here! You can have it. I don't want it anymore. Take it and all that goes with it. She gave it to me, Thalia. Miss Phillips!

THALIA: Oh Millicent. My life is bleak. I have crawled into a bottle of scotch and I cannot get out. You rehabilitate here, don't you? Rehabilitate me, Millicent! Please!

MILLICENT: No! I don't rehabilitate! I just serve soup! And I'm not even very good at that! Ask anyone! They all hate my soup! You don't get it, do you, Thalia? I'm poison! Poison with a capital P! If you know what's good for you, you'll flee! As fast as you can.

THALIA: Very well. I'm going. I know somewhere I can go. It was good to see you again, Millicent.

She goes to leave. Music swells and she sings.

> *There's a brave smile looking back at me.*
> *It reminds me of the girl I used to be.*
> *Once I had a heart but I guess I broke it.*
> *Once I had a song but now I choke on it.*
>
> *And outside the snow is falling*
> *like my tears only frozen*
> *And I can't turn away from this lonely path*
> *I've chosen.*
>
> *In the warmth of a bar*
> *a steady hand to hold.*
> *So tonight, just for tonight,*
> *let me not be alone.*

THALIA goes to leave.

MILLICENT: Thalia, wait! Stay with me! I will help you. Only you've got to help me, too. Help me to let go of the past.

THALIA: I will try.

MILLICENT: Oh! Smell the air! Thalia, it's spring! A time of new beginnings. We're going to start all fresh, Thalia. We're getting out of the Bowery. I know there's not much money, but we can take a small apartment somewhere, in a humble neighborhood where rents are low. I'll help you stop drinking, and you can help me write that book of poetry I've been meaning to write for so many years. Yes! Our life will be beautiful and lovely and nobody, nobody, nobody will ever be able to spoil it! Oh, Thalia, I'm happy.

They go to kiss. BUM *enters, brandishing a knife.*

BUM: Hey! Sister! Gimme all your money!
THALIA: Millicent, look out!
MILLICENT: It's all right, Thalia. We have no money here, sir. We're an operation of the Lord. We have a bowl of hot soup if that interests you.
BUM: I don't want your soup! I want your money!
MILLICENT: I tell you, we haven't any money.
BUM: If you haven't got any money then maybe there's something else I can have. (*Leering at* THALIA.) Who's your pretty friend?
MILLICENT: You leave her alone.
BUM: You're awful pretty.
MILLICENT: You touch her and I'll . . . I'll kill you.
BUM (*Laughs.*): What are ye gonna do? Kill me with that book?!

MILLICENT *whacks the bum with her diary. He collapses. Dead.*

THALIA: Millicent!
MILLICENT: My poems are deadly.

Blackout.

SCENE 7—I WANT TO LIVE

Scene: Sing Sing Prison, October 12, 1959, 7:12 A.M.

The style is atmospheric, noir. The sound of sirens and the clang of a prison door is heard in the blackout. MILLICENT *is handcuffed and nervously smoking.*

MILLICENT: It was an accident, I tell you! Haven't you ever heard of self-defense? I want to live! I want to live!

Blackout.

SCENE 8—THE BOOKSIGNING

Scene: A book signing at Rizzoli in NYC, c. 1969. DAMWELL *is signing copies of her best-selling autobiography.*

DAMWELL: And what's your name darling? Kitty? Grrrrowwwl! "To Kitty. Best of luck, Damwell Maxwell." Thanks so much for coming. Hello! How are you? And your name is . . . Richard! Handsome name, handsome fellow. Yes . . . I hope you enjoy it. Thanks so much for coming. Next?

THALIA: Perhaps you could sign one for me?

DAMWELL: That's what I'm here for. And your name is—Thalia? Oh, my goodness. Look everyone! It's Thalia! From Tilue-Pussenheimer! Chapter three! It's the tiny, little Hebrew girl! Oh my! How are you?

THALIA: I'm well, Damwell. You . . . you're a famous author now. What a life you've had. I've seen all your pictures.

DAMWELL: Oh, that was so long ago.

THALIA: My favorite one was *Two Planes Over Morocco.* Yes. That was my favorite.

DAMWELL: Oh yes, well, I think I really captured the role of the nurse in that one, don't you? I— (THALIA *collapses.*) Thalia? Thalia! Would someone please get me a glass of water! Oh, dear. You'll be all right, Thalia. I'll take you to my house in Southampton for a little while. The salt air will be just the thing. Taxi!

Blackout.

SCENE 9—SOUTHAMPTON

Scene: Southampton, later that day.

DAMWELL: Are you feeling better, dear?

THALIA: Yes, thank you, Damvell.

DAMWELL: You gave me quite a fright. What's wrong with you, anyway, dear? Do you have a condition?

THALIA: You're very kind. But really, my life story is too horrible to share. I don't want to burden you.

DAMWELL: Oh, but you must. It's just the thing to make you feel better. Why, when I was in the mental hospital, Dr. LeFarge couldn't emphasize enough the importance of disclosure. Well, I must've—

THALIA: You were in the mental hospital?

DAMWELL: Oh, for Pete's sake—haven't you read my book? Why, yes! You see, after I was blacklisted by that awful Senator Hungwell and the rest of them, well, my whole life simply went flush down the toilet. It seems that hideous Dick Moorehead—you remember Dick—was taking perverted photographs of myself and Tina—you remember Tina, the sophomore? And, well, there went my second marriage. Then they marched right in and took my lovely twins, Janey and Junie, and sent them to a state home. Can you believe it? Well, it was all a bit much for me and I began, you know, wearing my nightgown and slippers in public and things like that. Fortunately, Dr. LeFarge and all the wonderful staff at MeadowPines had me right as rain in twelve years. Well, I'm not complaining. It gave me plenty of time to write my book, *I, Damwell Maxwell*. And as you saw, it's just a raving success.

THALIA: It must have taken tremendous personal courage to endure such hardship. I'm afraid we all misjudged you back at Tilue-Pussenheimer.

DAMWELL: Thanks. Now. You look like you could use a l'il scotch and soda. How 'bout that?

THALIA: No!

DAMWELL: Hold the soda?

THALIA: Uh . . .

DAMWELL: Maybe this'll loosen your tongue a little. Remember. Disclosure.

THALIA (*THALIA sucks down the drink.*): Well, you see, after Will got run over by the delivery truck . . .

DAMWELL: Oh, my God!

THALIA: Yes. I thought I'd never love again. Then, I met Millicent. You remember Millicent.

DAMWELL: Oh, yes. The ethereal one. Always strumming on that awful guitar.

THALIA: Yes, Damvell. I met Millicent in a mission for wayward alcoholics. We fell in love, Damvell. She gave me Miss Phillips' necklace of tears. (*The necklace is even bigger.*)

DAMWELL: Oh, how nice for you.

THALIA: Yes. And, well, you must know she was on death row for murdering a bum. Damvell, they gave her the electric chair. My life is one horrible tragedy after another. I don't know how I stand it.

DAMWELL: Oh, there, there now. Come on. What did they teach us back at the academy, Thalia, hmm? (*Mushing THALIA's face into a brave smile.*) Brave smiles! That's right. Brave smiles. See? (*Smiling bravely.*) How do you think I've gotten through the relentless tragedy that's been my life? It's not just the antidepressants, let me tell you. Look at me, Thalia. I'm free. I've got all the money in the world and my book is a smash.

THALIA: Oh, Damvell. I'm starting to feel all varm and tingly.

DAMWELL: See? What did I tell you? Let me make you another. Say, Thalia—let's put a record on the hi-fi and do some dance impressions, just like we used to at the academy!

THALIA: Oh, I couldn't possibly.

DAMWELL: From now on, "I couldn't possibly" will not be in your vocabulary. (*DAMWELL pulls THALIA up. They dance through the end of the scene.*) Isn't it lovely to feel so free and gay? Just like when we were girls!

THALIA: Yes! I do feel gay. I feel light!

DAMWELL: Thalia, I'm gonna help you. I'm gonna help you write your very own book.

THALIA: Me?

DAMWELL: Why not? With all the tragedy you've had? It's certain to be a best-seller! Your very own autobiography. Let's see . . . we'll call it—NECKLACE OF TEARS!

SCENE 10—SOUTHHAMPTON

Scene: Two years later, in Southampton. A banner reading "two years later" appears from offstage. The necklace of tears is now huge.

THALIA: You shallow bitch! You empty publicity whore!

DAMWELL: Thalia, please! You've got to stop drinking!

THALIA: Why? Why should I stop the one thing in this life that gives me pleasure?

DAMWELL: Don't I . . . aren't I some consolation to you, my darling—

THALIA: Yes, Damvell. You are the consolation prize!

DAMWELL: All right! Just give me that goddam necklace!

THALIA: Mine, mine, mine, mine, mine! These are my tears, and you can't have them!

DAMWELL: It's not my fault that you are too drunk to go on the *Mike Douglas Show* to promote that book! It's not my fault that I have to go on instead of you, and I'm going to wear the goddam necklace!

THALIA: You're jealous, Damvell. That's what you are! A pathetic washed-up-celebrity-has-been! You're jealous because *Necklace of Tears* outsold *I, Damwell Maxwell*! Well, now Thalia is the star! Thalia is who they want! Damvell can go and be on the game shows! Ha, ha, ha!

DAMWELL: My God, Thalia! What's happened to us! We used to love each other! We used to be so good for each other . . .

Phone rings.

THALIA: Who is that? One of your fucking girlfriends?

DAMWELL: Shut up! Would you please shut up for one minute? Helloo?

THALIA: If that's Mike Douglas, you tell him I'm not here!

DAMWELL: Yes, this is Damwell Maxwell.

THALIA: You slut!

DAMWELL: Oh yes. Yes I've been waiting for your call.

THALIA: I'm queen of the house! I'm the queen.

DAMWELL: Yes? Yes? Oh no. No. I—it can't be. Yes. Thank you.

THALIA: One of your fucking girlfriends, huh?

DAMWELL: Thalia . . .

THALIA: Oh, now she's crying. Boo hoo hoo. Poor little miss rich girl is crying her eyeballs out. Always feeling sorry for herself.

DAMWELL: We're gonna have to add another bead to that necklace of tears . . .

THALIA: You get your paws off my neckla— What do you mean?

DAMWELL: Oh, Thalia. It's so horrible.

THALIA: What? What is so horrible? What could possibly be more horrible than our lives?

DAMWELL: Oh honey. You know those mood swings you've been having? And the headaches?

THALIA: Yeah . . .

DAMWELL: . . . And, you know this big lump on your head?

THALIA: I've been drinkin' a lot.

DAMWELL: It's not the drinking, Thalia.

THALIA: What is it?

DAMWELL: You have a malignant brain tumor.

THALIA: Fuck! . . . Maybe we can put it in the book.

DAMWELL: Good idea! You can be an inspiration to others with brain tumors.

THALIA: Yeah and you can make some more money off me!

DAMWELL: Thalia . . .

THALIA: Get offa me.

DAMWELL: I always loved you so much.

THALIA: Oh shit, I'm gonna die.

DAMWELL: No, Thalia, no. Look outside the window, darling. Look how beautiful it is outside. Look at the seagulls, look at— (*THALIA falls in a faint.*) Oh my God!! They didn't say it was gong to happen now!

THALIA: (*Mumbles.*)

DAMWELL: Oh thank God. Don't die. I love you so much. Godammit! Don't die, you bastard! Don't die! (*Pounds on her.*) I love you so very much. Don't die. Don't die, Thalia. I never thought I would be the one to survive. I thought I was the spoiled one who would just fall apart under the least bit of strain. Oh, I don't want to be the only one left!

THALIA: Mother . . . Mother . . . I see you, Mother.

DAMWELL: How can you see your mother? You're an orphan.

THALIA: Flowers . . . lovely white flowers . . .

DAMWELL: Oh, yes, lovely white flowers . . .

THALIA: I'll pick them, Muti. I'll get them. I'll pick them, Muti. Muti? The soldiers are coming, Muti.

DAMWELL (*Fiercely whispered.*): Stay back!

THALIA: Muti? Muti? (*Pause.*) Damwell?

DAMWELL: Yes, I'm here, darling.

THALIA: Will?

DAMWELL: Well . . .

THALIA: Babe?

DAMWELL: Oh, yes she's here.

THALIA: Millicent?

DAMWELL: Yes. Hi. Millicent's right here.

THALIA: Who's the bravest smiler?

DAMWELL: You are honey!

THALIA: All the little orphan girls have gone to heaven. We're all little angels in the sky now. Finally happy. Finally free to live and to love. Real life begins now. (*THALIA dies.*)

DAMWELL: *Thalia!*

(*the tragic end*)

~

TURTLES ARE FREE

Words and music by Peg Healey

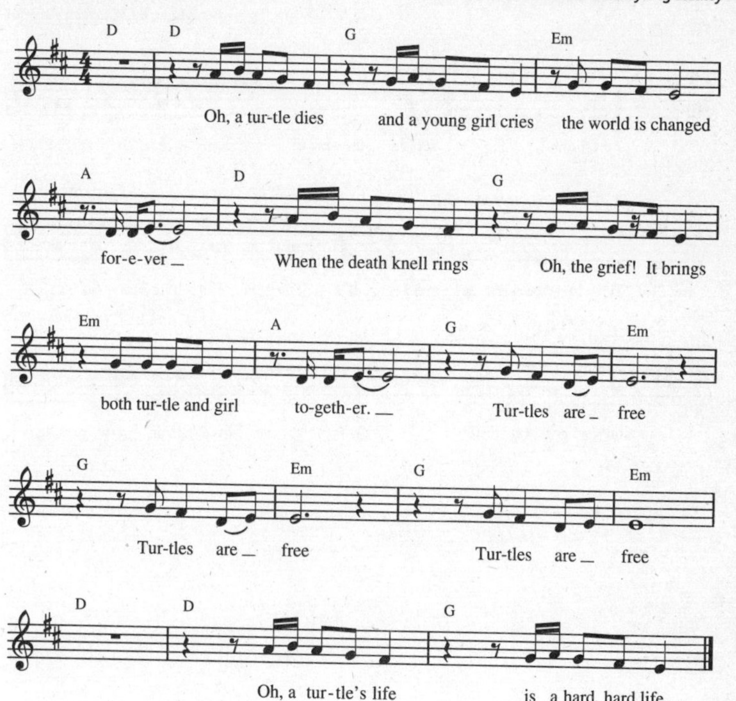

WHO'S THE BRAVEST SMILER

Words by the Five Lesbian Brothers
Music by Maureen Angelos

BRAVE SMILES

Words and music by Peg Healey

VIN MARCONI'S SONG

Word and music by Peg Healey and Dominique Dibbell

B♭m7
E♭7
hand a - long the Seine prov - ing to me I was a les - bi -
A♭
Gdim7
an. But long it could not
A♭
Gdim7
last She loved me deep She loved me
A♭
Gdim7
fast I awoke one morn-ing to find her
Gdim7
gone I had to find a rea - son to go
E♭7
Gdim7
on And then I met them I shan't for -
A♭
B♭m7
E♭7
get them I loved them one and all when I could
A♭
Gdim7
get them In the vast pa - rade of stars We were so
A♭
Gdim7
young The world was ours We were so gay in ev - ery way Ca -
E♭7
A♭
rous - ing with the flot - sam and the jet - sam

Gdim7 A♭
But as the years roll cruel - ly by
Gdim7 A♭
with count-less love, and count-less sad good-byes. The
Gdim7 A♭
mir - ror tells me truth - ful - ly I've grown I
E♭ Edim B♭m7 Adim7 E♭7
plan to live my la - ter years a - lone And then I
Gdim7 A♭
saw you How I a - dore you When you
B♭m7 E♭7 A♭
fix your hair I want to do it for you! Is this true
Gdim7 A♭
love at last? How I'm a - fraid to ask My
Ddim7 A♭/E♭
knees are weak I can-not speak I
B♭m7 Bdim7
took the stage blood's boil - ing rage Is
A♭/E♭ E♭7 E♭7 A♭
this true love or is it just— old age?

THALIA'S LAMENT
Words and music by Dominique Dibbell
Slowly
Fm Fm C7
There's a brave smile _ look-ing back at me. It re -
C7 Fm Fm
minds me of the girl I used to be Once I had a heart, _ but I guess I
B♭m C7 Fm
broke it Once I had a song, _ but now I choke on it And out -
A♭ A♭7 Fm B♭m
side, the snow is fal-ling like my tears on - ly fro - zen, _ and I
B♭m B♭m/A♭ Gdim C7
can't turn a-way from this lone - ly path I've cho - sen In the
Fm C7
warmth of a bar, a stead - y hand to hold. So, to -
C7 C7/E Fm
night, just for to - night, let me not be a - lone.

CATER-WAITER

Eric Lane

CATER-WAITER is a part of *The Gary and Rob Show,* a play comprised of ten ten-minute pieces. CATER-WAITER was commissioned by WATT Theater Company, Donal Egan Artistic Director. It premiered at Westbeth in New York City, May 1993. The cast was as follows:

GARY . . . . .Thomas Keith
ROB . . . . Mark Bateman

The play was named Finalist in the Actors Theatre of Louisville National Ten-Minute Play Contest.

Characters

GARY, a cater-waiter who has been doing this too long. Late twenties to early thirties. Smart, funny. Masks his anger with humor.
ROB, new to catering. Early to mid twenties. Sweet, gentle, cute.

Setting

Kitchen area at a Republican fund-raiser in Connecticut

Time

1987–1990

~

SCENE I

1987
Breaktime. A table. Two chairs.
A glass with a little water used as an ashtray.

GARY *sits on the table, facing out. He smokes. His jacket is slung over one of the chairs. Bow tie unhooked but still on. Top shirt button undone.*

ROB *quickly eats dinner—leftovers from the gala: veal, straw potatoes (french fries), and vegetable medley (mixed vegetables).* GARY *looks over at him, then straight out. Takes a drag on his cigarette.*

GARY: I told Karl, "Karl," I says. "You stick me on another Republican fund-raiser, I don't care if it is the middle of Connecticut, I'm walking. You got eighty-seven gay men and three lesbians serving dinner to a buncha Reagan cronies, doesn't that strike you as the least bit ironic? I mean, it's like B'nai Brith serving the fucking Nazis." How're the french fries?

ROB: I thought they're straw potatoes.

GARY: Out there they're straw potatoes. Back here they're french fries.

ROB: They're o.k. A little cold but . . . Aren't you gonna eat?

GARY: (*Shakes his head "no." To a passing waiter we don't see*): Hey, Miss Thing. That beeline to the dessert's fastest I seen you moving all night. (*To* ROB) My name's Gary, by the way.

ROB: (*Wipes hand, offers it*): Rob.

GARY: Hey, Rob.

ROB: Hey, Gary.

GARY: I don't remember seeing you on the bus.

ROB: I live just ten minutes from here.

GARY: Fancy schmancy.

ROB: Ah, no, it's my parents' house.

GARY: You live with your parents?

ROB: Well, they're in Florida most of the time.

GARY (*With accent*): Boca—

ROB (*Smiles, nods*): You been there? (*GARY rolls his eyes*) Right.

GARY: Must be hard getting to auditions from here.

ROB: I didn't say I was an actor.

GARY: Honey, you're in a tux on a Saturday night, and you're not one of the guests. The odds are in my favor.

ROB: How about you?

GARY: I'm just a cater-waiter. This is my whole life. I live to french-serve women whose hair doesn't move when their head does. No, actually, I'm a performance artist.

ROB: What do you do?

GARY: Well, it's kinda like giving a big party for your friends, except they have to pay, and you're the only one gets to talk. I tried being an actor, but it just didn't work.

ROB: Why was that?

GARY: There was this basic concept I just couldn't get a handle on. See, like when you're onstage with another actor, well, you must've had this, and they're talking, you have to listen to them.

ROB: So they're one-man shows.

GARY: I just did a piece downtown about codependency called "Healing the Oprah Within." It was autobiographical, of course. And right now, I'm working on a new piece based on the life of Rose Marie.

ROB: The one with the bow.

GARY: That's her. See, the other night I turned on *The Dick Van Dyke Show* and found I was really identifying with her. It was definitely scary. So I thought I'd do a piece about it. (*To passing friend*) Hey, Miss Thing. One hairdo at a time, please. (*To ROB*) You can just picture her this morning with her hair wrapped around a Chock Full o'Nuts can. So what about you?

ROB: What?

GARY: Shows. Like what kind?

ROB: You don't want to hear.

GARY: O.K. (*A beat*) No, really. What kind of shows do you do?

ROB: Well, musicals mostly. I have a second call-back Monday for *No, No, Nanette.*

GARY (*Quickly sings*):

No, No, Nanette, that's all I hear
I hear it the whole day through

ROB: It's just a chorus thing but . . .

GARY: Hey, it's a job. (*ROB knocks tables twice*) Knock on imitation pine board. (*Sees others heading back*) Oh, jeez. We better get back. (*Doesn't move. Continues smoking.*)

ROB (*Re: french fries*): Sure you don't want any?

GARY (*Shakes head "no"*): You know, sometime maybe, if you're in a show, let me know, I'll come see it.

ROB: Sure. That'd be great. Same here.

GARY (*Takes flier out of coat pocket, hands it to him*): I just had them printed this morning.

ROB: I like the bow. Very Rose Marie.

GARY: You like it? (*ROB smiles*) The reservation number, that's my apartment, too, if you want to get together sometime. If you're in the city. Like for coffee.

ROB: I don't get into the city all that much.

GARY: Sure, living out here.

ROB: I mean, David and I've been spending a lot of time together. You know David, one of the captains.

GARY: Oh, sure. David. He's a nice guy. A few control issues. Well, just one or two. But really nice. Look, I hope you didn't think—

ROB: No, it's o.k.

GARY: 'Cause I didn't mean—

ROB: Maybe we'll see each other on another job real soon.

GARY: I don't think so. I told Karl. "Karl," I says. "You got me till the end of the month. Then I'm leaving catering for good." "Yeah, yeah, yeah," he says. "You always say that." Well, this time it's for real.

ROB: Good for you.

GARY: Yeah, good for me.

SCENE 2

1988
On break. Rob eats dinner quickly. Gary smokes.

GARY: I hate this job. (*Inhales*) I hate this place. (*Inhales*) I hate these people. (*Inhales*) I told Karl, "Karl," I says. "This is the last year I'm doing this. I don't care if you are stuck. You find somebody else." (*Smells shirt*) God, I need to wash this.
ROB: You want some french fries?
GARY (*Shakes head "no"*): Where's Miss David tonight?
ROB: He wasn't feeling so good.
GARY: I should've tried that with Karl. Actually, I did try that with Karl. Has he gone to the doctor?
ROB: Nah, it's no big deal. Just a little cold, that's all.
GARY (*Nods*): I never seen so many Nancy Reagan red dresses in one room at the same time. I guess they figure their days are numbered. It's kinda like that Fred and Ginger number with all the women dressed like her. Which one is that? *Swingtime?* (*ROB shrugs*) Maybe *Swingtime.*
ROB: I got a call-back Tuesday for *Carnival.* National tour.
GARY: The Anna Maria Alberghetti part, I'm sure.
ROB: Chorus. But it's a job.
GARY: Hey, it's a job. I hate this job. (*He smokes.*)

SCENE 3

1989
On break. Gary smokes a cigarette. He looks over to where Rob would sit. He isn't there. Gary looks out, smokes.

SCENE 4

1990
On break. Gary smokes. Rob eats.

GARY: How you doing?

ROB: O.K. (*Re: french fries*) You want? (*GARY shakes his head "no."*)

GARY: I was sorry to hear about David.

ROB: It's o.k.

GARY: Yeah, well . . . (*ROB starts to cry. GARY gently touches his sleeve*) It's o.k., honey. It's o.k.

ROB: I—

GARY: It's o.k. Maybe him and Karl are together. Maybe this time, they're the ones being served.

(*Lights fade.*)

BAD DREAM

Craig Lucas

The first performance of *BAD DREAM* was on WBAI radio, May 11, 1992. It was directed by Scott Ziegler and Gordon Hunt, produced by the Atlantic Theater Company. The cast was as follows:

ROBERT . . . . Steven Goldstein
MALCOLM . . . . Ray Anthony Thoms

Characters

ROBERT
MALCOLM

~

Darkness. Sound of someone breathing. The breaths comes faster, then a quick expulsion of air and a relaxing of breath: the end of a nightmare.

ROBERT: Are you awake? (*Pause.*) Honey? . . .
MALCOLM (from a deep sleep, inaudible): What's wrong?
ROBERT: I'm having heebie-jeebies.
MALCOLM: Ohhhh . . . it's okay. (*Pause.*)
Tell me . . . (*Pause.*) It's gonna be great, you'll see.
ROBERT: It won't.
MALCOLM: You have a bad dream?
ROBERT: It was horrible.
MALCOLM: What?
ROBERT: No, go to sleep.
MALCOLM: It's okay . . . What happened?
ROBERT: It was all . . . There was like this . . . It was like this horrible engine room. . . . It was filling up with water. . . .

Every time I tried to turn one of these gears or open one of these portals, they were all too small and there was all this, like, grease. . . . It was getting hotter and hotter. . . . And you had left me these messages which I had written on my stomach or on my chest—how to get out—and I forgot they were there and I wiped my hands, trying to get this goop off and . . . smeared your words.

MALCOLM: Awww. (*Pause.*) Do you . . . ? What do you think the ship represents?

ROBERT: I don't know.

MALCOLM: What are your associations?

ROBERT: I don't know. . . . Just tell me.

MALCOLM: Well . . . It's something large and important. . . . You're trapped inside . . . and its sinking. . . . What—?

ROBERT: The two party system?

MALCOLM: De doctor thinks dat maybe what you want is for me to write your report for you . . . save your ship from sinking . . .

ROBERT: Uh-huh.

MALCOLM: And that you feel bad maybe because you've been jerking off . . .

ROBERT: Where do you get that?

MALCOLM: Well, Freud feels strongly that in a dream . . . sticky goopy stuff . . .

ROBERT: I see.

MALCOLM: —almost always represents sticky goopy stuff. And in light of the fact that we have not been having maybe the amount of necessary activity which . . .

Good-sized silence.

ROBERT: I left the tape in the VCR. Right?

MALCOLM: . . . Yeah, you did, but—

ROBERT: I'm sorry.

MALCOLM: It's okay, I don't care.

ROBERT: I'm just out of my mind. Nothing makes me feel like . . .

MALCOLM: I don't care, really, it's your body. You can . . . beat it 'til it . . . blisters. . . . (*Pause.*) It's a horrible dream. You'll finish your report.

ROBERT: Oh, I've put it off so long. . . . I mean, I don't have a *clue*. . . . Do you want to go to sleep?

MALCOLM: Mm-hm. (*Pause.*)

ROBERT: I don't even know where *not* to start with it. (*Pause.*)

MALCOLM: Is there anything I can help with?

ROBERT: Shoot me . . . (*Pause.*)

MALCOLM: When is it due?

ROBERT: Two weeks ago yesterday.

MALCOLM: You got an extension, I thought.

ROBERT: It doesn't matter, because I'll never finish it.

MALCOLM: Yes you will.

ROBERT: I'm a complete fraud. I don't know anything about—

MALCOLM: You always say this—

ROBERT (*without stopping*): —this kind of system. I've been bullshitting my way through—

MALCOLM: You always do this and then you forget you do it.

ROBERT: Not like this.

MALCOLM: Yes, you do. And you always say that.

ROBERT: I do?

MALCOLM: Yes. Remember we went to Maine and you were in a panic about that thing—

ROBERT: I wasn't like this, though.

MALCOLM: You were out of your mind. You wished Catherine a belated happy birthday and apologized—

ROBERT: Right.

MALCOLM (*without stopping*): —for forgetting and it was like three days after the party you threw.

ROBERT: Yeah. (*Pause.*) I was.

MALCOLM: You were certifiable. Remember you rented that horrible shack up at that lake because—

ROBERT: Uh!

MALCOLM: —you *had* to be away to learn that software and then you called your answering machine . . . ?

ROBERT: No.

MALCOLM: Oh, there was a message from the phone man saying they'd buzzed the buzzer and you were sure the dog had destroyed the apartment—

ROBERT: Oh, yeah.

MALCOLM: That drove him nuts and you called the super and had him check on the apartment and the dog was with *you*? (*Pause.*)

ROBERT: Thank you. I feel better.

MALCOLM: Good. (*Pause.*)

ROBERT: I am. I'm insane.

MALCOLM: Sweet dreams. (*Pause.*)

ROBERT: They're going to fire me, though, I know they are. I'm sorry. (*Pause.*)

MALCOLM: They just gave you a raise.

ROBERT: That's why. They're paying me too much and the recession . . . (*Pause.*) I just . . . My mind, one thing to the next: I won't finish the report, they'll fire me, I won't be able to keep up our bills, we'll lose our health insurance . . . (*Pause.*) When you do you have your blood done again? (*Pause.*) Sweetheart? (*Pause.*) You can't be asleep yet.

MALCOLM: I'd like to be.

ROBERT: Just tell me. (*Pause.*)

MALCOLM: Last week, Robert. (*Pause.*)

ROBERT: When were you gonna tell me that?

MALCOLM: When you were back on the planet.

ROBERT: Is it bad?

MALCOLM: It's not great.

ROBERT: You can tell me.

MALCOLM: Fifty-six. (*Pause.*)

ROBERT: Oh, baby . . .

MALCOLM: It's okay. Ken says a lot people walk around for years with low T-cells. I just . . . have to keep doing the pentamidine—

ROBERT: Right.

MALCOLM: —and . . . resting and eating right and . . .

ROBERT: That's right. Oh sweet baby . . .

MALCOLM: I feel fine. . . . The ship isn't sinking yet.

ROBERT: I know.
MALCOLM: You'll survive. . . .
ROBERT: I know I will.
MALCOLM: I know you'll miss me. (*Pause.*) You'll meet somebody great.
ROBERT: I don't want to meet somebody great. (*Pause.*)
MALCOLM: Your report'll be great.
ROBERT: You're great.
MALCOLM: Yes, I am. (*Pause.*) So are you.
(*Silence.*)
ROBERT: I love you.
MALCOLM: Shut up. (*Pause.*) Please?

ROBERT is crying, trying not to make any noise.

MALCOLM: Come on.
ROBERT: I'm sorry. I'm sorry.

MALCOLM turns on the light.

MALCOLM: Why do you do all the crying, and I'm the one who's sick?
ROBERT: I know.
MALCOLM: Please stop, honey.
ROBERT: I can't.
MALCOLM: All right.
ROBERT: I can't even imagine a world without you.
MALCOLM: I can't imagine a world without me either.
ROBERT: You must be so fucking angry with me.
MALCOLM: I'm not, though.
ROBERT: I know you're not, that's the amazing thing.
MALCOLM: I'm glad you're not sick.
ROBERT: But why? (*Pause.*) Why aren't I sick? It doesn't make any sense. I've slept with half of America. (*Pause.*)
MALCOLM: I'm sick of feelings. . . . You know?
ROBERT: . . . Uh-huh.
MALCOLM: I'm sick of support groups.

ROBERT: Me too.

MALCOLM: I'm sick of sickness. I'm sick of articles. I'm sick of the news. I'm sick of constantly being reminded. I'm sick of Magic Johnson.

ROBERT: Oh, he's so cute, though.

MALCOLM: And funerals. I'm sick of me.

ROBERT: I'm not.

MALCOLM: I am.

ROBERT: I'm not. (*They kiss.*)

MALCOLM: Can we . . . ? (*ROBERT nods.*)

MALCOLM: I meant turn out the light.

ROBERT: Oh.

MALCOLM: Sorry.

ROBERT turns out the light. Pause.

MALCOLM: But we can.

ROBERT: Really? . . . You sure you want to?

MALCOLM: Well . . .

Rustle of sheets.

ROBERT: God, I have never known anybody who could get hard so fast.

MALCOLM: Yeah . . .

ROBERT: Ooof.

MALCOLM: Play with my balls . . . (*Pause.*) Mm.

ROBERT: Can I suck you?

MALCOLM: No.

ROBERT: Please?

MALCOLM: No, Robert.

ROBERT: How's that?

MALCOLM: That's great. (*Pause.*) Let me lick you. . . . Bring it up here. . . .

ROBERT: Wait . . . Be careful—your beard . . .

MALCOLM: Did I scratch you?

ROBERT: No just . . . Oh, that feels so—*God.* Yes, suck me. . . . Wait . . .

MALCOLM: Come.

ROBERT: No, with you.

MALCOLM: Come on my face.

ROBERT: Are you close?

MALCOLM: Uh-huh.

ROBERT: Are you sure? Are you ready? . . . Oh, Jesus your mouth feels so . . . Ouch . . .

MALCOLM: Did I —?

ROBERT: No, it's okay . . .

MALCOLM: Are you sure? Do you want to look at it?

ROBERT: No. I want this, I want to make you come . . . (*Breathing, rustling.*) Oh, I love you.

MALCOLM: I love you too . . .

ROBERT: I love you so much.

MALCOLM: Oh yeah . . . Oh . . . Oh . . . Oh . . .

ROBERT: Shoot it . . .

MALCOLM: Yeah . . .

ROBERT: Yeah . . .

MALCOLM: Oh . . .

The sounds of MALCOLM'S *orgasm. Overlapping the end of it.*

ROBERT: Baby . . .

MALCOLM: Jesus . . .

ROBERT: Did you . . . ? (*Cracks up.*) Did you shoot in my *hair*?

MALCOLM: Did I?

ROBERT: Are you like working for NASA or something?

MALCOLM (*also laughing*): Did I really? It didn't get in your eye or anything.

ROBERT: I don't think you can get it from your eye, can you?

ROBERT *turns the light on. With the blanket up over* MALCOLM'S *knees, he wipes himself up; the Kleenexes are treated like nuclear waste.*

MALCOLM: Don't you want to come?

ROBERT takes the Kleenexes from MALCOLM and deposits them in the trash bin.

MALCOLM: Wash your hands.

ROBERT goes off. Sounds of water running. MALCOLM lies still. ROBERT returns.

ROBERT: Can you?
MALCOLM: What?
ROBERT: Get it from your eye.
MALCOLM: No. Did you get it in your eye?
ROBERT: I don't . . . I can't tell . . .
MALCOLM: Did you rinse it?
ROBERT: Yes. I'm fine.

They kiss, snuggle, lights still on.

ROBERT: Goodnight, honey.
MALCOLM: Don't you want to come?
ROBERT: Maybe in the morning. (*Pause.*) Lights out?
MALCOLM: I might read.
ROBERT: You sure?
MALCOLM: Mm-hm.

ROBERT has his head on MALCOLM's chest.

ROBERT: You're the best.
MALCOLM: Yep. (*Pause.*)
ROBERT: This feels so good. (*Pause.*) I don't give a shit about the report.
MALCOLM: Good.

ROBERT: It'll write itself.
MALCOLM: Right. (*He sighs.* ROBERT*'s eyes are closed. Silence.*)
MALCOLM: Honey?
ROBERT: Mmm?
MALCOLM: Never mind. (*Silence. No one moves. End of scene.*)

IT'S OUR TOWN, TOO

(A PLAY IN ONE ACT)

Susan Miller

IT'S OUR TOWN, TOO was first staged by The Fountainhead Theater in Los Angeles.

Characters:

STAGE MANAGER	MOLLY
EMILY	CHANCE
ELIZABETH	DOC MCADOO
GEORGE	2 ANGRY CITIZENS
LOUIS	

~

No curtain. No scenery. The STAGE MANAGER *walks on and as she talks, begins placing the minimal boxes or chairs that will suggest a sense of place. House lights remain on until she begins to speak.*

STAGE MANAGER: This play is called *It's Our Town, Too* and all you need to know about who wrote it is she's still here and constantly wondering.

Beat

This first scene is called An Ordinary Afternoon and you'll see two of our main characters, Emily and Elizabeth.

A train whistle is heard.

It's 4 A.M. in our town. The stars were out like a promise and someone kissed someone they'd never thought of kissing before. Teachers doubted their lessons and Mrs. Malone could be heard singing the overture to *Carousel*. If you were passing through our town, and you happened to stop at the general store for some of Brenda Samson's peach pie, you might be lulled into thinking that folks here were small and narrow and wouldn't give a rightful place to the world's concerns.

But we're no different from anyone else, trying to grasp the meaning of things. We're mean and lost and fragile and shrewd. We're lonely and aiming too high, bitter and good. We come up thinking the world is sweet but it's every human's experience to meet disappointment.

Sound of a bird.

Sometimes there's a commotion sets in over a new possibility. Like the summer Abigail Cruthers swore she spotted a UFO, when it turned out to be Emily Rosen's hopes making themselves known in a burst of light.

Beat

Which brings me to Emily and Elizabeth.

I suppose there aren't any two people on the planet put together in one place for very long, who don't have their disagreements, who don't feel sometimes like maybe they made the worst mistake of their lives or wish the person they thought was so sweet just a few hours before, would pack up and leave. There isn't anybody who hasn't looked across the dinner table and thought I don't know if I love her anymore. And it can drive good people to saying cold words. But it's not really the fact. It's no more true than the first day when you looked at somebody and thought, "She's the one."

Thought, "I'm saved." We're just scared is all, every one of us.

School bell, sound of young people.

Now we're going to go back to the day two of our kind really saw each other for the first time. And knew that there was some future in it.

Beat

Oh, uh, this is high school and well, you all remember what that was like. In your heart of hearts aren't you still standing by your locker waiting for that certain one to walk by and maybe, just maybe stop to say your name?

STAGE MANAGER *backs away as* EMILY *and* ELIZABETH *walk on, as if carrying books. They are seventeen and breathless.*

EMILY: I liked what you said in class today.

ELIZABETH: Did you? God, 'cause I was looking at you the whole time. Trying not to. I wasn't too—well, too full of myself was I?

EMILY: Oh, no. Not at all. You were just talking like . . . like you. I mean, it was very smart and everything but sweet, too. It was like, you were saying, okay, there are some things I know pretty well but then you wanted us to see that there are lots of things you don't know, either, and it's okay not to know them. In fact maybe it's important not to know them, to be a real human being. I was just so proud of you for that.

ELIZABETH: You're something, Emily. You know that. You're just about the best person I ever met.

EMILY: Did you ever think that maybe it's someone else who puts us up there? I mean, just by being near to something good and true, brings out our real nature?

ELIZABETH: You have a great way about you, Emily.

EMILY: Well, I don't know about that.

ELIZABETH: I hope when we graduate we'll still be friends.

EMILY: I wouldn't want to live without talking to you every day.

ELIZABETH: I guess that's just about how I feel.

We HEAR parents call out: "EMILY! ELIZABETH!"

EMILY: So, it's good we had this talk, then.

ELIZABETH: Sometimes I think the earth is just gonna spin me off and I'll fly by night and keep you safe, Emily.

EMILY: I'd rather if you stayed here on the ground with me. If you could, I mean. If you didn't think it was holding you back, that is.

ELIZABETH *gives her a quick kiss. They are both stunned.*

ELIZABETH: I had to, that's all.

EMILY: Oh, my.

Lights dim on the girls, as they leave and the STAGE MANAGER *speaks from the corner of the stage.*

STAGE MANAGER: Well, that's how these things get started. Somebody fastens inside of you, and you're lost. 'Course it's always pleasing to watch two such fresh ones as Emily and Elizabeth. If we didn't know so much about the terrible turn the heart takes, we could be happier for them. (*Beat*) Anyhow, twenty years have passed. A wedding's about to take place. Emily and Elizabeth set up house over on Taft Street. And you remember Georgie, the newspaper boy, well he lives across the way with his life partner—that'd be Louis. And today all these fine friends are preparing to send their offspring out into the world together. (*Calling out.*) Chance! This is Emily and Elizabeth's son and the bridegroom in today's event.

Chance enters.

STAGE MANAGER: Chance, I thought the audience might like to know how it's been growing up with two mothers.

CHANCE: Well, I don't think of it like that, exactly. They're my parents is all. Oh, sometimes we fight about if I leave my clothes all over the floor. We laugh pretty much too, like, about—well you had to be there. Mom, that's Emily—she kind of spurs me on, you know. Won't let me quit when I'm down low. Being the son of a doctor, you see how people have it a lot harder than you. Mama—she's more moody, sorta like me. But she's a poet and you know how they are. I'm working as a stringer for the *Times.* I think I'd like to write about medicine.

STAGE MANAGER: Okay, Chance. Thank you for—

CHANCE: One more thing. The day my Mom and Mama were arrested. The day the very same country I call home, broke up ours—saying we weren't a real family—that was a hard day. Nearly broke my faith. Molly and I, that's my bride-to-be, we were thinking rash thoughts. It was our parents pulled us through it.

STAGE MANAGER: How's that?

CHANCE: Sat us down and said, You know what's true. You know what's right. And same as always they wouldn't stop talkng until everyone came around to their way.

An intense young woman approaches.

STAGE MANAGER: Well, now here's young Molly. And she'll be wanting to say something too.

MOLLY (*To audience*): Hi. Uhm. I guess you probably want to know how I turned out and all. Okay, sure, sometimes I wished I had Eleanor Jones' parents, but who doesn't? I mean, when one of your fathers is being overprotective or a real pain in the butt about doing your homework. Still, when we have our children, if one of them wants to climb Mount Everest or fix machines or stay at home and tend the next generation, well, as long as she's a friend you can count on and gives something back to the world in her own particular way, I'll be proud to call her mine. And if her heart opens up to someone decent—woman or man—I'll be glad my whole life for them to pair off and meet the world together.

STAGE MANAGER: Well, kids, that was fine. Just fine. Now you better run off. Gotta a wedding to get ready for.

Lights up in area of EMILY *and* ELIZABETH*'s house.*

CHANCE (*Presenting himself*): Is my tie straight?

EMILY (*Moving to adjust it*): Here, you never could do that right. (*She fights back tears.*)

CHANCE: Mom! You're not going to start again?

EMILY: I'm not. Really, I'm not.

ELIZABETH: Well, a mother's got a right to cry at her son's wedding.

CHANCE: Did Nana cry at yours?

EMILY: We didn't have an official wedding. No one would perform it. (*Beat*) But we took vows.

ELIZABETH: A person takes vows every day. Really. Over the first cup of coffee. When she looks up at you from reading the newspaper.

EMILY (*To Chance*): There. You're gorgeous.

CHANCE: I don't feel so good.

EMILY: I know. It'll pass.

ELIZABETH (*Launching into a game they used to play—this time to quell his nerves*): Okay, Bauer steps up to the plate, Jerhovic gets his sign, throws it. Bauer swings, it's a—

CHANCE (*Very animated*): Strike! Jerhovic tosses a curve, Bauer goes for it misses. Strike two. Another one fired down the pike and—

ELIZABETH: Bauer connects! It's going going—

CHANCE: Caught. He's out. We win!

Lights up on the area of GEORGE and LOUIS's house. They are finishing the last beat of a song they used to sing to MOLLY, now designed to quell HER nerves.)

MOLLY: Daddy, how did you and Dad do it? I mean, all these years with the same person, day after day, night after night. Doesn't it get terribly predictable? The same face and how he smells and what he's going to say next?

GEORGE: Yes!

LOUIS: I never know what he's going to say next.

MOLLY: But, isn't it awfully terribly monotonous?

GEORGE: Molly, you and Chance, you're going to have afternoons when it seems everything is just the way it was the day before. Days when the pipes go bad and that sofa you ordered doesn't arrive and— Bless those days, Molly.

MOLLY: I'm going to miss you guys.

LOUIS: What do you mean? We're not going anywhere.

MOLLY: Well, I know that. But you won't be shouting up to me to wake up, lazy bones or forcing me to listen to some article that makes you crazy mad.

GEORGE: Don't worry, we're gonna call you up on the telephone and make you listen to some article that makes us crazy mad.

We hear the wedding march.

MOLLY: I'm scared.

LOUIS: Perfectly reasonable response.

GEORGE: We're holding you up, sweet girl. We're on your side.

STAGE MANAGER steps forward.

STAGE MANAGER: Maybe before the wedding Doc McAdoo can fill you in a little on some history.

DOC MCADOO comes on.

DOC MCADOO: I guess you want to know how they did it. Had their babies. Well, I guess you know where babies come from. I don't have to tell you that. But where children come from—how they survive—well, that's a mother's explanation, a father's humor, a thousand sleepless nights and constant arms of welcome. (*Beat*) But for you more technically minded, Emily and Elizabeth adopted Chance when he was two days old. George and Louis, well they got Molly when she was a few weeks. Now I've delivered lots of human beings. And it doesn't matter how they get delivered. Some arrive the old-fashioned way and still find sorrow, even get beat up by their own flesh and blood. No, it's not about where a person comes from—it's who they come home to that gives them the odds in this life. And for what it's worth, Chance here and Molly, they lucked out.

There is an audible cacophony of sounds from the parents in question. DOC MCADOO *looks over in their direction.*

Excuse me, Em. El. George, Louis—I stand corrected. (*To audience*) they hate when anyone puts it like that. See, they figure *they're* the ones who got lucky. Anyhow, that's the story.

He leaves the stage. The two fathers stand with their daughter. And the two mothers, with their son. Their children remain still, while the parents speak to one another.

EMILY: Well, did you ever think we'd be seeing this day?
GEORGE: They're the most beautiful creatures I ever saw.
ELIZABETH: Louis, I thought we put you in charge of him.
LOUIS: Sorry. He's out of control.
ELIZABETH: Now if you keep this kind of thing up, Georgie Warren, we won't make it through the ceremony.
EMILY: I wasn't sure we'd make it to this day.
ELIZABETH: We're okay now. We're fine.
EMILY: Oh, I hope it lasts!

LOUIS: Can't guarantee anything.

ELIZABETH: So when the time comes, do you want to be called Granpa or Zada or—

EMILY: Stop!

GEORGE: Do you think we did all right by them?

EMILY: We did the best we could, Georgie.

GEORGE: I don't know.

LOUIS: Gotta let them blame us for one thing or another. It's a tradition.

ELIZABETH: Don't they just stop your heart?

LOUIS puts his arm around GEORGE. EMILY touches ELIZABETH.

EMILY: You know what I think? I think we did good.

Suddenly an eruption, as a citizen steps forward.

ANGRY RIGHTEOUS CITIZEN: Just hold everything. Doesn't anybody care that this here is a play celebrating sodomizers. There's known felons in our community and some of you turning your heads the other way. People wake up. This isn't right, not before God, not under the laws of the land of the free and the home of the brave.

ANOTHER PARTY HEARD FROM: Isn't anyone else tired of this crap? We've got a real people here, people. This is not normal. These children are going to have serious mental scars. And they're gonna have children, God knows what kind of deviants they'll be. No, sir. This is not right.

STAGE MANAGER: Excuse me, you're interrupting a wedding. (*To audience*) They tried that before when Emily and Elizabeth put a bid on their house. And when George and Lou went to the open house down at the elementary school. There's never any lack of trouble for what ought be a person's own business. Yeah. George's father never spoke to him again after he found out. Emily's mother, well she kept in touch but wouldn't look Elizabeth in the eye. It's a hard thing when your own turn away. It's a powerful hold they got on our hearts and minds—Mother. Father. The world is unforgiving enough without the people who brought us up in it, taking the other side. So, let's not allow that part of the world in today. Just for a little while, let's give these families a break. Seems to me we'd all sleep better at night knowing our children had someone decent to worry over them each and every day, each and every time they laid their head down to rest from the day's struggle. What does it matter, all the rest of it?

Music starts again. STAGE MANAGER *turns his back to the audience and toward the couples.*

STAGE MANAGER: I now pronounce you part of the human race that has the good fortune and the daily struggle of being married. (*Turns his head back to the audience*) We wish them all the best, don't we?

The lights shift, as the couples move out. The STAGE MANAGER *rearranges the boxes or chairs on stage.*

STAGE MANAGER: Well now, this is a hard part. This last scene, if you haven't already figured it out—is called "The End of Things." Of course, that's only one way of seeing it. Once you've known someone they never stop being a part of how you look at things. That goes for the living as well as the dead. And who knows but that we're being watched over somehow or carried out into the eternal universe, by every soul we ever mattered to or mattered to us. (*Beat*) But, our sad friends don't know any of this today. So bear with them.

There are chairs or boxes now arranged with "The Dead" seated and staring ahead. Among them, ELIZABETH *and* LOUIS*. Nearby laying flowers at a fresh gravesite, are* EMILY, GEORGE, *and* MOLLY.

This is a funeral for young Chance. Who was walking down the street one chilly day bringing home the newspaper with a story he was proud to write and caught someone's anger in a stray bullet.

GEORGE (*Comforting MOLLY*): Shh, shh. Dear Girl.

MOLLY: Why? Why him?

GEORGE: I don't know.

EMILY: What are we going to do now?

GEORGE: Go on.

MOLLY: I don't think I can.

GEORGE: Em—help us.

EMILY gathers them up in her arms.
Chance walks among the dead.

ELIZABETH: Over here, Chance. Next to me.

CHANCE (*Overcome*): Mother!

ELIZABETH: It's all right, it's all right.

CHANCE: We missed you so!

ELIZABETH: Yes.

CHANCE: Look at them! What can I do for them?

ELIZABETH: Let them go.

CHANCE: But they're burning in my throat. I see them behind my eyelids.

ELIZABETH: And you always will. But in a while it won't hurt as much.

GEORGE moves over to put flowers on LOUIS's grave.

LOUIS: I'm here, honey. I'm right here.

STAGE MANAGER: Louis died of a disease that took too many too young. And Elizabeth, from breast cancer. Too many, too young.

CHANCE: The last moment I spent on earth, was so . . . small. So normal. I never got to tell anyone what I really felt. What did I ever give anyone?

ELIZABETH: You were loved. And you loved in return. That's about all anyone can ask of the days we have. And don't you for a minute regret one casual morning or nights there wasn't some deep thought in the air. Why, even if you just sat near someone watching television—why even then, dear boy, you were a comfort. Someone was thinking: He means the world to me. And I mean the world to him. And we don't have to speak of it.

EMILY moves in front of ELIZABETH and CHANCE and falls to her knees.

EMILY: Do you know how much? How very much?
ELIZABETH: We know. Don't we Chance?
STAGE MANAGER: The human heart has a way of making itself large again, even after it's broken itself into a million pieces. Once a person knows a kiss and a kind word, you can't blame him for never wanting to live without them again. Our friends here will go on a long time past their partners, and they'll make room again for kisses and kind words, but the heart never forgets, never gives up the territory marked off for the ones who came before. They'll always have a place. And their kisses and kind words, beat on.

EMILY gathers up GEORGE and MOLLY.

EMILY: Come home now. Come home with me.

They walk off.

CHANCE: Mother?
ELIZABETH: What is it, honey?
CHANCE: Remember that game we used to play?
ELIZABETH: I remember.
CHANCE: Can we?
ELIZABETH: Of course. Of course we can.

Lights dim on the dead.

STAGE MANAGER: Well, it's turning into the next day. People are picking up their mail, making plans. Having opinions. This is who we are, I guess. This is us. It's a mystery isn't it?

Sound of a train whistle. A bird. A conversation. As lights dim.

The end.

GIVING UP THE GHOST

A STAGE PLAY IN THREE PORTRAITS

Cherríe Moraga

If I had wings like an angel
over these prison walls
I would fly
(*song my mother would sing me*)

Giving Up the Ghost had its world premiere on February 10, 1989, at The Studio, Theatre Rhinoceros in San Francisco, with the following cast (in order of appearance):

MARISA . . . . Belinda Ramírez
CORKY . . . . Linda Huey
AMALIA . . . . .Anna Olivarez

It was directed by Anita Mattos and José Guadalupe Saucedo, with sets by Yolanda López, lights by Stephanie Johnson, and sound by Chuy Varela.

An earlier version of *Giving Up the Ghost* was produced by the Front Room Theatre in Seattle. It opened on March 27, 1987, and was directed by Laura Esparza.

The play was developed in part through the "Broadcloth Series" hosted by At the Foot of the Mountain Theatre in Minneapolis. It was given staged readings on June 16 and June 24, 1984, directed by Kim Hines.

Giving Up the Ghost was published in book form by West End Press of Albuquerque in 1986. This current version of the play is based to a large degree on the Theatre Rhinoceros production.

Characters

MARISA, Chicana in her late twenties

CORKY, MARISA as a teenager

AMALIA, Mexican-born, a generation older than MARISA

THE PEOPLE, those viewing the performance or reading the play

Set

The stage set should be simple, with as few props as possible. A crate is used for street scenes downstage. A raised platform, stage left, serves as the bed in a variety of settings, including a hotel room, a mental hospital, and both AMALIA's and MARISA's apartments. A simple wooden table and two chairs, stage right, represent AMALIA's kitchen. Windows, doorways, and furniture appear in the imagination when needed. The suggestion of a Mexican desert landscape is illuminated upstage during scenes evoking indigenous México. Scrims can be used for the dreamlike sequences. Aside from the minimal set pieces mentioned above, lighting and music should be the main features in providing setting. Music should be used to re-create the "streetwise ritmo" of the urban life of these Chicanas, spanning a generation of Motown, soul, Tex-Mex, and Latin rock. It should also reflect the profound influence of traditional Mexican folk music—rancheras, corridos, mariachi, etc.—as well as the more ancient indigenous sounds of the flauta, concha, and tambor. Throughout the long monologues (unless otherwise indicated) when the nonspeaking actors remain on stage, the lighting and direction should give the impression that the characters both disappear and *remain within hearing range of the speaker. In short, direction should reflect that each character knows, on an intuitive level, the minds of the other characters.*

~

RETRATO I "LA PACHUCA"

PROLOGUE

This is the urban Southwest, a Chicano barrio within the sprawling Los Angeles basin. Street sounds fill the air: traffic, children's schoolyard voices, street repairs, etc. MARISA sits on a wooden crate, centerstage. She wears a pair of Levi's, tennis shoes, and a bright-colored shirt. Her black hair is pulled back, revealing a face of dark intensity and definite Indian features. She holds a large sketchbook on her lap. CORKY *enters upstage. Their eyes meet. As* MARISA'*s younger self,* CORKY *tries to act tough but displays a wide openheartedness in her face which betrays the toughness. She dresses "Cholo style"—khaki pants with razor-sharp creases, pressed white undershirt. Her hair is cut short and slicked back. She approaches the upstage wall, spray can in hand, feigning the bravado of her teenage male counterparts. She writes in large, Chicano graffiti-style letters, as* MARISA *writes in her sketchbook.*

Dedicación

Don't know where this woman
and I will find each other again,
but I am grateful to her   to something
that feels like a blesing

that I am, in fact, not trapped

which brings me to the question of prisons
politics
sex.

CORKY *tosses the spray can to* MARISA.

CORKY (With *MARISA.*): I'm only telling you this to stay my hand.
MARISA: But why, cheezus, why me?
Why'd I hafta get into a situation where all my ghosts come to visit?
I always see that man . . . thick-skinned, dark, muscular.
He's a boulder between us.
I can't lift him and her, too . . . carrying him.

He's a ghost, always haunting her . . .
lingering.

Fade out.

SCENE I

A Chicano "oldie" rises. Crossfade to CORKY *coming downstage, moving "low and slow" to the tune.*

CORKY: the smarter I get the older I get the meaner I get
tough a tough cookie my mom calls me
sometimes I even pack a blade
no one knows I never use it or nut'ing
but can feel it there there in my pants pocket
run the pad of my thumb over it to remind me I carry somet'ing
am sharp secretly
always envy those batos who get all cut up at the weddings
getting their rented tuxes all bloody
that red 'n' clean color
against the white starched collars
I love that shit!

the best part is the chicks all climbing into the ball of the fight
"¡Chuy, déjalo! Leave him go, Güero!" tú sabes
you know how the chicks get all excited 'n' upset 'n' stuff
they always pulling on the carnales 'n' getting nowhere
'cept messed up themselves 'n' everybody looks so
like they digging the whole t'ing tú sabes
their dresses ripped here 'n' there . . . like a movie
it's all like a movie

when I was a real little kid I useta love the movies
every Saturday you could find me there
my eyeballs glued to the screen
then later my friend Arturo 'n' me
we'd make up our own movies
one was where we'd be out in the desert
'n' we'd capture these chicks 'n' hold 'em up for ransom

we'd string 'em up 'n' make 'em take their clothes off
"strip" we'd say to the wall all cool-like
funny . . . now when I think about how little I was at the time
and a girl but in my mind I was big 'n' tough 'n' a dude
in my *mind* I had all their freedom
the freedom to see a girl   kina
the way   you see
an animal   you know?

like imagining
they got a difernt set
of blood vessels or somet'ing   like   so
when you mess with 'em
it don' affect 'em the way   it do   you
like like they got a difernt gland system or somet'ing that
that makes their pain cells
more dense

hell I dunno

but you see
I never could
quite
pull it off

always knew I was a girl
deep down inside
no matter how I tried to pull the other off

I knew
always knew
I was an animal that kicked back . . .

(*With* MARISA.) . . . cuz it hurt! (CORKY *exits.*)

MARISA (*From the platform, coming downstage.*): I never wanted to be a man, only wanted a woman to want me that bad. And they have, you know, plenty of them, but there's always that one you can't pin down, who's undecided. (*Beat.*) My mother was a heterosexual, I couldn't save her. My failures follow thereafter.

AMALIA (*Entering.*): I am a failure.

AMALIA is visibly "soft" in just the ways that MARISA appears "hard." She chooses her clothes with an artist's eye for color and placement. They appear to be draped over her, rather than worn: a rebozo wrapped around her shoulders, a blouse falling over the waist of an embroidered skirt. Her hair is long and worn down or loosely braided. As a woman nearing fifty, she gives the impression of someone who was once a rare beauty, now trading that for a fierce dignity in bearing.

AMALIA: I observe the Americans. Their security. Their houses. Their dogs. Their children are happy. They are not *un* . . . happy. Sure, they have their struggles, their problemas, but . . . it's a life. I always say this, it's a life. (*She sits at the table stacked with art books, puts on a pair of wire-rim glasses, leafs through a book.*)

MARISA: My friend Marta bought her mother a house. I admire her. Even after the family talked bad about her like that for leaving home with a gabacha, she went back cash in hand and bought her mother a casita kina on the outskirts of town. Ten grand was all it took, that's nothing here, but it did save her mother from the poverty her dead father left behind. I envy her. For the first time wished my father'd die so I could do my mother that kind of rescue routine.

I wanna talk about betrayal, about a battle I will never win and never stop fighting. The dick beats me every time. I know I'm not supposed to be sayin' this cuz it's like confession, like still cryin' your sins to a priest you long ago stopped believing was god or god's sit-in, but still confessing what you'd hoped had been forgiven in you. . . . (*Looking to AMALIA.*)

That prison . . . that passion to beat men at their own game.

AMALIA: I worry about La Pachuca. That's my nickname for her. I have trouble calling her by her Christian name. (*Savoring it.*) Marisa. (*"Rain sticks" in the background.*) I worry about La Pachuca. I worry what will happen to the beautiful corn she is growing if it continues to rain so hard and much.

CORKY (*Entering.*): one time Tury 'n' me stripped for real
there was this minister 'n' his family down the street
they was presbyterians or methodists or somet'ing
you know one of those gringo religions
'n' they had a bunch a kids
the oldest was named Lisa or somet'ing lightweight like that
'n' the littlest was about three or so, named Chrissy
I mean you couldn't really complain about Chrissy
cuz she wasn't old enough yet to be a pain in the cola
but you knew that was coming

Lisa'd be hassling me 'n' my sister Patsy all the time
telling us how we wernt really christians
cuz cath-lics worshipped the virgin mary or somet'ing
I dint let this worry me though cuz we was being tole at school
how being cath-lic was the one true numero uno church 'n' all
so I jus' let myself be real cool with her
'n' the rest of her little pagan baby brothers 'n' sisters
that's all they was to me as far as I was concerned
they dint even have no mass
jus' some paddy preaching up there with a dark suit on
very weird
not a damn candle for miles
dint seem to me that there was any good happening in that place at all

so one day Tury comes up with this idea how we should strip "for real"

I wasn't that hot on the idea but still go along with him
checkin' out the neighborhood looking for prey
then we run into Chrissy 'n' Tury 'n' me eye each other
the trouble is I'm still not completely sold on the idea
pero ni modo cuz I already hear comin' outta my mouth
real syrupy-like
"come heeeeere Chrissy, we got somet'ing to shooooow you"
well, a'course she comes cuz I was a big kid 'n' all
'n' we take her into this shed

I have her hand 'n' Tury tells her . . .
no *I* tole her this
I tell her we think she's got somet'ing wrong with her
"down there"
I think . . . I think I said she had a cut or somet'ing
'n' Tury 'n' me had to check it out
so I pull her little shorts down 'n' then her chones
'n' then jus' as I catch a glimpse of her little fuchi
fachi . . .
it was so tender-looking all pink 'n' real sweet like a bun
then stupid Tury like a menso goes 'n' sticks his dirty finger
on it
like it was burning hot

'n' jus' at that moment . . . I see this little Chrissy-kid
look up at me like . . . like I was her mom or somet'ing
like tú sabes she has this little kid's frown on her face
the chubby skin on her forehead all rumpled up
like . . . like she knew somet'ing was wrong with what we
was doing
'n' was looking to me to reassure her
that everyt'ing was cool 'n' regular 'n' all
what a jerk I felt like!

She pushes "Tury" away, bends down to "Chrissy."

so, I pull up her shorts 'n' whisper to her
"no no you're fine really there's nut'ing wrong with you
but don' tell nobody we looked
we don' want nobody to worry about you"
what else was I supposed to say? ¡Tonta!
'n' Tury 'n' me make a beeline into the alley 'n' outta there!

She exits.

SCENE 2

Crossfade to AMALIA *rising from the bed. It is morning.*

AMALIA: I remember the first time I met her, the day she first began to bring me her work. It was early morning, too early really, and there was someone at the door. At first I think it is my son, Che. Like him to appear at my doorstep with the least amount of warning. (*She goes to the "window," looks down to the front steps.* MARISA *appears, carrying a portfolio.*) But it was Marisa, standing there with a red jacket on, I remember, a beautiful color of red. Maybe if I had not dreamed the color the night before I might not even have bothered to open the door so early, such a hermit I am. (*To* MARISA.) ¿Sí?

MARISA: Hello. I got these . . . paintings. I . . . heard you could help me.

AMALIA: ¿Quién eres?

MARISA: Marisa. Marisa Moreno.

AMALIA: It's a little early ¿qué no?

MARISA: I'm sorry. Frank Delgado—

AMALIA: Súbete.

AMALIA *"buzzes"* MARISA *in.* AMALIA *puts on a robe, brushes back her hair.* MARISA *enters.*

MARISA: Good morning.

AMALIA: It's too early to tell.

MARISA: I'm sorry.

AMALIA: That's two "sorrys" already and I don't even got my eyes on yet.

MARISA: Sor . . .

AMALIA (*Smiling.*): Pásale. Pásale.

MARISA (*Handing her a small paper sack.*): Here, this is for you.

AMALIA: Siéntate.

MARISA: It's pandulce.

AMALIA (*Looking inside.*): Conchas. They're my favorites.

AMALIA puts the pastry on the table. MARISA sits down, holds the portfolio awkwardly in her lap. During the following scene there are brief lapses in the conversation.

AMALIA: ¿Quieres café?

MARISA: Gracias. No.

AMALIA: Pues, yo . . . sí. (*Goes to prepare the coffee.*) I can't even talk before I have a cup of coffee in me. Help yourself to the pandulce.

MARISA (*Indicating the books on the table.*): Are all these yours?

AMALIA: The books? Claro.

MARISA: They're wonderful.

AMALIA: Take a look at them if you want.

MARISA carefully props up her portfolio onto a chair and begins to leaf through one of the books. AMALIA reenters, looking for her glasses.

MARISA: You got a lotta . . . things.

AMALIA: What? Yes. Too much. My son, Che, he calls me a . . . rat pack.

MARISA: A pack rat.

AMALIA: Whatever you call it, I can't even find my glasses.

MARISA (*Pointing to the painting on the upstage wall.*): And this?

AMALIA: Well, I couldn't afford a room with a view, so . .. bueno, pues I improvised a little. ¿Te gusta? (*She finds her glasses in her robe pocket, puts them on.*)

MARISA: Yeah. Mucho.

AMALIA (*Observing her.*): You don't seem quite as awesome as Delgado described you.

MARISA: He told you about me?

AMALIA: Ay, all los boys at El Centro were talking about you, telling me how I should see your work . . . this new "Eastlos import."

MARISA: I didn't think they liked me.

AMALIA: Pues, I didn't say they *liked* you.

MARISA: Oh.

AMALIA: I think you scared them a little. Una pintora bien chingona, me dijo Frank.

MARISA: That's what he said?

AMALIA: Más o menos. Bueno . . . (*Indicating the portfolio.*) Abrélo. Let's see what makes those machos shake in their botas so much.

As MARISA *opens the portfolio, the lights crossfade to* CORKY *entering.*

CORKY: the weird thing was that after that episode with Chrissy
I was like a maniac all summer
snotty Lisa kept harassing me about the virgin mary 'n' all
'n' jus' in general being a pain in the coolie
things began to break down with her 'n' her minister's family
when me 'n' Patsy stopped going to their church meetings on wednesday nights
we'd only go cuz they had cookies 'n' treats after all the bible stuff
'n' sometimes had arts 'n' crafts where you got to paint
little clay statues of blond jesus in a robe
'n' the little children coming to him
the drag was that you also had to do these prayer sessions
where everybody'd stand in a circle squeezing hands
'n' each kid'd say a little prayer
you know like "for the starving people in china"

Patsy 'n' me always passed when we got squeezed
jus' shaked our heads no
cuz it was against our religion to pray with them
well, one time, this Lisa punk has the nerve to pray that Patsy 'n' me
would (*Mimicking.*) "come to the light of the one true Christian faith"
shi-it can you get to that? 'course we never went again

AMALIA *puts on an apron, becomes* CORKY'S *"mother."*

CORKY: but I remember coming home 'n' telling my mom . . .
"MOTHER": It's better mi'jitas, I think, if you don' go no more.
CORKY: 'n' it was so nice to hear her voice so warm
like she loved us a lot
'n' that night being cath-lic felt like my mom
real warm 'n' dark 'n' kind

Fade out.

SCENE 3

At rise, MARISA *straddles the kitchen chair, addresses* THE PEOPLE. AMALIA *is upstage by the bed. During* MARISA'*s monologue,* AMALIA *ties her hair back into a tight bun, applies a gray powder to her face, and draws dark circles under her eyes.*

MARISA: The women I have loved the most have always loved the man more than me, even in their hatred of him. I'm queer I am. Sí, soy jota because I have never been crazy about a man. (*Pause.*) My friend Sally the hooker told me the day she decided to stop tricking was when once, by accident, a john made her come. That was strictly forbidden. She'd forgotten to resist, to keep business business. It was very unprofessional . . . and dangerous. No, I've never been in love with a man and I never understood women who were, although I've certainly been around to pick up the pieces. My sister was in love with my brother.

CORKY (*Entering.*): My mother loved her father.

MARISA: My first woman—

CORKY: The man who put her away.

MARISA: The crazy house. Camarillo, Califas. Sixteen years old.

Blue light. Haunting music. AMALIA *becomes* "NORMA," MARISA*'s "first woman." She sits on the bed in a kind of psychotic stupor.* CORKY *goes over to her.* MARISA *narrates.*

MARISA: When I come to get my cousin Norma, she has eyes like saucers, spinning black and glass. I can see through them, my face, my name. She says . . .

"NORMA": I am Buddha.

CORKY: How'd you get that black eye? ¿Quién te pegó?

"NORMA": I am Buddha.

Fade out.

SCENE 4

CORKY *is alone on stage. She takes out a yo-yo, tries a few tricks. She is quite good.*

CORKY: since that prayer meeting night
when Patsy 'n' me wouldn't get squeezed into the minister's jesus
Lisa's nose was gettin' higher 'n' higher in the air

one day Patsy 'n' her are playing dolls up
on the second story porch of Mrs. Rodríguez's house
it was nice up there cuz Mrs. R would let you move the tables
'n' chairs 'n' stuff around to play "pertend"

my sister had jus' gotten this nice doll for her birthday
with this great curly hair
Lisa only had this kina stupid doll
with plastic painted-on hair 'n' only one leg
she'd always put long dresses on it to disguise the missing leg
but we all knew it was gone

anyway, one day this brat Lisa throws my sister's new doll into this mud puddle right down from Mrs. R's porch (*She lets out the yo-yo. It dangles helplessly.*)

Patsy comes back into our yard crying like crazy
her dolls all muddy 'n' the hair has turned bone straight
I mean like an arrow!
I wanted to kill that punk Lisa!
so me 'n' Patsy go over to Lisa's house
where we find the little creep all pleased with herself
I mean not even feeling bad
suddenly I see her bike which is really a trike
but it's huge . . . I mean hu-u-uge!
to this day, I never seen a trike that big
it useta bug me to no end that she wasn't even *trying*
to learn to ride a two-wheeler
so all of a sudden . . . (*Winding up with the yo-yo like a pitcher.*)
that trike 'n' Lisa's wimpiness come together in my mind
'n' I got that thing (*Throwing the pitch.*)
'n' I threw the sucker into the street

I dint even wreck it none (*She stuffs the yo-yo in her back pocket.*)
but it was the principle of the thing

a'course she goes 'n' tells her mom on me
'n' this lady who by my mind don' even seem like a mom
she dint wear no makeup 'n' was real skinny 'n' tall

'n' wore her hair in some kina dumb bun
she has the nerve to call my mom 'n' tell her what I done

AMALIA, as CORKY's "mom," appears upstage in an apron. She is stirring a pot in her arms. She observes CORKY.

CORKY: so a'course my mom calls me on the carpet
wants to know the story
'n' I tell her 'bout the doll 'n' Patsy 'n' the principle of the thing
'n' Patsy's telling the same story 'n' I can see in my mom's eyes
she don' believe I did nut'ing so bad but she tells me . . .
"MOTHER": We got to keep some peace in the neighborhood, hija.
CORKY: cuz we was already getting pedo from the paddy neighbors
'bout how my mom hollered too much at her kids . . . her own kids!
I mean if you can't yell at your own kids who *can* you yell at?
but she don' let on that this is the real reason
I hafta go over to the minister's house and apologize
she jus' kina turns back to the stove 'n' keeps on
with what she was doing

"MOTHER": Andale, mija, dinner's almost ready. (*CORKY hesitates.*) Andale. Andale.

CORKY (*Coming downstage.*): so, a'course I go . . .
I go by myself
with no one to watch me to see if I really do it
but my mom knows I will cuz she tole me to
'n' I ring the doorbell 'n' Mrs. Minister answers
'n' as I begin to talk that little wimp Lisa runs up
'n' peeks out at me from behind her mother's skirt
with the ugliest most snottiest shit-eating grin
I'd ever seen in a person

while all the while *I* say *I'm* sorry
'n' as the door shuts in front of my face
I vow I'll never make that mistake again . . .

(*With* MARISA.) I'll never show nobody how mad I can get!

Blackout.

SCENE 5

MARISA is pacing about AMALIA's room. AMALIA sits on the floor mixing paints. She wears a paint-splattered apron.

MARISA (*To THE PEOPLE.*): I have a very long memory. I try to warn people that when I get hurt, I don't forget it. I use it against them. I blame women for everything. My mistakes. Missed opportunities. My grief. I usually leave just when I wanna lay a woman flat. When I feel that vengeance rise up in me, I split. I desert.

AMALIA: Desert. Desierto. For some reason, I could always picture mi cholita in the desert, amid the mesquite y nopal. Always when I closed my eyes to search for her, it was in the Mexican desert that I found her. I *had* intended to take her . . . to México. She would never have gone alone, sin gente allá.

MARISA: This *is* México! What are you talking about? It was those gringos that put up those fences between us!

AMALIA brings MARISA to the table, takes out a piece of charcoal from her apron, puts it into MARISA's hand. MARISA begins to sketch.

AMALIA: She was hardly convincing. Her nostalgia for the land she had never seen was everywhere. In her face, her drawings, her love of the hottest sand by the sea.

Coming around behind her, AMALIA wraps her arms around MARISA's neck. Indigenous flutes and drums can be heard in the background.

AMALIA: Desierto de Sonora. Tierra de tu memoria. (*Turning* MARISA's *face to her.*) Same chata face. Yaqui. (*They hesitate, then kiss their first kiss.*)

MARISA: I've just never believed a woman capable of loving a man was capable of loving . . . me. Some part of me remains amazed that I'm not the only lesbian in the world and that I can always manage to find someone to love me. (*Pause.*) But I am never satisfied because there are always those women left alone . . . and unloved.

Lights slowly fade to black. Musical interlude.

~

Retrato II "La Loca"

SCENE 6

A sunny morning. AMALIA *is kneeling on a chair, bent over the table, painting in thick strokes and occasionally sipping at a cup of coffee. Her hair is combed into a braid and tied up.* MARISA *lies on the bed, hands behind her head.*

AMALIA: I've only been crazy over one man in my life. Alejandro was nothing special. Era pescador, indio. Once we took a drive out of the small town he lived in, and he was terrified, like a baby. I'm driving through the mountains and he's squirming in his seat, "Amalia, ¿pá dónde vamos? Are you sure you know where we're going?" I was so amused to see this big macho break out into a cold sweat just from going no more than twenty miles from his hometown. Pero ¡Ay, Dios! How I loved that man! I still ask myself what I saw in him, really. (*Pause.*) He was one of the cleanest people I had ever met. Took two, three baths a day. You have to, you know. That part of la costa is like steam baths some seasons. I remember how he'd even put powder in his shorts and under his huevos to keep dry. He was that clean. I always loved knowing that when I touched him I would find him like a saint. Pure, somehow . . . that no matter where he had been or who he had been with, he would always have washed himself for me. He always smelled . . . so clean. (*She wipes her hands, sits at the foot of the bed.*) When I went back home that first time, after my son was already grown, I had never dreamed of falling in love. Too many damn men under the bridge. I can see them all floating down the river like so many sacks of potatoes. "Making love," they call it, was like having sex with children. They rub your chi-chis a little, then they stick it in you. Nada más. It's all over in a few minutes. ¡Un río de cuerpos muertos!

MARISA: Sometimes I only see the other river on your face. I see it running behind your eyes. Remember the time we woke up together and your eye was a bowl of blood? I thought the river had broken open inside you.

AMALIA: I was crazy about Alejandro. But what I loved was not so much him . . . I loved his children. I loved the way he had made México my home again. (*Pause.*) He was not a strong man really. He was soft. An inside softness, I could feel even as his desire swelled into a rock hardness. Once he said that with me he felt as though he were "a heart that knew no sex." No man-woman, he meant, only heat and a heart and that even a man could be entered in this way. (*Indigenous music rises in the background.*) I, on the other hand, was *not* clean, forgot sometimes to wash. Not when I was around others, pero con mí misma, I became like animals. Uncombed. El olor del suelo.

MARISA: I remember the story you told me about the village children, how they had put una muñeca at the door of your casita. How you had found it there . . . there, in your likeness and you thought—

AMALIA: I must be mad.

Suddenly, the beat of tambores. CORKY *enters, wearing a native bruja mask. She dances across the stage with rattles in her hand. As she exists,* MARISA *goes to* AMALIA, *unbraids her hair*

MARISA: So we take each other in doses. I learn to swallow my desire, work my fear slowly through the strands of your hair.

MARISA bends to kiss AMALIA on the neck. AMALIA pulls away, comes downstage.

AMALIA: Of course, soon after, Alejandro ran to every whore he could find, but not without first calling me that: "puta, bruja." He claimed I was trying to work some kind of mala suerte on him, that I was trying to take from him his manhood, make him something less than a man. (*Pause, to MARISA.*) I have always felt like an outsider.

MARISA starts toward her, then changes her mind and exists.

AMALIA (*To THE PEOPLE.*): Ni de aquí, i de allá. Ask me in one word to describe to you the source of all my loneliness and I will tell you, "México." Not that I would have been any happier staying there. How *could* I have stayed there, been some man's wife . . . after so many years in this country, so many years on my own? (*Pause.*) I'll never forget the trip, the day our whole tribe left para el norte.

Sudden spiritedness. A Mexican mariachi instrumental rises. AMALIA ties a bandana around her head. She is a young girl.

AMALIA: All of us packed into the old blue Chevy. I was thirteen and la regla had started, the bleeding, and I was ashamed to tell my mother. Tía Fita had been the one to warn me that at my age, any day, I could expect to become sick. "Mala," she said, and that when it happened I should come to her and she would bless me and tell me how to protect myself. It came the morning of our long jornada to California.

AMALIA sees the "blood" coming down her leg. She takes the bandana from her head, looks around nervously, then stuffs it under her skirt, flattening it back into place.

AMALIA: Tía Fita was not speaking to my mother so angry was she for all of us leaving. We had asked her to come with us. "What business do I have up there with all those pochos y gringos?" My father said she had no sense. It broke her heart to see us go. So, there was no running to Tía Fita that morning. It seemed too selfish to tell her my troubles when *I* was the one leaving *her*.

Southwestern desert and distant highway sounds can be heard. AMALIA, trying to hide from the others, pulls the bandana out from under her skirt. Kneeling by the "river," she secretly begins to wash the blood from it. Sound and lights gradually fade out.

SCENE 7

MARISA sits at the table in soft light sipping at a beer. She is dressed for the evening in a man's suit jacket. She wears a kind of classic androgynous look. AMALIA enters in a slip, crosses to the bed where she begins to dress.

MARISA: If I were a man, things wouldn've been a lot simpler between us, except . . . she never would've wanted me. I mean, she would've seen me more and all, fit me more conveniently into her life, but she never would've, tú sabes . . . wanted me.

AMALIA: Sometimes I think, with me, that she only wanted to feel herself so much a woman that she would no longer be hungry for one. Pero, siempre tiene hambre. Siempre tiene pena.

MARISA: She'd come to me sometimes I swear like heat on wheels. I'd open the door and find her there, wet from the outta nowhere June rains, and, without her even opening her mouth, I knew what she had come for. I never knew when to expect her this way, just like the rains. Never ever when I wanted it, asked for it, begged for it, only when she decided.

AMALIA: I always had to have a few traguitos and then things would cloud between us a little and I could feel her as if underwater, my hands swimming towards her in the darkness, discovering breasts, not mine . . . not these empty baldes, pero senos firmes, like small stones of heat. Y como un recién nacido, I drink and drink and drink y no me traga la tierra.

Lights suggests memory. Nighttime freeway sounds, car radio music. MARISA *and* AMALIA *hold each other's eyes. Voice-over.*

MARISA: I'll keep driving if you promise not to stop touching me.
AMALIA: You want me to stop touching you?
MARISA: No, if you promise *not* to stop.

AMALIA *crosses in front of* MARISA. *She prepares herself a drink.* MARISA *waches her.*

MARISA: It's odd being queer. It's not that you don't want a man, you just don't want a man in a man. You want a man in a woman. The woman part goes without saying. That's what you always learn to want first. Maybe the first time you see your dad touch your mom in that way. . . .
CORKY (*Entering.*): ¿Hiiiijo! I remember the first time I got hip to that! My mom standing at the stove making chile colorado and flippin' tortillas. She asks my dad . . .
AMALIA (*As "*MOM,*" to* MARISA.): ¿Quieres otra, viejo?
CORKY: Kina like she's sorta hassled 'n' being poquit fría, tú sabes, but she's really digging my dad to no end. 'N' jus' as she comes over to him, kina tossing the tort onto the plate, he slides his hand, real suave-like, up the inside of her thigh. Cheezus! I coulda died! I musta been only about nine or so, but I got that tingling, tú sabes, that now I know what it means.

As CORKY *exits, she throws her chin out to* MARISA *"bato style."* MARISA, *amused, returns the gesture. The lights shift.* MARISA *puts on a tape. A*

Mexican ballad is played—"Adios Paloma" by Chavela Vargas. AMALIA *hums softly along with it.*

MARISA: Hay un hombre en esta mujer. Lohe sentido. La miro, cocinando para nosotras. Pienso . . . ¿cómo puede haber un hombre en una persona, tan feminina? Su pelo, sus movimientos de una serenidad imposible de describir.

AMALIA (*Softly singing.*):

Ya se va tu paloma, mi vida
lleva en sus alas dolor
lleva en sus ojos tristeza
y esun lamento su voz.

MARISA (*Going to her.*): Tu voz que me acaricia con cada palabra . . . tan suave . . . tan rica. (*Takes her by the hand.*) Vente.

The music rises. They dance for a few moments, then MARISA *takes* AMALIA *to the bed. The music fades as* MARISA *slowly removes* AMALIA*'s blouse.*

MARISA: Con ella, me siento como un joven lleno de deseo. I move on top of her. She wants this. The worn denim and metal buttons are cotton and cool ice on my skin. And she is full of slips and lace and stockings. . . .

AMALIA: Quítate los pantalones.

MARISA: And yet it is she who's taking me.

A soft jazz rises. MARISA *takes off her jacket. They kiss each other, at first tenderly, then passionately. They hold and caress each other.* MARISA *takes* AMALIA*'s hand, brings it to her chest. The music softens.*

MARISA: I held the moment. Prayed that if I looked long and hard enough at your hand full inside me, if I could keep this pictured forever in my mind . . . how beneath that moon blasting through the window, . . . how everything was changing at that moment in both of us.

AMALIA: How everything was changing . . . in both of us.

The jazz rises again. The lights fade as they hold a deep kiss.

RETRATO III "LA SALVADORA"

SCENE 8

CORKY writes graffiti-style on upstage wall.

I have this rock in my hand
it is my memory
the weight is solid
in my palm   it cannot fly away

because I still remember
that woman
not my savior, but an angel
with wings
that did once lift me
to another
self.

MARISA and AMALIA appear in shadow on opposite sides of the stage.

AMALIA: You have the rest of your life to forgive me.
MARISA: Forgive you for what?
AMALIA: Por lo que soy.

Blackout.

SCENE 9

AMALIA enters carrying a small suitcase. She sets it down at the foot of the bed, removes her rebozo and holds it in her lap.

AMALIA: All I was concerned about was getting my health back together. It was not so much that I had been sick, only I lacked . . . energy. My body felt like a rag, squeezed dry of any feeling. Possibly it was the "change" coming on. But the women in my family did not go through the change so young. I wasn't even fifty. I thought . . . maybe it was the American influence that causes the blood to be sucked dry from you so early. Nothing was wrong with me, really. My bones ached. I needed rest. Nothing México couldn't cure.

She lies down, covers herself with the rebozo. MARISA *enters, barefoot.*

MARISA: For the whole summer I watched the people fly in bright-colored sails over the Califas sea, waiting for her. Red- and gold- and blue-striped wings blazing the sky. Lifting off the sandy cliffs, dangling gringo legs. Always imagined myself up there in their place, flying for real. Never ever coming back down to earth, just leaving my body behind. (*Pause.*) One morning I awoke to find a bird dead on the beach. I knew it wasn't a rock because it was light enough to roll with the tide. . . . I saw this from a distance. Later that day, they found a woman dead there at the very same spot, I swear. Una viejita. (*A soft grey light washes over* AMALIA.) A crowd gathered 'round her as a young man in a blue swimsuit tried to spoon the sand from her throat with his finger. Putting his breath to her was too late. She very grey and wet, como la arena . . . y una mexicana. I could tell by her housedress. How did she drown? Then I remembered what Amalia had told me about bad omens. (*A sudden ominous tambor,* AMALIA *bolts up in bed.*) I stopped going. I stopped waiting.

MARISA *exits.*

AMALIA: When I learned of Alejandro's death, I died too. I just started bleeding and the blood wouldn't stop, not until his ghost had passed through me or was born in me. I don't know which. That Mexican morning I had awakened to find the hotel sheets red with blood. It had come out in torrents and thick clots that looked like a fetus. But I was not pregnant, my tubes had been tied for years. Yet, lying there in the cool dampness of my own blood, I felt my womanhood leave me. And it was Alejandro being born in me. Does this make sense? I can't say exactly how I knew this, except . . . again . . . for the smell, the unmistakable smell of the man, as if we had just made love. And coming from my mouth was *his* voice . . . "¡Ay mi Marisa! ¡Te deseo! ¡Te deseo!" (*Her eyes search for* MARISA.) *Marisa!*

Lights rise. Morning in Mexico City. AMALIA *gets up from bed.*

AMALIA: It is barely dawn and the sun has already entered my hotel window. Afuera los hombres are already at work tearing up the Mexican earth with their steel claws. (*Indigenous music.*) Pero La Tierra is not as passive as they think. "Regresaré," Ella nos recuerda. "Regresaré," nos promete. When they "discovered" El Templo Mayor beneath the walls of the city, they had not realized that it was She who discovered them. Nothing remains buried forever. Not even memory. Especially not memory.

Fade out.

SCENE 10

The indigenous music blends into Chicano urban sounds. MARISA *enters. Her posture is noticeably more guarded than in the previous scene. The music fades. There is a pause as* MARISA *scans the faces of* THE PEOPLE.

MARISA: Got raped once. When I was a kid. Taken me a long to say that was exactly what happened, but that was exactly what happened. Makes you more aware than ever that you are one hunerd percent female, just in case you had any doubts. One hunerd percent female whether you act it . . . or like it . . . or not. Y'see, I never ever really let myself think about it, the possibility of rape, even after it happened. Not like other girls,

I didn't walk down the street like there were men lurking everywhere, every corner, to devour me. Yeah, the street was a war zone, but for different reasons, . . . for muggers, mexicanos sucking their damn lips at you, gringo stupidity, drunks like old garbage sacks thrown around the street, and the rape of other women and the people I loved. They weren't safe and I worried each time they left the house . . . but never, never me. I guess I never wanted to believe I was raped. If someone took me that bad, I wouldn't really want to think, you follow me? But the truth is . . .

CORKY (*Entering.*): I was took.

MARISA crosses to the platform. CORKY "stakes out the territory."

CORKY: I was about twelve years old
I was still going to cath-lic school then
'n' we wore those stupid checkered jumpers
they looked purty shitty on the seventh 'n' eighth grade girls
cuz here we was getting chi-chis 'n' all

'n' still trying to shove 'em into the tops of these playsuits
I wasn't too big pero the big girls looked terrible!

anyway in the seventh grade I was trying to mend my ways
so would hang after school 'n' try to be helpful 'n' all to the nuns
I guess cuz my cousin Norma got straight A's
'n' was taking me into her bed by then
so I figured . . . that was the way to go
she'd get really pissed when I fucked up in school
threatened to "take it away" tú sabes if I dint behave
can you get to that? ¡Qué fría! ¿no?

anyway Norma was the only one I ever tole
about the janitor doing it to me
'n' then she took it away for good

I'd still like to whip her butt for that
her 'n' her goddamn hubby 'n' kids now shi-it
puros gabachos, little blond-haired blue-eyed things
the oldest is a little joto if you ask me
sure he's barely four years old but you can already tell
the way he goes around primping all over the place
pleases me to no end
what goes around comes around
"Jason" they call him
no, not "Ha-són" pero "Jay-sun"
puro gringo

anyway so I was walking by Sister Mary Dominic's classroom
"the Hawk" we called her cuz she had a nose 'n' attitude like one
when this man a mexicano motions to me to come on inside
"Ven p'aca," he says
I dint recognize him but the parish was always hiring
mexicanos to work around the grounds 'n' stuff
I guess cuz they dint need to know English
'n' the priests dint need to pay 'em much
they'd do it "por Dios" tú sabes
so he asks me, "Señorita, ¿hablas español?" muy polite y todo
'n' I answer, "Sí poquito," which I always say to strangers
cuz I dunno how much they're gonna expect outta me
"Ven p'aca," he says otra vez
'n' I do outta respect for my primo Enrique
cuz he looks a lot like him but somet'ing was funny
his Spanish I couldn't quite make it out cuz he mumbled alot
which made me feel kina bad about myself tú sabes
that I was Mexican too but couldn't understand him that good

he's trying to fix this drawer that's loose in the Hawk's desk
I knew already about the drawer
cuz she was always bitchin' 'n' moanin'
about it getting stuck cuz the bottom kept falling out
so he tells me he needs someone to hold the bottom of the drawer up
so he can screw the sides in
(*She goes to the "desk," demonstrates.*)
so standing to the side I lean over
and hold the drawer in place así
then he says all frustrated-like, "No, así, así."
it turns out he wants me to stand in front of the drawer
with my hands holding each side up así
(*She stands with her legs apart, her pelvis pressed up against the edge of the "desk."*)
'n' believe it or not this cabrón sits behind me on the floor
'n' reaches his arm up between my legs
that I'm straining to keep closed
even though he keeps saying all business-like
"Abrete más por favor las piernas. Abretelas un poco más."
'n' like a pendeja   I do

(*She grips the edge of the "desk."*)
I feel my face getting hotter
'n' I can kina feel him jiggling the drawer
pressed up against me down there
I'm staring straight ahead don' wanna look at what's happening
then worry how someone would see us like this
this guy's arm up between my legs
'n' then it begins to kina brush past the inside of my thigh
I can feel the hair   that first
then the heat of his skin
(*Almost tenderly.*) the skin is so soft I hafta admit
young kina like a girl's like Norma's shoulder

I try to think about Norma 'n' her shoulders
to kina pass the time hoping to hurry things along
while he keeps saying, "Casi termino. Casi termino."
'n' I keep saying back, "Señor me tengo que ir, mi mamá me espea."
still all polite como mensa!
until finally I feel the screwdriver by my leg like ice
then suddenly the tip of it   it feels like to me
is against the cotton of my chones

"Don't move," he tells me. In English. His accent gone. 'n' I don'

from then on all I see in mind's eye . . .
were my eyes shut?
is this screwdriver he's got in his sweaty palm
yellow   glass   handle
shiny metal
the kind my father useta use to fix things around the house
remembered how I'd help him how he'd take me on his jobs with him
'n' I kept getting him confused in mind
this man 'n' his arm with my father
kept imagining he was my father returned come back
the arm was so soft but this other thing . . .
hielo   hielo   ice!
I wanted to cry, "¡Papi! ¡Papi!"
'n' then I started crying for real
cuz I knew I musta done somet'ing real wrong
to get myself in this mess

I figure he's gonna shove the damn thing up me
he's trying to get my chones down, "Por favor señor please don'."
but I can hear my voice through my own ears
not from the inside out but the other way around
'n' I know I'm not fighting this one

I know I don' even sound convinced
"¿Dónde 'stás, papi? ¿Dónde 'stás?"
'n' finally I hear the man answering, "Aquí estoy. Soy tu papá."
'n' this gives me permission to go 'head to not hafta fight

by the time he ges my chones down to my knees
I suddenly feel like I'm floating in the air
my thing kina attached to no body
flapping in the wind like a bird a wounded bird
I'm relieved when I hear the metal drop to the floor
only worry *who will see me doing this?*
(*Gritting her teeth.*) *get-this-over-with-get-this-over-with*
'n' he does gracias a dios bringing me down to earth

linoleum floor   cold
the smell of wax
polish

y ya 'stoy lista for what long ago waited for me
there is no surprise
'n' I open my legs wide wide open
for the angry animal that springs outta the opening in his pants
'n' all I wanna do is have it over so I can go back to being myself
'n' a kid again

then he hit me with it
into what was supposed to be a hole
(*Tenderly.*) that I remembered had to be
cuz Norma had found it once wet 'n' forbidden
'n' showed me too how wide 'n' deep like a cueva hers got
when she wanted it to only with me she said

MARISA: Only with you, Corky.

CORKY: but with this one there was no hole he had to make it
'n' I saw myself down there like a face with no opening

a face with no features
no eyes no nose no mouth
only little lines where they shoulda been
so I dint cry
I never cried as he shoved the thing
into what was supposed to be a mouth
with no teeth
with no hate
with no voice
only a hole
a hole!

He made me a hole!

MARISA *approaches, wraps a rebozo around* CORKY'*s shoulders, holds her.*

MARISA: I don't regret it. I don't regret nuthin'. He only convinced me of my own name. From an early age you learn to live with it, being a woman. I just got a head start over some. And then, years later, after I got to be with some other men, I admired how their things had no opening . . . only a tiny tiny pinhole dot to pee from, to come from. I thought . . . how lucky they were, that they could release all that stuff, all that pent-up shit from the day, through a hole that *nobody* could get into.

SCENE II

MARISA *and* CORKY *remain onstage. The lighting slowly shifts. Indigenous music, lively tambores.* AMALIA *enters wearing a rebozo. She covers* MARISA'*s shoulders with one as well. All three, now in rebozos, have become indias. They enter a dream.* CORKY *comes downstage, kneels. She begins making tortillas, slapping her hands together.* MARISA *and* AMALIA *join her on each side, forming a half circle. They, too, clap tortillas to the rhythm of the tambores. They are very happy. The rhythm quickens, accelerates.*

MARISA and AMALIA slowly bend toward each other, their faces crossing in front of CORKY's. They kiss. Suddenly the scene darkens, the drumming becomes sinister, the clapping frantic. Thunder. Lightning. The gods have been angered. The three scatter. The stage is a maze of colliding lights, searching out the women. CORKY has disappeared. AMALIA cowers beneath her rebozo. MARISA appears upstage in shadow. She is out of breath. She is being hunted, her arms spread, her body pressed up against an invisible wall.

MARISA: Amalia, let me in! ¡Abre la puerta! ¡Vienen a agarrarme!

AMALIA wrestles in bed with her "pesadilla."

MARISA: ¡No me dejes, Amalia! ¡No me dejes sola! Let me in!

AMALIA: *can't bear to hear her, covers her ears.*

MARISA: Amalia! . . . Amalia! . . . Let . . . me . . . in!

The lights fade out and rise again. CORKY can be seen in shadow standing where MARISA had been seconds before. She holds a beer bottle in the air above her head. She comes down with it, like a weapon. The sound of glass breaking. Blackout.

AMALIA (*In the darkness.*): ¿Quién es? ¿Quién es? Who is it? ¿Eres tú, Che?

Lights rise. AMALIA is sitting up in bed. There is an opened, unpacked suitcase on the floor and a photo of a man with a candle next to it on the table. MARISA appears in the doorway. She is very drunk, almost in a stupor.

AMALIA: Marisa.
MARISA: Where the . . . where have you been? (*AMALIA gets out of bed, puts on a robe.*)
AMALIA: What are you doing here?

MARISA (*Menacingly.*): I'm asking you a question.

AMALIA: Don't come near me.

MARISA: I said, where have you been?

AMALIA: What do you want?

MARISA: I wanna know . . . (*She stalks* AMALIA.) I wanna know where you been.

AMALIA: You're drunk.

MARISA: Good observation, maestra. Now are you gonna answer me?

AMALIA: Stay away from me. Don't touch me.

MARISA: I'm not gonna touch you. No, no. These hands? No, no, Doña Amalia . . . us jotas learn to keep our hands to ourselves.

AMALIA: ¡Adió!

MARISA: Answer me!

AMALIA: You know where I was.

MARISA: I waited for you. I waited three goddamn months! Count them! June, July—

AMALIA: I can count.

MARISA: Well, jus' cuz it aint all hanging out on the outside don' mean I don' feel nuthin'. What did you expect from me anyway?

AMALIA: Well, not this.

MARISA: Well, honey, this is what you got. Aint I a purty picture?

AMALIA: Estás borracha. Estás loca.

MARISA: Bueno, 'stoy loca. Tal vez quieres que te hable en español, eh? A lo mejor you could understand me then. I'm sorry, y'know, us pochas don' speak it as purty as you do.

AMALIA: What are you talking about?

MARISA: I'm talking about going to the goddamn mailbox every day, thinking every llamadita would be you. "Ven, Chatita. Meet me in México." You lied to me.

AMALIA: I didn't lie.

MARISA: No?

AMALIA: No. (*She turns away.*)

MARISA: What then?

There is a pause.

MARISA: Look at you. You don' got nuthin' to say to me. You don' feel a thing.

AMALIA: It's three o'clock in the morning, what am I supposed to feel?

MARISA (*After a beat.*): Nuthin'. You're supposed to feel nuthin'.

AMALIA: I'm going to get you some coffee.

MARISA: I don' want no coffee! You went back to him, didn't you?

AMALIA: Ay, Marisa, por favor no empieces.

MARISA (*Seeing the photo.*): What is this? A little altar we have for the man? (*She picks it up.*)

AMALIA: Don't.

MARISA: ¡Vela y toto! What is he, a saint now?

AMALIA: ¡Déjalo!

MARISA: You're still in love with him, aren't you?

AMALIA: Put it down, te digo.

MARISA (*Approaching.*): I'm asking you a question.

AMALIA: Stay away from me.

MARISA: Answer me! (*Grabs* AMALIA.) Are you in love with him or not?

AMALIA: ¡Déjame!

MARISA (*Shaking her.*): Did you sleep with him?

AMALIA: No! Stop it!

MARISA: Did you? Tell me the truth!

AMALIA: No! ¡Déjame! (*They struggle. The picture falls to the floor.* AMALIA *breaks* MARISA*'s hold.*) I'm not an animal! What gives you the right to come in here like this? Do you think you're the only peson in the world who's ever been left waiting?

MARISA: What was I supposed to think . . . that you were dead? That you were dead or you were with him, those were my two choices.

AMALIA (*Bitterly.*): He's the one who's dead.

MARISA (*After a pause.*): What?

AMALIA: He's dead.

AMALIA *slowly walks over to the picture, picks it up, replaces it by the candle. She sits down on the bed, her face impassive.*

AMALIA (*After a pause.*): When I got the news, I was in a hotel in Mexico City. I didn't stop to think about it, I took a bus right away to la Costa. Then I hired a boy to give me a lift in a truck. When I got to the river, I knew where to go. The exact spot. The place under the tamarindo where we used to make love. And for hours until dark I sat there by la orilla as I imagined he had that last time.

MARISA: He drowned.

AMALIA: He drowned himself.

MARISA (*Going to her.*): It's not your fault, Amalia.

AMALIA (*After a pause.*): Whose face do you think he saw in the belly of that river moments before it swallowed him?

MARISA: It's not your fault. (*There is a long silence.* MARISA *makes a gesture to touch* AMALIA, *but is unable to.*) I shouldn't have come. I'm sorry.

AMALIA: No, stay. Stay and keep an old woman company.

MARISA: I'll come back tomorrow . . . fix the window (*She starts to exit.*)

AMALIA: Soñé contigo.

MARISA: You did?

AMALIA: Last night. (*Pause.*) I dreamed we were indias. In our village, some terrible taboo had been broken. There was thunder and lightning. I am crouched down in terror, unable to move when I realize it is *you* who have gone against the code of our people. But I was not afraid of being punished. I did not fear that los dioses would enact their wrath against el pueblo for the breaking of the taboo. It was merely that the taboo *could* be broken. And if this law nearly transcribed in blood could go, then what else? What *was* there to hold to? What immutable truths were left? (*Pause. She turns to* MARISA.) I never wanted you the way I wanted a man. With a man, I just would have left him. Punto. (*Pause.*) Like I left Alejandro.

The lights slowly fade to black.

SCENE 12

MARISA sits on the platform. AMALIA's rebozo has been left there.

MARISA: I must admit I wanted to save her. That's probably the whole truth of the story. And the problem is . . . sometimes I actually believed I could, and *sometimes* she did too.

She was like no woman I had ever had. I think it was in the quality of her skin. Some people, you know, their skin is like a covering. They're supposed to be showing you something when the clothes fall into a heap around your four ankles, but nothing is lost, y'know what I mean? They jus' don' give up nuthin'. Pero Amalia . . . ¡Híjole!

She picks up AMALIA's rebozo, fingers it.

She was never ever fully naked in front of me, always had to keep some piece of clothing on, a shirt or something always wrapped up around her throat, her arms all outta it and flying. What she did reveal, though, each item of clothing removed was a gift, I swear, a small offering, a suggestion of all that could be lost and found in our making love together. It was like she was saying to me, "I'll lay down my underslip. ¿Y tú? ¿Qué me vas a dar?" And I'd give her the palm of my hand to warm the spot she had just exposed. Everything was a risk. Everything took time. Was slow and deliberate.

I'll never forget after the first time we made love, I was feeling muy orgullosa y todo, like a good lover, and she says to me—

AMALIA (*Voice-over, memory.*): You make love to me like worship.

MARISA: And I nearly died, it was so powerful what she was saying. And I wanted to answer, "Sí, la mujer es mi religion." If only sex coulda saved us.

Y'know, sometimes when me and her were in the middle of it, making love, I'd look up at her face, kinda grey from being indoors so much with all those books of hers, and I'd see it change, turn this real deep color of brown and olive, like she was cooking inside. Tan linda. Kind. Very very very kind to me, to herself, to the pinche planet . . . and I'd watch it move from outside the house where that crazy espíritu of hers had been out makin' tracks. I'd watch it come inside, through the door, watch it travel all through her own private miseries and settle itself, finally, right there in the room with us. This bed. This fucking dreary season. This cement city. With us. With me. No part of her begging to have it over . . . forget. And I could feel all the parts of her move into operation. Waiting. Held. Suspended. Praying for me to put my tongue to her and I knew and she knew we would find her . . . como fuego. And just as I pressed my mouth to her, I'd think . . . *I could save your life.*

(*Coming downstage.*) It's not often you get to see people this way in all their pus and glory and still love them. It makes you feel so good, like your hands are weapons of war. And as they move up into el corazón de esta mujer, you are making her body remember, it didn't have to be that hurt. ¿Me entiendes? It was not natural or right that she got beat down so damn hard, and that all those crimes had nothing to do with the girl she once was two, three, four decades ago.

Pause. Music rises softly in the background.

MARISA: It's like making familia from scratch
each time all over again . . .
with strangers, if I must.
If I must, I will.

I am preparing myself for the worst
so I cling to her in my heart
my daydream with pencil in my mouth

when I put my fingers
to my own forgotten places.

The lights gradually fade out. Music.

RESERVOIR

Ron Nyswaner

RESERVOIR was commissioned by Actors & Writers, a professional theater company in Olivebridge, New York. Ron Nyswaner directed its premiere in November, 1994. The cast was as follows:

SHARP . . . . Kevin O'Rourke
DOUG . . . . Frank Juliano

~

The setting is a bank of a reservoir on a summer night; moonlight on rocks and tree stumps. There are summer sounds, crickets or peepers.

At Lights Up, a young man named DOUG *stares at the water, listening to night sounds.*

Soon, he's found by SHARP, *slightly older.* SHARP *enjoys the reputation of a local ne'er-do-well.*

SHARP: What are you doing? (*DOUG doesn't answer.*) You okay?
DOUG: Sh!
SHARP: What . . . ?
DOUG: I'm *listening*, okay?
SHARP: Okay. Relax. (*A beat.*) Do you know what you're listening to? Not crickets. Peepers. It's a different sound. People think they're hearing crickets when they're hearing something else. People make that mistake all the time. People are stupid, aren't they? (*SHARP twists the ends of a joint, preparing to smoke it.*) I didn't hurt you, did I?
DOUG: Do you want to know what I was listening for?

SHARP: There are a lot of sounds out here, at night, when the cars stop crossing the bridge.

DOUG: Why did you quit school?

SHARP: I have a job, don't I?

DOUG: Spraying apples.

SHARP (*The joint.*): Want some?

DOUG: That stuff's poison. That you spray on the apples. It's a chemical called Alar. Just to keep the apples all, like, round and red. Meryl Streep testified in front of Congress. You spray poison on apples that little children eat so you can buy pot.

SHARP: What are you pissed about? I didn't make you do anything you didn't want to do. I mean, if you're going to change your mind after the ball's gone through the hoop, it's too late, bro. The ball's gone through the hoop. (*A beat.*) Are you bleeding down there?

DOUG: I can't see down there, can I?

SHARP: Check your underwear.

DOUG: You're an expert, aren't you?

SHARP: I get it when I want it. Most people don't complain.

DOUG gets to his knees, closes his eyes, and folds his hands in a fervent prayer in which his lips move silently.

When the short prayer is over, he opens his eyes, listening for something.

SHARP (*Cont.*): What are. . . ?

DOUG: Sh! (*More listening. Nothing.*) They're gone.

SHARP: No one's jogging.

DOUG: Not joggers. Not people. If you want to know, I pray here. This is where I was saved. The preacher brought us here to be baptized. I come here every Wednesday night, when I'm driving home from the basketball games. I'm on the basketball team.

SHARP: That's cool.

DOUG: I hate it. My father . . . I try to obey, and it teaches me humility. They never let me play. Maybe, at the end of a game, if we're way ahead. I drop the ball. I foul. People yell at me from the stands, cursing me because I fouled when we're twenty-seven points ahead.

SHARP: You should tell them to fuck off.

DOUG: Christ endured his suffering on the cross. If He can endure that, without complaining . . .

SHARP: But I think he *did* complain.

DOUG: No.

SHARP: Oh yeah, bro. He said something on the cross. You know how I know? I saw that show. The musical. And they put him on a big cross, and he was singing all this shit. . . .

DOUG: *Jesus Christ Superstar?!*

SHARP: Right! "My God, why have you forgotten me?" That's what he said. Sounds like a complaint to me.

DOUG: That's just a *play*! You think you know anything about Jesus because you saw one play? Have you ever read the Bible? Or, don't you read anything but comic books?

SHARP (*Rising to leave.*): I'll see you.

DOUG: I'm sorry!

SHARP: I'm going.

DOUG: Are you going back to the turn-off? Are you going to sit there in your truck and wait for someone else?

SHARP: I don't owe you anything. Do I?

DOUG: Don't go. Please. (*SHARP remains.*) One night I came here to pray and a man was throwing rocks into the reservoir. He asked me if I was saved and when I told him I was, he asked me if I had been blessed with a gift of the Holy Spirit. There are two kinds of Christians. Did you know that? You can be a Carnal Christian, professing to love Jesus but still living in the world for the pleasures of the flesh. But a Spiritual Christian not only loves Jesus, but lives in the Spirit, and the evidence of the Spirit living in him is a gift, like the gift of tongues. The man asked me to kneel beside him and pray for the Spirit to enter me. He looked like you, Sharp.

SHARP: My twin brother. The good one.

DOUG: You think this is all . . . what? Stupid? I heard the voices of angels giving me my call, that I was supposed to work for Jesus and bring sinners to God, that I have the ability to reach people. And every Wednesday night I'd come here. I never saw the man again, maybe he wasn't real, maybe he was an angel that God sent to me. Don't laugh. I don't know who he was. But I know I heard the voices. Until now. I knew what I was going to do. I was going to preach and bring people to God. Now what am I supposed to do?

SHARP: We could use another guy on the apple truck.

DOUG: I don't think you have the capacity to understand what I'm talking about.

SHARP: Fuck you! You don't know anything about me, do you?

DOUG: No.

SHARP: No. You don't. (*A moment.*)

DOUG: How many times have you. . . ? You know . . .

SHARP: I want to hear you say it.

DOUG: Say . . . ?

SHARP: Say "fuck."

DOUG: I don't.

SHARP: You *do*. I know you do it. I was there, wasn't I?

DOUG: That's when you kissed me.

SHARP: Hey . . . ! You're nuts, man. Fucking queer teenage Billy Graham, and I'm going home. Good-bye. So long. See you on *The 700 Club*.

DOUG: I won't tell anyone you kissed me.

SHARP: Listen. I'm serious now . . .

DOUG: If you stay. I won't tell anyone if you stay a few minutes.

SHARP: What if I kill you? Then, for sure, you won't tell anyone, you little deranged piece of shit.

DOUG: I'm going to teach you some Scripture. We're going to have a Bible study. Sit down, Sharp. I said, sit down. (*SHARP sits on a rock.*) "Wherever two or more are gathered in My name, there I shall be also."

SHARP: You're a fucking freak, you know that?

DOUG: Today's lesson comes from Paul's letter to the Corinthians, in which Saint Paul addresses the problems of a divided church, believers who were straying from the one true path that leads to eternal life. (*SHARP raises his hand.*) Mr. Sharp, you have a question?

SHARP: I know the Lord's Prayer.

DOUG: Very good.

SHARP: I learned it in prison.

DOUG: Now you're going to learn First Corinthians, chapter 13, verses 4 to 8. It's my favorite section of the Bible. (*Then.*) I can't. I can't say it. After what we did . . .

DOUG throws himself to the ground, his face in the dirt, crying.

SHARP: Hey. C'mon. Hey . . . Maybe it wasn't angels. The voices. How do you know it wasn't aliens? This county has one of the highest numbers of UFO sightings because of the reservoir. They're attracted to it from their ships. Maybe the aliens are trying to plant subliminal ideas in your mind, like an experiment, they tell you to do things and then see if you do them. Like, maybe they tell you to come here and pray and think you hear angels. And then one night they tell you to come here with me and get fucked and think you don't hear angels because they're, like experimenting with the idea of people who suddenly think that, because they got fucked they can't get messages from God anymore, shit like that. So maybe this is all constructed in your head and you shouldn't get so freaked. Doug?

DOUG: You're retarded. (*SHARP stands, pulling a jacket over his shoulders.*)

SHARP: That's right, man. You go on and cry. And you remember. You got what you asked for. You were waiting for me. I was not waiting for you. And I did *not* kiss you.

DOUG (*Swinging at SHARP.*): You'll rot in hell, do you know that? You'll burn in the fiery lake!

SHARP (*Throwing punches at DOUG.*): C'mon, bro. You wanna fight?

DOUG (*Ducking SHARP's punches.*): You'll die a thousand deaths . . . live an eternal life separated from God . . . surrounded by . . .

suffering, hearing the voices of the tormented crying out for water, "I'm thirsty, I'm thirsty, won't someone save me?"

One of SHARP's fists connects with DOUG's chin, sending DOUG to the ground.

SHARP: I'm sorry. Hey . . . (*DOUG lies on the ground, silent.*) Why do people have to prove something all the time? You asshole. Come on. Get up.

DOUG: No.

SHARP: What am I supposed to do? Leave you here?

DOUG: Yes.

SHARP: I'll tell you how I *know* I didn't kiss you. I don't kiss, okay? My girlfriend gets bent out of shape because I *don't* kiss, I'm not like, a kisser. I mean, there are so many things out there, so many fucking germs, and diseases and like, residue from pollution and germ warfare, I mean, we don't know what's in our food or anything. Do you know how many people have herpes sores right on their lips and they think you ought to, like, want to kiss them? Do you know how many people think, like, for some weed or some blow or twenty bucks I ought to enjoy having my dick sucked by some fat, ugly motherfucker, like I'm supposed to *enjoy* it? And for a beer, a lousy, motherfucking beer, I'm supposed to listen, oh yeah, uh-huh, listen to one sad motherfucking story after another, one lousy sad song, the fucking plant's closing down, the fucking wife's out of her gourd, whacked out on lithium, and mom, she's fucking eighty years old and moving into the spare room. Every sad motherfucker in this county thinks his life's a goddamn Loretta Lynn song, like it isn't the same shit that everyone else is rolling in. They're all suffering from tunnel vision, the only thing they see is their own four walls and their own sad, stinking life, and I'm just suppose to roll over and die, I am supposed to care for the price of a Rolling Rock! So then I have to hear this shit, how I'm not human because I don't kiss. I didn't kiss you, Douglas. If I don't kiss my girlfriend, why would I kiss you?

DOUG: I don't know why. But you did.

SHARP: Do you realize I could kill you and get away with it? I have a gun in my truck, man. What the fuck's wrong with you? (*A moment. Finally,* DOUG *pulls himself from the ground.*)

DOUG: I want to call you by your first name.

SHARP: Listen, man . . .

DOUG: What?

SHARP: You'd be a good preacher. I'd go to church if you was preaching.

DOUG: I'm not going to be a preacher.

SHARP: Man, don't like, change your whole life because of this. This wasn't anything. I'm not anything. I'm bullshit, man. I don't even have a fucking gun!

DOUG: What's your first name?

SHARP: Howard. Is that a bullshit name or what?

DOUG: Howard. I want to do it again.

SHARP: What?

DOUG: You want me to say it.

SHARP: That's right.

DOUG: I want you to fuck me again. (*Rises.*) C'mon.

SHARP: Why does everyone want something from me? I don't hurt people. But they're always coming at me. Why?

DOUG: I won't.

SHARP: You won't what?

DOUG: I won't criticize you. "Love bears all things, believes all things, hopes all things, endures all things."

SHARP: Is that my Bible lesson?

DOUG: First Corinthians, chapter thirteen.

SHARP: Perhaps I don't have the capacity to understand it.

DOUG: I'm sorry.

SHARP: Pick up the blanket.

DOUG: All right.

SHARP (*Rising.*): What's that?

DOUG: What?

SHARP: That light.
DOUG: Nothing.
SHARP: What are you talking about? Look at that.
DOUG: Just headlights in the fog. Someone's crossing the bridge.

DOUG exits.

SHARP stands there, watching the water.

The light gets brighter and brighter, shining directly into SHARP's eyes.

Then, it fades. SHARP listens for something.

SHARP: The peepers stopped.

SHARP puts out his joint with his fingertips, sliding it into his pocket, and exits.

ROSEN'S SON

Joe Pintauro

Setting: An apartment foyer on the Upper West Side of Manhattan, New York City.

Characters

MR. ROSEN is about sixty.
EDDIE is forty.
HARRISON is twenty-eight.

~

Two men, one old enough to be the father of the other, are sitting on the floor of an apartment foyer. The older man is lying with his head in the lap of the younger, like a child who has been crying. There is quiet in the foyer, although we are aware that something awful has just happened, something that caused the men to collapse to the floor. The older man is still in his wet raincoat; his umbrella is on its side next to him, dripping on the floor tiles. The younger man, who apparently just answered his buzzer, obviously had been entertaining dinner guests. He is dressed handsomely for dinner. Perhaps some coats, hats, and umbrellas of guests are hanging in the small foyer. Doors to the foyer, imaginary or not, are closed, one supposedly locked.

MR. ROSEN: Forgive me, Eddie.
EDDIE: Shhhhh.
MR. ROSEN: Do ya forgive me?
EDDIE: I think so.
MR. ROSEN: Where's the gun?
EDDIE: I've got it.
MR. ROSEN: Did I hurt you?

EDDIE: My lip's cut.

MR. ROSEN: I'm sorry.

EDDIE: Just take it easy. Relax.

MR. ROSEN: I've gone crazy. I miss my boy.

EDDIE: I miss him too, Mr. Rosen.

MR. ROSEN: So you get involved two months after he dies?

EDDIE: Your son was sick a long time.

MR. ROSEN: So you celebrate his death by moving a stranger in here to live with you?

EDDIE: He's no stranger.

MR. ROSEN: You call me "Mr. Rosen"?

EDDIE: All right. Ziggie. Take it easy.

MR. ROSEN: Strangers' coats in my son's foyer.

EDDIE: Just shut up.

HARRISON (*Off.*): Ed?

EDDIE: Yeah?

HARRISON (*Off.*): Who buzzed?

EDDIE: I'm taking care of it.

HARRISON (*Enters, speaking.*): Our guests are waiting. . . . Who is this man?

EDDIE: Ben's father (*To* MR. ROSEN.) This is Harrison.

HARRISON: Mr. Rosen?

MR. ROSEN: What else?

HARRISON: My deepest sympathies . . . for your recent trouble. Would you care to join us? (*He indicates the dining room.*)

EDDIE: No, Harrison . . .

MR. ROSEN: I come here with a gun, he invites me to dinner?

HARRISON: Does he have a *gun?*

EDDIE: I took it from him.

MR. ROSEN: Does he know who allows him to stand here in this foyer? My son. Because of his death you stand here. Is that true Eddie? I would vomit on that table in there.

HARRISON: He's off his rocker. . . .

EDDIE: This is not him.

MR. ROSEN: Young people, you have no hearts, no memory, but wait. You'll get yours. Just let me outta this death oven.

EDDIE: I'll call you later.

MR. ROSEN: Call nothing. Which way out of this hell?

EDDIE (*Grabbing his coat, to* HARRISON.): I've got to go with him.

HARRISON: You're *going*?

EDDIE: To see him home.

MR. ROSEN: Are you crazy? For me what is home?

HARRISON: Eddie, you can't just leave our dinner guests.

EDDIE: Shut up, will you, Harrison?

HARRISON: Are you aware of the tone you just used with me?

EDDIE: *I said shut up.*

HARRISON: I'm calling the police. He's threatened us.

EDDIE: Do that, Harrison, and I'll leave you. I swear to Christ.

HARRISON: Did you say you'll leave me?

MR. ROSEN: Easy come, easy go.

HARRISON (*Pointing at* ROSEN.): You are trespassing, and it's criminal.

MR. ROSEN: Bite your tongue, cutie. Who do you think you are to get your bloomers in such an uproar over me? What do you see standing before you? An old man in a raincoat. One wife. One child. Both dead. Both dead. Him I put in the diamond business. For you, bastard.

HARRISON: Does he mean me?

MR. ROSEN: Who do I mean, this umbrella? You start living with a man two months after his lover dies—are you the Blessed Virgin?

HARRISON: I knew Eddie a year.

MR. ROSEN: While my son was sick you fooled around, you pig in a fancy shirt.

EDDIE: He worked in our office.

HARRISON: You're wrong, Mr. Rosen.

MR. ROSEN: Drop in a hole the two of you. Young people. You replace other people like spark plugs. Half your age I said good-byes that would make you sweat blood. I cut the tattooed numbers off my wrist with a kitchen knife, then worried, without them, how would my sister find me. Don't worry. Your government brought the numbers back worse and you got them and no knife is sharp enough. . . . You. I tried to teach you, but only diamonds you learned, only money so you could marry Mister Bloomingdales here who tells me I trespass in my son's apartment? *Mazel tov.* Give me at least back my gun.

HARRISON: Don't give it to him.

EDDIE: Get inside, Harrison.

MR. ROSEN: Afraid to die so young, Mister Bloomingdales? My boy was not afraid. He smiled. Relax, Mister Bloomingdales, the gun was for my head not yours or his, though you are pigs enough to be slaughtered. . . .

EDDIE: Ziggie, please.

MR. ROSEN: Shame on people who eat with candles, not for God but to hide pimples and wrinkles. Young people who live together not for love but for sex, boff boff like pistons machines. You never get bored? (*To HARRISON.*) What are you smiling at?

EDDIE: Harrison, go now. (*HARRISON starts off.*)

MR. ROSEN: Not so fast, cutie. You wanna make a deal? You change places?

HARRISON: With who?

MR. ROSEN: My boy?

HARRISON: Oh, Eddie.

MR. ROSEN: You crawl into his grave and send my son home to his father?

HARRISON: I'm so sorry for you, Mr. Rosen. . . .

EDDIE: Harrison's a good person.

MR. ROSEN: Young people living in a magazine. Did you show him a picture of my boy? (*MR. ROSEN takes out his wallet.*)

EDDIE: Jesus!

HARRISON: I'm not afraid. I'd like to see him.

MR. ROSEN (*Showing him the photo.*): Look at a beautiful face. Eh?

HARRISON: Very nice.

MR. ROSEN: You . . . (*To EDDIE.*) What's his name?

EDDIE and HARRISON: Harrison.

MR. ROSEN (*To EDDIE.*): *Goyisha?* (*EDDIE nods yes.*) Harrison. Where do they get these names?

HARRISON: It's a family name.

MR. ROSEN: Your nose is a fortune cookie next to my son. I'm serious.

EDDIE: Okay, Ziggie, let's call it quits.

MR. ROSEN: A basketball is your neck. My way of speaking. You play an instrument?

HARRISON: I've always regretted not . . .

MR. ROSEN: The flute, my son . . . Avery Fisher Hall. Clippings to drown in.

HARRISON: He's extraordinary. He's beautiful. (*Handing back the photo.*) Eddie, our guests are waiting.

MR. ROSEN: I came here to splash my brains over your table. That's what the gun was for, to put out your candles with my blood.

HARRISON: Please.

MR. ROSEN: But I changed my mind. In the river throw the gun. Me, I'll do like the elephants: Go to Miami. The sun will polish my bones. For a little fee, a lawyer will send you my tusks. They'll go nice here, either side of your door. Speaking of doors, kindly point the way a person gets out of here.

HARRISON: May I be excused please?

MR. ROSEN: Leave. *Mazel tov.* (*HARRISON exits. ROSEN stares long at EDDIE.*) You forgot the summers at the lake, the canoe, the three of us? The dinners? The holidays, birthdays? I had to accept you, didn't I? I had to swallow it. And I did. And you just forgot those days?

EDDIE: I didn't forget any of it.

MR. ROSEN: Were we really together then?

EDDIE: I thought we were.

MR. ROSEN: I thought so, too. I thought so. (*EDDIE puts on his coat.*) Where you goin'?

EDDIE: To help you get a taxi.

MR. ROSEN: No taxi.

EDDIE: Then I'll call you later to see you got home safe.

MR. ROSEN: Never dare call me again in your life. You're nothing to me.

EDDIE: Don't say that.

MR. ROSEN: Liar. You want I should disappear so bad.

EDDIE: No.

MR. ROSEN: Look at his face. Such a liar. After this minute, never, never again will you see this face of your *"Mr. Rosen."* But before I go I want you should tell me a truth, so perfect as you never before spoke the truth to anyone in your life, and I'll give you the freedom of a thousand doves set loose on the mountaintops.

EDDIE: Ask me.

MR. ROSEN: Do you love that one in there? The truth before God.

EDDIE: I'm trying to love him. I'm the kind of man who has to have somebody. . . . I'm trying very hard. (*ROSEN moves in on EDDIE, beating him down with questions.*)

MR. ROSEN: Does he take care of you like—?

EDDIE: He's different. . . .

MR. ROSEN: Like my boy used to? Remember—

EDDIE: Different.

MR. ROSEN: Like you were God on Earth?

EDDIE: No.

MR. ROSEN: Does he laugh with those same funny eyes. . . .

EDDIE: Of course not.

MR. ROSEN: Bake bread like he used to?

EDDIE: No. (*Losing it.*)

MR. ROSEN: Play the flute on Sunday while you read the paper?

EDDIE: No.

MR. ROSEN: The truth before God.

EDDIE (*Shouts.*): *It'll never be the same for me again. Never.*

MR. ROSEN: This is true?

EDDIE: What do you think? (*EDDIE falls, crouches at ROSEN's feet, weeping.*) You bastard, you awful man.

MR. ROSEN: Good you cry. Now I'm happy. Good-bye, Eddie. Don't follow me. Don't call me. God bless you. You were my son. Really. You were. My other son. (*MR. ROSEN exits, lights fade on EDDIE.*)

TRAFFICKING IN BROKEN HEARTS

Edwin Sánchez

TRAFFICKING IN BROKEN HEARTS was originally produced by Bailiwick Theatre in Chicago, June 1992.

Characters

PAPO—a hustler, twenty-six years old
BRIAN—a lawyer, twenty-six years old
BOBBY—a runaway, sixteen years old
Assorted voices that will represent the voices of New York.

The play takes place primarily in the 42nd Street area of New York.

AT RISE

From the darkness neon begins to turn on and off. Voices are heard, some dirty talk, some high-pitched laughter. Drugs and sex are offered. All we see are flashing lights. The lights slowly come up to a dim. A fight is happening somewhere, a siren, someone asking for spare change while another voice is demanding that gentlemen drop their quarters. We see the facade of a peep show. A wire mesh garbage can is on the corner. PAPO, *his back to the audience, stretches and yawns. He opens his pants and positions his cock to maximum advantage. He clears his throat and spits. He leans against the peep show facade. Lights begin to dim.*

PAPO: Hey, you wanna see a movie?

Blackout.

A third of the stage is lit.

PAPO: The first time I walked down Forty-second Street I got scared and turned back. A woman lifted her skirt and started pissing and two cops were standing right there and they didn't do anything. She wasn't wearing panties and she was ugly. I turn around and walk back. I didn't go back for a while.

Second third is lit. BRIAN *at work. Sitting behind a desk he places a call. Music under.*

BRIAN: Hello.
VOICE 1: Card number, please.
BRIAN (*Fumbles in pocket for wallet, removes a card.*): Uh, 0655182.
VOICE 1: Thank you. Go ahead.
BRIAN: Hello.
VOICE 2: Hi.
BRIAN: Hi.
VOICE 2: You got a real sexy voice.
BRIAN: You too. Can you tell me what you look like?
VOICE 2: Sure. I'm six feet tall, 180, bodybuilder, 9 inches.
BRIAN: Sounds good.
VOICE 2: What are you in the mood for today?
BRIAN: I just want to hear your voice.
VOICE 2: You want me to talk dirty to you?
BRIAN: No, just talk to me.
VOICE 2: Look, what scene do you want?

The music builds. Hard. Hypnotic. VOICE 2 *fades and* BRIAN *will speak but won't be heard over the music.* BRIAN*'s phone receiver exchanges hands and his right hand goes under his desk. He opens his pants and begins to masturbate. The music becomes louder and* BRIAN *is sweating. He moans and trembles as he cums. A second after he does a light from an open doorway appears on him. He freezes. Music stops.*

SECRETARY'S VOICE: They're waiting for you in the conference room, Mr. Ritter.

BRIAN: Tell them I'll be right in.

Light from doorway disappears.

VOICE 2: Are you still there? Hello.

(BRIAN hangs up. He pulls a handkerchief from his pocket and cleans himself. Last third of the stage is lit. BOBBY is sitting on the floor, hugging himself and crying.

BOBBY: Why do you want to marry her, Reggie? What's the matter with me? What's the matter with me?

42nd Street Peep Show. PAPO is leaning against the front. Enter BRIAN from off stage. He slows down in front of Peep Show. He enters. PAPO waits a couple of seconds then follows. BRIAN is walking past the magazines. He stops to flip through one. PAPO reaches in front of him to get one.

PAPO: 'Scuse me.

BRIAN looks at PAPO out of the corner of his eye. PAPO brushes past him on the way to the booths. BRIAN waits a couple of seconds then fumbles putting magazine back. BRIAN enters the booth area and pretends to read the display cards on the different booths.

Psst.

BRIAN looks in the booth next to him where the door is ajar. PAPO is inside booth, playing with himself through his pants.

Hey man, you wanna see a movie?

BRIAN stands watching as PAPO begins to unfasten his pants.

MAN'S VOICE: Let's drop some quarters, gentlemen.

PAPO gestures with his head for BRIAN to come in. BRIAN is frozen in place.

PAPO: C'mon man. I ain't giving no fucking free show.
BRIAN: The sign says one person per booth. What if they catch us?
PAPO: Nobody pays attention to that.

BRIAN looks both ways and quickly enters the booth.

You got some quarters, man? You gotta drop some quarters in the machine else we can't close the door.

BRIAN begins to look through his pockets.

BRIAN: Yeah, I got a couple.
PAPO: Well, drop 'em in.

BRIAN does. The lights go out in the booth and a loop begins to play. They are standing in front of the screen so the film images are on their faces. PAPO leans against the wall, still massaging himself.

Go ahead and touch it. It ain't gonna bite you.

BRIAN stares at him openmouthed. PAPO reaches over and grabs one of BRIAN's hands. He places it over his crotch and moves it up and down.

You got some money?
BRIAN: Uh-huh.
PAPO: Okay then.

BRIAN awkwardly grabs PAPO and tries to kiss him. PAPO pushes him off.

Look man, I don't kiss no faggots.

BRIAN: Aren't you a faggot?

PAPO: No dickface, I'm a hustler. Look, you got some money, right?

BRIAN: Yeah.

PAPO: Okay, gimme twenty.

BRIAN: What for?

PAPO: To go down on me.

BRIAN: I don't know if I want to do that.

MAN'S VOICE: Let's drop some quarters, gentlemen.

BRIAN deposits another quarter.

PAPO: Not you. When the lights go up that's when you put in another quarter.

BRIAN: I'm sorry. Look, I've never done this before.

PAPO: Yeah, sure. It's still twenty. No discounts.

BRIAN: Can I kiss you?

PAPO: I told you, I don't kiss no faggots.

BRIAN shrugs helplessly and turns to leave. PAPO presses against him. He begins feeling him up, looking for his wallet.

Hey c'mon, man. Relax.

BRIAN: Do you have someplace else we can go?

PAPO does not find a wallet in BRIAN's pants.

PAPO: That would be more money.

BRIAN: That's okay.

PAPO: Man, you don't have any money. Don't be fucking bullshitting me.

Lights come up in booth.

BRIAN: Yes I do.

PAPO: Yeah? Show me.

BRIAN is about to reach for his money when a banging is heard on their booth door.

MAN'S VOICE: Let's drop some quarters in there.
PAPO (*Under his breath.*): Fuck you.
BRIAN: I don't have any more quarters.
PAPO: Great.

He reaches into his pocket and pulls one out.

You owe me a quarter, motherfucker.

He deposits it.

Let me go out first. I'll meet you outside then I'll take you to my room.
BRIAN: Okay.
PAPO: Hey man, you owe me a quarter.

PAPO EXITS. BRIAN touches the screen. Outside PAPO is waiting. BRIAN comes out of the Peep Show.

BRIAN: I got more change from a man in there. Here's your quarter.
PAPO: Yeah, look, it'll be fifty for me and ten dollars for the room.
BRIAN: I haven't got much time left.
PAPO: Don't worry, it won't take much time.
BRIAN: Maybe we should leave it for another time.
PAPO: You ain't got the money, right? Goddamn, fucking queer.
BRIAN: Please be quiet. No, I got it. It's right here.

BRIAN takes his wallet from his jacket pocket but when he looks inside he only finds a ten.

I'm sorry but all I have is a ten.
PAPO: Yeah, well you owe me that for the feel you copped in the booth.

BRIAN: Look, I got a credit card. I could buy you something.
PAPO: I don't want nothing. Fuck the credit card. What you gonna buy me?
BRIAN: I don't know. There's a clothing store over there, pick something.
PAPO: And you buy it for me?

They approach store.

How about that suit?
BRIAN: That's a hundred and twenty-five.
PAPO: Oh yeah.
BRIAN: How about that sweater?
PAPO: That's sixty-five.
BRIAN: It'll look good on you.
PAPO: So will the suit, man.
BRIAN: Wait here.

BRIAN enters shop. Lights fade. Up on Flophouse. BRIAN and PAPO enter. PAPO is admiring his sweater. BRIAN is uneasy.

BRIAN: Where's the washroom?
PAPO: This fucking sweater is ace.
BRIAN: Where can we clean up?
PAPO: Right there in the sink. They's supposed to give you a little soap and a towel but they won't if you don't ask for it.
BRIAN: Look.
PAPO: Papo.
BRIAN: Yeah, Papo. I have never done this before. With any man. Ever. I just want to be safe.
PAPO: Well, you shouldn't a bought me the sweater first, but it's okay. A lot of guys would have gotten the sweater and skipped but not me. I'll treat you right.
BRIAN: I don't want to get a disease.
PAPO: Excuse me?
BRIAN: I don't know where you've been and I know that's none of

my business; but I don't want to die because I had sex. That's too high a price to pay.

PAPO: Hey man, you think I got AIDS?

BRIAN: I'm not saying you do. I'm just saying—

PAPO: I ain't no fucking leper.

BRIAN: I've waited this long I can wait until they find a cure.

PAPO: So fucking wait.

BRIAN: Are you healthy?

PAPO: Jesus Christ, you wanna fucking note from my mother?

BRIAN: I'm afraid.

PAPO: Well look, what the fuck do you want me to do?

BRIAN: I'm afraid.

PAPO: Look, what do you want to do? Do you wanna jerk off?

BRIAN: I don't have to buy you a sweater so I can jerk myself off.

PAPO: Lissen, I ain't got all day and you ain't got all day; so what is it you want?

BRIAN: Just be a little patient. I've never done this before.

PAPO: Yeah yeah, sure sure.

BRIAN: Please don't ruin it for me.

PAPO: What the fuck am I doing? You're the one looking at me like an open sore or something.

BRIAN: I'm afraid to touch you. All the years of waiting so that I could become financially safe and now my idea of sex has become dangerous. I'm becoming so obsessed with sex that I'm suffocating. I walk down Forty-second Street and I can't breathe.

PAPO: You ain't missing much.

BRIAN: I'm beginning to fantasize at work.

PAPO: Hey, fucking ease up. Look, I'm clean. You ain't gonna catch nothing from me. I use these.

PAPO throws a package of condoms on the bed.

BRIAN: Great.

PAPO: Let's get this show on the road. I'll pop your cherry and you'll feel like a new man.

PAPO carefully takes off his sweater and folds it neatly. BRIAN picks up the package of condoms.

BRIAN: I am trusting my life to a piece of rubber that is thin enough to read through.
PAPO: C'mon, motherfucker. They're tropical colors no less.
BRIAN: I can't. I want to, but I can't.

PAPO stares at him.

PAPO: Fine. Fuck you, too. But I am keeping this sweater.
BRIAN: Don't be mad.
PAPO: Hey, of course not. But lissen, I better not see you on the deuce again cause sweater or no sweater I'll kick your motherfucking ass in.
BRIAN: Don't be that way.
PAPO: Come telling me I'm a fucking walking den of AIDS. What, you work for the *Post*, motherfucker?
BRIAN: Papo, can I just hold you.
PAPO: No.
BRIAN: I just want to feel you next to me.
PAPO (*Relenting.*): Fuck you.

BRIAN tentatively approaches PAPO. PAPO smirks, but lets himself be hugged.

Shit, it was an expensive sweater.

BRIAN begins to caress PAPO who slowly begins to respond.

Look, motherfucker—
BRIAN: Brian.
PAPO: You ain't gonna catch that shit from me. I'm clean. Really. No tracks. Look at my arms.
BRIAN: Just hold me.
PAPO: You a virgin, right? I never met a fucking virgin before.

BRIAN: If I'm fucking I can't be a virgin.
PAPO: You know what I fucking mean.

PAPO and BRIAN begin to kiss. PAPO begins to undress BRIAN, who panics and tries to break free. PAPO holds him. BRIAN pushes him, breaks free and runs out. PAPO follows him. On the street.

PAPO: C'mon back, man. You still got some time left.
BRIAN: You weren't supposed to do that.
PAPO: Okay. Okay.
BRIAN: I know where you were heading.
PAPO: Jesus fucking Christ. I'm sorry I touched you. I thought that's what you paid me for.
BRIAN: Lower your voice.
PAPO: Look, you turn me on. Not many tricks do that. I gotta fake it with most of 'em. But you, look.

He points to his crotch.

I don't wear underwears so I know when something is fucking getting to me.

BRIAN is panic-stricken. He walks away from PAPO and pretends to look in a store window. PAPO follows him.

What's the matter?
BRIAN: Will you cover that?
PAPO: C'mon. Nobody gives a fuck.

BRIAN walks away, PAPO follows.

Man, you don't want to see it, you don't want to touch it. Get yourself a fucking woman.

BRIAN tries to stretch PAPO's sweater down to cover his crotch.

Hey, watch it with the fucking sweater.

BRIAN: Uh, look I thought it was the right time for me but I guess it's not.

PAPO: Hey c'mon. There's no motherfucking contest going on. We ain't out to break a speed limit or shit like that.

BRIAN: Papo, I am a twenty-six-year-old white male virgin.

PAPO: You're twenty-six? You look older.

BRIAN: There are not too many of us out there.

PAPO: It's probably cause of the fucking suit and tie.

BRIAN: Look, I've got to go.

PAPO: You wanna meet again or something?

BRIAN: I'm . . . I'm not ready.

PAPO: Give you a discount. I could use some pants to go with this sweater.

BRIAN: And buy yourself some underwear. People are staring at us.

PAPO: Fuck 'em. You wanna get back together again?

BRIAN: I have to get back to work.

PAPO: Hey, I'm not good enough for you, faggot.

BRIAN walks away. PAPO follows.

Look, I'm sorry. I'm sorry. My mouth is like on automatic pilot.

BRIAN grabs PAPO's hand and shakes it.

BRIAN: Good-bye and good luck.

BRIAN hurriedly crosses the street.

PAPO: Yeah, you too.

PAPO waits for a bit and then follows BRIAN to where he works. BRIAN rushes into the building not knowing he has been followed. PAPO smiles at the building.

Lights up on BOBBY *who is packing a knapsack full of panties.*

BOBBY: Dear Reggie, thanks a lot for telling me yourself that you were gonna get married. It meant a whole lot to me that you called even though Mom and Dad were trying to keep it a secret. We both know how they are. Reggie, I think you are making a big mistake. There is no way this Lisa can love you the way I love you and no way you can love her the way you love your Baby. I wish Mom and Dad hadn't a taken away those pictures. They meant a whole lot to me. They had to hold me down to get them and I bit Dad whenever I could. I'm going to save you, Reggie, before you make the worst mistake of our lives. Love, Baby.

Lights up on PAPO *sitting at a table, drinking coffee.*

PAPO: I always take a coffee at Blimpie's on Forty-second off Eighth. Right across the street from Port Authority. Pick up some change from the Jersey crowd. I used to hang out at Playland next to the old Anco theatre, but fuck, the crowd there just kept getting younger and younger. Fucking Menudo convention. One of those snot-nosed little bastards tried to charge me. Waving his skinny ass in my face and then tells me "forty bucks." I broke his head. They don't want me at Playland no more. Fuck 'em. I don't care. I'm here for the duration.

Lights come up on BOBBY, *who is holding a carving knife.* PAPO *remains lit, drinking his coffee silently.*

BOBBY: No, not a whole set of knives. I think all my sister-in-law needs is a carving knife. The whole family is getting together for her birthday and I'm always giving her clothes and stuff so I figured this year I'd give her something for the house. She likes cooking so I'm sure she'll be able to utilize it. My sister-in-law really is gonna be surprised. I think mine is gonna be the best gift of all.

Lights out on BOBBY.

PAPO: And anyways right outside of Playland there's this girl preaching to everybody with a motherfuckin' bullhorn. Yeah, that bitch. Goddamn. It's like, is Jesus Christ deaf?

Lights up on BRIAN. *He is at his desk, lost in thought. The phone on his desk rings seven times without any sign of* BRIAN *hearing it. After the phone has stopped ringing there is a pause,* BRIAN *suddenly talks into the intercom.*

BRIAN: Did the phone just ring?

PAPO: After I recharge my batteries at Blimpie's I head to P.A. You gotta be careful though cause they put motherfucking cops everywhere. Keep moving and keep looking at the schedule so it looks like you got someplace to go. I once got pinched after I sucked a cop dry. Hell, yes! He starts in to read me my motherfucking rights and I looked at that motherfucker and I started yelling "Rape" and he got nervous and he left.

Lights up. PAPO *and* BOBBY *meet. The men's room at the Port Authority. Five* P.M. *on Friday.* BOBBY *looks like what he is, lost. He is wearing a jacket that is too hot for the weather and carrying a knapsack. In his right hand he carries the knife in a brown paper bag. He is hot and tired. He squats down on the floor and puts his knapsack between his legs and the paper bag on top of it. He is removing his jacket when* PAPO *enters and walks right into him.*

PAPO: Hey motherfucker, you couldn't find someplace else to park?

BOBBY: You bumped into me.

PAPO *does not listen and continues walking.*

BOBBY: You did.

PAPO has walked down the length of the stalls and returns. He is upset. Again he bumps into BOBBY.

PAPO: Goddamn it, kid. Get the fuck outta my way.
BOBBY: You bumped into me.
PAPO: What?
BOBBY: Last time too.

PAPO grabs BOBBY's face.

PAPO: If I see you again I'm gonna kick your fuckin' ass in.

Someone clears his throat in the last stall. PAPO releases BOBBY and washes his hands.

VOICE: Psst.
BOBBY: What's that?
PAPO: Why don't you go over there and find out, cunt?
VOICE: Psst, hey kid.
PAPO: He means you, white boy.
BOBBY: He dropped some money.
PAPO: No fool, he's makin' an offer you ain't gonna refuse.
BOBBY: I'm hungry.
PAPO: Tell him that. Maybe the motherfucker will buy you dinner.
BOBBY: I spent all my money on a gift.
VOICE: Psst.
BOBBY: You wanna see?
PAPO: Show it to the guy with the leak.
BOBBY: What do I have to do for the money?
PAPO: Nothing you haven't done before, only now some fool motherfucker's gonna pay to help.
BOBBY: I could use the money.
PAPO: So go ahead.
BOBBY: Can I?
PAPO: Hey faggot, I ain't your father.

BOBBY begins to inch toward the stall.

BOBBY: I'm sorry I bumped into you.

PAPO watches BOBBY's slow progress in the mirror.

PAPO: Oh, what the hell.

PAPO grabs BOBBY's arm and steers him out of the men's room.

Come on, Georgie, we don't want you to miss your motherfucking bus. You know how ma gets.

BOBBY: Bobby.

PAPO: Yeah, just move it white boy.

Outside the men's room.

PAPO: Let's circulate. That guy in the last stall. The one you was going to is a cop. The second you touched that twenty he was gonna pinch your lily-white ass.

BOBBY: Why would a cop wanna pinch me?

PAPO: Arrest, fool. Fuck. Straight off the motherfuckin' bus. He'd have you for soliciting and as a runaway.

BOBBY: How do you know he's a cop?

PAPO: They all wear the same fucking shoes. All the time. Like the whole fucking police force gets a discount if they all buy them. Ugly-ass shoes.

BOBBY: I'm still hungry.

PAPO: So, go earn some money, bitch. Just watch out for the shoes.

PAPO walks away, BOBBY follows.

Good-bye, kid.

BOBBY: I'll give you my jacket if I can stay with you for a while.

PAPO: I don't want you fucking jacket.

BOBBY: I want ice cream.

PAPO: Bitch, what is your problem. Lookee here.

PAPO goes to trash basket and takes out a piece of paper.

Pencil.

BOBBY: I got a pen.

PAPO: Whatever.

BOBBY reaches into his pocket and gives PAPO a pen. PAPO looks at the arrival board and writes down a number.

PAPO: Okay kid, every time you walk up to somebody you tell him this is the bus you're waiting for. He'll tell you it ain't due for hours you tell him you're waiting for your mother and you haven't got any money and you're hungry. With a face like yours, baby, they'll buy you something. Don't go with one of them unless they show you money. First get the money then find out what you gotta do to earn it. Capiche? Keep your eyes on their shoes, too. If a cop stops you show him this piece of paper and point to the fucking sign. Then just tell him you're gonna sit down and read comic books. They should leave you the fuck alone.

BOBBY: Who am I waiting for again?

PAPO: Your mother, asshole.

BOBBY: Right. You want to wait with me?

BOBBY: You are a fool. This is just pretend so the cops don't get you. Gimme back the paper. You're gonna fuck it up.

BOBBY: I won't. Honest.

PAPO: Shit. I should just let them drag you down to juvenile. Trade down there rape you ragged.

BOBBY begins to tremble. He drops his bag.

Hey shithead, don't go having a fucking seizure on me. You a fucking epileptic or something?

BOBBY: I'm just hungry, Reggie. Buy me some ice cream.

PAPO: Sure baby, sure. They got some Howard Johnson shit on the second floor.

BOBBY: My mother's not coming to pick me up. Can I stay with you?

PAPO: What the fuck. I ain't scored and I'm horny and you're cute. Okay. One night. One. Uno.

BOBBY picks up bag. Blackout. Light up on BRIAN in a cap and gown, holding a diploma. It is his Graduation Day.

DEAN'S VOICE: . . . class valedictorian, Brian Ritter.

BRIAN: Esteemed professors, honored guests, fellow students—

BRIAN's voice will continue but his mouth will stop moving. His own voice and his taped voice will alternate, rising and falling like waves.

BRIAN'S VOICE: We have before us what appears to be a horizon with no borders, no limits. Our education and our potential guarantee us entrance to—

BRIAN: To nothing. My tie is too tight. I remember I was angry because the gown wasn't long enough to hide where my mother had lowered the hem of my cousin David's "perfectly good suit, and we can't afford a new one anyway." I am the class valedictorian in a hand-me-down suit.

BRIAN'S VOICE: . . . as pioneers of our own future we stand to—

BRIAN: Voted most desperate to fit in. I always knew I was different and I always hid it. Ever since my parents caught me playing doctor with a neighbor boy. They wouldn't speak to me for a week.

BRIAN'S VOICE: Rewards and—

BRIAN: I was dirty. I didn't exist.

BRIAN'S VOICE: Making you proud of us—

BRIAN: Sometimes I would get so crazy I would kiss my G.I. Joe doll. Or I would cry and stand in a corner. I discovered religion. I would pray and God would make it all better. I would be like everybody else.

BRIAN'S VOICE: . . . our family, our friends—

BRIAN: No, better.

BRIAN'S VOICE: We are a community—

BRIAN: I'm never coming back here. I am going to work, nothing but work for five years. Put some money away. Buy my life back from you.

BRIAN'S VOICE: . . . and I urge you all—

BRIAN: What kind of parents would not talk to a seven-year-old child for a week?

BRIAN'S VOICE: I know I speak for all of us when I—

BRIAN: No! Let me finish. I don't care if you ever talk to me again but let me finish. I am getting out of here. I will become a somebody. I will win my independence. And when I have I'll get myself a man. A life-sized G.I. Joe. If I can just wait. If I can go hungry just for a little while I'll be all right.

BRIAN'S VOICE: . . . and in closing—

BRIAN: There's no reason anyone should know. Don't make the world angry at you, Brian. Wait.

BRIAN'S VOICE: Wait.

BRIAN: Wait.

BRIAN'S VOICE: Thank you.

Blackout. Lights up on Flophouse. PAPO *and* BOBBY.

BOBBY: Why can't I stay with you? I'll sleep on the floor. You won't even know I'm here.

PAPO: That's cause you won't be. Go get your own room, though you'll probably get kilt by some doped-up jerk. Go home, kid.

BOBBY: Why don't you want me?

PAPO: Oh shit, c'mon kid, if you're gonna start getting all pussy on me.

BOBBY: You saved my life.

PAPO: I shoulda let the cop throw you into juvenile hall.

BOBBY: They'd kill me in there.

PAPO: Man, all those Puerto Ricans and Blacks get together and they'd rip your fucking ass in half.

BOBBY: I'd be like a baby doll to them.

PAPO: Yeah, right.

BOBBY: No, it's true. My two older brothers would rape me cause I was so beautiful. Ever since I was twelve. One would hold me down and the other would rape me.

PAPO: Yeah, life's a bitch.

BOBBY: They took polaroid pictures. They would wait until my parents were gone and make me put on my mother's clothes.

PAPO: Real Norman Rockwell stuff, white boy.

BOBBY: My parents divorced when they found the pictures. Why did they do that? They sent my brothers away to a military school and me to a nuthouse. My father got married again. He has a little girl, a real one. Doesn't ever want me to come over. My mother puts a lock on her closet door when I'm home with her.

PAPO: Sure, stupid. She's afraid you're gonna steal her clothes.

BOBBY: I wouldn't do that.

PAPO: I was just goofing on you, kid.

BOBBY: My brother's getting married. That's where I was supposed to be going when I got off the bus. He found somebody else. He used to call me his Baby.

PAPO: You is all a bunch of sick fucks.

BOBBY: Reggie always treated me nice. He got me a valentine once.

PAPO: I didn't know they made them for brothers. Lissen you're a cute kid. You'll find yourself a nice rich guy who'll take care of you. You're a fine piece of blue-eyed ass, you'll do okay.

BOBBY: I want to be your wife.

PAPO: What, do I look like your brother? Is there a blue-eyed blond football player in me that I'm not seeing? Man, last night was just a freebie, don't let it go to your head. This is just too fucking stupid for words.

BOBBY: I can cook.

PAPO: Great, so can Burger King.

BOBBY: You can pimp me. You said yourself that I was a fine piece of ass. We can make a lot of money.

PAPO: I can make a lot of money.

BOBBY: Right, you can make a lot of money.

PAPO: No, forget it. That's all I need, for the fucking cops that's got it in for me already to see me pimping a little white minor.

BOBBY: I'm not a minor.

PAPO: Save it, Baby.

BOBBY: I can steal for you.

He pulls a small radio out of his pocket.

Look, I took this from the guy sitting next to me on the bus. For you.

PAPO: Yeah?

BOBBY: I took it right out of his pocket. I could make you a lot of money, between stealing and making tricks.

PAPO: That's turning tricks, man. You stole this? Then how come it has your name in magic marker on the back?

BOBBY: I wrote it.

PAPO: Yeah? Bullshit. Let me see the marker you used.

BOBBY: I threw it away. It was evidence.

PAPO: Right. You can't steal and you're gonna make a fucking great hustler proposing to every john you get.

BOBBY: I'm sorry, sir.

PAPO: Don't call me sir. I ain't your fucking father, Baby.

BOBBY: I didn't lie about cooking. I know how to cook.

PAPO: Then fucking go get yourself a job at some dago place. Go to a Greek diner and slice up some gyros.

PAPO turns to leave. BOBBY pulls the knife from his jacket. He stabs at PAPO, barely missing him.

You fucking crazy?!

BOBBY: Why can't I stay with you?

BOBBY jumps in front of the door.

PAPO: I don't want to have to hurt you, kid. Don't be pulling no knives on me.

BOBBY: Call me "Baby."

PAPO tries to push BOBBY who stabs wildly at him. He slashes PAPO's sweater sleeve. PAPO falls backward on the floor. BOBBY holds the knife poised at PAPO's throat.

Please call me "Baby."

PAPO: Baby.

BOBBY: I was going to Reggie's wedding. I was. I was going to stop his marriage to that imposter. It's a good thing I met you. Now I can be yours.

PAPO: Yeah, Baby. Whatever you say.

BOBBY: You're just like Reggie was, too. You can be real rough in bed but every so often you'd kiss as if you hoped I wouldn't notice. You'd kiss my eyelids. So softly. Give me a kiss, sir.

They kiss with the knife still at PAPO's throat.

I wanna do what we did last night. Whatever you want me to do. Can I call you Reggie?

PAPO: Sure.

BOBBY: And you can call me Baby. I'll make you a good wife.

BOBBY helps PAPO stand.

Take off your sweater, Reggie.

PAPO: My what?

BOBBY: Your sweater, Reggie.

PAPO slowly does.

I didn't hurt you, did I?

PAPO: No, it okay. (*Pause.*) Baby.

BOBBY groans. PAPO grabs BOBBY by the back of his hair and pulls him toward him, kissing him roughly on the mouth and then very gently on the eyelids. BOBBY is still holding the knife. PAPO continues to kiss him now on the neck and shoulders. PAPO kisses BOBBY's right arm, his hand and kisses the blade of the knife.

Give me the knife, Baby. (*BOBBY gives PAPO the knife.*) Lay down.

BOBBY does. His arms reach up for PAPO. Blackout. Lights up outside of Peep Show. PAPO is hanging out as BRIAN comes down the street. He sees PAPO and tries to walk quickly by. PAPO sees him and chases him.

PAPO: Hey Brian. Brian, wait up. (*He falls in step next to him.*) Hey man, you deaf or something?

BRIAN: I thought you people never recognize customers on the street.

PAPO: Well, fuck you very much, too.

BRIAN: I'm sorry. How are you doing?

PAPO: Okay. How about you?

BRIAN: Fine. Look I've got to run.

PAPO: Run my ass. This is your lunch break. The only place you gotta run is to a peep show.

BRIAN: Papo.

PAPO: Which is cool cause that's where I met you.

BRIAN: Hey, you need a couple of bucks?

PAPO: Shit, can't I talk to you without your wallet getting all itchy?

BRIAN: Sorry. What do you want?

PAPO: Well man, I see you're in the market for some action.

BRIAN: Papo.

PAPO: No strings.

BRIAN: I was kind of looking for somebody else.

PAPO: Yeah, well fuck you. (*BRIAN walks away. PAPO follows.*) Hey look man, I'm sorry. I haven't seen you in a while. I guess I'm jumpy, that's all. Friends?

BRIAN: Sure. Look, I don't have much time left.

PAPO: We can just duck in here. I got some quarters.

BRIAN: How about your place?

PAPO: Uh, no. A friend is kinda staying there. A real sweet kid, a little psycho is all.

BRIAN: Why are you letting him stay?

PAPO: I don't know.

BRIAN: Is he your lover?

PAPO: Get real. Baby spends all day in panties.

BRIAN: Baby?

PAPO: The kid. The kid, okay. Hey, you jealous or something?

BRIAN: No.

PAPO: Yes you are. I sleep with this guy every night and he lets me do anything I want to him. You are jealous.

BRIAN: Papo, I really don't care.

PAPO: Yeah, I know you don't.

BRIAN: I should start getting back. I left a lot of work on my desk.

PAPO: Hey, a quickie. My treat.

BRIAN: Some other time.

PAPO: Let me walk you back then.

BRIAN stops PAPO.

BRIAN: No.

PAPO pushes BRIAN's hand away.

PAPO: Man, I just wanna be your friend. You think you're too good for me? Fine. Fuck you. I got me a piece of sixteen-year-old white meat who'll take anything I give him. Baby treats me just fine; so fuck you. Fuck you, motherfucker.

BRIAN *hurries off with* PAPO *still screaming after him.*

Yeah, you're too good to talk to me but you ain't too good to get my dick up your ass. Fuck you, man, just fuck you. Look, how about if I call you sometime?

Blackout. Lights up as each person speaks.

BRIAN: It's crazy, but I know he follows me. He thinks I don't notice, but I do. What does he want from me? He can't be in love. People like that don't fall in love and nobody falls in love with me. So what does he want?

BOBBY: I'm making him everything I ever wanted in a brother.

PAPO (*Holding a brick.*): This is where I grew up. This brick belongs to a building in the Bronx. Six story walk-up. Fucking got asthma from living there. Going up and down those motherfucking stairs every day. I went there a couple of years ago and the fucking building was bricked up. I hadn't been there in ten years and I expect to go back and knock on the door, tell the new people I had lived there and if I could have a fucking look around. So I go back and it's all like fucking bricked up and I thought I should have gone back sooner.

BRIAN: Am I supposed to be the gateway to the white world for him?

BOBBY: And he loves me, too.

PAPO: I went back last summer and the whole place was torned down. That's when I got the brick. Sure you can tear a building down but you can't knock it down from here.

PAPO *points to heart with brick.*

PAPO: People don't fucking understand that. My parents live in P.R. now. I send them money, they don't ask questions. My baby sister lives with them. She's getting married soon.

BOBBY: I would like for us to get married. To be together for always so no one can separate us.

BRIAN: The thing is Papo doesn't know about the times I follow him. When I stand there without him seeing me and just watch him. He doesn't know the times he's helped me jerk off.

BOBBY: Don't tell Papo but I went upstate the other day. I wanted to see Reggie. I wanted to tell him it was all right. That I forgave him for getting married cause I was gonna get married, too. I'm on the bus and just as we enter into town I see Reggie outside of his car. I get off and run to him. Ronald, my other brother, was with him.

PAPO: Baby's like a pet, you know.

BOBBY: They wanted to take me back to the hospital. They say I'm sick. They say what we did together was sick and Reggie can't meet my eyes. Ronald's doing all the talking. And I tell them I got a good man, a true man. Someone who really loves me.

BRIAN: Maybe if Papo and me ran away together.

BOBBY: Ronald grabs me and I kick him in the balls. He's down. He yells for Reggie to hold me and when he does I naturally kiss him. Like always. And he looks at me and yells, "Run!" He sets me free and holds back Ronald and I hitched a ride with a trucker to the Lincoln Tunnel. I'm luckier than they are. I get to go home to someone who loves me.

Blackout. Lights up. PAPO *is in the receptionist area of* BRIAN*'s office.*

RECEPTIONIST: Pickup or delivery.

PAPO: No, I'm here to see Brian.

RECEPTIONIST: Do you have an appointment with Mr. Ritter?

PAPO: Nah, it's a surprise. Just tell him Papo is here. Uh, Mr. Papo Santiago.

PAPO *can feel people looking at him. He tries to act nonchalant but finally smirks at a few people. He takes a paper cup and gets water from a watercooler. He is nervous and fidgets with the glass, accidentally puncturing it and spilling the water.*

Oh shit, I'm sorry. You got a rag or something? These little glasses are for shit.

BRIAN enters. He tries to hide his anger as he steers PAPO outside. He pushes him into a stairwell.

PAPO: Hey man, what's with you? No hello—
BRIAN: Don't you ever—
PAPO: . . . no nothing. Just take me off to—
BRIAN: . . . ever come to where I work again.
PAPO: Huh?
BRIAN: How did you find it? Did you follow me?
PAPO: Wait a second. Are you pissed off that I came to visit?
BRIAN: This is not a place for you to visit. This is where I work.
PAPO: Big fucking deal.
BRIAN: I'm serious. You are never to come—
PAPO: Fuck off, man. I just wanted to surprise you.
BRIAN: . . . here again. What the hell were you thinking of. Look at the way you look.
PAPO: What the hell's the matter with the way I look?
BRIAN: You look like a goddamn faggot.

PAPO punches BRIAN.

PAPO: Look, motherfucker, I come by cause I was gonna take you to lunch.
BRIAN: Dressed like that?
PAPO: Fuck you fuck you fuck you.

BRIAN tries to cover PAPO's mouth but he pushes his hand away. BRIAN tries to regain his composure.

BRIAN: Papo . . . I can't receive any visitors where I work. This is not playtime, this is work.
PAPO: I fucking know that, I'm not stupid. And don't be telling

me you (*PAPO hits BRIAN.*) can't get any visitors cause everybody knows—

BRIAN: Will you just get out?

PAPO: . . . that you people all got your private little bars in your office for your guests. I seen that on the TV.

BRIAN reaches into his pocket and takes out his wallet. He gives PAPO some money.

BRIAN: Go buy something.

PAPO tries to jam the wallet into BRIAN's mouth.

PAPO: Look you piece of shit I ain't no piece of shit.

He takes the money and wipes his ass with it.

PAPO: This is what I think of your money.

BRIAN: I'm sorry. I'm sorry. Please keep your voice down.

PAPO: I went out and bought underwears, okay? Something I ain't never done for anybody.

BRIAN: Okay, okay.

PAPO: No, it's not okay. I'm sorry you're embarrassed by me, faggot.

BRIAN: Please, get out of here.

PAPO pushes BRIAN against the wall. He pulls an open package of underwear from his jacket. There are still two left in the package. He throws them at BRIAN.

PAPO: Here, these are yours, motherfucker.

PAPO storms out. BRIAN picks up his wallet, the money and the underwear. He removes one of the underwear from the jacket and kisses it.

The following scene is done with lights and sound. PAPO is standing between two subway cars on an express train. As the lights and the sound builds so do his screams. He opens his pants and struggles until he manages to rip off his underwear. Lights fade. Train sound fade.

Lights up on BRIAN *in his bedroom. He is undressing. He removes* PAPO*'s underwear from his pocket and puts them on. He fondles himself. He adjusts his mirror on the bureau so it can reflect on him. He lies on the bed and caresses himself, pinching his nipples.*

BRIAN: Oh, baby. You know that I want you so much. And you want it too, yes you do. You drive me crazy. I want to kiss every inch of your body.

Music begins underneath.

BRIAN: I've been watching you for so long. Now it's just you and me. All I want is to touch you and hold you.

BRIAN *runs his hands over his body. His eyes are shut tight.*

Oh, yes, and kiss you.

He takes a pillow and begins to kiss it. He places another pillow between his legs.

Nobody can see us. It's you and me. Don't we look good together? Look in the mirror. Don't we look good?

BRIAN *opens his eyes.* PAPO*'s voice is heard.*

PAPO'S VOICE: You wanna see a movie?

BRIAN *sits bolt upright. He looks straight into the mirror, his desperation is rising.*

BRIAN: I've got to get out. I've got to get out.

He reaches madly for the phone and dials.

VOICE: Hello, card number please.
BRIAN: Yes, 0655482.
VOICE: Thank you. Please hold.
MAN'S VOICE: Hi.
BRIAN: I want you to touch me.
MAN'S VOICE: Yeah.
BRIAN: I want you right here.
PAPO'S VOICE: You turn me on. Not many tricks do that.
BRIAN: I gotta get out. I gotta get out of here.

BRIAN *jumps from the bed and throws on a pair of slacks and a jacket. He hurriedly puts on some shoes and runs to the door. He stands frozen in place in the open doorway, unable to set foot outside his apartment.*

I can't, Papo. I can't.
PAPO'S VOICE: I sleep with this guy every night. He lets me do anything I want to him.

BRIAN *screams out in to the hallway.*

BRIAN: Papo!

He slams the door and collapses against it.

Blackout. Lights up on Flophouse. BOBBY *is wearing panties and panties are hung to dry from every available place. Enter* PAPO *who is still upset over his turndown at* BRIAN*'s office.* BOBBY *senses trouble and tries to keep his distance.* PAPO *paces and begins to pull down the panties.*

PAPO: I come home to a fucking laundromat.
BOBBY: I gotta put it somewhere to dry.
PAPO: They got dryers. God invented dryers, okay?

BOBBY *is on his hands and knees picking up the panties.*

BOBBY: I wash these at home, darling. All my fine washables are done by hand.

PAPO: These are not yours. They belong to a woman. You know, a woman.

PAPO roughly grabs BOBBY and makes him stand. He grabs BOBBY's balls.

You're supposed to be a fucking guy.

PAPO pushes him aside.

BOBBY: I can be who I want to be, I can create myself. What's the matter, Reggie?

PAPO: Don't fucking call me Reggie! I'm confused enough as it is.

BOBBY: Are you hungry? Did you have a tough football practice? Why won't you tell Baby what's wrong?

PAPO grabs BOBBY.

PAPO: You ain't my baby. I am not your goddamn fucking brother, see. Goddamn loony tunes. I want you out of here. You take your underwear and you make tracks back to the white world but you leave me the fuck alone.

MAN'S VOICE: Hey, you faggots wanna keep it down in there?

BOBBY: What would you do without me? You can't cook.

PAPO sits on the bed with his head in his hands.

PAPO: Leave me alone, man. Just leave me alone.

BOBBY kneels next to him.

BOBBY: I'm not a man, I'm your Baby.

PAPO puts his arm around BOBBY's shoulder and begins to rock him.

You just wait. Someday we'll get our own house, and a sheepdog and two children.

PAPO: Fucking loony tunes.

BOBBY: And a station wagon. I'll drive you to the train station and you can catch the eight-fifteen into the city. I'll go home and get the kids off to school and clean the house and go shopping and make dinner. You know, I can really cook.

BOBBY gets up and goes to hot plate. He returns with a pot.

Look, Reggie, I made your favorite. Rice-A-Roni.

PAPO begins to tremble. He knocks the pot from BOBBY's hand and begins to beat him.

PAPO: I am not Reggie! You got that you little motherfucker? You are getting out of this place today, right now.

BOBBY is trying to block his blows.

BOBBY: Please, Reggie, please don't hit me. I'll do whatever you want.

PAPO: Goddamn fucking retard. (*He points to himself.*) Papo! You got that? (*He smacks him for emphasis.*) Papo!

He throws open the door and begins to throw BOBBY's panties into the hallway. BOBBY is crying and hanging on to PAPO's leg.

BOBBY: Please, Papo, please don't.

Steps are heard outside the door.

MAN'S VOICE: Hey, you wanna beat the little queer up? Fine. Just keep it down.

PAPO: This little motherfucker is outta here.

BOBBY is still crying and wrapped around PAPO's leg.

BOBBY: Why don't you want me, Reggie? Why? I wore the panties you wanted.
PAPO: I bought underwears!
BOBBY: You should have married me.
MAN'S VOICE: I personally don't care. I just don't want no trouble.

PAPO tries to move his leg but BOBBY holds on fast.

PAPO: It's okay, Baby.
BOBBY: Why didn't you tell me you didn't like Rice-A-Roni?
MAN'S VOICE: Are you working this kid? Cute kid, you know?
PAPO: Hey man, throw me those motherfucking panties.

PAPO catches them. He gently rubs BOBBY's head with them.

BOBBY: Are you mad at me, Reggie?
PAPO: No, Baby, I'm not mad.
BOBBY: I'll do whatever you want me to do, you know that.
PAPO: Yeah, Baby, I know that.

BOBBY slowly stands and huddles under PAPO's arm.

MAN'S VOICE: Hey look, Papo, how much for the kid?
PAPO: Baby's not for sale.
MAN'S VOICE: C'mon guy.
PAPO: But you can watch.
BOBBY: Reggie.
PAPO: Sssh.
MAN'S VOICE: How much?
PAPO: Today's rent.
MAN'S VOICE: Forget it.
PAPO: Goodnight then, motherfucker.
MAN'S VOICE: And I can watch.
PAPO: That's what I said.

MAN'S VOICE: Okay.

BOBBY: No, Reggie.

PAPO: Look, Baby, what was the name of your other fucking brother?

BOBBY: Ronald.

PAPO pushes BOBBY backward on the bed. Lights go out on bed. The only light is now coming from the doorway. Fade to Blackout.

Outside Peep Show. BRIAN is walking by, very slowly. PAPO exists Peep Show. They see each other. BRIAN smiles, PAPO smirks and looks away. BRIAN starts to walk away.

PAPO: What's the matter, man? You don't say hello?

BRIAN: I thought you were mad at me.

PAPO: I should be.

BRIAN: I've been looking for you.

PAPO: You can't have been looking too hard. I'm always right here.

BRIAN: You're not wearing the sweater.

PAPO: Yeah, well I don't wear it everyday, you know. I gotta give it a rest.

BRIAN: So, how are you doing?

PAPO: Look are you buying or what?

BRIAN: I just wanted to see you, to talk. I thought you might be happy to see me.

PAPO: Well I ain't.

BRIAN looks down at PAPO's crotch.

BRIAN: I think you are.

PAPO: That's not fair, man. I don't wear underwears.

BRIAN: I just wanted to say I'm sorry about the other day.

PAPO (*Shrugs.*): Fuck it. (*BRIAN turns to enter Peep Show.*) Hey, where the fuck are you going? Hot damn. You come all the way down here to apologize and then you go try to pick up somebody else.

BRIAN: Sssh. I thought you were still mad at me.
PAPO: I fucking should be.
BRIAN: Would you like to go to dinner?
PAPO: Time is money.
BRIAN: Can you take some time off?
PAPO: What you think, I punch a fucking time clock?
BRIAN: You got such a mouth on you.
PAPO: Yeah, good lips, huh?
BRIAN: Do I have to pay you to take you to dinner?
PAPO: Hey, don't stand in front of me, you're blocking my fucking view.

When BRIAN shifts he begins to stare at somebody else.

You know, it's not like I ain't got other motherfuckers waiting for me. You fucking show up out of nowheres and—

PAPO notices BRIAN staring at someone else. He slaps the back of his head.

Hey, motherfucker, you planning on taking the whole fucking deuce to dinner?
BRIAN: No, just you. If you'll come.
PAPO: Like if I'm gonna turn down free food.
BRIAN: Do you want to go home and change?
PAPO: No, do you?

Blackout. Lights up on Restaurant. PAPO and BRIAN seated at a small round table. Very nice place. Linen tablecloth and napkins. In the background BOBBY is softly lit. He sits on the bed, smoking, waiting for PAPO. He remains seated throughout the scene.

PAPO: Is this how you white people eat every day. (*He touches tablecloth and napkins.*) Look, it's all material.
BRIAN: Lower your voice.

PAPO (*In a basso profundo.*): It's all material. (*BRIAN laughs.*) Seriously, how much does it cost to eat here?

BRIAN: It's my treat. Don't worry about it.

PAPO: The waiter looked at me like I belonged cause I came in with you. Hey, where's my napkin holder? You got one of them glass napkin rings. Where's mine?

BRIAN: Here, you can have mine.

PAPO: No, I'll just take one of the little motherfuckers off another table.

BRIAN: Papo, don't.

PAPO: They ain't in use.

BRIAN: Take mine. (*PAPO gets up and returns with one.*)

PAPO: Ta-da.

BRIAN: Sssh.

PAPO: Am I embarrassing you, faggot? (*BRIAN looks away. PAPO sits.*) Look man, I'm sorry. Really. I won't call you that again. I swear.

BRIAN: Just tell me what you want from the menu.

PAPO: Now you're mad at me.

BRIAN: No, I'm not.

PAPO: Don't fucking be that way.

BRIAN (*Sharply.*): Can you talk without cursing?

PAPO: When did I fucking curse?

BRIAN: You don't even hear it anymore.

PAPO: I hear what I want to hear. You should try it sometime.

BRIAN: You mean some fucking time.

PAPO: That ain't cursing.

BRIAN: Fuck is a verb, not an adjective.

PAPO: Fool, if anybody knows that I do.

BRIAN: Let's make a deal. Let's see if we can have a nice meal with no cursing.

PAPO: Serious, man, I don't call that cursing. Cursing is when I'm mad at somebody. Like when I used to call you "faggot." I used that as a curse.

BRIAN: Could you also try to speak a little softer?

PAPO: Maybe if that guy could hold off on the piano for a bit. (*Calls to piano player.*) Hey, man.

BRIAN: Papo. Shut up. Now. (*PAPO stares at BRIAN a second, then smiles.*)

PAPO: You getting all butch on me all of a sudden?

BRIAN: Maybe this wasn't such a good idea.

PAPO: I'll be good. Look, I won't say another word. So, what do you do?

BRIAN: I'm a lawyer.

PAPO: Fucking judge must go crazy when he sees you.

BRIAN: Papo.

PAPO: Right.

BRIAN: I've been in New York a little over a year. Just bought a coop.

PAPO: Nice, nice.

BRIAN: Pretty much a stay-to-myself type. I'm very discreet. Don't have too many gay friends.

PAPO: I ain't gay.

BRIAN: Okay.

PAPO: I'm not.

BRIAN: Fine.

PAPO: When did you know you were a fag . . . uh, a queer?

BRIAN: Do you care? (*PAPO shrugs.*) I always knew it. Sometimes I feel like I'm going to die if I can't have sex; then other times I think I'll die if I do have it.

PAPO: Man, you is how old and you're still a virgin?

BRIAN sees waiter. He elbows PAPO.

BRIAN: I'll have the house salad with vinaigrette dressing, onion soup, and duck in raspberry sauce.

PAPO: Me, too. (*Waiter disappears. BRIAN takes a drink of water.*) So when can I pop your cherry? (*BRIAN chokes on water.*) Hey man, I don't mean right here.

BRIAN: Let's just see if we can make it through this dinner without you giving me a heart attack. Okay?

PAPO: Yeah, okay. I have that effect on people sometimes.
BRIAN: Making them choke?
PAPO (*Sly smile.*): That too.
BRIAN: Uh, do you have any family here?
PAPO: I don't wanna talk about them.
BRIAN: Okay.
PAPO: Do you like talking about your parents?
BRIAN: I said okay.

Pause.

PAPO: What do you talk about when you're with your white friends?
BRIAN: What do you mean?
PAPO: I'm no dummy. Talk English to me and I'll understand you.
BRIAN: I don't think you're stupid.
PAPO: Yeah, well you fucking better not. Talk to me.
BRIAN: Okay, how old are you?
PAPO: Jesus fucking Christ!
BRIAN: Lower your voice.
PAPO: I'm surprised you got any fucking friends. I'm not as old as I look.
BRIAN: I just wanted to know how long you've been at it.
PAPO: You mean fucking fags?

BRIAN tenses. PAPO puts his hand on BRIAN's arm and mouths "Sorry".

BRIAN: This is not working.
PAPO: Sure it is, just fucking relax.
BRIAN: You get angry at everything I say.
PAPO: No, I don't. I started at fifteen.
BRIAN: Why?
PAPO: I don't know. I was a real delicacy then. Flavor of the month. The last Coca-Cola in the desert. I made a lot of money.
BRIAN: What's a lot of money?
PAPO: I once made three hundred dollars in one day.

BRIAN whistles appreciatively. PAPO smiles.

BRIAN: That is a lot of money.

PAPO: I gave most of it to my parents. They bought a new living room set.

BRIAN: What did you have to do to earn it?

PAPO gives BRIAN a dirty look.

Sorry.

PAPO: Most people think that all Puerto Ricans are strung-out hustlers. I read, you know. I do fucking crossword puzzles. I don't do drugs. You don't have to be embarrassed by me. I'm not stupid.

BRIAN: I never said you were stupid.

PAPO: You like me, right?

BRIAN: Yeah.

PAPO: Then talk to me. Trust me, I'll understand you.

BRIAN: What do you want me to say?

PAPO: You're a lawyer. Why did you become a lawyer?

BRIAN: To make money.

PAPO: See? We got things in common.

BRIAN laughs.

BRIAN: Money buys freedom. I put myself through law school. I almost had to drop out twice.

PAPO: Why?

BRIAN: Money.

PAPO: I thought all white people had money.

BRIAN: We don't. I once had to carry two jobs at once and keep my grades up.

PAPO: Shit.

BRIAN: Now I've got a good job and I make good money.

PAPO: Yeah?

BRIAN: I'm not rich, but I can buy things for myself now and then. Pamper myself. Take friends to dinner.

PAPO smiles.

BRIAN: Things I read about but could never afford to do. (*PAPO's hand begins to fondle BRIAN under the table.*) Don't do that. (*PAPO continues.*)

PAPO (*Teasing.*): Why not? You no like?

BRIAN: Please put your hands on top of the table.

PAPO: Lower your voice. (*BRIAN reaches under the table to remove PAPO's hand.*) It looks even worse with both of our hands under here. (*BRIAN whips his hand out. PAPO continues groping.*) This is better.

BRIAN: Please stop.

PAPO: No one can see us. Relax. Drink a little fucking water. You feel real healthy down here.

BRIAN: The waiter is coming.

PAPO: Tell him to go the fuck away.

BRIAN: We're not quite ready yet. (*PAPO continues groping.*) Please, this is enough. Stop it.

PAPO: Take me back to your place?

BRIAN shakes his head "no."

BRIAN (*Whispers.*): Yes.

PAPO: Do you have any fantasy you want to live out?

BRIAN: I just don't want to die.

PAPO freezes.

PAPO: Do you really want me to stop?

BRIAN: If you stop I'll die.

Blackout. BOBBY hears a noise in the hallway and hurriedly puts out the cigarette. He opens the window and tries to air the room by waving his hands. He is stopped by the silence in the hallway. He listens by the door.

He goes back to his cigarette, is about to start smoking again, but stops. He gently drops the cigarette out the window. He waves good-bye to it as it falls. Lights fade out on BOBBY.

Lights up on BRIAN *who is asleep among his sheets.* PAPO *enters, he carries a supermarket bag and places it on the floor. He exits and returns wheeling a portable TV set and positions it in front of the bed.*

He is carrying the remote control for it in his mouth. He exits again and returns with two plates, two spoons and a knife. He puts the plates on the bed, trying to be as quiet as possible so as not to awaken BRIAN. PAPO*'s mood is very up. He takes a pint of ice cream and a pound cake from the bag. He cuts the cake in half, putting a half on each plate. He opens the ice cream and divides it the same way.*

He puts the knife aside, puts the ice-cream container in the bag and quickly, but quietly strips. He gently gets into bed and puts both plates on his lap. He aims the remote control at the TV. Loud cartoon music is heard. BRIAN *jumps up.*

PAPO: Good morning.
BRIAN: What the hell? Lower that goddamn thing!
PAPO: Shit. And you talk about my motherfucking mouth.
BRIAN: What's going on here?
PAPO: I made breakfast in bed. Here. (PAPO *hands* BRIAN *a plate.*) And they're doing Bugs Bunny. The old ones.
BRIAN: Could you lower that a little?
PAPO: Man, if I put it any lower I won't be able to fucking hear it. (PAPO *lowers the volume.*) You got a real problem with sound, you know that?

BRIAN *lies back and watches* PAPO, *who is lost in his cartoons.*

BRIAN: I've got to take a shower.
PAPO: You've had three since we got here.

PAPO *continues eating. He watches the cartoons and reacts to them. He takes* BRIAN*'s hand with his free hand.*

PAPO: You still think God is gonna strike you dead?
BRIAN: What?

PAPO *laughs at the cartoon.*

PAPO: What's up doc?
BRIAN: I have to go to work.

PAPO *tries to kiss him with his mouth full of ice cream.* BRIAN *turns his head.*

PAPO: Time for a quickie?

BRIAN *jumps from the bed and pulls the sheet around him.*

BRIAN: Do you want to, uh, do you want to take a shower first? (PAPO *takes the remote and ups the volume.* BRIAN *takes it from him and shuts off the TV.* PAPO *studies his ice cream.*) I don't want to be late.
PAPO: I guess you're done with this spic, huh?

BRIAN *gets his wallet and places it gently on the bed next to* PAPO.

BRIAN: Papo, I am petrified of you.

He tries to smooth PAPO*'s head but* PAPO *violently shakes him off.*

PAPO: So you kicking me out, right? (*Silence.*) Are you kicking me out?
BRIAN: Yes. (PAPO *puts his plate on the bed and gets dressed. He begins to put on a shoe.*) Will you please take some money from me?

Without looking up, PAPO *throws the shoe at* BRIAN. PAPO *gets himself under control and puts on his other shoe.* BRIAN *brings the shoe to him and stands by* PAPO *with it in his hand.*

PAPO *takes it and puts it on. He never looks up at* BRIAN. *When* PAPO *stands, he punches* BRIAN *in the stomach.* BRIAN *doubles over as* PAPO *exits.*

Flophouse.

BOBBY *is sleeping while hugging a pillow.* PAPO *enters. He stares at* BOBBY *and quietly walks to the bed where he gently kisses* BOBBY, *who continues sleeping.* PAPO *goes to the hot plate and takes a saucepan from it. He uncovers it and begins to eat Rice-A-Roni directly from it. He sits on the bed, next to* BOBBY, *who slowly wakes up.*

PAPO: Hey, Baby.

BOBBY *shimmies up to* PAPO *and lays his head in his lap.*

BOBBY: How'd it go today, Reggie?
PAPO: Not too good, Baby. A lot of distractions. Didn't get jackshit done. Just ran around with my finger up my ass. (BOBBY *giggles.* PAPO *begins to feed him like a baby. Tenderly, playfully.*) You keeping out of mischief?
BOBBY: Uh-huh.
PAPO: Good boy.
PAPO: Gimme a kiss, Reggie.

A knock is heard.

PAPO (*To door.*): Hold on a second. (PAPO *gives* BOBBY *a kiss.* BOBBY *throws his arms around* PAPO*'s neck.* PAPO *must pull him off.*) Look Baby, that's the man from downstairs, and he wants his rent.
BOBBY: Ronald.

PAPO: Right. Look, I bullshitted the day away, and we has got to pay the rent.

BOBBY: Don't let him in.

PAPO kisses BOBBY on the shoulder.

PAPO: Baby, he's just gonna touch you a little, that's all. (*Another knock is heard. PAPO yells to door.*) Hey fucking dickhead, fucking chill out for a second. (*PAPO goes to door and opens it. Doorway light comes into room.*) You all fucking ready and set to explode? (*PAPO pulls the sheet off BOBBY, who is facedown and eating from the pan. A whistle from the man is heard.*) Good, huh?

PAPO motions for the man to enter, and he turns to leave. BOBBY reaches out and takes PAPO's hand.

BOBBY: Okay, but you stay. You stay. You promise. (*The lights from the doorway and the room begin to dim. BOBBY closes his eyes and squeezes PAPO's hand.*) This is for you.

Blackout. Lights up on each as they speak.

PAPO: He doesn't love me.

BRIAN: Sometimes I get the feeling that I'm his revenge against the white world.

PAPO: This is how I see it. He won't say he loves me, won't touch me, but he can't help wanting me. Then after we did it he took half a dozen showers and sat and sulked and looked at me as if I had just stolen a course of years from his life. Hey, but wait a second, lemme rewind my past and I'll erase it. I'll be nice and clean for the big white hunter. And I still won't be good enough for him.

BOBBY: You're plenty good enough for me.

PAPO: I ain't even me for you.

BOBBY: Don't say that. You're my dream lover. There's nothing wrong with that. I look up to you, I idolize you.

PAPO: So let's see what I got here. With this guy I'm an open sore. The one thing I am I can't be with him. I'm good at sex, real good, but I can't do it with him because it makes him nervous. But I can go to nice places with him, I can go to stores and not have store detectives follow me as if I were gonna steal something. He's one of them and if I'm with him I must be okay, too. White by marriage. Which with Baby would be pretty useless. I mean, to be white and poor I might as well stay the way I fucking am. Then you start falling in love. You know, the stupid stuff. What kind of guy falls in love with another guy? With two other guys; yeah, cause once you start with that shit it takes on a fucking life of it's own. My life.

Night. PAPO *enters phone booth. Lights up on* BRIAN, *in bathrobe, in his bedroom.* BRIAN'*s phone rings.*

PAPO: Hi, Brian, this is Papo.
BRIAN: Ah, listen, I'm about getting ready to leave.
PAPO: Yeah, where to?
BRIAN: I'm meeting some friends for dinner.
PAPO: So you wanna hang out later?
BRIAN: We'll be out late.
PAPO: That's okay.
BRIAN: I don't think so.
PAPO: C'mon man. Fuck, if you're just half as horny as I am we'll set the sheets on fire.

BRIAN *hangs up.* PAPO *is left holding a dead receiver. He starts to hit the phone with the receiver. He fishes into his pocket for another quarter and calls* BRIAN.

BRIAN: Papo, please.
PAPO: Don't you ever, ever fucking hang up on me. (BRIAN *hangs up.* PAPO *inserts another quarter while hitting the phone booth in a rage. He yells at someone waiting to use the phone.*) I ain't fucking finished yet. You wanna do something about it, huh? Wait

your goddamn turn, cunt. (*PAPO flails with one hand at someone waiting for the phone while dialing with the other hand. The phone rings and rings.*) Please pick up.

BRIAN finally picks up.

BRIAN: Papo.

PAPO: Do you want me to go over there, is that it? Do you want me to show up where you work? I will, you know I will. Don't fuck with me, Brian.

Pause.

BRIAN: What do you want from me?

PAPO: Why can't I see you?

BRIAN: Papo.

PAPO: I ain't so fucking bad. And you like me, I know you do.

BRIAN: Look, Papo . . . Okay, I'll meet you at the Peep Show in twenty minutes.

PAPO: I'm right outside your apartment. I'm calling from the corner.

BRIAN: You're what?!

PAPO: Don't get mad, man. I'm just hanging out.

BRIAN: Are you spying on me?

PAPO: No, no, I swear.

BRIAN: Walk away from my building. I'll meet you at Thirty-fourth and Fifth in ten minutes.

PAPO: Yeah, okay.

BRIAN: If I see you at the phone booth when I leave the building I'll turn around and go right back in.

PAPO: And I'll fucking crack your head in. (*Pause.*) Thirty-fourth and Fifth.

BRIAN: Thirty-fourth and Fifth.

PAPO: Well, fucking hurry up. (*BRIAN hangs up.*) Cause I miss you.

Thirty-fourth and Fifth. PAPO is wearing BRIAN's sweater. Enter BRIAN.

PAPO: Yo man, fancy meeting you here.

BRIAN: Hi, Papo.

PAPO: Check out the sweater, man. I'm wearing the sweater you bought for me.

BRIAN: What do you want?

PAPO: Hey, just a little action. That's all. (*He playfully grabs* BRIAN *who moves away.*)

BRIAN: Are you crazy? This is not the Peep Show.

PAPO: Oh yeah, I forgot. Decent people hang out here.

BRIAN: That's not it.

PAPO: People who never have sex.

BRIAN: Look, I've got to get up early tomorrow.

PAPO: So what? You were gonna meet your white friends for dinner, weren't you?

BRIAN: They're friends, period. And I called and canceled.

PAPO: Shit. You weren't gonna meet nobody. You were probably at home playing with your meat when I called. (BRIAN *starts to walk away,* PAPO *follows.*) Let's go back to your place.

BRIAN: I don't ever want you in my home again.

PAPO: And have a little party. Take one of the side streets, there are less people there.

On a dimmer street. PAPO *grabs* BRIAN *and kisses him.*

BRIAN: This has got to stop.

PAPO: Okay.

BRIAN: I mean it. Don't call me, don't follow me.

PAPO: Fine. Don't desire me.

BRIAN *twitches.*

BRIAN: Your ego, like your brain, is in your crotch.

PAPO: No man, I don't think so.

BRIAN: You don't think, period.

PAPO: Cause I ain't the only one doing the following.

BRIAN: You're crazy.

PAPO: And I ain't the one who checked out the meat the first chance I got. (*BRIAN turns to leave, PAPO grabs his arm.*) I get my rocks off seven times a day. How do you do?

BRIAN: I . . .

PAPO slowly pulls BRIAN toward him.

PAPO: I don't think you do too well. I think you probably got a real tired hand.

BRIAN: I can't. Please. I just want to go back to the way it was.

PAPO: The only trouble with being alone is there's no one there to kiss back.

BRIAN: Before I met you.

PAPO holds BRIAN and kisses him.

PAPO: Now you kiss me.

BRIAN: I can't.

PAPO: I'm not gonna fucking move. You kiss me. (*They stare at each other. BRIAN slowly moves toward PAPO.*) Keep your eyes open, baby. I want you to see who you're kissing. (*BRIAN kisses PAPO. The kiss builds in passion until PAPO breaks free.*) No, you don't wanna see me. Tell me you don't wanna see me.

BRIAN (*In a small voice.*): I don't want to see you.

PAPO: You know, you're really full of shit, man. You'd rather be home jerking off by yourself. Is that it?

BRIAN: No.

PAPO kisses him.

PAPO: Is that it?

BRIAN (*Whispers.*): No.

PAPO: No what?

BRIAN: Don't go.

PAPO: Why not?

BRIAN: Please.

PAPO: Are you horny? (*Silence.*) Let me hear you say it, man. Are you horny?

BRIAN: I'm horny.

PAPO puts his arms around BRIAN.

PAPO: What do you want me to do about it? Put your arms around my neck.

BRIAN: We're in the middle of the street.

PAPO: It's dark man. (*BRIAN does.*)

PAPO: Maybe I can help you do what you do alone.

BRIAN: Yes, please.

PAPO: But where? You told me you don't want me in your home. I'm too dirty for your home, right? (*PAPO kisses BRIAN as they embrace. A car goes by, someone yells "Faggot." BRIAN tries to break free. PAPO holds him. BRIAN stops struggling and they kiss again.*) I'll see you around, Brian.

PAPO begins to walk away, BRIAN follows.

Have to go back where I belong. Got a nice, seventeen-year-old white boy waiting up for me. You better hurry home, too. You don't want to keep your hand waiting.

BRIAN follows PAPO and begins to hit him. PAPO tries to hold his hands and they begin to fight. PAPO wraps his arms around BRIAN, pinning his arms down.

PAPO: Say it.

BRIAN: Fuck you.

PAPO: Say it or I walk. (*Pause.*)

BRIAN: Please come home with me.

PAPO lets BRIAN go.

PAPO: Why?
BRIAN: Cause I want you.
PAPO: How much do you want me?
BRIAN: I want you.
PAPO: I don't believe you.
BRIAN: I want you.
PAPO: I still don't believe you.

BRIAN *looks to his right and left and gets on his knees.*

BRIAN: I want you.

PAPO *kneels with* BRIAN. *They embrace.*

Blackout

FLOPHOUSE

BOBBY: Please don't go, please don't go, please don't go.
PAPO: This is my last chance. I ain't no sweet-looking little kid anymore. I've got mileage on me and it's beginning to show.
BOBBY: You got somebody else.
PAPO: Yeah.
BOBBY: I love you, Reggie.
PAPO: Well, he loves me too. And he knows my name.
BOBBY: Do you like him better than you like me?
PAPO: I must.
BOBBY: He's never gonna love you like I love you.
PAPO: I didn't have to come back here to tell you, you know. What the hell do I have here that I have to take with me?
BOBBY: You mean besides my heart?

PAPO *hits* BOBBY.

BOBBY: I don't want to fight with you, Reggie.

PAPO: C'mon Shithead. You fucking pissed off, right? Go ahead, hit me. Hit me.

PAPO continues to jab at BOBBY who grabs PAPO's hand and kisses it.

BOBBY: I love you.

PAPO pushes him away.

PAPO: Cut the fucking shit. You love Reggie, not me. What the fuck am I supposed to do, turn tricks until we're old and gray?

BOBBY: I'm yours, Papo. I'm your Baby.

PAPO: I never asked for you, you fucking fruitcake.

BOBBY reaches between the mattress and box spring and pulls out his knife. He tries to stab himself. PAPO wrests the knife from him. He sits on the floor cradling BOBBY.

BOBBY: Oh please don't go. Oh please, Reggie. I love you, Papo.

PAPO: Sssh, sssh. Ronald's a good guy. He loves you too, Baby.

BOBBY: You're the one for me, Reggie.

PAPO: No, I'm the one for me, period.

PAPO gets up, takes the knife, and heads to the door.

PAPO: You'll be okay, guy. You're probably right. Nobody's gonna love me like you do. Even if you don't know who I am.

BOBBY: I don't know who you are? I don't know who you fucking are?! I can be you, anybody can be you. What's so fucking tough about pushing people away? But can you be me? Come on, Papo, can you be me? Can you love anybody the way I love you? I know who you are. I love you.

PAPO: Get the fuck outta my face.

BOBBY: I know who you are, Papo. I love you.

PAPO: And you call me by somebody else's name?

BOBBY: Would it have made such a big motherfucking difference if I called you Papo? (*PAPO exits.*) When did I stop being your Baby?

He goes to window. Lights dim as he opens it.

Lights up on street. PAPO enters and begins to walk. A siren approaches and crowd voices are heard.

VOICE 1: What happened?
VOICE 2: Some little white boy in panties jumped out the window.
VOICE 1: I think he's dead.
VOICE 3: One less faggot.

PAPO pauses, staring straight ahead. After a few beats he continues walking, totally expressionless. He slowly begins to shake. He runs toward the Flophouse and cradles BOBBY's body. The music from the beginning of the play starts, with the voices and the sirens. PAPO rocks BOBBY's body and then puts him down. PAPO rises and crosses over to BRIAN's bedroom. As he does he removes his shirt and jacket, replacing it with a white dress shirt, a tie and a suit jacket. Note: *They should not be buttoned or tied. He sits on the edge of BRIAN's bed, the top half of his body and the lower part of his body from two different worlds. The lights on the Flophouse area begin to dim.*

PAPO: Bring back my heart, you little motherfucker. (*Music rises as lights dim.*)

FALLING MAN

Will Scheffer

To Fred Einhorn and the fabulous falling people

FALLING MAN was originally presented by The Ensemble Studio Theatre, in New York City, in May 1994. It was directed by David Briggs. The cast was as follows:

FALLING MAN . . . . Will Scheffer
MAN IN BLACK . . . . Kevin Weldon

FALLING MAN was presented by HBO New Writer's Project and Wavy Line Productions, in Los Angeles, in October 1994. It was directed by Beth Milles. The cast was as follows:

FALLING MAN . . . . .Michael Malone Starr

~

The sound of air, as it rushes past ears. Lights come up on a FALLING MAN. *His hair flies up in the wind. He is thin and his skin is very white. He wears underwear. He is falling. White clouds float behind him.*

FALLING MAN: You get used to the sound of the wind as it rushes past your ears. And the ominous sense of velocity becomes familiar after a while. You watch as the stars whiz by you like flying candles. You listen to the planets as they sing their songs. You think of yourself, at any moment I am going to come crashing down into the Earth, but you never do. At least not yet.

Wind.

You begin to wonder about gravity. You become obsessed with it. You say to yourself over and over: I'm falling I'm falling, but soon you get used to not having your feet on the ground anymore. In fact, ground itself, becomes a concept that no longer has any meaning to you.

Wind.

For some reason you can't seem to stop talking, as if talking were the only action that could give you your bearings in a constantly shifting environment without recognizable landmarks. You convince yourself that if you are talking, if someone can hear you, you must still be alive. You scream: I'm alive I'm alive, to no one in particular. You discover that you don't like to look down, but prefer to look up, for obvious reasons. And then quite suddenly, for a moment, without warning—you have this unbearable urge to Cha Cha once more.

Blackout.

Cha Cha music. When the lights come up again the FALLING MAN *sits on a chair in a pool of light. He wears a hospital gown and addresses the audience. Occasionally he operates a slide projector.*

Before I started falling, I was a Ballroom Dancing Champion, expert at ten dances. They were, in order of my expertise and preference: Cha Cha, Salsa, Mambo, Samba, Paso Doble, Rhumba, Tango, Slow Waltz, Quick Waltz, and Fox Trot. On a perfect night in 1983, at the age of twenty-two, I became the Cha Cha champion of the world. (*Slide:* FALLING MAN *at twenty-two. TA DA!*) No one much remembers that now, but it's true. Even before this, however, I was famous for my Cha Cha. My dancing partner Svetlana defected from the former

Soviet Union in 1981, specifically to dance the Cha Cha with me. And, at that time, we were legendary. You would have loved Svetlana. (Slide: Svetlana, a big Soviet girl!) She had an accent just like Norma Shearer in *Idiot's Delight*. You know, all Vonderfuls and Werys. "I am so Wery Wery crazy about you" she would often say to me. Sometimes I wondered if she had actually defected from Russia or if she hadn't really just hitchhiked to Manhattan from Duluth and made the whole thing up. But she was acknowledged to be the Soviet Champion of the Jive-Rock step (*Slide: Svetlana dancing!*), a dance step that for some reason only Baltic women could master. That and the fact that only Svetlana could really look sexy in Jordache Jeans, wearing a shade of lipstsick that was five times too red for even the most fabulous 1940s movie star, proved to me, at least, that she was genuinely Eastern European.

The MAN IN BLACK *enters, wheeling an intravenous stand and proceeds to attach the hook up to the* FALLING MAN*'s arm.* FALLING MAN *pauses for moment and then continues.*

As I said before, we won the title of Cha Cha champions of the world on a perfect night in January of 1983. (*Slide:* FALLING MAN *and Svetlana. The winners!*) And we indeed ourselves, were perfect that night, as we moved across the dance floor of the Cincinnati Hilton Hotel. The floor was so highly polished that a few couples actually fell that evening. But not us. My strong arms that night, supported Svetlana in poses of inspired and delirious sexuality. (*Slide: Dancing!*) Our footwork was impeccable and unrivaled. We glittered and sparkled and shined. And of course, although the steps we navigated on that mirror-smooth floor were uncompromisingly difficult—we did not once stumble or trip, or even slip or falter.

Inspired, the FALLING MAN *rises to his feet.*

Perhaps there could have been more of a natural passion between us, yes, but our acting was flawless and inspired. Not for a second was there a false move to our grace, to our speed and authority. And I now realize that in my life up until that moment there had never ever been even the remotest possibility of falling, on the dance floor or off. It wasn't even a question. I would not have allowed it. I was not that kind of a person. No.

Music fades up as the FALLING MAN dances with the intravenous stand.

That night we floated, Svetlana and I. We glided. We dazzled. And for a moment, at the very climax of our passionate Cha Cha embrace, when I heard the entire crowd gasp together at our impossible beauty—I was almost happy.

Applause. The MAN IN BLACK enters and carries him back to the chair. MAN IN BLACK removes the intravenous hook-up.)

You must forgive me for talking so much. It's just that since I—started falling—, I don't dance anymore. And so it seems I'm endlessly talking, endlessly meandering on about my past as a dancer. I hope I'm not boring you. Really all I'd like to do is to entertain you. You see, that's what Ballroom Dancing is really about, it's—entertainment and—it makes people feel good about life, about living, about being alive, do you know? And I am a born entertainer. I even used to dance to *West Side Story*, as a child, for the relatives. My mother encouraged me. As a matter of fact, I'd like to entertain you right now, even in my condition, as it were. Yes! That's what I'd really like to do, more than anything else. "Oh, I'd like to do a Cha Cha but the lesions hurt my feet!" (*He laughs.*) Only kidding. Sorry. Bad joke. Anyway. That night, Svetlana and I celebrated in my hotel room.

MAN IN BLACK gives FALLING MAN a sip of water from a glass with a straw.

We drank champagne from Svetlana's silver Cha Cha slipper, which she stained red with her lips. We got drunk, and before Svetlana could stain me red, I convinced her that we should make an appearance at the post-competition party in the Buckeye Room of the Cincinnati Hilton.

MAN IN BLACK carries the FALLING MAN to another chair, lights shift. There is a basin beneath the chair. Throughout the following the MAN IN BLACK will gently and delicately sponge-bathe the FALLING MAN. The action should be slow and intimate.

When we made our entrance the party was in full swing and the waves seemed to part for us, as we made our way into the room. Compliments flowed endlessly along with the alcohol but I felt vaguely uncomfortable that night with Svetlana on my arm. Sometimes it seems to me that Destiny has a way of making you ready for her arrival. Of creating the conditions necessary for her to be able to play out her cards. Because I can't expain why I felt, as I did at that moment, at that exact moment in the Buckeye Room of the Cincinnati Hilton Hotel on the night of my triumphant Cha Cha, that my young life until then had been nothing more than a championship performance, a perfect ten absolutely, but just a performance nonetheless. A graceful, well-choreographed, impeccable dance for the relatives. And no sooner than I had this impression, or rather as I was having it, I saw an enchanting stranger from across the room, the crowded room as it were, and our eyes locked. He was not precisely a stranger, for I recognized him, although I had never met him, as Paolo, a Brazilian dancer, whose Mambo I had appreciated. You might find this hard to believe, but I must admit to you now, that at the ripe age of twenty-two and even in that day and time, I was still a virgin on that fateful night in Cincinnati, in 1983. And as Paolo and

I slowly and inexorably made our way towards each other, my heart beat with a fear experienced perhaps only by twenty-two-year-old virgins, who have never entirely admitted to themselves that they are homosexual—and their mothers. But there was no turning back. Destiny had opened her arms wide to greet me and soon so had Paolo, who kissed me warmly on both cheeks with congratulations. This action on his part caused an immediate and uncontrollable erection on my part, so to speak. And I understood by the look in Paolo's eyes that indeed he, had coveted my Cha Cha as much as I had admired his Mambo.

The MAN IN BLACK *comes around and lifts* FALLING MAN *to his feet.*

Quickly and without too much effort I lost Svetlana, who was demonstrating the Jive-Rock step to a group of enthusiastic older men, and made my way to Paolo's room.

As the lights shift, the MAN IN BLACK *carries* FALLING MAN *to a small table. He supports* FALLING MAN *as he lights a candle and puts a record on a small record player. A very romantic Brazilian Samba begins to play softly. The* FALLING MAN *continues to speak to the audience.*

I don't really know how to put into words what happened next. If I could I would dance it for you; I would dance that night for you and not trivialize it with words. After all, Paolo and I barely spoke ourselves. Sometimes I think love is about inventing a private language, a language lovers make up as they go along, that only they can speak and understand—isn't that what love is? Just a language, an intricate intoxicating language that you have forgotten and now you must remember. But surely you understand what I am saying? That night almost immediately upon entering his room, I fell into Paolo's arms and we began to dance.

FALLING MAN *dances with the* MAN IN BLACK.

That was the language we spoke all that night. A language that was all our own. We danced our words as if our tongues had been burned from our mouths.

FALLING MAN removes MAN IN BLACK's shirt.

I wonder if you can understand what that felt like to me—please try to understand because tonight I want us to be like lovers—but I wonder if you can, can know what it felt like for me to dance the Cha Cha with him. I who was the champion of the world in that dance. To dance the Samba, the Mambo, the Tango with him. To dance with a man. For me, who had danced a thousand Sambas, with a thousand lovely women, in a thousand sparkling rooms, for me, to dance with a man for the first time in my life.

FALLING MAN lets his robe fall to the ground.

How can I explain to you. How can I describe it as I fell. As I fell for the first time in my young life. As I fell into the eyes of him, as I fell into the deep of his smell, into the strong arms of him, into his mouth. As we fell into each other.

They kiss.

As we danced.

After a moment, the FALLING MAN removes the record with a scratch and they freeze. FALLING MAN puts on his robe and comes down to talk to the audience. The MAN IN BLACK stands behind him.

You must forgive me. You must forgive me for talking so much. I know it's silly but sometimes I think if I stop talking I'll die. That you will forget me. That you will forget that I was a champion dancer, expert at ten dances, Cha Cha, Salsa, Mambo, Samba, Paso Doble, Rhumba, Tango, Slow Waltz,

Quick Waltz and Fox Trot, in order of my preference. I am afraid you will forget me and my Cha Cha. I am afraid that you will judge me. That you will condemn me for falling that night. That astonishing night in 1983. I want so much to entertain you, but you must understand that night, it was as if I had to fall. As if a person like me had just been waiting to fall all his life. And it felt not so much as if I were falling, but more like I was being born, but of course you understand that, don't you?

Pause.

I'm afraid I must be boring you. I'm afraid I'm running out of time. I'll just tell you this. Paolo died a year later.

MAN IN BLACK exits.

It was so fast. I didn't even have a chance to learn Portuguese. Not long after that, Svetlana took me to the clinic to get tested. And I've been falling ever since.

Black out. Wind. Gentle Cha Cha music from West Side Story. *Lights come up again on the* FALLING MAN. *Stars twinkle behind him.*

You know, sometimes I see the other falling people around me and I want to grab onto them as we fall. I want to dance with them up here in the sky. I want to choreograph some fabulous Busby Berkeley–type number up here in the sky. So everyone can look up and just see these fabulous falling people. I think that would be terrific, but it's so hard to organize.

Wind.

I have to stop talking. I do have one thing to ask you, though. When I am finished talking, remember that I used to dance the Cha Cha, that I was the Cha Cha champion of the world.

And remember the sound of my voice—so that all of this talking will not have been in vain. Remember my Cha Cha. Remember my voice. Remember me.

The sound of the wind rises. The MAN IN BLACK *turns and the* FALLING MAN *appears to fall into his arms.*

Blackout.

End.

THE BALTIMORE WALTZ

Paula Vogel

To the memory of Carl—because I cannot sew.

> Ron Vawter: . . . I always saw myself as a surrogate who, in the absence of anyone else, would stand in for him. And even now, when I'm in front of an audience and I feel good, I hearken back to that feeling, that I'm standing in for them.
>
> —David Savran, *Breaking the Rules*

THE BALTIMORE WALTZ was produced at the Circle Repertory Company (Tanya Berezin, artistic director; Terrence Dwyer, managing director), in New York City, in February 1992. It was directed by Anne Bogart; the set design was by Loy Arcenas; the costume design was by Walker Hicklin; the lighting design was by Dennis Parichy; the sound design and score was by John Gromada; the dramaturg was Ronn Smith and the production stage manager was Denise Yaney. The cast was as follows:

ANNA . . . . Cherry Jones
CARL . . . . Richard Thompson
THIRD MAN/DOCTOR . . . . Joe Mantello

THE BALTIMORE WALTZ was produced at the Perseverance Theatre (Molly D. Smith, artistic director; Deborah B. Baley, producing director), in Douglas, Alaska, on October 18, 1990. The workshop production was directed by Annie Stokes-Hutchinson; the set design was by Bill Hudson; the costume design was by Barbara Casement and Kari Minnick; the lighting design was by John E. Miller; the sound design was by Katie Jensen and the stage manager was Carolyn Peck. The cast was as follows:

ANNA . . . . Deborah Holbrook
CARL . . . . Rick Bundy
THE THIRD MAN/DOCTOR . . . . Charles Cardwell

In 1986, my brother Carl invited me to join him in a joint excursion to Europe. Due to pressures of time and money, I declined, never dreaming that he was HIV positive. This is the letter he wrote me after his first bout with pneumonia at Johns Hopkins Hospital in Baltimore, Maryland. He died on January 9, 1988.

As executor of his estate, I give permission to all future productions to reprint Carl's letter in the accompanying program. I would appreciate letting him speak to us in his own words.

The Baltimore Waltz—a journey with Carl to a Europe that exists only in the imagination—was written during the summer of 1989 at the MacDowell Colony, New Hampshire.

—Paula Vogel

March 1987

Dear Paula:

I thought I would jot down some of my thoughts about the (shall we say) production values of my ceremony. Oh God—I can hear you groaning—everybody wants to direct. Well, I want a good show, even though my role has been reduced involuntarily from player to prop.

First, concerning the choice between a religious ceremony and a memorial service. I know the family considers my Anglican observances as irrelevant as Shinto. However, I wish prayers in some recognizably traditional form to be said, prayers that give thanks to the Creator for the gift of life and the hope of reunion. For reasons which you appreciate, I prefer a woman cleric, if possible, to lead the prayers. Here are two names: Phebe Coe, Epiphany Church; the Rev.

Doris Mote, Holy Evangelists. Be sure to make a generous contribution from the estate for the cleric.

As for the piece of me I leave behind, here are your options:

(1) Open casket, full drag.
(2) Open casket, bum up (you'll know where to place the calla lillies, won't you?)
(3) Closed casket, interment with the grandparents.
(4) Cremation and burial of my ashes.
(5) Cremation and dispersion of my ashes in some sylvan spot.

I would really like good music. My tastes in these matters run to the highbrow: Fauré's "Pie Jesu" from his *Requiem*, Gluck's "Dance of the Blessed Spirits" from *Orfeo*, "La Vergine degli Angeli" from Verdi's *Forza*. But my favorite song is "I Dream of Jeannie," and I wouldn't mind a spiritual like "Steal Away." Also perhaps "Nearer My God to Thee." Didn't Jeannette MacDonald sing that di-vinely in *San Francisco?*

Finally, would you read or have read A. E. Housman's "Loveliest of Trees"?

Well, my dear, that's that. Should I be lain with Grandma and Papa Ben, do stop by for a visit from year to year. And feel free to chat. You'll find me a good listener.

Love,
Brother

Characters

ANNA
CARL, her brother
THE THIRD MAN/DOCTOR, who also plays:

Harry Lime
Airport Security Guard

Public Health Official
Garçon
Customs Official
The Little Dutch Boy at age fifty
Munich Virgin
Radical Student Activist
Concierge
Dr. Todesrocheln
and all other parts

The Baltimore Waltz takes place in a hospital (perhaps in a lounge, corridor or waiting room) in Baltimore, Maryland.

Notes

The lighting should be highly stylized, lush, dark, and imaginative, in contrast to the hospital white silence of the last scene. Wherever possible, prior to the last scene, the director is encouraged to score the production with music—every cliché of the European experience as imagined by Hollywood.

Anna might be dressed in a full slip/negligee and a trench coat. Carl is dressed in flannel pajamas and a blazer or jacket. The stuffed rabbit should be in every scene with Carl after Scene 6. The Third Man should wear latex gloves throughout the entire play.

~

SCENE 1

Three distinct areas on stage: ANNA, *stage right, in her trench coat, clutching the* Berlitz Pocket Guide to Europe; CARL, *stage left, wearing pajamas and blazer;* THE THIRD MAN/DOCTOR, *in his lab coat and with stethoscope, is center.*

ANNA *reads from her book. Her accents are execrable.*

ANNA: "Help me please." (*ANNA recites from memory.*) Dutch: "Kunt U mij helpen, alstublieft?" "There's nothing I can do." French— (*ANNA searches in vain.*) I have no memory. (*Anna reads from* Berlitz.) "Il n'y a rien à faire." "Where are the toilets?" "Wo sind die Toiletten?" I've never been abroad. It's not that I don't want to—but the language terrifies me. I was traumatized by a junior high school French teacher, and after that, it was a lost cause. I think that's the reason I went into elementary education. Words like brioche, bidet, bildungsroman raise a sweat. Oh, I want to go. Carl—he's my brother, you'll meet him shortly—he desperately wants to go. But then, he can speak six languages. He's the head librarian of literature and languages at the San Francisco Public. It's a very important position. The thought of eight-hundred-year-old houses perched on the sides of mountains and rivers whose names you've only seen in the Sunday *Times* crossword puzzles—all of that is exciting. But I'm not going without him. He's read so much. I couldn't possibly go without him. You see, I've never been abroad—unless you count Baltimore, Maryland.

CARL: Good morning, boys and girls. It's Monday morning, and it's time for "Reading Hour with Uncle Carl" once again, here at the North Branch of the San Francisco Public Library. This is going to be a special reading hour. It's my very last reading hour with you. Friday will be my very last day with the San Francisco Public as children's librarian. Why? Do any of you know what a pink slip is? (*CARL holds up a rectangle of pink.*) It means I'm going on a paid leave of absence for two weeks. Shelley Bizio, the branch supervisor, has given me my very own pink slip. I got a pink slip because I wear this— (*He points to a pink triangle on his lapel.*) A pink triangle. Now, I want you all to take the pink construction paper in front of you, and take your scissors, and cut out pink triangles. There's tape at every table, so you can wear them too! Make some for Mom and Dad, and your brothers and sisters. Very good. Very good, Fabio. Oh, that's a beautiful pink triangle, Tse Heng.

Now before we read our last story together, I thought we might have a sing-along. Your parents can join us, if they'd like to. Oh, don't be shy. Let's do "Here We Go Round the Mulberry Bush." Remember that one? (*He begins to sing. He also demonstrates.*) "Here we go round the mulberry bush, the mulberry bush, the mulberry bush:/ Here we go round the mulberry bush, so early in the morning." "This is the way we pick our nose, pick our nose, pick our nose:/ This is the way we pick our nose, so early in the morning." Third verse! (*He makes a rude gesture with his middle finger.*) "This is the way we go on strike, go on strike, go on strike:/ this is the way we go on strike, so early in the—" What, Mrs. Bizio? I may leave immediately? I do not have to wait until Friday to collect unemployment? Why, thank you, Mrs. Bizio. Well, boys and girls, Mrs. Bizio will take over now. Bear with her, she's personality-impaired. I want you to be very good and remember me. I'm leaving for an immediate vacation with my sister on the east coast, and I'll think of you as I travel. Remember to wear those pink triangles. (*To his supervisor.*) I'm going. I'm going. You don't have to be rude. They enjoyed it. We'll take it up with the union. (*Shouting.*) *In a language you might understand, up-pay ours-yay!*

ANNA: It's the language that terrifies me.

CARL: Lesson Number One: Subject position. I. Je. Ich. Ik. I'm sorry. Je regrette. Es tut mir leid.

ANNA: But we decided to go when the doctor gave us his verdict.

DOCTOR: I'm sorry.

CARL: I'm sorry.

DOCTOR: There's nothing we can do.

ANNA: But what?

CARL: How long?

ANNA: Explain it to me. Very slowly. So I can understand. Excuse me, could you tell me again?

DOCTOR: There are exudative and proliferative inflammatory alterations of the endocardium, consisting of necrotic debris, fibrinoid material, and disintegrating fibroblastic cells.

CARL: Oh, sweet Jesus.

DOCTOR: It may be acute or subacute, caused by various bacteria: streptococci, staphylococci, enterococci, gonococci, gram negative bacilli, etc. It may be due to other micro-organisms, of course, but there is a high mortality rate with or without treatment. And there is usually rapid destruction and metastases.

CARL: Anna—

ANNA: I'm right here, darling. Right here.

CARL: Could you explain it very slowly?

DOCTOR: Also known as Lŏffler's syndrome, i.e., eosinophilia, resulting in fibroblastic thickening, persistent tachycardia, hepatomegaly, splenomegaly, serious effusions into the pleural cavity with edema. It may be Brugia malayi or Wucheereria bancrofti—also known as Weingarten's syndrome. Often seen with effusions, either exudate or transudate.

ANNA: Carl—

CARL: I'm here, darling. Right here.

ANNA: It's the language that terrifies me.

SCENE 2

CARL: Medical Straight Talk: Part One.

ANNA: So you're telling me that you really don't know?

DOCTOR: I'm afraid that medical science has only a small foothold in this area. But of course, it would be of great benefit to our knowledge if you would consent to observation here at Johns Hopkins—

CARL: Why? Running out of laboratory rats?!

ANNA: Oh, no. I'm sorry. I can't do that. Can you tell me at least how it was . . . contracted?

DOCTOR: Well—we're not sure, yet. It's only a theory at this stage, but one that seems in great favor at the World Health Organization. We think it comes from the old cultus ornatus—

CARL: Toilet seats?

ANNA: Toilet seats! My God. Mother was right. She always said—

CARL: And never, ever, in any circumstances, in bus stations—

ANNA: Toilet seats? Cut down in the prime of youth by a toilet seat?

DOCTOR: Anna—I may call you Anna?—you teach school, I believe?

ANNA: Yes, first grade. What does that have—

DOCTOR: Ah, yes. We're beginning to see a lot of this in elementary schools. Anna—I may call you Anna? With assurances of complete confidentiality—we need to ask you very specific questions about the body, body fluids, and body functions. As mature adults, as scientists and educators. To speak frankly—when you needed to relieve yourself—where did you make wa-wa?

ANNA: There's a faculty room. But why—how—?

DOCTOR: You never, ever used the johnny in your classroom?

ANNA: Well, maybe once or twice. There's no lock, and Robbie Matthews always tries to barge in. Sometimes I just can't get the time to—surely you're not suggesting that—

DOCTOR: You did use the facilities in your classroom? (*The doctor makes notes from this.*)

CARL: Is that a crime? When you've got to go, you've got to—

ANNA: I can't believe that my students would transmit something like this—

DOCTOR: You have no idea. Five-year-olds can be deadly. It seems to be an affliction, so far, of single schoolteachers. Schoolteachers with children of their own develop an immunity to ATD . . . Acquired Toilet Disease.

ANNA: I see. Why hasn't anybody heard of this disease?

DOCTOR: Well, first of all, the Center for Disease Control doesn't wish to inspire an all-out panic in communities. Secondly, we think education on this topic is the responsibility of the NEA, not the government. And if word of this pestilence gets out inappropriately, the PTA is going to be all over the school system demanding mandatory testing of every toilet seat in every lavatory. It's kindling for a political disaster.

ANNA (*Taking the doctor aside.*): I want to ask you something confidentially. Something that my brother doesn't need to hear. What's the danger of transmission?

DOCTOR: There's really no danger to anyone in the immediate family. You must use precautions.

ANNA: Because what I want to know is . . . can you transmit this thing by . . . by doing—what exactly do you mean by precautions?

DOCTOR: Well, I guess you should do what your mother always told you. You know, wash you hands before and after going to the bathroom. And never lick paper money or coins in any currency.

ANNA: So there's no danger to anyone by . . . what I mean, Doctor, is that I can't infect anyone by—

DOCTOR: Just use precautions.

ANNA: Because, in whatever time this schoolteacher has left, I intend to fuck my brains out.

DOCTOR: Which means, in whatever is left, she can fuck her brains out.

SCENE 3

CARL and the DOCTOR.

CARL (*Agitated.*): I'll tell you what. If Sandra Day O'Connor sat on just one infected potty, the media would be clamoring to do articles on ATD. If just one grandchild of George Bush caught this thing during toilet training, that would be the last we'd hear about the space program. Why isn't someone doing something? I'm sorry. I know you're one of the converted. You're doing . . . well, everything you can. I'd like to ask you something in confidence, something my sister doesn't need to hear. Is there any hope at all?

DOCTOR: Well, I suppose there's . . . always hope.

CARL: Any experimental drugs? Treatments?

DOCTOR: Well, they're trying all sorts of things abroad. Our hands are tied here by NIH and the FDA, you understand. There is a long-shot avenue to explore, nothing, you understand, that I personally endorse, but there is an eighty-year-old urologist overseas who's been working in this field for some time—

CARL: We'll try anything.

DOCTOR: His name is Dr. Todesrocheln. He's somewhat unorthodox, outside the medical community in Vienna. It's gonna cost you. Mind you, this is not an endorsement.

ANNA: You hear the doctor through a long-distance corridor. Your ears are functioning, but the mind is numb. You try to listen as you swim towards his sentences in the fluorescent light in his office. But you don't believe it at first. This is how I'd like to die: with dignity. No body secretions—like Merle Oberon in *Wuthering Heights*. With a somewhat becoming flush, and a transcendental gaze. Luminous eyes piercing the veil of mortal existence. The windows are open to the fresh breeze blowing off the moors. Oh. And violins in the background would be nice, too. (*Music: Violins playing Strauss swell in the background.*)

SCENE 4

The Phone Call.

THE THIRD MAN: Lesson Number Two: Basic dialogue. The phone call. Hello. I would like to speak to Mr. Lime, please.

CARL: *Entschuldigen Sie, bitte*—operator? Operator? Hello? *Guten Tag? Kann ich bitte mit Herr Lime sprechen?* Harry? Harry? *Wie geht es dir?* Listen, I . . . can you hear . . . no, I'm in Baltimore . . . yeah, not since Hopkins . . . no, there's—well, there is something up. No, dear boy, that hasn't been up in a long time—no, seriously—it's my sister. ATD.

THE THIRD MAN: ATD? Jesus, that's tough, old man. You've got to watch where you sit these days. She's a sweet kid. Yeah. Yeah. Wait a second. (*Offstage.*) Inge? Inge, baby? *Ein Bier, bitte,* baby. *Ja. Ja.* You too, baby. (*Pause.*) Okay, Dr. Todesrocheln? Yeah, you might say I know him. But don't tell anybody I said that. There's also a new drug they've got over here. Black market. I might be able to help you. I said might. But it's gonna cost you. (*Cautiously, ominously.*) Do you still have the rabbit?

CARL: I'll bring the rabbit.

THE THIRD MAN: Good. A friend of mine will be in touch. And listen, old man . . . if anybody asks you, you don't know me. I'll see you in a month. You know where to find me.

THE THIRD MAN and CARL: (*Simultaneously.*): Click.

SCENE 5

THE THIRD MAN: Lesson Number Three: Pronouns and the possessive case. I, you, he, she and it. Me, you, their. Yours, mine, and ours.

VOICE OF ANNA: There's nothing I can do. There's nothing you can do. There's nothing he, she or it can do. There's nothing we can do. There's nothing they can do.

ANNA: So what are we going to do?

CARL: Start packing, sister dear.

ANNA: Europe? You mean it?

CARL: We'll mosey about France and Germany, and then work our way down to Vienna.

ANNA: What about your job?

CARL: It's only a job.

ANNA: It's a very important job! Head of the entire San Francisco Public—

CARL: They'll hold my job for me. I'm due for a leave.

ANNA: Oh, honey. Can we afford this?

CARL: It's only money.

ANNA: It's your money.

CARL: It's our money.

SCENE 6

THE THIRD MAN: Lesson Four: Present tense of *faire*. What are we going to do? *Qu'est-ce qu-on va faire.*

ANNA: So what are we going to do?

CARL: We'll see this doctor in Vienna.

ANNA: Dr. Todesrocheln?

CARL: We have to try.

ANNA: A urologist?

CARL: He's working on a new drug.

ANNA: A European urologist?

CARL: What options do we have?

ANNA: Wait a minute. What are his credentials? Who is this guy?

CARL: He was trained at the Allgemeines Krankenhaus during the Empire.

ANNA: Yeah? Just what was he doing from, say, 1938 to 1945? Research?

CARL: It's best not to ask too many questions. There are people who swear by his work.

ANNA: What's his specialty?

CARL: Well, actually, he's a practitioner of uriposia.

ANNA: He writes poems about urine?

CARL: No. He drinks it.

ANNA: I'm not going.

CARL: Let's put off judgment until we arrange a consultation . . . my God, you're so messy. Look at how neat my suitcase is in comparison. You'll never find a thing in there.

ANNA: I refuse to drink my own piss for medical science. (*CARL grabs a stuffed rabbit and thrusts it in ANNA's suitcase.*) What are you doing?

CARL: We can't leave bunny behind.

ANNA: What is a grown man like you doing with a stuffed rabbit?

CARL: I can't sleep without bunny.

ANNA: I didn't know you slept with . . . stuffed animals.

CARL: There's a lot you don't know about me.

SCENE 7

THE THIRD MAN: Lesson Five: Basic dialogue. At the airport. We are going to Paris. What time does our flight leave? *Nous allons à Paris. A quelle heure depart notre vol?* (*THE THIRD MAN becomes an AIRPORT SECURITY GUARD.*)

AIRPORT SECURITY GUARD: Okay. Next. Please remove your keys and all other metallic items. Place all belongings on the belt. Next. (*CARL and ANNA carry heavy luggage. CARL halts.*)

CARL: Wait. I need your suitcase. (*He opens ANNA's luggage and begins to rummage around.*)

ANNA: Hey!

CARL: It was a mess to begin with. Ah— (*He retrieves the stuffed rabbit.*) There.

ANNA: Are you having an anxiety attack?

CARL: You hold it. (*He and ANNA stamp, sit and stand on the baggage. CARL manages to relock the bag.*)

ANNA: What is wrong with you?

CARL: X-rays are bad for bunny.

AIRPORT SECURITY GUARD: Next. Please remove all metallic objects. Keys. Eyeglasses. Gold fillings.

CARL: Go on. You first.

AIRPORT SECURITY GUARD: Metallic objects? (*ANNA passes through, holding the stuffed rabbit. CARL sighs, relieved. CARL passes through. The airport security guard stops him.*) One moment, please. (*The AIRPORT SECURITY GUARD almost strip-searches him. He uses a metallic wand which makes loud, clicking noises. Finally, he nods. He hands ANNA and CARL their bags, still suspiciously looking at CARL.*)

ANNA: Okay, bunny—Paris, here we come!

SCENE 8

THE THIRD MAN: At the hotel. (*Simultaneously with CARL's next lines.*) Lesson Six: Direct pronouns. I am tired. And my sister looks at herself in the mirror.

CARL: *Sixième Leçon: Pronoms—compléments directs. Je suis fatigué. Et ma soeur—elle se regarde dans la glace.* (CARL *climbs into a double bed with the stuffed rabbit.* ANNA *stares into a mirror.* THE THIRD MAN, *apart, stands in their bedroom.*)

THE THIRD MAN: The first separation—your first sense of loss. You were five—your brother was seven. Your parents would not let you sleep in the same bed anymore. They removed you to your own bedroom. You were too old, they said. But every now and then, when they turned off the lights and went downstairs—when the dark scared you, you would rise and go to him. And he would let you nestle under his arm, under the covers, where you would fall to sleep, breathing in the scent of your own breath and his seven-year-old body.

CARL: Come to bed, sweetie. Bunny and I are waiting. We're going to be jet-lagged for a while.

ANNA (ANNA *continues to stare in the mirror.*) It doesn't show yet.

CARL: No one can tell. Let's get some sleep, honey.

ANNA: I don't want anyone to know.

CARL: It's not a crime. It's an illness.

ANNA: I don't want anybody to know.

CARL: It's your decision. Just don't tell anyone . . .what . . . you do for a living. (ANNA *joins* CARL *in the bed. He holds her hand.*)

ANNA: Well, there's one good thing about traveling in Europe . . . and about dying.

CARL: What's that?

ANNA: I get to sleep with you again.

SCENE 9

CARL: Medical Straight Talk: Part Two. (THE THIRD MAN *becomes a* PUBLIC HEALTH OFFICIAL.)

PUBLIC HEALTH OFFICIAL: Here at the Department of Health and Human Services we are announcing Operation Squat. There is no known cure for ATD right now, and we are acknowledging the urgency of this dread disease by recognizing it as our 82nd national health priority. Right now ATD is the fourth major cause of death of single schoolteachers, ages twenty-four to forty . . . behind school buses, lockjaw and playground accidents. The best policy, until a cure can be found, is of education and prevention. (*ANNA and CARL hold up posters of a toilet seat in a circle with a red diagonal slash.*) If you are in the high-risk category—single elementary schoolteachers, classsroom aides, custodians and playground drug pushers—follow these simple guides. (*ANNA and CARL hold up copies of the educational pamphlets.*)

Do: Use the facilities in your own home before departing for school.

Do: Use the facilities in your own home as soon as you return from school.

Do: Hold it.

Don't: Eat meals in public restrooms.

Don't: Flush lavatory equipment and then suck your digits. If absolutely necessary to relieve yourself at work, please remember the Department of Health and Human Services ATD slogan: Do squat, don't sit.

SCENE 10

Music: Accordion playing a song like "La Vie en Rose." ANNA and CARL stroll.

CARL: Of course, the Left Bank has always been a haven for outcasts, foreigners and students, since the time that Abélard fled the Île de La Cité to found the university here—

ANNA: Oh, look. Is that the Eiffel Tower? It looks so . . . phallic.

CARL: And it continued to serve as a haven for the avant-garde of the twenties, the American expatriate community that could no longer afford Montparnesse—

ANNA: My god, they really do smoke Gauloises here.

CARL: And, of course, the Dada and Surrealists who set up camp here after World War I and their return from Switzerland—

(*THE THIRD MAN, in a trench coat and red beret, crosses the stage.*)

ANNA: Are we being followed?

CARL: Is your medication making you paranoid? (*Pause.*) Now, over here is the famous spot where Gertrude supposedly said to her brother Leo— (*THE THIRD MAN follows them.*)

ANNA: I know. "God is the answer. What is the question?"—I'm not imagining it. That man has been trailing us from the Boulevard Saint-Michel.

CARL: Are you getting hungry?

ANNA: I'm getting tired.

CARL: Wait. Let's just whip around the corner to the Café Saint-Michel where Hemingway, after an all-night bout, threw up his shrimp heads all over Scott's new suede shoes—which really was a moveable feast. (*THE THIRD MAN is holding an identical stuffed rabbit and looks at them.*)

ANNA: Carl! Carl! Look! That man over there!

CARL: So? They have stuffed rabbits over here, too. Let's go.

ANNA: Why is he following us? He's got the same—

CARL: It's your imagination. How about a little déjeuner? (*ANNA and CARL walk to a small table and chairs.*)

SCENE II

GARÇON: (*With a thick Peter Sellers French.*) It was a simple bistro affair by French standards. He had le veau Prince Orloff, she le boeuf à la mode—a simple dish of haricots verts, and a Médoc to accompany it all. He barely touched his meal. She mopped the sauces with the bread. As their meal progressed, Anna thought of the lunches she packed back home. For the past ten years, hunched over in the faculty room at McCormick Elementary, this is what Anna ate: on Mondays, pressed chipped chicken sandwiches with mayonnaise on white; on Tuesdays, soggy tuna sandwiches; on Wednesdays, Velveeta cheese and baloney; on Thursdays, drier pressed chicken on the now stale white bread; on Fridays, Velveeta and tuna. She always had a small wax envelope of carrot sticks or celery, and a can of Diet Pepsi. Anna, as she ate in the bistro, wept. What could she know of love?

CARL: Why are you weeping?

ANNA: It's just so wonderful.

CARL: You're a goose.

ANNA: I've wasted over thirty years on convenience foods. (*The* GARÇON *approaches the table.*)

GARÇON: Is everything all right?

ANNA: Oh god. Yes—yes—it's wonderful.

CARL: My sister would like to see the dessert tray. (ANNA *breaks out in tears again. The* GARÇON *shrugs and exists. He reappears two seconds later as* THE THIRD MAN, *this time with a trench coat and blue beret. He sits at an adjacent table and stares in their direction.*)

ANNA: Who is that man? Do you know him?

CARL: (CARL *hastily looks at* THE THIRD MAN.) No, I've never seen him before. (THE THIRD MAN *brings the stuffed rabbit out of his trench coat.*)

ANNA: He's flashing his rabbit at you.

CARL (CARL *rises.*) Excuse me. I think I'll go to les toilettes.

ANNA: Carl! Be careful! Don't sit! (CARL *exits.* THE THIRD MAN *waits a few seconds, looks at* ANNA, *and then follows* CARL *without expression.*) What is it they do with those rabbits? (A SPLIT SECOND LATER, THE GARÇON *reenters with the dessert tray.* ANNA *ogles him.*)

GARÇON: O-kay. We have *la crème plombière pralinée, un bavarois à l'orange, et ici* we have *une Charlotte Malakoff aux Framboises.* Our *specialité* is *le gâteau de crêpes à a Normande.* What would mademoiselle like? (ANNA *has obviously not been looking at the dessert tray.*)

ANNA (*Sighing.*): Ah, yes.

GARÇON (*The* GARÇON *smiles.*): *Vous êtes Américaîne?* This is your first trip to Paris?

ANNA: Yes.

GARÇON: And you do not speak at all French?

ANNA: No. (*The* GARÇON *smiles.*)

GARÇON (*Suggestively.*): *Bon.* Would you like *la specialité de la maison?*

SCENE 12

CARL: Exercise: *La Carte. La specialité de la maison.* Back at the hotel, Anna sampled the Garçon's *specialité de la maison* while her brother browsed the Louvre. (ANNA *and the* GARÇON *are shapes beneath the covers of the bed.* CARL *clutches his stuffed rabbit.*) Jean-Baptiste-Camille Corot lived from 1796 to 1875. Although he began his career by studying in the classical tradition, his later paintings reveal the influence of the Italian style.

ANNA (*Muffled.*): Ah! Yes!

GARÇON (*Also muffled.*): Ah! *Oui!*

CARL: He traveled extensively around the world, and in the salon of 1827 his privately lauded techniques were displayed in public.

ANNA: Yes—oh, yes, yes!

GARÇON: *Mais oui!*

CARL: Before the Academy had accepted realism, Corot's progressive paintings, his clear-sighted observations of nature, revealed a fresh almost spritely quality of light, tone and composition.

ANNA: Yes—that's right—faster—

GARÇON: *Plus vite?*

ANNA: Faster—

GARÇON: *Encore! Plus vite!*

ANNA: Wait!

GARÇON: *Attends?*

CARL: It was his simplicity, and his awareness of color that brought a fresh wind into the staid academy—

GARÇON: *Maintenant?*

ANNA: Lower—faster—lower—

GARÇON: *Plus bas—plus vite—plus bas—*

CARL: He was particularly remembered and beloved for his championing the cause of younger artists with more experimental techniques, bringing the generosity of his advancing reputation to their careers.

ANNA: Yes—I—I—I—I—!

GARÇON: *Je—je! Je!! Je! (Pause.)*

CARL: In art, as in life, some things need no translation.

GARÇON: Gauloise?

CARL: For those of you who are interested, in the next room are some stunning works by Delacroix.

SCENE 13

Back at the Hotel.

CARL: Lesson Seven: Basic vocabulary. Parts of the body. (*CARL, slightly out of the next scene, watches them. ANNA sits up in bed. The GARÇON is asleep beneath the sheet.*)

ANNA: I did read one book once in French. *Le Petit Prince.* Lying here, watching him sleep, I look at his breast and remember the Rose with its single, pathetic thorn for protection. And here—his puckered red nipple, lying poor and vulnerable on top of his blustering breastplate. It's really so sweet about men. (*She kisses the GARÇON's breast. The GARÇON stirs.*)

GARÇON: *Encore?*

ANNA: What is the word—in French—for this? (*She fingers his breast.*)

GARÇON: For *un homme—le sein.* For *une femme—la mamelle.*

ANNA: *Le sein?*

GARÇON: *Oui. Le sein.*

ANNA: (*She kisses his neck.*) And this?

GARÇON: *Le cou.*

ANNA: *Et ici?*

GARÇON: *Bon. Décolleté—* (*ANNA begins to touch him under the sheet.*)

ANNA: And this?

GARÇON (*The GARÇON laughs.*): *S'il vous plâit* . . . I am tickling there. Ah. *Couille.*

ANNA: Culle?

GARÇON: *Non. Couille. Le cul* is something much different. *Ici c'est le cul.*

ANNA: Oh, yes. That's very different.

GARÇON (*Taking her hand under the sheet.*): We sometimes call these also *Le Quatrième État*. The Fourth Estate.

ANNA: Really? Because they enjoy being "scooped"?

GARÇON: *Bien sûr.*

ANNA: And this?

GARÇON (*With pride.*): Ah. *Ma Tour Eiffel*. I call it *aussi* my Charles DeGaulle.

ANNA: Wow.

GARÇON: My grandfather called his Napoleon.

ANNA: I see. I guess it runs in your family.

GARÇON (*Modestly.*): *Oui. Grand-mère—qu'est-ce que c'est le mot en anglais?* Her *con*—here—*ici*—do you know what I am meaning?

ANNA: You're making yourself completely clear—

GARÇON: We called hers the *Waterloo de mon grand-père*— (*ANNA digs under the sheet more.*)

ANNA: And this?

GARÇON (*The GARÇON is scandalized.*): *Non.* There is no word *en français. Pas du tout.*

ANNA: For this? There must be—

GARÇON: *Non!* Only the Germans have a word for that. (*CARL enters and casually converses with ANNA. Startled, the GARÇON covers himself with the sheet.*)

CARL: Hello, darling. Are you feeling better? (*CARL walks to the chair beside the bed and removes the GARÇON's clothing.*)

ANNA: Yes, much. I needed to lie down. How was the Louvre? (*The GARÇON carefully rises from the bed and takes his clothing from CARL, who is holding them out. He creeps cautiously stage left and begins to pull on his clothes.*)

CARL: Oh, Anna. I'm so sorry you missed it. The paintings of David were amazing. The way his paintbrush embraced the body—it was just incredible to stand there and see them in the flesh.

ANNA: Ah yes—in the flesh. (*She smiles at the confused GARÇON.*)

CARL: Well, sweetie. It's been a thoroughly rewarding day for both of us. I'm for turning in. How about you? (*The* GARÇON *is now fully dressed.*)

ANNA: Yes, I'm tired. Here—I've warmed the bed for you. (*She throws back the sheet.*)

CARL: *Garçon—l'addition!*

ANNA (*To the* GARÇON.): *Merci beaucoup.* (ANNA *blows him a kiss. The* GARÇON *takes a few steps out of the scene as* CARL *climbs into bed.*)

SCENE 14

THE THIRD MAN: Anna has a difficult time sleeping. She is afflicted with night thoughts. According to Elisabeth Kübler-Ross, there are six stages the terminal patient travels in the course of her illness. The first stage: Denial and Isolation. (THE THIRD MAN *stays in the hotel room and watches* CARL *and* ANNA *in the bed. They are sleeping, when* ANNA *sits upright.*)

ANNA: I feel so alone. The ceiling is pressing down on me. I can't believe I am dying. Only at night. Only at night. In the morning, when I open my eyes, I feel absolutely well—without a body. And then the thought comes crashing in my mind. This is the last spring I may see. This is the last summer. It can't be. There must be a mistake. They mixed the specimens up in the hospital. Some poor person is walking around, dying, with the false confidence of my prognosis, thinking themselves well. It's a clerical error. Carl! I can't sleep. Do you think they made a mistake?

CARL: Come back to sleep— (CARL *pulls* ANNA *down on the bed to him, and strokes her brow. They change positions on the bed.*)

THE THIRD MAN: The second stage: Anger.

ANNA (ANNA *sits bolt upright in bed, angry.*): How could this happen to me! I did my lesson plans faithfully for the past ten years! I've taught in classrooms without walls—kept up on new audio-visual aids—I read Summerhill! And I believed it! When the principal assigned me the job of the talent show—and nobody wants to do the talent show—I pleaded for cafeteria duty, bus duty—but no, I got stuck with the talent show. And those kids put on the best darn show that school has ever seen! Which one of them did this to me? Emily Baker? For slugging Johnnie MacIntosh? Johnnie MacIntosh? Because I sent him home for exposing himself to Susy Higgins? Susy Higgins? Because I called her out on her nose picking? Or those Nader twins? I've spent the best years of my life giving to those kids—it's not—

CARL: Calm down, sweetie. You're angry. It's only natural to be angry. Elisabeth Kübler-Ross says that—

ANNA: What does she know about what it feels like to die?! Elisabeth Kübler-Ross can sit on my face! (*CARL and ANNA change positions on the bed.*)

THE THIRD MAN: The third stage: Bargaining.

ANNA: Do you think if I let Elisabeth Kübler-Ross sit on my face I'll get well? (*CARL and ANNA change positions on the bed.*)

THE THIRD MAN: The fourth stage: Depression. (*CARL sits on the side of the bed beside ANNA.*)

CARL: Anna—honey—come on, wake up.

ANNA: Leave me alone.

CARL: Come on, sweetie . . . you've been sleeping all day now, and you slept all yesterday. Do you want to sleep away our last day in France?

ANNA: Why bother?

CARL: You've got to eat something. You've got to fight this. For me.

ANNA: Leave me alone. (*CARL lies down beside ANNA. They change positions.*)

THE THIRD MAN: The fifth stage: Acceptance. (*ANNA and CARL are lying in bed, awake. They hold hands.*)

ANNA: When I'm gone, I want you to find someone.

CARL: Let's not talk about me.

ANNA: No, I want to. It's important to me to know that you'll be happy and taken care of after . . . when I'm gone.

CARL: Please.

ANNA: I've got to talk about it. We've shared everything else. I want you to know how it feels . . . what I'm thinking . . .

when I hold your hand, and I kiss it . . . I try to memorize what it looks like, your hand . . . I wonder if there's any memory in the grave?

THE THIRD MAN: And then there's the sixth stage: Hope. (*ANNA and CARL rise from the bed.*)

CARL: How are you feeling?

ANNA: I feel good today.

CARL: Do you feel like traveling?

ANNA: Yes. It would be nice to see Amsterdam. Together. We might as well see as much as we can while I'm well—

CARL: That's right, sweetie. And maybe you can eat something—

ANNA: I'm hungry. That's a good sign, don't you think?

CARL: That's a wonderful sign. You'll see. You'll feel better when you eat.

ANNA: Maybe the doctor in Vienna can help.

CARL: That's right.

ANNA: What's drinking a little piss? It can't hurt you.

CARL: Right. Who knows? We've got to try.

ANNA: I'll think of it as . . . European lager.

CARL: Golden Heidelberg. (*CARL and ANNA hum/sing a song such as the drinking song from* The Student Prince.)

SCENE 15

THE THIRD MAN: And as Anna and Carl took the train into Holland, the seductive swaying of the TEE-train aroused another sensation. Unbeknownst to Elisabeth Kübler-Ross, there is a seventh stage for the dying. There is a growing urge to fight the sickness of the body with the health of the body. The seventh stage: Lust. (*ANNA and CARL are seated in a train compartment. CARL holds the stuffed rabbit out to ANNA.*)

ANNA: Why?

CARL: Just take it. Hold it for me. Just through customs.

ANNA: Only if you tell me why.

CARL: Don't play games right now. Or we'll be in deep, deep dodo. (*ANNA reluctantly takes the stuffed rabbit and holds it.*)

ANNA: You're scaring me.

CARL: I'm sorry, sweetie. You're the only one I can trust to hold my rabbit. Trust me. It's important.

ANNA: Then why won't you tell me—?

CARL: There are some some things you're better off not knowing.

ANNA: Are you smuggling drugs? Jewels?

CARL (*Whispers.*): It's beyond measure. It's invaluable to me. That's all I'll say. (*In a louder tone.*) Just act normal now.

CUSTOMS OFFICIAL: *Uw paspoort, alstublieft.* (*ANNA and CARL give him their passports. CARL is nervous. ANNA smiles at the CUSTOMS OFFICIAL a bit lasciviously.*) Have you anything to declare?

ANNA (*Whispering.*): Yes—captain, I'm smuggling contraband. I demand to be searched. In private.

CUSTOMS OFFICIAL (*The CUSTOMS OFFICIAL blushes.*): Excuse me?

ANNA: Yes. I said—*waar is het damestoilet?*

CUSTOMS OFFICIAL: Oh . . . I thought . . . (*The CUSTOMS OFFICIAL giggles.*)

ANNA: Yes?

CUSTOMS OFFICIAL: First left. (*The CUSTOMS OFFICIAL returns their passports.*) Have a very pleasant stay. (*ANNA waves bunny's arm good-bye. The CUSTOMS OFFICIAL looks at her, blushes again, and retreats. CARL relaxes.*)

CARL: You're good at this. Very good.

ANNA: When in Holland, do like the Dutch . . . Mata Hari was Dutch, you know.

SCENE 16

CARL: *Questions sur le Dialogue. Est-ce que les hommes Hollandais sont comme les Français?* Are Dutch men like the French? (*ANNA and THE LITTLE DUTCH BOY at age fifty. He wears traditional wooden shoes, trousers and vest. His Buster Brown haircut and hat make him look dissipated.*)

THE LITTLE DUTCH BOY AT AGE FIFTY: It was kermis-time, the festival in my village. And I had too much bier with my school friends, Piet and Jan. *Ja.* Soo—Piet thought we should go to the outer dyke with cans of spray paint, after the kermis. So we went.

Here in Noord Brabant there are three walls of defenses against the cruelty of the North Sea. The first dyke is called the Waker—the Watcher; the second dyke is de Slaper—the Sleeper; and the last dyke, which had never before been tested, is known as the Dromer—the Dreamer.

And when we got to the Dreamer, Piet said to me: "Willem, you do it." Meaning I was to write on the walls of the Dreamer. This is why I was always in trouble in school—Piet and Jan would say, "Willem, you do it," and whatever it was—I would do it.

Soo—I took up a can of the paint and in very big letters, I wrote in Dutch that our schoolmaster, Mijnheer Van Doorn, was a gas-passer. Everyone could read the letters from far away. And just as I was finishing this, and Piet and Jan were laughing behind me, I looked—I was on my knees, pressed up against the dyke—and I could see that the wall of the Dreamer was cracking its surface, very fine little lines, like a goose egg when it breaks from within.

And I yelled to my friends—Look! And they came a bit closer, and as we looked, right above my head, a little hole began to peck its way through the clay. And there was just a small trickle of water. And Jan said: "Willem, put your thumb in that hole." And by that time, the hole in the dyke was just big enough to put my thumb in. "Why?" I asked of Jan. "Just do it," he said. And so I did.

And once I put my thumb in, I could not get it out. Suddenly we could hear the waves crashing as the Sleeper began to collapse. Only the Dreamer remained to hold off the savage water. "Help me!" I yelled to Jan and Piet—but they ran away. *"Vlug!"* I cried—but no one could hear me. And I stayed there, crouching, with my thumb stuck into the clay. And I thought what if the Dreamer should give in, too. How the waves would bear my body like a messenger to the village. How no one would survive the flood. Only the church steeple would remain to mark the spot where we had lived. How young we were to die. (*Pause.*)

Have you ever imagined what it would be like to be face-to-face with death?

ANNA: Yes—yes I have.

THE LITTLE DUTCH BOY AT AGE FIFTY: And have you ever prayed for deliverance against all hope?

ANNA: I—no. I haven't been able to get to that stage. Yet.

THE LITTLE DUTCH BOY AT AGE FIFTY: But the Dreamer held. And finally there came wagons with men from the village, holding lanterns and sand and straw. And they found me there, strung up by my thumb, beside the big black letters: "Mijnheer Van Doorn is een gas-passer." And they freed me and said I was a hero, and I became the boy who held back the sea with his thumb.

ANNA: Golly. You were very brave.

THE LITTLE DUTCH BOY AT AGE FIFTY: I was stupid. Wrong place, wrong time.

ANNA: How long ago did this happen?

THE LITTLE DUTCH BOY AT AGE FIFTY (*Sadly.*): Let us just say it happened a long time ago.

ANNA: You've faced death. I wish my brother were here to meet you.

THE LITTLE DUTCH BOY AT AGE FIFTY: Where is he? *Wo ist dein bruder?*

ANNA: Oh, he stayed in Amsterdam to see the Rijksmuseum and the Van Gogh Museum.

THE LITTLE DUTCH BOY AT AGE FIFTY: And you did not go? You should see them, they are really fantastic.

ANNA: Why? What's the use? I won't remember them, I'll have no memory.

THE LITTLE DUTCH BOY AT AGE FIFTY: So you are an American?

ANNA: Yes.

THE LITTLE DUTCH BOY AT AGE FIFTY: So do you want to sleep with me? All the women *toeristen* want to sleep with the little Dutch boy who put his thumb in the dyke.

ANNA: Do you mind so much?

THE LITTLE DUTCH BOY AT AGE FIFTY (*Shrugs.*): Nee. It's a way to make a living, is it *niet?*

ANNA (*Quietly.*): Let's go then.

SCENE 17

CARL: *Répétez. En Français.* Where is my brother going? *Où va mon frère? Bien.*

ANNA: I had just returned from my day trip and left the Central Station. The sun sparkled on the waters of the canal, and I decided to walk back to the hotel. Just then I saw my brother. (*CARL enters in a trench coat, sunglasses, holding the stuffed rabbit.*) I tried to catch up with Carl, dodging bicycles and pedestrians. And then, crossing the Amstel on the Magere Brug, he appeared. (*THE THIRD MAN enters, in a trench coat, sunglasses, and with black gloves, holding a stuffed rabbit.*) I trailed them from a discreet distance. (*THE THIRD MAN and CARL walk rapidly, not glancing at each other. CARL stops; THE THIRD MAN stops a few paces behind. CARL walks; THE THIRD MAN walks. CARL stops; THE THIRD MAN stops. Finally, they face each other and meet. Quickly, looking surreptitiously around, CARL and THE THIRD MAN stroke each other's stuffed rabbits. They quickly part and walk off in opposite directions, but not before THE THIRD MAN attempts to grab CARL's rabbit and run. ANNA rushes to C., looking in both directions.*) I tried to follow the man in the trench coat, and crossed behind him over the Amstel, but I lost sight of him in the crowd of men wearing trench coats and sunglasses. I want some answers from my brother. Whatever trouble he's in, he has to share it with me. I want some answers back at the hotel. He's going to talk.

SCENE 18

CARL: Questions *sur le dialogue.* You must learn. *Sie müssen lernen.* (*ANNA enters the empty hotel room. On the bed, propped up on pillows, lies a stuffed rabbit.*)

ANNA: Carl? Carl? Are you back? (*ANNA stops and looks at the stuffed rabbit.*)

CARL (*From the side.*): You were not permitted to play with dolls; dolls are for girls. You played with your sister's dolls until your parents found out. They gave you a stuffed animal—a thin line was drawn. Rabbits were an acceptable surrogate for little boys. You named him Jo-Jo. You could not sleep without him. Jo-Jo traveled with you to the seashore, to the hotel in New York City when you were seven, to your first summer camp. He did not have the flaxen plastic hair of your sister's Betsey-Wetsy, but he had long, furry ears, soft white on one side, pink satin inside. He let you stroke them. He never betrayed you. He taught you to trust in contact. You will love him always.

ANNA (*ANNA moves toward the stuffed rabbit.*): My brother left you behind, did he? Alone at last. Okay, bunny, now you're going to talk. I want some answers. What have you got that's so important? (*Just as ANNA reaches for the stuffed rabbit, THE THIRD MAN—in trench coat, sunglasses, and black gloves—steps out into the room.*)

THE THIRD MAN (*Threateningly.*): I wouldn't do that, if I were you. (*ANNA screams in surprise.*) Now listen. Where is your brother? I have a message for him. Tell him he's running out of time. Do you understand? (*ANNA, scared, nods.*) Good. He'd better not try to dupe us. We're willing to arrange a swap—his sister for the rabbit. Tell him we're waiting for him in Vienna. And tell him he'd better bring along the rabbit to the other side. (*THE THIRD MAN disappears. ANNA, shaken, sits on the bed and holds the stuffed rabbit. She strokes it for comfort. CARL enters, in a frenzy. He carries his stuffed rabbit. ANNA stares as CARL tosses the decoy rabbit away.*)

CARL: Don't ask me any questions. I can't tell you what's happening. Are you able to travel? Good. We have to leave Amsterdam tonight. There's a train in an hour. We'll go to Germany. Are you packed?

SCENE 19

ANNA and THE THIRD MAN (*Simultaneously.*): *Wann fahrt der nächste Zug nach Hamburg?* (*German band music swells as ANNA and CARL sit in their railroad compartment, side by side. ANNA, pale, holds the stuffed rabbit in her lap.*)

CARL: Ah, Saxony, Bavaria, the Black Forest, the Rhineland . . . I love them all. I think perhaps now would be a good time to show the slides.

ANNA: I'm so sorry. I hate it when people do this to me.

CARL: Nonsense. People like to see slides of other people's trips. These are in no particular order. We'll only show a few, just to give a taste of the German countryside.

ANNA: Carl took over two hours' worth of slides.

CARL: If you'll just dim the lights, please. (*THE THIRD MAN wheels in the projector and operates it throughout the travelogue.*) Well. Bonn's as good a place to start as anywhere. This is the view from the snug little hotel we stayed in. The gateway to the Rhine, the birthplace of Beethoven, and the resting place of Schumann. (*Slide: the view of downtown Baltimore from the Ramada Inn near John Hopkins Hospital, overlooking the industrial harbor.*)

ANNA: Looks a lot like Baltimore to me.

CARL: My sister jests. As you can see in the slide, one night we splurged and stayed in a rather dear inn near the Drachenfels mountains, where Lord Byron had sported. (*Slide: a close-up of the balcony railing looking into the Ramada Inn hotel room.*)

ANNA (*Deadpan.*): This is the room I slept in while I stayed with my brother Carl. (*Slide: gutted ruins of inner-city Baltimore near the Jones-Fall Expressway; rubble and obvious urban blight.*)

CARL: Alas, poor Köln. Practically wiped out by airplane raids during World War II, and yet, out of this destruction, the cathedral of Köln managed to survive—one of the most beautiful Gothic churches in the world, with a superb altar painted by the master artist of Köln, Stefan Lochner. (*Slide: an impoverished storefront church, a black evangelical sect in Baltimore.*) Let's see—what do we have next? (*Slide: a Sabrett's hot dog cart with its blue-and-orange umbrella in front of Johns Hopkins Hospital.*) Oh, yes. Let's talk about the food. Whereas I snapped momentos of the regal pines of the Black Forest, Anna insisted on taking photos of everything she ate.

ANNA: I can remember things I feel.

CARL: Well, then, let's talk about the food. Germany has a more robust gustatory outlook than the delicate palate of France. The Germans positively celebrate the pig from snout to tail. I could not convince Anna to sample the Sulperknochen, which is a Rheingau concoction of ears, snout, tail and feet.

ANNA: Ugh. (*Slide: a close-up of vender placing a hot dog on a bun and lathering it with mustard; there are canned sodas in a wide variety.*)

CARL: And of course, everything is washed down with beer. (*Slide: Anna sipping a Bud Light.*)

ANNA: It was delicious.

CARL: Enough of food. May we talk about culture, sister, dear? Next slide, please. (*Slide: the Maryland National Armory, the state penitentiary.*) Ah, Heidelberg. Dueling scars and castles. Spectacular ruin which serves as the locale for open-air concerts and fireworks (*Slide: the Baltimore smokestack.*) . . . and by a quaint cable car, you can reach the peak of Königstuhl, 2,000 feet high, with its breathtaking view of the Neckar Valley. (*Slide: the Bromo Seltzer tower in Baltimore. Slide: the interstate highways viewed from the tower.*) Every cobblestoned street, every alleyway, was so pristine and clean. (*Slide: the row houses on Monument Street. Slide: a corridor of Johns Hopkins Hospital, outside the basement laboratories.*) Wasn't it, Anna?

ANNA (*Deadpan.*): Yes. Sterile. (*Slide: a hospital aide washing the floor.*)

CARL: Even the Black Forest looked swept. We splurged once again and stayed at the Waldhorn Post here, outside of Wildbad. (*Slide: exterior of Johns Hopkins Hospital.*) The hotel dates back to 1145—the chef there is renown for his game dishes. (*Slide: Anna in front of a vending machine dispensing wrapped sandwiches in the Johns Hopkins Hospital cafeteria.*)

ANNA: I wasn't too hungry.

CARL: I was ravenous. (*Slides: Route* 95 *outside the harbor tunnel; the large toll signs are visible.*) Let's see—the Romantic Road . . . die Romantisehe Strasse . . . a trek through picture-book Bavaria and the Allgau Alpen . . . Füssen to Wurzburg.

ANNA: Honey, perhaps they've seen enough. It's hard to sit through this many—

CARL: Wait. Just one more. They've got to see Neuschwanstein, built by mad King Ludwig II. It's so rococo it's Las Vegas. (*Slide: the castle at Disneyland.*) I believe that Ludwig was reincarnated in the twentieth century as Liberace. Wait a moment, that's not the castle.

ANNA: Yes, it is.

CARL (*Upset.*): It looks like—how did that get in here?

ANNA: I don't know which castle you're referring to, but it's definitely a castle. (*Slide: a close-up of the castle, with a large Mickey Mouse in the picture.*)

CARL: That's not funny, Anna! Are you making fun of me?

ANNA: Don't get upset. (*Slide: Donald Duck has joined Mickey Mouse with tourists.*)

CARL: I went to Europe. I walked through Bavaria and the Black Forest. I combed through Neuschwanstein! I did these things, and I will remember the beauty of it all my life! I don't appreciate your mockery!

ANNA: It's just a little—

CARL: You went through Germany on your back. All you'll remember are hotel ceilings. You can show them your Germany— (*He rushes off, angry.*)

ANNA: Sometimes my brother gets upset for no apparent reason. Some wires cross in his brain and he—I'm sorry. Lights, please. (*The Third Man wheels the projector offstage.*) I would like to show you my impressions of Germany. They were something like this—

SCENE 20

In Munich, ANNA *is under the sheet beside the* MUNICH VIRGIN, *who is very young.*

ANNA: Are you comfortable?

MUNICH VIRGIN: *Ja, ja . . . danke.*

ANNA: Good. Have you been the bellhop here for a long time?

MUNICH VIRGIN: Not so very long a time. My vater owns the hotel, and says I must learn and work very hard. Soon I will be given the responsibility of the front desk.

ANNA: My. That's exciting. (*Pause.*) Are you cold?

MUNICH VIRGIN: *Nein.* Just a . . . *klein nervös.* My English is not so very good.

ANNA: Is this your first time? You always remember your first time. (*Pause.*) I'm very honored. (*Pause.*) Listen. I'm a schoolteacher. May I tell you something? A little lesson? When you're a much older man, and you've loved many women, you'll be a wonderful lover if you're just a little bit nervous . . . like you are right now. Becuase it will always be the first time.

MUNICH VIRGIN: You are a very nice woman.

ANNA: The human body is a wonderful thing. Like yours. Like mine. The beauty of the body heals all the sickness, all the bad things that happen to it. And I really want you to feel this. Because if you feel it, you'll remember it. And then maybe you'll remember me.

SCENE 21

ANNA *and the* MUNICH VIRGIN *rise.* CARL *gets into the bed with his stuffed rabbit.* ANNA *gets ready to leave.*

THE THIRD MAN: Conjugations of the verb *verlassen.* To leave, to abandon, to forsake. The present tense.

CARL: Are you leaving me alone?

ANNA: Yes. Just for a little while. I need to take a walk. I'm restless. It's perfectly safe.

CARL: Okay, sweetie. Don't be too long. Bunny and I are ready for bed.

ANNA: I won't stay out long. I'll be right back.

THE THIRD MAN: The future tense of the verb *verlassen*.

CARL: Will you be leaving me alone again tonight? I'm ready for bed.

ANNA: I will be leaving you alone. Just for a little while.

CARL: Who will it be tonight? The bellhop? The desk clerk? Or the maitre d'?

ANNA: Don't be mean. You said you didn't make judgments.

CARL: I don't. I just want to spend time with you.

ANNA: I'll be back in time for a bedtime story.

THE THIRD MAN: The past tense of the verb *verlassen*.

CARL: Again? Again? You left me alone last night. And the night before.

ANNA: I can't help it. I've been a good girl for the past thirty years. Now I want to make up for lost time.

CARL: And what am I supposed to do while you're out traipsing around with every Thomas, Deiter *und* Heinrich?

ANNA: Hug bunny.

THE THIRD MAN: There are three moods of the verb *verlassen*: the indicative, the imperative, and the subjunctive. Anna and Carl are never in the same mood.

CARL: Leave me alone.

ANNA: Carl, don't be like that.

CARL: Why? It doesn't matter what I want. You are going to leave.

ANNA: I never stay out very long.

CARL: All I can say is if this establishment charges us for room service, they've got some nerve—

ANNA: I've got to take what opportunities come along—

CARL: I wish you wouldn't go—

ANNA: Please understand. I don't have much time. I spend as much time with you as I can, but while I still have my health . . . please?

SCENE 22

THE THIRD MAN: As children they fought.

CARL: We never fought, really.

ANNA: Not in a physical way. He was a sickly child.

CARL: She was very willful.

ANNA: No roughhousing. But he knew all of my weak points. My secret openings. He could be ruthless.

CARL: She'd cry at the slightest thing.

ANNA: He has a very sharp tongue.

CARL: But when one of you is very, very sick, you can't fight. It's not fair. You've got to hold it in. We never fight.

ANNA: But we had a doozy in the hotel room in Berlin.

CARL: Well, my god, Anna, even though you're sick, I have the right to get angry.

ANNA: We'd been traveling too long. We were cranky. The rooms were closing in.

CARL: I'm just saying that we should spend a little more time together. I don't get to see you alone enough. You're always restless.

ANNA: Fine. You go out without me for a change.

CARL: I'm going out for a walk.

ANNA (*Starting to weep.*): I don't care.

CARL: When she was little, this would be the time I'd bribe her. With a comic book or an ice cream. I always had pennies saved up for these little contingencies.

ANNA: But sometimes, for the sake of my pride, I would be inconsolable. I would rush off and then feel just awful alone. Why didn't I take the bribe? (*To* CARL.) I'm going out.

CARL: To fuck?

ANNA: No, dear. The passive voice is used to emphasize the subject, to indicate the truth of the generalization. I'm going out. To get fucked.

SCENE 23

Music: Kurt Weill. ANNA *goes over to a small cabaret table. There is a telephone on the table. The* RADICAL STUDENT ACTIVIST *sits at another identical table, smoking, watching her.*

ANNA: I'm going to enjoy Berlin without him. I'll show him. I'm going to be carefree, totally without scruples. I'll pretend I've never taught first-graders. (*Beat.*) I'm going to have a perfectly miserable time. (*The* RADICAL STUDENT ACTIVIST *picks up the telephone. The telephone at* ANNA's *table rings.*) Oh my goodness. My miserable time is calling me. (ANNA *picks up the phone.*) Yes?

RADICAL STUDENT ACTIVIST: Are you alone, Fraülein?

ANNA: Well, uh, actually—yes, I am.

RADICAL STUDENT ACTIVIST: *Gut. Du willst mal richtig durchgefickt werden, ja?*

ANNA: I'm sorry. I don't speak a word of German. (*The* RADICAL STUDENT ACTIVIST *laughs.*)

RADICAL STUDENT ACTIVIST: *Ja.* Even better. I said, would you like to get fucked?

ANNA: Do you always come on to single women like that?

RADICAL STUDENT ACTIVIST: Would you like it better if I bought you tall drinks with umbrellas? Told to you the stories of how hard a time my parents had during the war? Tell you how exciting I find foreign women, how they are the real women, not like the pale northern *mädchen* here at home? How absolutely bourgeois.

ANNA: I see. Why do you come here?

RADICAL STUDENT ACTIVIST: I don't come here for the overpriced drinks. I come here because of the bored western women who come here, who leave their tired businessmen husbands in the hotel rooms behind.

ANNA: You're cute. In a hostile way.

RADICAL STUDENT ACTIVIST: Fucking is a revolutionary act.

ANNA: Your hovel or my hotel?

SCENE 24

In the Hotel Room. ANNA, *awake, lies in the middle of the bed. To her left,* CARL *sleeps, curled up. To her right, the* RADICAL STUDENT ACTIVIST, *curled on her breast, slumbers.* ANNA *is awake with an insomniacal desperation.*

ANNA (*Singing softly.*): Two and two are four; four and four are eight; eight and eight are sixteen; sixteen and sixteen are thirty-two—

RADICAL STUDENT ACTIVIST (*Groggy.*): *Wo ist die Toilette?* (*The* RADICAL STUDENT ACTIVIST rises and stumbles off.)

ANNA: In lovemaking, he's all fury and heat. His North Sea pounding against your Dreamer. And when you look up and see his face, red and huffing, it's hard to imagine him ever having been a newborn, tiny, wrinkled, and seven pounds. That is, until afterwards. When he rises from sleep and he walks into the bathroom. And there he exposes his soft little derrière, and you can still see the soft baby flesh. (*As the* RADICAL STUDENT ACTIVIST *comes back into the room.*) I've gotta put a name to that behind. What's your name? *Wie heissen Sie?*

RADICAL STUDENT ACTIVIST (*Starts dressing in a hurry.*): *Auf Wiedersehen*. Next thing you'll ask for my telephone number.

ANNA: No, I won't. I was just curious—

RADICAL STUDENT ACTIVIST: *Ja, ja . . . und* then my sign of the zodiac. I'll get cards from Hallmark *und* little scribblings like "I'll never forget the night we shared."

ANNA: Forget it.

RADICAL STUDENT ACTIVIST: There is something radical in two complete strangers committing biological necessity without having to give into bourgeois conventions of love, without breeding to produce workers for a capitalist system, without the benediction of the church, the family, the bosses—

ANNA: I have something to confess to you. I lied to you.

RADICAL STUDENT ACTIVIST: About what?

ANNA: I'm not here on business. I don't specialize in corporate takeovers. I don't work on Wall Street. I only told you that because I thought that was what you wanted to hear.

RADICAL STUDENT ACTIVIST: Okay. So you do estate planning? Income tax?

ANNA: No. You just committed a revolutionary act with a first-grade schoolteacher who lives in low-income housing. And I'm tired. I think you should go.

RADICAL STUDENT ACTIVIST: And your husband?

ANNA: Not too loud. And he's not my husband. He's my brother. A maiden librarian for the San Francisco Public. (*As the RADICAL STUDENT ACTIVIST starts to leave.*) And by the way—the missionary position does not a revolution make. (*The RADICAL STUDENT ACTIVIST leaves. ANNA, depressed, lies down. CARL rises from the bed.*)

SCENE 25

CARL: And as she lay in the bed, sleepless, it swept over her—the way her classroom smelled early in the morning, before the children came. It smelled of chalk dust—

THE THIRD MAN: It smelled of Crayola wax, crushed purple and green—

CARL: The cedar of hamster cage shavings—

THE THIRD MAN: The sweet wintergreen of LePage's paste—

CARL: The wooden smell of the thick construction paper—

THE THIRD MAN: The spillings of sticky orange drink and sour milk—

THE THIRD MAN and CARL (*Simultaneously.*): And the insidious smell of first-grader pee.

CARL: It smelled like heaven.

ANNA: And the first thing I did each morning was put up the weather map for today on the board under the flag. A bright, smiling sun, or Miss Cloud or Mr. Umbrella. On special days I put up Suzy Snowflake. And when I opened my desk drawer, scattered like diamonds on the bottom were red, silver, and gold stars. (*Beat.*) I want to go home, Carl, I want to go home.

CARL: Soon, sweetie. Very soon.

ANNA: I've had enough. I've seen all of the world I want to see. I want to wake up in my own bed. I want to sit with you at home and we'll watch the weather. And we'll wait.

CARL: We've come so far. We have to at least go to Vienna. Do you think you can hold out long enough to meet Dr. Todesrocheln? (*ANNA, miserable and homesick, nods.*) That a girl. I promise you don't have to undertake his . . . hydrotherapy unless you decide to. I have a friend in Vienna, a college chum, who might be able to get us some of black market stuff. It's worth a shot.

ANNA: Then you'll take me home?

CARL: Then I'll take you home.

SCENE 26

Music: A song such as the zither theme from The Third Man. *CARL and ANNA stand, with their luggage, in front of a door buzzer.*

CARL: First we'll just look up Harry. Then we'll cab over to Dr. Todesrocheln. (*CARL rings the buzzer. They wait. CARL rings the buzzer again. They wait. An aging CONCIERGE comes out.*) *Entschuldigung. Wir suchen* Harry Lime? Do you speak English?

CONCIERGE: *Nein. Ich spreche kein Englisch.* (*CARL and the CONCIERGE start to shout as if the other one was deaf.*)

CARL: Herr Lime? Do you know him? Herr Harry Lime?

CONCIERGE: *Ach. Ach. Ja,* Herr Harry Lime. You come . . . too *spät.*

CARL: He's gone? Too *spät?*

CONCIERGE: *Fünf minuten* too *spät. Er ist tot—*

CARL: What?

CONCIERGE: *Ja. Ein auto mit* Harry *splatz-machen auf der Strasse. Splatz!*

ANNA: *Splatz!?*

CARL: *Splatz?!* (*It dawns on CARL and ANNA what the CONCIERGE is saying.*)

CONCIERGE: *Ja, ja. Er geht über die strasse, und ein auto . . . sppplllaattz!*

ANNA: Oh, my *god.*

CONCIERGE (*Gesturing with hands.*): *Ja. Er hat auch eine* rabbit. Herr Rabbit *auch—spllaattz!* They are . . . *diggen ein grab in den Boden. Jetz.*

CARL: Now? You saw this happen?

CONCIERGE: *Ja.* I . . . saw it *mit merinen* own *Augen. Splatz.* (*As he exits.*) *"Splatzen, splatzen, über alles . . . "*

CARL: Listen, darling. I want you to take a cab to the doctor's office.

ANNA: Where are you going?

CARL: *Ich verlasse.* I'll find out what happened to Harry.

ANNA: I wish you wouldn't leave . . .

CARL: I'll come back. Okay?

SCENE 27

ANNA climbs onto a table and gathers a white paper sheet around her. She huddles.

ANNA: Some things are the same in every country. You're scared when you see the doctor, here in Vienna just like in Baltimore. And they hand you the same paper cup to fill, just like in America. Then you climb up onto the same cold metal table, and they throw a sheet around you and you feel very small. And just like at home, they tell you to wait. And you wait. (*As ANNA waits, dwarfed on the table, the scene with HARRY LIME and CARL unfolds. Music, such as* The Third Man *theme, up.*)

SCENE 28

On the Ferris wheel in the Prater. CARL holds the stuffed rabbit closely.

CARL: Why are we meeting here?

HARRY LIME: Have you looked at the view from up here? It's quite inspiring. No matter how old I get, I always love the Ferris wheel.

CARL: I just came from your funeral.

HARRY LIME: I'm touched, old man. Was it a nice funeral?

CARL: What are you doing?

HARRY LIME: It's best not to ask too many questions. The police were beginning to do that. It's extremely convenient, now and then in a man's career, to die. I've gone underground. So if you want to meet me, you have to come here. No one asks questions here.

CARL: Can you help us? (*HARRY LIME at first does not answer. He looks at the view.*)

HARRY LIME: Where is your sister? She left you alone?

CARL: She's—she needs her rest. You were my closest friend in college.

HARRY LIME: I'll be straight with you. I can give you the drugs—but it won't help. It won't help at all. Your sister's better off with that quack Todesrocheln—we call him the Yellow Queen of Vienna—she might end up drinking her own piss, but it won't kill her.

CARL: But I thought you had the drugs—

HARRY LIME: Oh, I do. And they cost a pretty penny. For a price, I can give them to you. At a discount for old times. But you have to know, we make them up in my kitchen.

CARL: Jesus.

HARRY LIME: Why not? People will pay for these things. When they're desperate people will eat peach pits, or aloe, or egg protein—they'll even drink their own piss. It gives them hope.

CARL: How can you do this?

HARRY LIME: Listen, old man, if you want to be a millionaire, you go into real estate. If you want to be a billionaire, you sell hope. Nowadays the only place a fellow can make a decent career of it is in Mexico and Europe.

CARL: That's . . . disgusting.

HARRY LIME: Look. I thought you weren't going to be . . . sentimental about this. It's a business. You have to have the right perspective. Like from up here . . . the people down on the street are just tiny little dots. And if you could charge $1,000, wouldn't you push the drugs? I could use a friend I can trust to help me.

CARL: When we were at Hopkins together, I thought you were God. You could hypnotize us into doing anything, and it would seem . . . charming. Carl, old man, you'd say, "Just do it." Cutting classes, cribbing exams, shoplifting, stupid undergraduate things—and I would do it. Without knowing the consequences I would do it.

HARRY LIME: Oh, you knew the consequences, old man. You knew. You chose not to think about them.

CARL: I've grown old before my time from the consequences. I'm turning you in.

HARRY LIME: I wouldn't do that, old man. (*HARRY LIME pats a bulge on the inside of his trench coat.*) By the time you hit the ground, you'll be just a tiny little dot. (*CARL and HARRY LIME look at each other, waiting.*) And I think you have something I want. The rabbit, *bitte*.

CARL: No. You're not getting it. I'm taking it with me. (*HARRY LIME puts his arms in position for a waltz and begins to sway, seductively.*)

HARRY LIME: Come on, give it up. Come to my arms, my only one. Dance with me, my beloved, my sweet— (*CARL takes the stuffed rabbit and threatens to throw it out the window of the Ferris wheel. A Strauss waltz plays very loudly, and HARRY LIME and CARL waltz-struggle for the rabbit. CARL is pushed and HARRY LIME waltzes off with the rabbit.*)

SCENE 29

Meanwhile, back at DOCTOR TODESROCHELN.

ANNA: You begin to hope that the wait is proportionate to the medical expertise. My God. My feet are turning blue. Where am I? An HMO? (*ANNA waits.*) The problem with being an adult is that you never forget why you're waiting. When I was a child, I could wait blissfully unaware for hours. I used to read signs and transpose letters, or count tiles in the floor. And in the days before I could read, I would make up stories about my hands—Mr. Left and Mr. Right. (*Beat.*) Mr. Left would provoke Mr. Right. Mr. Right would ignore it. The trouble would escalate, until my hands were battling each other to the death. (*Beat.* ANNA *demonstrates.*) Then one of them would weep. Finally, they became friends again, and they'd dance— (ANNA*'s two hands dance together; she is unaware that* DR. TODESROCHELN *has entered and is watching her. He clears his throat. He wears a very dirty lab coat with pockets filled with paper and a stale doughnut. He wears a white fright wig and glasses. He also wears one sinister black glove. With relish, he carries a flask of a golden liquid.*) Oh, thank goodness.

DR. TODESROCHELN: *Ja.* So happy to meet you. Such an interesting specimen. I congratulate you. Very, very interesting.

ANNA: Thank you.

DR. TODESROCHELN: We must have many more such specimens from you—for the urinocryoscopy, the urinometer, the urinoglucosometer, the uracidimeter, uroazotometer, and *mein* new acquirement in *der* laboratorium—*ein* urophosphometer.

ANNA: My goodness. (DR. TODESROCHELN *has put the flask down on a table. Quietly, his left hand reaches for it; the right hand stops the left.*)

DR. TODESROCHELN: *Ja.* Nowadays, we have learned to discover the uncharted mysteries of the fluids discharged through the urethra. We have been so primitive in the past. Doctors once could only analyze by taste and smell—but thanks to the advancement of medical science, there are no limits to our thirst for knowledge.

ANNA: Uh-huh. (DR. TODESROCHELN*'s left hand seizes the flask. Trembling, with authority, his right hand replaces the flask on the table, and soothes the left hand into quietude.*)

DR. TODESROCHELN: So much data has been needlessly, carelessly destroyed in the past—the medical collections of Ravensbruck senselessly annihilated—and that is why as a scientist, I must be exacting in our measurements and recordings.

ANNA: What can I hope to find out from these . . . specimens?

DR. TODESROCHELN: Ah, yes—the layman must have his due! Too much pure research und no application makes Jack . . . *macht* Jack . . . (*DR. TODESROCHELN loses his train of thought.*) Fraülein Anna—I may call you Fraülein Anna?— Let us look at the body as an alchemist, taking in straw and mud *und Schweinefleisch* and processing it into liquid gold, which purifies the body. You might say that the sickness of the body can only be cured by the health of the body. To your health! (*His left hand seizes the flask in a salute, and raises the flask to his lips. In time, the right hand brings the flask down. A brief struggle. It appears the flask might spill, but at last the right hand triumphs.*)

ANNA: You know, even though I really grew up in the suburbs of Baltimore, I like to think of myself as an open-minded person—

DR. TODESROCHELN: The ancient Greeks knew that the aromatic properties of the fluid could reveal the imbalances of the soul itself . . . (*The left hand sneaks toward the flask.*)

ANNA: I'm always very eager to try new foods, or see the latest John Waters film—

DR. TODESROCHELN: —its use in the purification rites of the Aztecs is, of course, so well known that it need not be mentioned— (*The hand has grasped the flask and begins to inch it off the table.*)

ANNA: And whenever I meet someone who cross-dresses, I always compliment him on his shoes or her earrings—

DR. TODESROCHELN: It is the first golden drop that marks the infant's identity separate from the womb— (*The hand has slipped the flask beneath the table. His right hand is puzzled.*)

ANNA: But still, it's important to know where your threshold is . . . and I think we're coming dangerously close to mine. . . .

DR. TODESROCHELN: Until the last precious amber releases the soul from the body—ashes to ashes, drop to drop—excuse me— (*His left hand, with the flask, swings in an arc behind his body; he *swivels his body to the flask, his back turned to us. We can hear him drink in secrecy. With his back turned.*) Ahhh . . . (*He orders himself. Composed, he turns around to face* ANNA *again, and demurely sets down the flask. Its level is noticeably lower.* ANNA *is aghast.*) I can sense your concern. I have been prattling on without regard to questions you must surely have—

ANNA: Is that your real hair?

DR. TODESROCHELN: Of course, I cannot promise results, but first we must proceed by securing more samples—

ANNA: I don't believe that's your real hair.

DR. TODESROCHELN: I will need first of all twenty-four hours of your time for a urononcometry—

ANNA (*Increasingly scared.*): You look familiar to me—

DR. TODESROCHELN: Although I can tell you from a first taste—er, test, that your uroammonica level is high—not unpleasantantly so, but full-bodied—

ANNA: Oh, my god . . . I think I know who you are . . . you're . . . you're . . . (ANNA *rises to snatch his toupée.* DR. TODESROCHELN *suddenly stands, menacing. And the light changes.*)

DR. TODESROCHELN: *Wo ist dein bruder?* (*He takes off his wig and glasses and appears as the Doctor in the first scene, peeling off the black glove to reveal latex gloves underneath.*) You fool! You left your brother in the room alone! *Wo ist dein bruder?* (*Music:* The Emperor Waltz *plays at a very loud volume.* ANNA, *frightened, races from the doctor's office to the hotel room. We see* CARL, *lying stiff beneath a white sheet. To the tempo of the Strauss,* ANNA *tries to wake him. He does not respond.* ANNA *takes off the sheet and forces him into a sitting position, the stuffed rabbit clenched beneath his arms.* CARL *remains sitting, stiff, eyes open, wooden; he is still in his pajamas. Then he slumps.* ANNA *raises him again. He remains upright for a beat, and begins to fall.* ANNA *stops him, presses his body against hers, pulls his legs over the bed, tries to stand him up. Frozen, his body tilts against hers. She tries to make him cross the floor, his arms around her neck. She positions him in a chair, but his legs are locked in a perpendicular angle and will not touch the floor. She presses his legs to the floor. He mechanically springs forward. Then suddenly, like the doll in "E.T.A. Hoffman," the body of* CARL *becomes animated, but with a strange, automatic life of its own.* CARL *begins to waltz with* ANNA*. Gradually, he winds down, and faltering, falls back to the bed. There is the sound of a loud alarm clock; the* DOCTOR *enters, and covers* CARL *with a sheet. Then he pulls a white curtain in front of the scene, as the stage lights become, for the first time, harsh, stark and white.)*

SCENE 30

In the Hospital Lounge. The DOCTOR *holds the stuffed rabbit and travel brochures in his hands. He awkwardly peels off his latex gloves.*

DOCTOR: I'm sorry. There was nothing we could do.

ANNA: Yes, I know.

DOCTOR: I thought you might want to take this along with you. (*The* DOCTOR *hands* ANNA *the stuffed rabbit.*)

ANNA (*To the stuffed rabbit.*): There you are! (ANNA *hugs the stuffed rabbit and sees the doctor watching her.*) It's Jo-Jo. My brother's childhood rabbit. I brought it to the hospital as a little surprise. I thought it might make him feel better.

DOCTOR: Sometimes little things become important, when nothing else will help—

ANNA: Yes. (*They pause and stand together awkwardly.*) At least Carl went in his sleep. I guess that's a blessing.

DOCTOR: If one has to die from this particular disease, there are worse ways to go than pneumonia.

ANNA: I never would have believed what sickness can do to the body. (*Pause.*) Well, Doctor, I want to thank you for all you've done for my brother.

DOCTOR: I wish I could do more. By the way, housekeeping found these brochures in your brother's bedside table. I didn't know if they were important.

ANNA (ANNA *takes the brochures.*): Ah, yes. The brochures for Europe. I've never been abroad. We're going to go when he gets—

(ANNA *stops herself. With control.*) I must learn to use the past tense. We would have gone had he gotten better.

DOCTOR: Anna—may I call you Anna?— I, uh, if there's anything I can do—

ANNA: Thank you, but there's nothing you can do—

DOCTOR: I mean, I really would like it if you'd call me for coffee, or if you just want to talk about all this— (*The* DOCTOR *trails off.* ANNA *looks at him. She smiles. He squirms.*)

ANNA: You're very sweet. But no, I don't think so. Not now. I feel it's simply not safe for me right now to see anyone. Thanks again and good-bye. (ANNA *starts to exit. The* DOCTOR, *wistful, watches her go. The lighting begins to change back to the dreamy atmosphere of the first scene. Softly, a Strauss waltz begins.* CARL, *perfectly well, waits for* ANNA. *He is dressed in Austrian military regalia. They waltz off as the lights dim.*)

THERE ARE MANY HOUSES IN MY TRIBE

Shay Youngblood

THERE ARE MANY HOUSES IN MY TRIBE was presented by Brown University for the Once Upon A Weekend Festival of Short Plays in October 1992. Inspired from a painting by Miles Davis. Artistic Director Aishah Rahman; Direction, sound design and costumes by Daniel Alexander Jones.

ESTELLE . . . . Daniel Alexander Jones
NIA . . . . Miré Regulus

Characters

ESTELLE, African American woman or man
NIA, African American woman

Voices whisper and Body Drums beat softly in the darkness. The sounds grow louder and louder. Lights up on ESTELLE *asleep. Her dreadlocked hair spills from an African headwrap. She wears a loose white dress. She is barefoot. The sounds stop abruptly. A Timer rings. Without opening her eyes* ESTELLE *pickups up the Timer, puts it to her ear and sits up in bed. We see a mask on the back of her head. The women find a rhythm with their voices, hands, and bodies to accompany each other. They speak as if performing poetry.*

ESTELLE (*Speaks in different accents, inflections.*): Buenos dias? Allo? Hie? Jambo? Hello? Hello, is anybody out there?

Drum music and Voices echo throughout the rest of the scene as NIA *enters wearing a loose, colorful dress and lots of musical jewelry on her arms, in her ears, and around her ankles. Her head is wrapped, she is barefoot.* NIA *wears a mask on the back of her head also. She approaches* ESTELLE *from behind, caresses then cups the face of the mask in her hands, then kisses the Mask on the lips.*

NIA: Twelve days. (*Pause.*) Estelle didn't comb her head for twelve days. Neither did she eat or speak to anyone, but the gods. She wet her mouth with water and allowed damp kisses from my lips.

ESTELLE *mimes a cobra growing out of her hair, then aimed at her face as if it is hypnotizing her.*

ESTELLE: On the thirteenth day snakes began to grow from the roots of my hair.

NIA: They writhed and wound their way down her body, scoring erotic images in the floor.

ESTELLE *looks into a large mirror, stroking the imaginary snakes coming out of her hair. She watches as they crawl down her arms and writhe in a large pile at her feet. She is amazed at their color and shapes. She picks up one of the snakes and watches it crawl up her arm and down the other side. She moves with the body drum music and voice rhythms as she carries the snakes delicately.*

ESTELLE (*Mimes snakes making love with her arms. A Rain Stick can be used to simulate hissing.*): They made love there on the floor. Hundreds of them. Copperheads with coral tongues. Diamond-backs and blue boa constrictors with silver eyes. White-fanged water moccasins and dusty red rattlers screamed with pleasure. (*Sound of the Rain Stick.*) Then they crawled back into my head and slept, exhausted, content.

NIA: Twelve days. (*Pause.*) Do you hear me? For twelve days that girl didn't comb her hair. She didn't eat or speak to anyone but the gods. She wet her mouth with water and allowed damp kisses from my lips.

NIA caresses, then cups the face of the Mask, kissing the Mask on the lips. NIA begins to dance with the mask/ESTELLE's back as they both dance and sway to the rhythms.

NIA: On the thirteenth day she built a house with upside-down windows and sprinkled salt in the four directions.

ESTELLE tosses salt in the four directions clockwise and moves with the story as NIA dances with the shadows.

ESTELLE: When tears were rivers and mud made my mask, I ate the bark of trees. I washed naked in the river at dusk. I clothed my body in red clay and smooth white pebbles and leaves of grass and cowrie shells. I walked through the forest without direction. Branches braided into my hair, leaves became the soles of my feet. On the seventh day my eyes rested on a mystery. They stood like trees across my path. Seven women. Tall, thick, black women with wide hips and long delicate fingers. They invited me down a certain path. After many days we came to a village. There were no men there. No children or animals. Seven barren women. Seven huts formed a circle around a huge fire in that dusty place. The women offered me food and a place by the fire. At night they told stories and when it came my turn to tell a tale no sound came out. I opened my mouth to speak and in the place of words snakes spilled from my lips and slithered toward the women, wrapping around their ankles, circling their inner thighs and caressing their bellies. Seductive hissing whispers were drowned out by passionate cries as the women made the night aware of their pleasure. I watched as if from a great distance the union of snake and woman and I wept at the beauty and sensuousness of it all. Before the light of day each of the seven women had borne seven children and the next night those seven bore seven more and so on and so on, for seven days and seven nights. Beautiful girl children with gleaming white teeth and handsome boy children with proud wide noses. They grew into a tribe of two-headed people with snakes in their hair and colorful tongues that spoke many languages. The languages of trees, the languages of hearts, the languages of men and women. The face of beauty, the face of truth, the face of innocent dreams. The drums beat even their dreams.

ESTELLE/NIA: There are many houses in my tribe.

ESTELLE: Many tongues in my head.

NIA: Twelve days. (*Pause.*) For twelve days Estelle didn't comb her head. Neither did she eat or speak to anyone, but the gods.

NIA *and* ESTELLE *kiss, lips to lips and sway to the music. Drum Music stops. The Timer rings. Lights slowly fade as* ESTELLE *speaks.*

ESTELLE: I dreamed that there were snakes in my hair and the languages of trees on my tongue and two-headed people in my tribe. I dreamed I made a world.

Black

CONTRIBUTORS

VICTOR BUMBALO is the recipient of an Ingram Merrill Award for playwriting. His works have been produced throughout the United States, England, and Australia. Plays include *Adam and the Experts*, *Niagara Falls*, and *What Are Tuesdays Like?* He has won two MacDowell Fellowships and residencies at Yaddo and the Helene Wurlitzer Foundation.

~

CLAIRE CHAFEE is from New York. She studied acting and directing in London, has a B.A. from Oberlin College, studied writing in the M.F.A. program at Brown University, and became an associate artist at The Magic Theatre in San Francisco, where *Why We Have* a *Body* and *Even Among These Rocks* were both premiered. She is currently working on a musical commissioned by Berkeley Rep.

~

CONSTANCE CONGDON's latest plays include *Dog Opera*, *Tales of the Lost Formicans*, *Losing Father's Body*, and *Casanova*. Her works have been produced in Moscow, Helsinki, Hong Kong, Edinburgh, and London, as well as throughout the United States. She has been awarded the NEA Playwriting Fellowship, a Rockefeller Playwriting Award, and Newsday's Oppenheimer Award.

~

KEITH CURRAN's work has been produced Off-Broadway and at top regional theaters around the country. His plays *Dalton's Back* and *Walking the Dead* were produced at Circle Rep, while *Sidekick* won the National One-Act Play Contest at Actor's Theatre of Louisville. *The Stand-In* premiered at Naked Angels in New York.

~

STEVEN DIETZ is a playwright and director who lives in Seattle. His plays include *Lonely Planet*, *Foolin' Around with Infinity*, *More Fun Than Bowling*, and *God's Country*, about the white supremacist movement in the United States. He has been awarded playwriting fellowships from the McKnight, Jerome, and W. Alton Jones foundations; as well as directing fellowships from the McKnight Foundation and TCG.

~

LINDA EISENSTEIN is a composer and playwright whose plays and new music-theater works include *Three the Hard Way*, *Star Wares: The Next Generation* (with James Levin), the opera *Street Sense* (with Migdalia Cruz), and *The Last Red Wagon Tent Show in the Land* (with Teddi Davis). She resides in Cleveland, Ohio.

~

THE FIVE LESBIAN BROTHERS are Maureen Angelos, Babs Davy, Dominique Dibbell, Peg Healey, and Lisa Kron. They met at the WOW Cafe Theater and came together as a company in 1989. *The Brothers* are committed to creating provocative lesbian theater through collaboration. Their repertoire includes *Voyage to Lesbos*, *Brave Smiles*, and *The Secretaries*. They have performed their plays extensively in New York and around the country.

~

ERIC LANE is the award-winning author of *The Gary & Rob Show*, *Lights Along the Highway*, and *Dancing on Checkers' Grave*. His screen adaptation of *Cater-Waiter*, starring David Drake, is currently in production. Honors include a Writers Guild Award, the LaMama Playwright Development Award, and two Yaddo Fellowships.

~

CRAIG LUCAS is a graduate of Boston University, where he studied with poets George Starbuck and Anne Sexton. He is author of the plays *God's Heart*, *Missing Persons*, and *Blue Window*. Screenplays include *Longtime Companion* and the adaptations of his award-winning plays *Reckless* and *Prelude to a Kiss*.

~

SUSAN MILLER is the Obie-winning author of *Nasty Rumors and Final Remarks*, *For Dear Life*, and *Flux*, produced by Joseph Papp and the New York Shakespeare Festival. *Cross Country* and *Confessions of a Female Disorder*, by the Mark Taper Forum. *My Left Breast*, which won an Obie and the Susan Smith Blackburn Award, premiered in Louisville's 1994 Humana Festival. Her plays have also been done by Second Stage and Naked Angels.

~

CHERRÍE MORAGA is a playwright, poet, essayist, and cultural organizer. Her plays include *Giving up the Ghost*, *Shadow of a Man*, and *Heroes and Saints*. Honors include an NEA Playwrights' Fellowship, the 1990 Fund for New American Plays Award, the Dramalogue, the Pen West, and the Critics Circle awards.

~

RON NYSWANER wrote the screenplay for *Philadelphia*, for which he was nominated for the Golden Globe, Writers Guild, and Academy awards. He has written the screenplays for *Smithereens*, *Mrs. Soffel*, and wrote and directed *The Prince of Pennsylvania*. His play, *Oblivion Postponed*, was presented at the Bay Street Theatre Festival, and will be produced Off-Broadway in 1995.

~

JOE PINTAURO is a playwright, novelist, and poet. His plays include *Raft of the Medusa*, *Men's Lives*, *Snow Orchids*, and *Cacciatore*. He has written two novels, *Cold Hands* and *State of Grace*, and several award-winning books of poetry, among them *To Believe in God* and *The Rainbow Box*.

~

EDWIN SÁNCHEZ is the recipient of the Kennedy Center's Fund for New American Plays Grant for *Clean* which was produced by Hartford Stage. His other plays include *Unmerciful Good Fortune*, *Trafficking in Broken Hearts*, and *The Road*. He received the 1994 Princess Grace Playwriting Fellowship and is a playwriting fellow of the New York Arts Council.

~

WILL SCHEFFER is an award-winning playwright, screenwriter, and actor. His one-act *Falling Man* was produced in the 1994 Ensemble Studio Theater Marathon and HBO's New Writers Project. Mr. Scheffer's full-length plays include *Multiple Personality* and *Easter*. He is a member of the Public Theater's Emerging Playwrights Lab, E.S.T., and the Actors Studio.

~

PAULA VOGEL is a playwright, screenwriter, and professor. Her plays include *The Baltimore Waltz* (nominated for the Pulitzer Prize in 1992), *Hot 'n' Throbbing*, *And Baby Makes Seven*, and *Desdemona*. She has headed the Brown University Playwriting Workshop since 1985. Awards include two NEA Playwriting fellowships, two MacDowell Colony fellowships, and the Rhode Island Governor's Arts Award.

~

SHAY YOUNGBLOOD is author of the plays, *Shakin' the Mess Outta Misery* and *Talking Bones* (Dramatic Publishing Company) and a collection of short stories, *The Big Mama Stories* (Firebrand Books). *Shakin'* was adapted for film by Ms. Youngblood for Columbia Pictures. She is the recipient of the 1994 Edward Albee Award for Playwriting.

Grateful acknowledgment is made for permission to reprint the following copyrighted works:

What Are Tuesdays Like? by Victor Bumbalo. Copyright © 1992 by Victor Bumbalo. By permission of Rosenstone/Wender. For information, address Rosenstone/Wender, 3 East 48 Street, New York, NY 10017.

Why We Have a Body by Claire Chafee. Copyright © 1994 by Claire Chafee. By permission of the playwright. For information, address The Joyce Ketay Agency, 1501 Broadway, Suite 1910, New York, NY 10036.

Lonely Planet by Steven Dietz. © Copyright, 1994, by Steven John Dietz. The reprinting of *Lonely Planet* in this volume is by permission of the author and Dramatists Play Service, Inc. The stock and amateur performance rights in this play are controlled exclusively by Dramatists Play Service, Inc., 440 Park Avenue South, New York, NY 10016. No stock or amateur production of the play may be given without obtaining, in advance, the written permission of the Dramatists Play Service, Inc. and paying the requisite fee. Inquiries regarding all other rights should be addressed to Brad Kalos, International Creative Management, 40 West 57 Street, New York, NY 10019.

It's Our Town, Too by Susan Miller. Copyright © 1993 by Susan Miller. By permission of the playwright. For information, address The Joyce Ketay Agency, 1501 Broadway, Suite 1910, New York, NY 10036.

Giving Up the Ghost by Cherríe Moraga. Copyright © 1986, 1994 by Cherríe Moraga. Appearing in the author's *Heroes and Saints and Other Plays*, West End Press, 1994; an earlier version was published by West End Press, 1986. By permission of Cherríe Moraga. For information, address the playwright c/o Penguin USA, 375 Hudson Street, New York, NY 10014.

Rosen's Son by Joe Pintauro. Copyright © 1989 by Joe Pintauro. Inquiries concerning rights should be addressed to William Morris Agency, Inc., 1325 Avenue of the Americas, New York, NY 10019, attention: Gilbert Parker.

The Baltimore Waltz by Paula Vogel. Copyright © 1992 by Paula Vogel. Inquiries concerning rights should be addressed to William Morris Agency, Inc., 1325 Avenue of the Americas, New York, NY 10019, attention: Peter Franklin.